D1430709

THE BITTER AIR OF EXILE

The Bitter Air of Exile: Russian Writers in the West 1922-1972

Edited by SIMON KARLINSKY
and ALFRED APPEL, JR.

University of California Press
Berkeley · Los Angeles · London

University of California Press
Berkeley and Los Angeles, California
University of California Press, Ltd.
London, England

Originally published as "Russian Literature and
Culture in the West: 1922–1972," Volumes 27
(Spring 1973) and 28 (Fall 1973) of *TriQuarterly*.
Copyright © 1973 by Northwestern University Press
Revised version Copyright © 1977 by the
Regents of the University of California

ISBN: cloth, 0–520–02846–5
       paper, 0–520–02895–3
Library of Congress Catalog Card Number: 74–84147
Printed in the United States of America

Title page photo: St. Petersburg, by Ernst A. Jahn   1 2 3 4 5 6 7 8 9 0

. . . some are in Tashkent, some in New York
And the bitter air of exile
Is like poisoned wine.

Anna Akhmatova,
"Poem Without a Hero"

I: SIX MAJOR ÉMIGRÉ WRITERS

II: SOME *EMIGRÉ* POETRY

III: SELECTION OF *EMIGRÉ* PROSE

Source list
Nikolai Morshen poems from *Punctuation: Colon* (*Dvoetochie*), Washington, 1967. Igor Chinnov's poems I and III from *The [Musical] Score* (*Partitura*), New York, 1970; poem II published in *The New Review* (*Novyi zhurnal*), New York, No. 100, September 1970. The Yuri Odarchenko poems from *Quite a Day* (*Denyok*), Paris, 1949. Anatoly Steiger's poem ("How can I shout . . .") from *Two Times Two Makes Four* (*Dvazhdy Dva = Chetyre*), 1950. All other Steiger poems from his collection *Ingratitude* (*Neblagodarnost'*), Paris, 1936. N. Teffi's "Time" from *All About Love* (*Vsyo o Lyubvi*), Paris, n.d. (ca. 1950). Georgy Ivanov: *St. Petersburg Winters,* originally Paris, 1928; the expanded section on Esenin from the second edition, New York, 1952. Ivanov's poems: "Thank god there is no tsar . . ." from *Embarkation for Cythera,* Paris, 1937; all others from *Poems 1943–1958,* New York, 1958. Marina Tsvetaeva: "Poems grow . . . ," originally in the journal *Contemporary Annals,* No. 52, Paris, 1933; "Psyche," originally in her collection *Versts* (*Vyorsty*), Moscow, 1922; "To Mayakovsky," originally in the journal *Volya Rossii,* XI-XII, Prague, 1930; "A Poet on Criticism," originally in *Blagonamerennyi,* II, Brussels, 1926. Letter to Anna Teskovà from Marina Tsvetaeva's *Letters to Anna Teskovà,* Prague, 1969. Boris Poplavsky: "In the Distance," "The Rose of Death," and "Rondeau Mystique III" from *Flags,* Paris, 1931; "Biography of a Clerk," "Rembrandt," and "Another Planet" from *Dirigible of Unknown Destination,* Paris, 1965; "How awful, getting tired . . ." from *Snowy Hour,* Paris, 1936. The chapter from *Homeward from Heaven,* originally in the collection *Krug,* Vol. 1–2, Paris, n.d. (ca. 1935). Vladimir Markov: "Mozart," originally in *The New Review,* New York, XLIV, 1956. Vladislav Khodasevich's essay on Tolstoy from his collected *Literary Essays and Memoirs,* New York, 1954. Konstantin Korovin's memoir on Chekhov originally published in *Russia and Slavdom* (*Rossiya i slavianstvo*), Paris, July 13, 1929; reprinted in *Literary Heritage* (*Literaturnoe nasledstvo*), Vol. 68, Moscow, 1960. D. S. Mirsky's essay on Tsvetaeva originally in *Contemporary Annals,* No. 27, Paris, 1926.

Grateful acknowledgment is made for permission to reprint the following materials: excerpts from *Grasse Diary,* by Galina Kuznetsova, and *The Face of Firebird,* by Alla Ktorova, reprinted by permission of Viktor Kamkin, Rockville, Maryland.

We would also like to thank the Center for Slavic and East European Studies, University of California, Berkeley, for its assistance in the preparation of this volume.

Photo credits
The Museum of Modern Art/Film Stills Archive: *The Scarlet Empress; The Last Command; The North Star; You Can't Take It with You; Touch of Evil; Tarzan and the Apes; Safety Last; Brats.* National Film Archives: *The Hands of Orlac; Love; The Killers; The Last Command; I Am a Fugitive from a Chain Gang; The North Star; The Hitler Gang; Mission to Moscow; Song of Russia; Casablanca; A Night at the Opera; The Scarlet Empress,* Buster Keaton. Doug Lemza and Films, Inc.: *Fra Diavolo.* Culver Pictures; Stravinsky *et al.* Kevin Brownlow: *Surrender.* Impact Films: *Transport from Paradise.*

Foreword: who are the émigré writers?
SIMON KARLINSKY

Some were established authors with international reputations: Dmitry Merezhkovsky, Konstantin Balmont, Ivan Bunin. Others had just begun making a name for themselves at the time of the Revolution: Georgy Adamovich, Mark Aldanov, Georgy Ivanov. Still others were very young people who had perhaps managed to publish a few poems before they left Russia for good and who were to develop into writers only abroad: Nina Berberova, Yuri Felsen, Boris Poplavsky. Aesthetically, they represented the entire spectrum of twentieth-century Russian literature, from the most traditionalist and conservative to the most wildly experimental. Their politics were likewise varied; yet the majority, like the majority of the pre-Revolutionary intelligentsia, had little use for the tsarist autocracy and welcomed the revolution of February 1917 that swept it away. But after Lenin's takeover in October 1917, even such limited civil liberties and freedom of expression as had gradually been gained since the reforms of the 1860's were soon abolished, turning the Revolution into a nightmare for many Russians. By 1921 preliminary censorship of books and the periodical press, abolished after the unsuccessful 1905 Revolution, was restored in Russia in far stricter form than had existed under the tsars. By 1922 it become clear to those who cared about such things that the new Soviet government had confiscated Russian literature, both past and present, and was determined to control and direct the content and, eventually, the style of everything that Russian writers and artists would produce in the future. It was at this point that many creative people who had hoped to make their contributions in the new revolutionary Russia saw no choice but to leave the country.

Émigré literature of the twenties and thirties appears in retrospect as an unbelievable and heroic phenomenon. It had some magnificent journals (the Paris *Contemporary Annals* and the Prague *Will of Russia* were two of the most durable), a number of fine publishing houses, and a galaxy of excellent poets, novelists, philosophers, and critics. But the most important ingredient that a thriving literature needs—readers—was in short supply. The Russian emigration was not large enough numerically to support a literature on such a scale. The work of *émigré* writers could not be imported into the Soviet Union, which otherwise would have been its logical market. Such *émigré* readers as did exist preferred light, entertaining reading—adventure novels and humorous sketches. There is something almost unreal about the way such serious young *émigré* writers as Nabokov, Poplavsky, and Yanovsky (to mention three of the more familiar names) managed to launch their literary careers in the face of such staggering odds and to accomplish as much as they did.[1]

The awarding of the Nobel Prize to Ivan Bunin in 1933 crowned and brought to a close the earlier, most prosperous period of Russian *émigré* literature. By the nineteen-thirties, the Western intellectual community, which had no objection to the numerous successful Russian painters, composers, and dancers who were active in the West, came to regard the existence of an exiled Russian literature in its midst with a mixture of hostility and studied indifference. It was during that decade of Stalinist purges and proliferating forced labor camps that large numbers of American,

British, and French intellectuals (including such men as George Bernard Shaw, Theodore Dreiser, André Gide, and Thomas Mann) came to regard the U.S.S.R. as the finest example of a free and just social organization that humanity had so far been able to devise. A Russian writer who preferred to live abroad rather than contribute to the glorious experiment that was unfolding in his native country was automatically seen as a reactionary exploiter from the past and an obstacle to human progress in the present.

When, in the late nineteen-twenties, Ivan Bunin and Konstantin Balmont managed to publish in an obscure French journal some documents about the suppression of literary freedom in the U.S.S.R., they were denounced in print by the venerable Romain Rolland for aiding the cause of international reactionaries and blocking humanity's path to light and freedom.[2] In 1936 a major British literary journal rejected a story by Vladimir Nabokov because it had a policy against publishing any work by Russian émigrés.[3] And when, in 1943, the translation of Mark Aldanov's novel *The Fifth Seal* was selected by the Book-of-the-Month Club, a number of prominent American intellectuals (none of whom had read the novel or previously heard of Aldanov) signed a protest against this selection of a book written by a presumed enemy of the Soviet Union.[4] It was during the forties, we might recall, that George Orwell's *Animal Farm* was rejected by five American publishing houses and a chapter critical of Soviet musical policies was deleted from the French edition of Stravinsky's *The Poetics of Music,* in both cases for fear of offending the sensibilities of the Soviet government.

Such Western self-censorship has become more rare in recent decades. But the conviction, inherited from the thirties, that a Russian writer who resides outside the Soviet Union cannot be of any interest to the Western reader remains widespread, Vladimir Nabokov's wide following notwithstanding. Had Alla Ktorova's recent novel *The Face of Firebird* or Nikolai Morshen's brilliant collection of verse *Punctuation: Colon* been published in Moscow, they would have been instantly translated into all the major languages; but they appeared in, of all places, Washington, D.C., and are therefore known to only a handful of Western readers of Russian who took the trouble to learn of their existence. Boris Pasternak and Alexander Solzhenitsyn must have considered this when they resisted their government's suggestion that they live abroad.

The present collection is aimed at dispelling some of this apathy and prejudice. No attempt at comprehensive representation has been made, nor was it felt to be desirable. Some of the more famous names are not included; a few rather obscure ones are. More space is given, proportionately, to the period between the two world wars, but Russian writers who left their country in more recent decades (such as Vladimir Markov, Nikolai Morshen, and Alla Ktorova) are also represented.

Much of the work in this collection would be unpublishable in the Soviet Union today, even if the authors were not *émigrés*.[5] Aspects of twentieth-century sensibility that have not been cleared by the government for domestic consumption; religious or mystical interests; portraits of famous Russian writers that clash with their officially decreed images; an individualistic or pessimistic personal outlook; surrealistic imagery—these are some of the things from which a government embargo on *émigré* literature still protects all Soviet citizens. Yet the literary quality of much *émigré* writing is such that only the hidebound attitudes of the Soviet cultural establishment prevent its recognition as a major and permanent part of contemporary Russian literature. There is no earthly reason why Western readers, critics, and publishers should perpetuate their self-imposed quarantine against *émigré* writing. The door opened by the universal recognition of Vladimir Nabokov's importance should be wide enough to admit some of his equally interesting seniors, contemporaries, and juniors into the Western literary world.

Russian literature has been far richer and more varied in our century than is generally acknowledged. The political barriers to recognition of this richness and variety can now be seen as artificial and arbitrary. It is time they were removed.

Notes

1. See Anthony Olcott's essay on Poplavsky in the present volume for an outline of the problems the younger *émigré* writers had to face.

2. For details, see Nina Berberova, *The Italics Are Mine* (New York, 1969), pp. 231–37.

3. Gleb Struve, "Nabokov as a Russian Writer," in *Nabokov: The Man and His Work,* ed. L. S. Dembo (Madison, 1967), p. 46.

4. See, *inter alia,* Henry Seidel Canby, "The Fifth Seal," *Saturday Review of Literature,* April 24, 1943, p. 14. Whatever one may think of the artistic value of Aldanov's historical novels, there is no doubt that he understood the nature of democracy better and was more genuinely devoted to the cause of human freedom than his totalitarian-minded American critics and disparagers.

5. All work by living *émigré* writers is automatically unpublishable and often unmentionable in the Soviet Union. In a few select cases, the work of dead *émigré* writers has been reprinted there during the past decade (Khodasevich, Tèffi, and especially Tsvetaeva). The choice inevitably falls on such stories or poems that can be represented either as denunciations of life in the West or as testimony to the writer's patriotism and longing for his homeland. Even so, texts by *émigré* writers are frequently abridged by the censors. In Marina Tsvetaeva's essay "A Poet on Criticism," which appears in full here (pages 103–34), almost one-third of the text was deleted before it could appear in a Soviet journal.

An introduction to Alexei Remizov
ALEX M. SHANE

In one of his last autobiographical fragments, Remizov declared that he was not a storyteller, but a singer, an assertion borne out by the ever-present lyric strain in his work, particularly during the post-Revolutionary years. This lyric quality, in the sense of both emotion and musicality, determined the very nature of his artistic development, which was characterized by a great compassion for human suffering and by a passionate love for the purity of the Russian word. In striving to achieve the latter, Remizov focused on the syntax and intonation of the spoken language of provincial Russia and on the ancient pre-Petrine texts of old Russia, thereby creating a curious fusion of bookish and colloquial elements. Thus the rich nineteenth-century stylistic tradition of Nikolai Gogol (whose baroque syntax and grotesque characters still remain unsurpassed), Nikolai Leskov (renowned for the verbal virtuosity of his popular narratives), Pavel Melnikov-Pechersky (who vividly portrayed the life, language, and customs of the trans-Volga Old

Portrait of Alexei Remizov by Leonid Pasternak, 1923.

Believers), and Vladimir Dahl (a monumental figure in Russian lexicography and ethnography) found a worthy successor in Remizov. His ornamental prose not only stimulated and influenced the development of a host of young Russian writers in the 1910's and 1920's (Yevgeny Zamyatin, Mikhail Prishvin, Alexei Tolstoy, Vyacheslav Shishkov, and Yuri Olesha, to name a few), but is still palpable today in the works of such varied figures as Nabokov, Tertz (Sinyavsky), and Solzhenitsyn. That such a vital, pivotal figure in the Russian literary tradition has remained almost totally unknown to Western readers is indeed lamentable.

Alexei Mikhailovich Remizov was born in Moscow on June 24, 1877. His father, Mikhail Alexeyevich, an uneducated but well-known haberdasher, was twenty years older than Remizov's mother, Maria Alexandrovna. A graduate of one of Moscow's German secondary schools, she had been active among Nihilist groups and had married Remizov's father to spite her lover. Six years later, she abruptly left him, taking their four sons with her, and moved in with her older brothers who managed the family cotton mill. Her dowry was returned, and she was forced to live on meager means in an old wing adjacent to the mill, which had originally served as a paint shop. Despite a life of isolation and gloom, she managed to communicate her love of books and the theater to her youngest son, Alexei. As was the custom in Russian merchant-class families, the children had a strict religious upbringing, attending services each Saturday and twice on Sundays, at the parish church and at nearby Androniev Monastery. These excursions were the sole redeeming feature of a monotonous regime, and young Alexei always looked forward with great anticipation to the celebration of Easter, the annual apogee of his existence. Closely related to Remizov's piety, which became one of the major determinants of his development as a writer, were his sensitivity and compassion for the misfortunes of others, of which he first became aware while observing beggars on the church porch as well as his uncle's factory workers. Having noticed this deprivation and having felt it himself, he could not remain indifferent.

At the age of nineteen Remizov entered Moscow University in order to study natural sciences in the Division of Physical Sciences and Mathematics. He considered attempting the entrance examinations for the Agricultural Institute, but his political inclinations (he considered himself a Social Democrat) and his brother's enrollment in the Division of Jurisprudence drew him into economics. Through a quirk of fate, he was arrested at a student demonstration on November 18, 1897, permanently expelled from the university, and exiled to Penza for two years. Subsequent arrests, imprisonment, and exile took Remizov to Vologda, Ust-Sysolsk, Kharkov, Kiev, and Odessa. In 1905 he finally received permission to return to central Russia, and in February of that year, Alexei Remizov, a fledgling writer, settled in Petersburg, where he remained for sixteen years.

His works began appearing in Moscow and Petersburg journals and newspapers three years before his return from exile. From the beginning, they fell into two distinct categories: the derivative and the nonderivative. His derivative works include the vast store of folktales (Russian, Georgian, Armenian, Zyrian, Tibetan, and Siberian), parables, canonical and apocryphal narratives, legends, laments, letters, and mystery plays based upon existing literary materials, written and oral, which encompass the entire Russian tradition from the mythology of pagan times through Russianized forms of Byzantine Christianity to nineteenth-century Slavophilism. Remizov frequently amplified details or inserted additions which unified and emphasized the sense, imagery, and setting of the original text. Nonderivative works include his novels, short novels, stories, sketches, lyric fragments, dreams, and a whole series of biographical and autobiographical narratives. The inclusion of fiction, dreams, memoirs, and lyrics under one rubric may appear unorthodox at first glance, but Remizov's development after 1917 virtually demands it; for many of his works present a curious, at times surrealistic, blend of different genres and varied elements.

Marc Slonim has indicated that the tone of Remizov's work was determined "chiefly by two basic tendencies: his search for a 'national style' based on folklore tradition and philological studies, and his interest in religious and moral problems." * It should be added that both these tendencies crystallized during his captivity and exile from 1897 to 1905. On the one hand, his own chance arrest and the afflictions of his fellow "unfortunates" (as Russians called convicts) brought into sharp focus his vision of a world ruled by a senseless, indifferent fate and characterized by a lack of compassion and love among humans. Much of Remizov's early fiction, including his novel *The Pond* (*Prud,* 2d ed., 1911), the short novel *Sisters of the Cross* (*Krestovye sestry,* 1910), and stories such as "The New Year" ("Novyi God," 1907), "A Summer House at Public Expense" (1908), "The Judgment of God" ("Sud Bozhii," 1908), "Emaliol" (1909), "The Little Cockerel" ("Petushok," 1911), and "The Protected" ("Pokroven-naia," 1912) provide vivid descriptions of a grim world where chance misfortune at times appears to be the manipulation of a malignant, evil force. On the other hand, his wanderings in exile brought him in contact with provincial Russia and enclaves of indigenous natives which inspired a series of folktales based on Zyrian mythology, later gathered under the title "The Midnight Sun" ("Polunoshchnoe solntse," 1908), and further stimulated his interest in ethnography and the Russian oral tradition.

Significantly, Remizov's first book consisted of a collection of twenty-three folktales entitled *Follow the Sun* (*Posolon',* 1907), which was reprinted, with minor additions, together with a second cycle of thirty tales, "To the Ocean-Sea" ("K moriu okeanu," 1911) as Volume Six of his *Works* (*Sochineniya*). Each tale represents a finely wrought gem set in limpid, rhythmic prose. In "Vedogon," Remizov's lovely lyric description of the desolate landscape and of floating gossamer creates an appropriately autumnal tonality, which greatly enhances the pagan Slavic myth of guardian spirits (encountered among the Montenegrans, Serbs, and Poles and having a counterpart in the Zyrian Ort).

Dreams occupied a prominent place in Remizov's life and writ-

---

* Marc Slonim, *Modern Russian Literature: From Chekhov to the Present* (New York, 1953), p. 230.

ings. Since he had dreams every night, during his teens he began recording them each morning, a practice which he continued throughout his life. He believed that dreams and reality were firmly bound, interpenetrating one another, and that dreams, not being subject to conventional causal or temporal relations, were the sole means of communicating with the dead and penetrating the souls of the living. The protagonists in his early fiction frequently dream, and their dreams (or nightmares) usually reflect or complement the reality described, thereby retaining and enhancing the artistic unity of the work. It was not long, however, before Remizov began publishing collections of dreams as self-sufficient literary entities: "Perilous Fate" ("Bedovaia dolia," 1909), "From Eyes to Eyes" ("S ochei na ochi," 1913), "The Little Basket" ("Kuzovok," 1915), and ultimately a separate monograph named after the author of one of Russia's best known dream books, *Martyn Zadeka* (Paris, 1954). More interesting, however, were his post-Revolutionary attempts at fusing dream and reality within a single narrative such as *Russia in a Whirlwind* (*Vzvikhrennaia Rus'*, 1927) and *Along the Cornices* (*Po karnizam,* 1929). "Mu'allaqāt," the introductory piece to *A Flute for Mice* (*Myshkina dudochka,* 1953), provides a graphic example of the surrealistic juxtaposition of dream and reality in Remizov's post-Revolutionary memoir literature, as does "Sleepwalkers" ("Lunatiki"), taken from his reminiscences of his early Moscow years in the collection *With Clipped Eyes* (*Podstrizhennymi glazami,* 1953). The title of the piece refers to Remizov's belief that all men are born with shades over their eyes which prevent a real awareness of the world. By contrast, his "clipped eyes" enable him to view the events of everyday life, the misfortunes of others, and the nocturnal world of dreams in a perspective denied to most.

Religious elements permeate most of Remizov's works. In his nonderivative prose fiction, for example, time is usually measured by saints' days, while Christian humility and a readiness to accept God's will receive positive treatment, as do pious people who love and aid their fellowmen. Among the derivative works, the religious element found expression in an ever-increasing series of apocrypha and legends entitled *The Spiritual Meadow* (*Limonar'*, or *Lug dukhovnyi*, 1907, 1911); a cluster of parables and legends about St. Nicholas, the most beloved of Russia's saints: *St. Nicholas' Parables* (*Nikoliny pritchi*, 1917); and a series of apocrypha centering on the Mother of God, *Stella maria maris* (1928) but actually encompassing human history from the creation of the universe and the first man, through Adam's subsequent pact with Satan, to the coming of Christ and his crucifixion for man's salvation. Even in translation the three pieces from this collection, "Star Above All Stars," "Adam," and "The Angel of Perdition," provide excellent examples of Remizov's fine rhythmic prose, with its syntactic parallelism, acoustic and verbal repetition, and even visual structure.

After the Revolution of 1917, Remizov remained in Petersburg, serving in the repertory section of the government's Theatrical Department. Complaining of unbearable headaches, he emigrated from Russia on August 5, 1921. By the end of 1923, after a short stay in Estonia and almost two years in Germany, Remizov moved to Paris, where he remained until his death on November 26, 1957. Although he published more than forty volumes as an *émigré*, much of the material had already been written and published earlier in Russia. He continued work on new adaptations of apocrypha, but did not expand his various folktale cycles and completely shunned new endeavors in the area of traditional prose fiction genres such as the novel and short story. Instead, by and large, he developed a subjective hybrid memoir literature which combined a chronicle of Russia after the Revolution, biographical sketches, reminiscences, subjective essays on life and literature, autobiography, and his fantastic dream world. At least three volumes were devoted to a biography of his wife, Serafima Pavlovna Dovgello, a paleographer whom he had married while exiled in Vologda and who died in Paris during the Second World War. As interesting and as revealing of Remizov (the man and writer) as these works may be, they did not have any impact on the development of Russian literature either in the Soviet Union or among Russian exiles abroad. His role in Russian belles lettres had been determined primarily by what he had written and published in Russia prior to the Revolution.

His religious parables and apocrypha found no echo or imitators in the new socialist Russia, but his folktales did inspire and influence writers such as Prishvin and Shishkov. It was his prose fiction—the novels, short stories, and particularly works of intermediate length such as *The Unhushable Tambourine* (*Neuemnyi buben,* 1910), *Sisters of the Cross,* and *The Fifth Pestilence* (*Piataia iazva,* 1912)—that attracted the interest of the reading public and young writers, not so much for their themes as for their structure and style. His predilection for the grotesque and unusual, for static, segmented composition considerably influenced the younger generation—Boris Pilniak, for instance—and greatly contributed to the disintegration of the narrative form in postrevolutionary Russia. Recurrent imagery, motifs, and lyric refrains were a concomitant attribute of Remizov's segmentation. Of equal, if not greater, importance to the future development of Russian prose was his studied mastery of the *skaz* narrative technique, in which he sought to capture the intonations of the spoken language and the individualized verbal peculiarities of a specific narrator. His verbal techniques included frequent inversions (of subject and predicate, of modifier and noun), numerous diminutives, unusual but peculiarly Russian words found in pre-Petrine literature and documents, and colloquial words garnered from provincial Russian speech and the dialectal dictionaries of Vladimir Dahl and the Academy of Sciences. This emphasis on mode of expression helped mold a whole new breed of writers who sought to make their readers aware of the linguistic texture of their art. Thus Remizov's influence, readily apparent in the use of specific verbal and structural devices, went considerably deeper and affected the writer's basic attitude toward his craft. As Remizov aptly summarized: "For the writer the word is like paints for the artist-painter. Verbal art consists in weight, number, and measure. Words come to mind in droves, not alone. Art consists not only in the selection of words, but in their combination and composition."

from Follow the Sun, 1907

Vedogon: a prose poem
ALEXEI REMIZOV

The river's turned into shallow mud. The plowed furrows in the field have gone to grass.

The meadow has been mowed, the grain is gathered, the fall sowing is over, the lingonberry's gone.

And the wind has torn the leaves off the trees. It carried them, fluttering, through the air, dried them out and rolled them, rustling, away from the orphaned trees.

The lake is filled with leaves.

The golden, curly wood turned redder, rustier with each morning frost, thinned out with each sunny day. Gossamer floated through the wood; rose, clinging, to the treetops; and, rolling down the branches, slipped around the desolate trees.

In the mornings, at dawn, the gossamer, chilled in the night, grew ever lighter and more transparent; curling like worms, its threads swayed in abandoned, torn nests.

The rainy autumn has come riding on a piebald mare. The last bright days are gone.

The rainy, drowsy autumn.

The beasts have gone to sleep in their lairs—the shaggy ones are warm; to them it is still summer.

The wind plays in the fields and woods, sweeps rushing through the open space.

And the Vedogons have risen by the lairs, they stand and watch over the sleeping beasts. Every beast has his guardian-Vedogon.

But they get bored watching over the lairs in the rain. Bored and chilled. For want of something better to do, they start up fights among themselves, sometimes unto death.

Trouble—who'll submit and own himself beaten? And so a Vedogon will end his days, and the Vedogon's beast will end his —in his sleep.

Many a beast will perish in the autumn season, silently, unheard.

The wind is muted. The nights grow longer. Early frost.

The lucky ones, who were born in a shirt,* they also have their Vedogons, like the beasts.

And now, lucky one, you've gone to sleep. And your Vedogon has stolen out like a mouse and wanders through the world. What places won't he visit—what mountains, what stars! He'll wander to his heart's content, and take a look at everything, and then return to you. And you will waken in the morning happy after your fine-spun dream. A storyteller, you'll compose a tale; a singer, you will sing a song. But it is all from Vedogon—it's he who told you, who sang to you—the tale, the song.

Lucky one, born in a shirt, take heed—for if your sleep, your dream takes you too far, your days are numbered. The Vedogons are fighters; they'll meet and tease and get into a brawl, and then, before you know it, one is gone, has given up the ghost. And you, lucky one, teller of tales, singer of songs, will not wake. You will end your days in your sleep.

Many a lucky one dies in the autumn season, silently, unheard.

translated by Mirra Ginsburg

---

* "To be born in a shirt" is a formula from Russian folklore; it means "to be born in a caul," a traditional sign of preordained good luck. EDITOR.

from Perilous Fate, 1909

Three dreams
ALEXEI REMIZOV

Eaten by the wolf

I was sent into the woods for nuts.

"Go," they said, "gather us nuts, as many as you can."

And so I walk through the forest, searching, but it's very awkward. I keep stumbling, and there is not a single nut tree. At last I find one, but there isn't a single ripe nut; all are green.

"Well, anyway, I'll bring them green ones, if they're so anxious for them. . . ."

I bend a twig and want to pluck the nuts, when suddenly—pounce!—a wolf springs at me from behind a bush. I see I'm in a bad way, and I say:

"What's this, wolf? You don't really mean to eat me?"

But he doesn't seem to answer. And I talk to him again.

"Don't eat me, gray one," I say. "I'll be of use to you one day."

But to myself I think, how can I ever be of use to him?

And while I was thinking this . . . the wolf ate me.

19

My flowers

I walked along a cornfield just coming into bloom. A lark was singing, and the fragrance of fresh hay came from the mown meadow. I met two women carrying a basket full of wild flowers, and a little girl sat among the flowers.

"Where are you going?" I asked the women.

"To pick flowers," said the women with the basket.

And I followed them. We walked silently. And silently we came to a lake.

"There are your flowers!" the women pointed at the lake, laughing.

And I stood alone on the shore, and there were no flowers in the lake. Empty-handed, I turned toward home. The cornfield was swaying, coming into bloom, and a lark was singing. Suddenly I saw among the stalks of corn the girl who had sat in the women's basket. She ran to me, and threw her arms around my neck, and whispered into my ear:

"Take me with you!"

I took the girl on my shoulders, but didn't make a step before everything turned dark. Clouds swept the sky, and only a greenish light swirled like a funnel overhead. And some strange birds with serpents' tails rose from the ground, and everything flew up toward the swirling light. There was a great multitude of birds; they did not caw, but made strained, guttural sounds like deaf-mutes, and soon their tails shut out the light. The light went out, the birds fell silent. And in the night I heard again, from some immeasurable distance, the voice of the little girl.

"Take me with you!"

But I . . . I do not know where to go, what to do with my own self.

The mouse

The house is overrun with mice, they're scampering everywhere. I watched for one and caught her by the tail. And she—snap!— bit my finger. And from the spot where she had bitten, long hairs grew out. I dropped the mouse; she fell onto the floor, and sat there, wouldn't go away.

"You must be careful, not so rough. Be kind to her!" somebody said from under the floor.

So I took her paw gently, and stroked her, and right away she climbed up on my neck, and stretched her little snout, and wriggled her whiskers.

Note. To every dream there is the same conclusion: "And then I woke."

translated by Mirra Ginsburg

from Stella Maria Maris, 1928

THREE APOCRYPHA BY ALEXEI REMIZOV
translated by Mirra Ginsburg

Star Above All Stars

Judas—"he is Christ's first disciple"—and he betrayed.
   And when he understood, he flung down the money—
   "the blood on it clings to the hands!"—and went away.
   But where was he to go? He went seeking after death: "There is
      but one end!"
   He went seeking after death—but there was no death:
      He ran to the river—the river was gone;
      He ran to the woods—the woods bent down.
—Who will deliver him from his petrified black life?

Christ was led to the cross—
They asked Peter:
   "You knew Christ?"
"I know him not—have never heard about this man!" Peter denied.
   And when he understood—for only yesterday he vowed,
   "Though all should be tempted, he would never be tempted,"
   and "he would rather die, but he would never deny Him!"—
   he wept bitterly and went away—"it's not to be undone!"
   He went wherever his feet led him.

And three days he wept in a ditch, in a roadside pit:
    he could not rise with grief
    or lift his eyes.
—Who will lift him from his black ditch?

The Mother of God stands by the cross.
    Sees her Son hanging on the cross,
    sees the agony—and cannot help.
—Is there any grief darker and more hopeless than being
  powerless: "impossible to help!"
    And she fell before the Cross
    and her thoughts were in confusion. . . .
Night!—"When you were little, we rode from Bethlehem to Egypt
at night, lions and panthers ran before us, showed the way in
the desert; a star stopped, I sat down on a stone, unswaddled
you, and a lion came and put his head down at our feet, warm
as a robe, and another came—the most fearful one—and stretched
his paw in greeting—"the beasts understood. . . ."—Night! This
night of the ravaged despairing heart, when the last stars go out.
    And when the last stars went out,
    an archangel stood before her
    and gave her a branch—a star from heaven.
She raised her eyes and saw her Son on the cross—in light and
  glory!

And the Mother of God went from the cross, carried the star into
  the world—
    passed by the ditch where Peter wept:
    and Peter saw the star and came out of the ditch;
    she walked through trackless wilderness, where even a
      beast will not pass,
    Judas saw the star—and the light showed him the way. . . .
She came into this world—no one waited or hoped for
anything!—and with the star she lit our darkness:

STAR ABOVE ALL STARS

The mother of God and the Mother of Light
we shall magnify in song!

Adam

God created man in eight parts:
 from earth—the bones,
 from sea—blood,
 from sun—beauty,
 from clouds—thoughts,
 from wind—breath,
 from stone—wisdom and firmness,
 from light—meekness,
 from spirit—wisdom.
And after God created man, he had no name for him.

 Heavenly heights—the Father,
 Breadth of the earth—the Son,
 Depth of the sea—the Holy Ghost.
And God's creation—man—had no name.

And God called four angels:
 Michael,
 Gabriel,
 Raphael,
 Uriel.
And God said to the angels:
"Go forth and find a name for man!"

Michael went east—

and met a star; its name was Anatolē,* and he took from it

A

and brought it to God.

Gabriel went west—

and met a star, its name was Deisis, and he took from it

D

and brought it to God.

Raphael went to midnight—

and met a star, its name was Arktos, and he took from it

A

and brought it to God.

Uriel went to midday—

and met a star, its name was Mesevria, and he took from it

M

and brought it to God.

And God commanded Uriel to pronounce the word—man's name.

And Uriel said:

A   D   A   M

And Adam was the first man on earth.

* The names of the four stars are Slavonized Greek words for East, West, North, and South. EDITOR.

The Angel of Perdition

After He had risen from the dead, putting off the body of flesh, Christ appeared before His disciples. The Apostles Peter, Andrew, John, and Bartholomew were with the Mother of God, comforting her. And when they were all assembled together, Christ stood among them and said:

"Peace be with you! Ask me, and I shall teach you. Seven days will pass, and I shall ascend to my Father."

And no one dared to ask. And they followed Him meekly—in His divine steps—to the Mount of Olives. On the way, the Apostle Peter spoke to the Mother of God: let her beg of her Son "that the Lord reveal to them all that is in Heaven." But the Mother of God would not question. And they followed Christ in silence.

When they had ascended the Mount of Olives and sat together, Christ in the midst of them, Bartholomew spoke to Christ:

"Lord, show us the devil, that we shall see what he is and what his works are. He had no shame of Thee—he nailed Thee to the cross."

"O brave heart," said Christ, "thou mayest not behold him."

Bartholomew fell at the feet of the Savior, pleading:

"Unquenchable lamp! Everlasting light of salvation! Thou didst come into the world at the word of Thy Father; Thou hast done Thy work—turned Adam's sorrow to rejoicing, Eve's sadness to joy. Do this thing!"

And the Lord said to Bartholomew:

"It is thy wish to see the devil—thou shalt see him. But I tell thee: thou, and the Apostles, and the Mother of God shall fall down as dead."

And all of them beseeched:

"Lord, do this thing! Lord, show him!"

And, at the word of the Lord, angels appeared from the west. They raised up the earth like a scroll, and an abyss opened up— the pit of perdition. And forbidding the nether angels, Christ commanded Michael to sound his trumpet. And the Captain of the Armies of Heaven sounded his trumpet. And in that hour the Angel of Perdition, Satanael, was brought forth out of the abyss.

> —Free as the golden-eye, elder of the Heavenly Host,
> cast down for pride, where is thy freedom,
> where the crown of power? thy heavenly throne?

Six hundred and sixty angels held him, the harbinger of evil, creator of the dream—bound in fiery chains—and his height was six hundred cubits, his face—lightning! his hair—arrows! his lids —a wild boar! his right eye—the morning star! his left eye—a lion! and the mouth—a chasm! and the fingers—scythes! the wings —burning purple, the vestment—blood! And on his face, the writing of the Enemy, the seal of perdition.

> —And Satan proclaimed:
> *"I am the Lord God!"*

And there was a great quake—the earth shook. And in dread the Apostles and the Mother of God prostrated themselves upon the ground.

from With Clipped Eyes, 1951

The barber
ALEXEI REMIZOV

I write as I would read lists of the dead at a memorial service: the names of those I have given pain—not by intent or ill-will but through passion: ungovernable, driven, always thoughtless and irresponsible.

Near the Church of the Prophet Elijah in Vvedensky Lane, next to the Prokhorovs, Shvetsovs, and Morozovs, there was a barber shop. I remember it as I remember the church processions on Saint Elijah's Day. It was the only one in the whole Vorontsovo Field district. In its windows, fluffy elegant wigs and cut-glass vials, perfumes and elixirs; at Christmas and Shrovetide, funny and terrifying masks, and noses: noses like sausages, some with slits for eyes, others without eyes—attachable (those were the thickest). The owner, known to everyone in Syromyatniki and in Zemlyanka, was Pavel Alexandrovich Vorobyov. Dealing with the greatest variety of hair, shaping the most complicated coiffures, he was himself denied the blessing: not a single hair tickled his head, not a trace of delicate, clinging down, not a feathery black wisp, nothing but a smoothly polished skull as shiny as a barber's lathering bowl—Mambrino's helmet! Had his hair been eaten out to the very last by aromatic, caustic pomade? Or had the hairs conspired as one, and, tempted by the sticky brilliantine, slipped down into the beard? A veritable Proudhon! And a musician. I've never heard a greater variety of scissor music: he played with the scissors, both as he held them away, aiming at the head, and, having set his aim, plunging them into the thick. His haircuts took a long time; people waited their turn up to an hour. But even without the help of the humor purveyed by the various *Fragments, Alarm Clocks,* and *Dragonflies,* this hour flew by unnoticed. The chatter and trills of the scissors, the clitter of steel, the flash and swishing of the comb shortened the time; the minutes flowed not like minutes, but in a rush, in bursts.

How many times I asked him to give me a "polka cut," or crew cut, or, as we called it, "beaver cut," or, as it was known later, after the Revolution, a "Kerensky cut." Pavel Alexandrovich never argued. But, as if in spite, after some particularly melodious break, the scissors would swing over and bite deeper, right down to the skin. I suffered bitterly. Passing my hand over my naked head, I would lose all power of speech and leave the barber shop without a good-bye, a little Tartar. And Pavel Alexandrovich would smile after me, as singers and musicians smile after an especially successful performance.

Later I understood that Vorobyov was not at all bad, and not spiteful. And how, indeed, could I have failed to understand? He simply was unable to break off the music and stop his scissors, and everything would go not as intended, but as it came out—of itself. Should I have watched his hand? I could not see it in the mirror, or else I saw such things that . . . And, then, all of me turned into ears: dry violin bows flew over my head, flutes squealed like mice, clarinets clucked like bubbling, overwatered soil.

It became my dream to be a barber, a dream that neither overshadowed nor quenched my passion for drawing and calligraphy, or my love of theater and singing; it was the dream of a musician —to express his musical soul in any form, in any way.

In the Naydenov yard there were two chain dogs, famed throughout the neighborhood: Tresor and Polkan. Their kennel was behind the machine section of the factory, always brightly lit and throbbing dryly with its wheels and belts. The dogs were in a frenzy all night, clanking and barking. Everybody was afraid of them. Three small white dogs ran about the Naydenov yard, forever near their master's white house. Nobody ever wondered where their kennel was; they had a habit of attacking from behind and biting painfully. Nobody liked them. And at the other end, toward Syromyatniki, near the factory dormitories and the former dyer's shop where we lived—in "our" yard—the peaceful Malchik went about his duties as a watchdog. At certain given hours he barked in a "pleasant" baritone, and he never bit anyone. His kennel, next to the henhouse, was shared by Belka. All day long, Belka lay quietly, looking nowhere, her pointed muzzle resting on her outstretched paws; but at the slightest unfamiliar rustle, she'd leap up and fling herself like a stone underfoot, barking wildly. There was also a mutt, called Shavka. The fur hung on her body in ragged tufts, and only her kind black eyes looked out with lively attention from her "sheepskin." No one paid her any attention and no one knew who and what she really was. She never took part in "dog weddings," she never had puppies, and she never barked.

At lonely moments of my life I have thought of Shavka. I envied her, her obscure fate, her unprotesting patience, her mildness, her kind, silent greeting from under the unsightly pelt. . . . But this was later. Then—then—Shavka was the first on whom I tested my barbering art, the craft of Pavel Alexandrovich Vorobyov: scissors music.

I decided to give Shavka a "poodle cut." Shavka did not resist. She lay submissively under the scissors. No one had ever stroked her in her life, but I would shear a little island in her tangled waves and stroke her lightly. Or was it my music that charmed her? Of course, I did not succeed in making her a poodle. I turned her into something unspeakable, and very funny; suddenly everybody began to notice Shavka, and there was no end of laughter. Shavka herself evinced no displeasure, and her kind black eyes looked out as brightly from under the shaggy pelt, for, as is proper with a poodle, I did not touch her head and neck; I also left a tassel at the tip of her tail, a place for flies to settle, and for chasing flies. The season was warm, and the factory hands slept out in the open, in the yard. But after Saint Elijah's Day the weather cools, especially toward morning, and the yard was no longer a place to sleep. The ground was not the same, the stones were damp, the air stinging. Shavka felt it very acutely; she could not get warm in her poodle state; she crept into the kennel, but still felt cold. By the carpenter shop there was a pile of fresh wood shavings. She got out of the kennel and burrowed into them, but even the warm shavings gave no warmth! She shivered. . . .

We got up about two o'clock: all week after Transfiguration we went every night from Syromyatniki to the Kremlin for the night service and procession. I ran out first, lightly dressed, and immediately felt the chill outside. It was a clear August night; the whole sky shone—those winged autumn stars! And suddenly I heard the bark—but such a strange bark, like a song. Then my brothers came out, and again the chill and the bark. And that voice. . . . No one barked like that—neither Tresor nor Polkan, clanking their chains, nor those small white dogs disliked by everyone, nor our Malchik, nor Belka. Why, it was Shavka! Shavka was barking. And all the way to the Kremlin, and throughout the service in the Kremlin, listening to the chanted prayer, I thought about it—I understood: the kind black eyes were looking at me trustingly—and the strange voice. . . . When I first heard Kommissarzhevskaya in *The Poor Bride,* in her Italianate "He said to me" and "but he did not love"—how she sang out that "he did not love"—in that "chilled" heart without hope of finding warmth, in that bitter meekness, I recognized that voice.

Shavka—God's creature. And the conclusion, I must say it: such things don't happen to people. To our common joy, throughout those bitter nights, already by the time of the procession of the Miraculous Virgin of Kazan, Shavka had grown such a crop of tufts—my light hand!—that she went about like two Shavkas, such a warm coat for winter! And after that we became great friends. She had forgiven everything, she'd run to me without being called, her black, kind, loving eyes looked at me trustingly. Of course, she had forgotten, but could I, can I forget?

The novice of Androniev Monastery, Misha. Misha had come from Yelets with the dream of a monastic life. But finding himself in the cloister, he fell into despondency: the daily monastery life—its unwritten code—confused him. Had he ever thought of anything like that when he had longed to go to Moscow? The hieromonk Nikita, who had taken him under his wing as his attendant—a bitter drunk but a wise man—laid upon him the discipline of visiting us. We were like kin at the Androniev Monastery; all the monks knew us. And so the novice Misha, unbookish but possessed of a stubborn dream, appeared among us, in our former dyer's shop, with its paints, music, theater, chorus, and books.

At first he came on Sundays after vespers. We all took to him—so uncommon in our mischievous circle. And we were moved by his genuine meekness—nothing feigned, no cunning of any kind; he spoke whatever was in his heart, or else kept silent. He felt good among us, too, and started coming more often. Later, with my mother's consent, Father Nikita allowed him to live with us.

Misha was older, but we knew more, and we began to teach him. It was not easy for him. He studied diligently, and all his time was taken up: he went to the monastery for every service, and returned from the monastery to us, as to his cell. Living with us, he did not brood any more.

Misha had extraordinary hair—fine, wavy; stroke it, and it would caress your hand. In summertime it was too warm for hair, and troubling, too, especially at night, making for restless dreams. Not that the hair itself would weave those eerie specters, but that its thin hot sheath would waken primal memories, lead off into such deep, dense jungles—burn and chill the heart. It had to be cut. And so I offered to "trim it just a little in the back; I wouldn't touch it in front." Misha believed me. Submissively he bent his head, and I stepped up behind him with the scissors—Pavel Alexandrovich Vorobyov himself! And it began. When I was shearing Shavka's matted pelt, the scissors had to bite into it. But Misha's delicate, fine locks cut easily: they dropped like mowed grass, evoking visions of fields and flowers. My flowery music rustled silkily. I was oblivious of the passing minutes; an hour went by. And when I finished, I noticed nothing, and Misha could not see in the back. That night he slept serenely—no temptations.

In the morning, at early mass, wearing a splendid silver surplice, Misha came out with a large candle and stood on the ambo, facing the holy gates. And all who were in church—they all could see; and everybody rolled with laughter. "Jacob's ladder!" the monastery provisioner, a connoisseur of various kinds of fish, put a name to it. From neck to crown, steps ascended Misha's head, leading in imagination to the very heavens. Misha was shown the back of his head in a mirror, but it was no laughing matter to him. The only thing that could conceal the mutilation was a pointed "skufeika" —a monk's cap: in paintings of Judgment Day, such caps are worn by doomed heathens.

And this heathen cap made Misha's head burn as badly as— no, worse than—before the haircut. Whether because the velvet proved warmer than the hair, or because it was July, Moscow's Asiatic season, but now it was no longer a matter of restless sleep. Misha simply lost all sleep. He could not find relief from the unquenchable fiery heat, just as Shavka as a poodle could not find relief on autumn mornings from the shivering cold. I begged him: "Let me, I'll try to smooth it down!" And Misha was ready to submit himself again to my scissors, yet feared it might get even worse. "It will grow, it will even out!" Father Nikita consoled him and spoke of the deacon Vasily, whose face was like a woman's. "But then he died, and in the sight of all the dead man grew a beard . . . well, just a small one. . . ." And, licking his lips, dried out by pepper brandy, Father Nikita tugged at his own scanty, goatlike beard. Meantime, "Jacob's ladder," which had miraculously appeared on the head of the novice, roused all of Rogozhskaya and Taganka. The "miracle of Androniev Monastery" drew crowds of the curious to every service. People came even from the countryside to take a look at Misha.

The "heavenly ladder" awakened marvelous hopes. The visitors not only looked at Misha—and how they looked!—but even tried to touch him. The monastery had a rich store of vestments— ancient ones, the gifts of tsars, embroidered by the Moscow tsarevnas. For every service, Misha was arrayed as for great holidays. Solemnly he would appear with a tall candle on the ambo, now in pearl-studded crimson, now in azure with silver stars, now in raspberry red embellished with golden grasses, leaves, and grapes. A lilac pointed heathen cap concealed the "ladder," but this made it even more mysterious: "the ladder was hidden!" His eyes, inflamed from sleepless nights, burned with a wolfish spark; the heavy brocade weighing down his shoulders now sharply colored his face, now blanched it, drained it of the last drop of blood: greenish white, he stood with chattering teeth. No hiding place, always exposed to sight; and through the curious and the pious stares, always the mockery. It was too much, this service as a freak, even if a miraculous one. And he had no patience to endure until, as Nikita promised, "it would grow and even out." As the ultimate remedy, I offered Misha an extract brewed of nutshells. I had heard of this sure means of growing hair and remembered it, suspecting no mischief. But Misha would not yield to persuasion—to his good fortune. Or he would have become like Pavel Alexandrovich—with a naked, shiny skull, Mambrino's helmet! Who knows, even his thick eyebrows might have fallen out!

With clenched teeth, he stroked the back of his head, from nape to crown, from crown to nape, feeling the "ladder." And in his answers and his infrequent questions, the simplest words were full of grief, and in the grief—reproach and bitterness. Shavka—God's creature: what could she do in her extremity? And, never having barked, she suddenly burst into barking, and this barking, born of despair, was like the voice of a human. But Misha was a man.

... What saved him from despair was very simple: habit. People got used to the "miraculous" Misha and gradually stopped noticing, and then forgot him altogether. But could he forget? And who are those who say—a man forgets?

Through the moving mist, the column of incense, I see the surplice of green brocade with its white crosses, the burning candle, the green angry eyes—green, with a wolfish gleam. And all of this, in the enveloping cloud of chants—"more glorious than the cherubim"—melting the blackest, the most hardened heart until, as though split open, it flows and shines.

translated by Mirra Ginsburg

from With Clipped Eyes, 1951

Sleepwalkers
ALEXEI REMIZOV

> *He sees an ocean of light pouring in,*
> *filling the world; he sees sciences and arts en-*
> *gulfed; mathematics destroyed; lines broken,*
> *planes dissolved, bodies drowning. . . . The waves of*
> *light wrench entire formulas, root and all, out of*
> *calculations, wash away vast structures of equa-*
> *tions of all degrees, tear sines and cosines, tangents*
> *and cotangents from circles, ellipses, parabolae*
> *and hyperbolae; dislodge parallels, shatter*
> *cords, diameters, and radii. . . . figures are scat-*
> *tered, the multiplication table and logarithms*
> *fall apart; algebraic ABC's disintegrate; addition,*
> *subtraction, multiplication, and division merge*
> *together; pluses and minuses have split away from*
> *letters, values are lost, everything has turned*
> *into zero wholes, zero tenths, zero hundredths,*
> *zero thousandths. . . .*
> —*A. F. Weltman,* The Somnambulist (*1834*)

If you try to convince a sleepwalker of his nocturnal acrobatics, he will never believe you.

"Nonsense, you're sick in the head!"

That's what my brothers used to say when I attempted to describe to them their nights when the full moon was out.

I wanted to find out what they felt and how they saw themselves, those people led by the moon, that human breed mentioned obscurely only in fairy tales. I showed them their path along the eaves and told them how, with outstretched, swimming arms, they balanced themselves on such tiniest projections, at such heights that your breath stopped just to think of it. And always, not simply, but with pale wide-open empty eyes, or with lowered ones, with moonbeams streaming out of them. And why did they invariably do the same thing every time?

And from the way they listened to me, getting irritated if I was too persistent, but more often ridiculing me, the "little fibber," I realized that sleepwalkers remember nothing and can tell nothing about themselves; and no hints, no words can restore to them their own mysterious acts, so unlike ours.

It was thus, too, that the resurrected daughter of Jairus, and Lazarus who had been dead four days, could not remember, when questioned, their days and nights beyond the grave, which surely had been filled with events unlike ours, unknown to our days and nights.

At confession, and even simply in response to kind attention, the "possessed" and those "corrupted by an evil eye" would open their troubled hearts about things seen and heard, things that tormented them; but they remained forever silent about their mindless, unremembered ordeals—their ventral outcries, the conversations within them (from the gut) in different voices: human, animal, birdlike.

But sleepwalkers are totally without memory. Their mindlessness is like the great, self-preserving oblivion of humankind, to which Dostoyevsky's famed "children's tears," that ultimate argument of conscience and nonacceptance, is, in effect, nothing more than a touching literary image—without consequences.

Mindlessness and silence. If he mutters, the sleepwalker does not get far—he mostly shifts from foot to foot in the same spot. His own voice, even if hypnotic and trancelike, creates a barrier to lunar vision and confuses his path. But external sounds are no hindrance: a creaking bed, a chair turned over accidentally do not bar the way. Only a living call can return the sleeper to ordinary life. And I was warned never to try—it was like scaring someone from around a corner. Wakened abruptly, the sleeper screamed and trembled, doubled up, foamed at the mouth, choking in tears. And if you called him through the window, after he had started, he was lost—he'd crash down to his death.

Secretly I watched what went on in the nursery during full moon, which even our curtained windows were unable to screen out.

My brother, the one who considered himself superior to me— "cleverer by a year"—responded to the moon's mysterious call each time by climbing out of the window and walking along the cornice to the other side of the house. There he slid down the drainpipe into the yard and went into the henhouse. Carefully collecting every feather on the ground, he gathered them into a little pile; then, retracing his steps, he climbed back through the window and settled down in bed, falling into a peaceful sleep as if nothing had happened.

And the other brother, the one who wrote poems, climbed down from the window—on the second story!—at the opposite side, toward the street; climbed over the nail-studded fence, walked to our neighbor's roughhewn palisade, to the place where passersby usually "stopped," and just stood there. . . . After a while, all washed in moonlight, he scaled the fence again and walked past the henhouse to the woodpile; there he arranged the wood, setting log on log, a thick one on a thin one, then a still thicker one, like the menhirs at Karnak in the ocean (Moscow was also at the bottom of the ocean!), and, having built his incongruous row, he returned along the eaves, got in through the window, and serenely continued his lunar—now untroubled—sleep.

Their movements were like those of light, of flowing water— they nimbly rounded all obstacles. And if occasionally they'd meet on their journeys, they did not feel the contact, not even if they bumped foreheads: their common lunar sheath protected them.

And strangest of all: the mindlessness, the silence, and—to our eyes—the utter lack of purpose in their actions. And within this lack of purpose—always the same: the henhouse for one, and for the other the palisade, and the wood, mechanically, without the slightest deviation.

Another "walker" in our yard was Liska, the daughter of Nazarov the locksmith. On moonlit nights she climbed up on the roof, walked to the chimney, and crept into it. What she did in the chimney, no one could tell, but after a while she came out—flew out—and walked along the cornice, swam, with outstretched black arms, like an imp. And her whole sharp foxy little face was black with soot; only her shift, without a spot, glowed blue-white in the moon, and four thin rays, two from each eye, poured out eerily like molten silver from her tightly shut lids, and her black braids, blacker than ever, snaked, shining, down the white over her bony shoulders.

Andrevna, the Nazarov grandmother, took it into her head to break the girl of such things—a shame! At Liska's age, it was told, she herself had also been given to queer doings, but in those stories there was no hint of anything disgraceful; on the contrary, it was all fun. During full moon she'd rise and, like a ghost, with floating arms, she'd go directly to the larder where the eggs were kept. She'd put ten eggs or so into a sieve, then, face turned to the moon, she'd start shaking the sieve. The eggs would leap up with their round little chins like silver fish out of water, and—a marvel!—they would knock against each other and never break. It was a sight! But once a fellow thought he'd play a joke. He took a mouthful of water, and whooshed it out: aimed at the eggs, but struck her hands. The eggs, colliding, cracked, and yellow gold flowed down the shells. The dripping, sticky sieve slipped out of her hands and, as if burnt by fire, she clapped her empty hands and wakened with a sharp cry. That cured her. But eggs were one thing, and climbing into chimneys quite another. To break the girl of the habit, Andrevna put a basin full of water by her bed, and when she rose at the appointed hour and stepped into the water with her warm feet, she woke.

Andrevna weaned her of the chimney all right. Liska never once stepped on the roof again. But soon after that she had a "fit": suddenly, out of the blue, she started screaming—"for no reason." And no amount of water did any good this time. And though the girl, gasping, swore by the moon, "It isn't my fault, Grandma!" she was dragged off to the monastery to "exorcise the evil spell." And there she sank into the circle of the possessed.

Our nurse, Praskovya Semyonovna Mirskaya, . . . a meek and patient woman, "broken in" by a lifetime of servitude, had great faith in Andrevna, who had proven by Liska's example, and by her own experience as well, that water, being "kin in its nature to the moon," was a sure remedy against "moon trouble." On a moonlit night, she set out a basin of water, and settled down to sleep in her corner of the nursery.

At night, roused by a natural need, she got up and stepped right into the basin. And despite her firm faith in the sobering powers of water—or was it the moon's sorcery again?—the sleep-fuddled old woman imagined she was by the river, rinsing the wash. She turned around, but the wash wasn't there—nothing but a single sheet! No towels, no handkerchiefs, not even a miserable pair of underpants. Had the wind blown everything away, or had a sneak thief made off with it? She stretched her arms and went groping around the room until, unseeing, she knocked down the water pitcher and soaked her shift. "Girl," she cried, "I'm drowning!" And she drowned.

Since then, the nurse was nicknamed "the drowned one." The whole "outrage" with the basin, however, was attributed to me. I must confess, I did move the basin to the nurse's bed, but—honestly—the rest of it was not my fault!

Instead of water, wooden gratings were set into the nursery windows to put an end to the perilous nocturnal journeys, and it became impossible to climb out. But I discovered that, in violation of all self-evidence ("a part is always less than the whole"?), even the narrowest and smallest cage could not imprison the sleepwalker: the lunar hand passed freely where an ordinary finger would not enter. Hence, if there is a slightest chink, there is an exit for the lunar body. And only the inevitable effort to wriggle out somehow, in defiance of Euclid, made my brothers turn from the window.

Then followed an anguished wandering through the room: in

their nightshirts, with bare feet, catching the beckoning moonbeams with wide-open, pale, empty eyes, they walked about, stretching their swimming arms in despair.

I saw everything, but no one saw me: I was in this world. And it seemed to me that they were also unaware of one another in their lunar world. But I, watching from another world? . . .

At twilight, passing through the rooms, I noticed that I instinctively put out my arms—like them. And at night I was drawn to the window. I peered into the night; its seething, scurrying black life seemed filled with strange winged animal creatures —dragons, birds, serpents. On bright nights I stared at the moon, at its path, leading away and away. And, all of me possessed by the lunar dream, I strained to penetrate the depths of the dissolving light, to reach some center of disintegration (when everything "turned into zero wholes, zero tenths, zero hundredths, zero thousandths . . .") and glance into its bottomless core. And I felt that, just a moment more, and I would hear. . . . And I felt— this must be very much like their world.

Sleepwalkers are not told the truth; nobody would ever tell one, "You're a sleepwalker." Only Andrevna, trying to shame her Liska out of it, nagged at her: What did the girl do in the chimney at night, and with whom? And how come her shift stayed clean?

Sleepwalkers are asked no questions, they must not be frightened. And they are mentioned in hushed tones. But I, with my keen ear . . . (I listened to all talk.) My two brothers were always spoken of as sleepwalkers; and it was only about them that people whispered, "They walk."

My henhouse brother often cried—he was nicknamed "Crybaby"—and constantly complained: he pointed at his left temple, where it hurt, and was always sad. A good mathematician. Later a bookkeeper. My other brother, of the woodpile, did not complain, and was distinguished among us by his extraordinary susceptibility: when he read moving passages, he could not refrain from tears. He wrote tender verses himself, was always in love with someone, and sat for hours at the window, dreaming. He had a good voice. After graduation from the gymnasium, he entered medical school, but soon abandoned it and joined the Philharmonic. Later, an unsuccessful stockbroker.

With me, things were different. Even in appearance I was unlike either of them. And I never cried, except once, but that was so long ago that no one remembered it. On that sole occasion, I cried when awakened from sleep, frightened by a fire that I was shown through the window. The sugar refinery across the street was burning: a blue, enormous, airy, hissing mass, pierced by lightnings, pieces falling away from it—like a living thing. A stone itself would melt! I never cried and was not afraid of anything; people said that nothing fazed me, nothing could ever make a dent in me—"hopeless." In reality, despite my "thick skin," I felt everything, but seemed encased as in a coat of mail, and this was attributed to my "coarseness." But was it not, perhaps, because of this "coarseness," which was permeable to the most subtle excitations and yet seemed to lock everything within itself, without expression, that I, so open to the moon, was not a moon-walker like my defenseless brothers?

The sleepwalkers—those active dreamers—saw no dreams or, if they did, they had no recollection of them. But to me, no sleepwalker, was revealed an unforgettable, a magic world. And through the same moon—her sorcery—the moon floating in vastness "over the world of dreams."

Intoxicated with strange bitterness, I gazed at her: her green eyes flowed like a wave. . . . Scattering silver mist, she sped from star to star, herself "a star dream." Her flight was endless, and there were no bounds to my desire to reach her! Higher and higher, dissolving, she was flying from me, hopelessly. And, powdered with green efflorescence, I could not tear myself away. I stretched my arms to her and stared, chained by her power. Her bitter greenness sank into my heart. Then, blinded, I rose and followed, irresistibly, her silver beam—her hand. . . .

And can I ever forget our first meeting?

I had adopted Hoffmann as my own, because our eyes belong to the same light, a light of sharp trembling, of dazzling fire and lunar shimmer. And it was my mother who had first pronounced to me the name: Ernst Theodor Amadeus Hoffmann. And the gypsy Yelena Korneyevna, who kept a library on Moroseyka Street, at the corner where you turn to Clear Ponds, lent me the twelve-volume Hoffmann. "The Nutcracker" and "The Unknown Child"—these first tales later brought me into the circle of the Serapion Brethren. I know no writer who is closer to me than Hoffmann.

I remember, too: she flooded the room with patches of blue—my sheet and pillow turned blue, my hands, my fingers were shackled with blue rings. . . . With bottomless blue eyes she looked, without once taking them away, and I felt—they stared into my very heart. And now it was not I but she who strained to reach me: from star to star she flowed silently, scattering blue silver, and stood in my window, witching. And I could not tear myself away, and everything in me sang. And with the song, ringing with silvery bells, I rose to the window, I stretched my arms to her—and she receded slowly, drawing me after her with her blue beam—her sash. . . .

And how can I forget my first dream!

It was Gogol. Gogol, revealed to me by a Ukrainian song sung in Moscow by Maria Zankovetskaya. When I heard it, Gogol—of an alien sky (our own stars are no larger than a pinhead, and our sky has none of the deep blue of Sorochintsy!) and an alien mode (even our flowers are quiet: bluebells, clover, no mallows and no poppies; and the same is true of words, everything very simple!)—suddenly Gogol spoke to me, with his "May Night," and his "Viy," and his moonstruck Katerina. And I don't know of any other writer who has charmed me so irrevocably with his word.

And there is yet another image of her I will not forget. I dream of her like that—"always the same dream." Waking, I bitterly regret the dawn, I'd rather keep my eyes shut!

She appears from behind the Androniev belltower. I hear her. I go to the window. She stops. Her pale face is rimmed with pink, and near her eyes and mouth and over the eyebrows, a crooked cross of roses on the green. She sees me too. We look at one another. All!—more is not allowed! And I distinguish her whisper . . . half-words. And this shadow grips my heart again as in a vise. And my hands drop.

What did I know then? Or what had I done? But I understood that there was neither *yesterday* nor *tomorrow*—they were in the single *now*. And I had to answer—I was answerable both for what had been and what I had forgotten, and what would be and what I did not know. And this, as in a dream, was all at once all of my destiny.

Reproach, or conscience? Twisted roses on the green, and aching, intent, unblinking eyes: "murderer!" She dripped black, tarantula-poisoned fire into my soul. I turned numb, with closed eyes. And I felt, she was not gone, she was in the other window. And she would not go, she watched me.

Baudelaire's "L'Irrémédiable"? Dostoyevsky? And that pain, that reproach, that very word "murderer," from *Crime and Punishment*. . . . Who were the writers that had wounded me most deeply, calling to light my bitterest thought? Baudelaire and Dostoyevsky.

I cannot understand—or was this also the enchantment of the moon?—how I walked through the endless yard, passing the henhouse, where my brother counted moon feathers; past the factory dormitories, where Liska flew out of the chimney like an imp on moonlit nights; past the woodshed, where my other brother piled his lunar edifices; past the factory, by the cast-iron door where, before the eyes of my undimming memory, my friend Yegorka had lain on glittering chips of glass, while the peg-leg hen kept vigil over his small blue body, torn by the wheel, crushed by the belts, now covered with a piece of sacking; past the carpenter shop, the horse stable, the oaken front door of the white house; and suddenly I found myself in the front garden.

The house stood in a hollow within an ancient earth wall (Sadovaya Street Earth Bank), and on the slope before the house, all the way up to street level, there was a flower garden.

But I had never seen such flowers before. Freshly watered, they greedily opened their blue and blue-white calyxes and breathed deeply, powdered with airy silvery dust. Circling and turning, I followed the path, but not the usual one, covered with red, creaking sand; no, this path was softly black and undulated underfoot. I walked toward the cellar window. There, behind an iron grill, our distant relative (Ladygina) was living out her hundredth year. For her kindness and sweet temper, everybody called her "Granny"— the only being in that white house who did not meet us with vicious barking.

And, as ever, I glanced into the cellar behind the iron grill to greet her. But this was not old "Granny." Someone's mother sat there, winding a huge ball of thread. And in her blue eyes I saw the flash of joy with which they met my unexpected eyes. She stood up and, still looking at me, gave me an apple from behind the grill. I took the apple in my hand. And walked away. "Golden Sap!"

But now I did not walk along the darkling path—I walked right through the flowers, holding the apple in my hand. Nor did I go up to the street. All in a whirl of silver dust and flower breath, I floated down into an unknown abyss, and sensed behind me, following my descent, a pair of eyes, like ringing bluebells.

And of a sudden, in a gust of fragrant wind, I felt that something was growing out of my head. And I saw myself: on my head, rising out of me, branches were swaying. I seized the one over my right eye and plucked it out with the root: green—a magic plant, a fern!

translated by Mirra Ginsburg

from The Flute for Mice, 1953

Mu'allaqāt*
ALEXEI REMIZOV

My "contrariness" began in inconceivable eternity, when the fiery little star of my spirit flared up in the mist of the world. I have carried this contrariness through all the forms of my life, and I am carrying it into eternity; in all my transformations there is "unsubmission"—the untamable opposing force of my "I." I affirm my freedom in willfulness and, obeying no one, go my own way.

And suddenly the earth slipped out from under my feet and I hung suspendid in air—"Mu'allaqāt!" In Mecca ancient Arabic manuscripts hang suspended in air, "mu'allaqāt."

Above the earth: what depends on me on earth? Nothing. Hence, no power. My will, my freedom is with me.

For one suspended in the air, it is easier to look into himself and judge himself.

I was never possessed by self-importance, the misfortune of fools. I have always felt my limitations. Everyone I met—I speak

---

* This Arabic word means "posters" or here, apparently, "texts" hanging on a wall. EDITOR.

of memorable encounters—seemed more gifted than I. When I found myself in the first place, it embarrassed me, my whole being turned inside out: no, I had no right to it. And driven into a corner, I felt in my right place; and the feeling was pierced with pain. I understood that I lived only when hounded, humbled, and "life" and "pain" became one and the same to me. And when there was no pain, it was as though I were not living.

I am suspended, I see myself in the air, but some particle of my being remains on earth. Else I would not be thinking and would not be writing.

To eat and to drink, to freeze and seek warmth and peace; helpless all around. And in the helplessness there is pain. Hence, this particle of my being, too, lives buried alive.

I am a man buried alive.

Because I trust words, I am easily beguiled. There are no vain words, each one lives. And I weigh and measure words. This is my trade—"a counter of words." I cannot understand how words can be spoken "any old way," or what it means that "words have been mixed up and robbed of value."

My trust comes of forgetting that the valuation of words is something that is my own, not general.

What does the one who is buried alive say?

"I am ready for everything," I say. "Ready to accept everything, and I will accept. And I ask for nothing."

But I can tell from here what a storm there is beneath this meek silence and readiness for all.

And I know that in my nature everything is unsubmissive, to the very core. And I may be doomed, but I will never accept my end.

"My eyes, what did you look at, what did you see when I walked on earth?"

Looking no longer, my eyes replied:

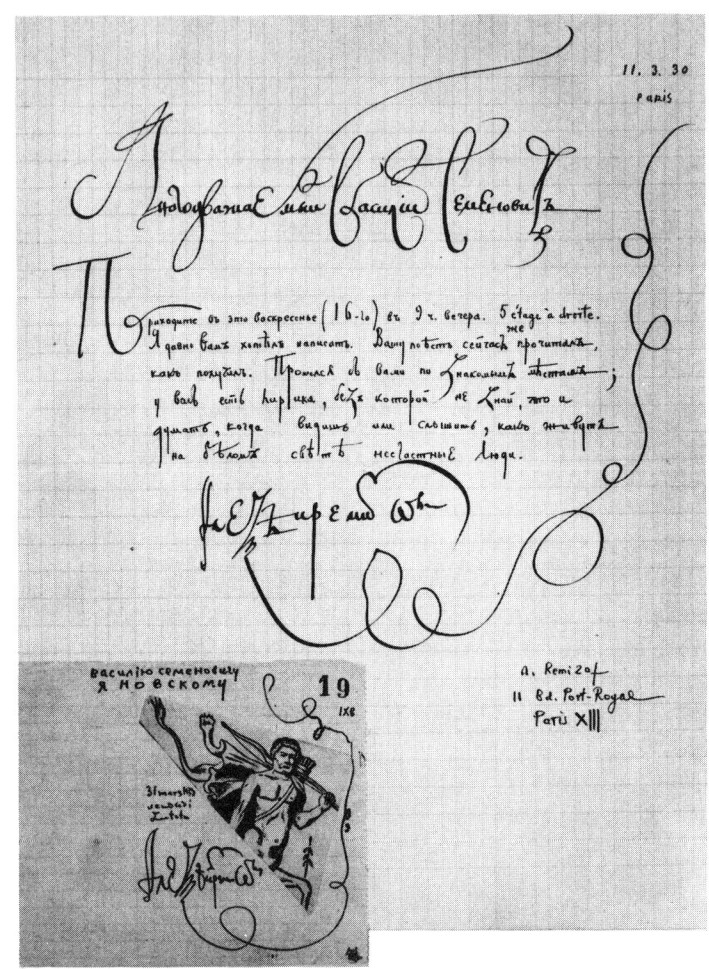

Letter by Remizov to V. S. Yanovsky, 1930.

Remizov's letter to Vladimir Markov, written when Remizov was going blind, 1956.

"We looked and looked, and could not get enough of the beauty of God's world. So many wonders, so much love! We saw pain too: it screams and it is hidden. And with mute pain, dazzled by ineffable light, we helplessly turned downward and were extinguished."

"And you, my ears, what did you hear?"

"The earth is filled with sounds," the ears replied. "Its song flies to the stars, and with the starry glitter descends to earth. All the sounds of the earth are steeped in bitterness. Is it because the earth is bitter, or the stars joyless? Or is it neither the earth nor the stars, but the very substance of life that is poisoned?"

I am suspended in the air above the earth, and I am also on earth, buried alive. I have two pairs of eyes and four ears, one heart and one mind.

He talked himself out—splintered himself out—screamed out, and fell silent with his stifled "I accept":

"I submit to my fate, I accept it." That means I deserve it. It means "the hounded, the cornered one" must still endure a certain term on earth.

I see it from above, the particle of me that is buried alive, my shadow; yet he is convinced that I am his shadow. Well, let him, it won't change anything. I see him fumbling there—in a closed circle; buried alive, no exit: hands slashed, bruised.

"I'm sick of begging," he says. "If anyone brings something, fine. If they forget, or can't be bothered, I'll get along somehow. It doesn't matter."

And I too am ready. I'd go and swat him down, my self that is buried alive.

"The most profound thing," he says, "is my unbelief. And it is ineradicable. And my insatiable nature—all or nothing—in words, in thought, in dreams, unchangeably. But the living is alive by constant change, don't I know it? And in despair I long for one thing—extermination."

He repeats my words, but with him they come out of his squashed heart.

"What?"

"I believe in miracles, I love all that lives."

She comes late in the evening. She settles on the sofa opposite me, under the silver snakeskin; takes out a piece of iron communion bread and, with her eyes fixed on me, starts gnawing at it.

In the field of my kaleidoscopic constructions she is a living black spot, and my green-shaded lamp blanches her face a deadly white.

Breaking away from manuscript or book, I can't help watching her: she knows everything about me, more perhaps than I do. As our eyes meet, I cannot tell myself apart from her—everything in us is interfused.

Her work will never end: the bread is iron, and I . . . it's useless, even thinking of an end. And we shall leave each other only in a single instant, at a stroke.

What is her voice like? She has never uttered a word with me. Or is she mute?

My dreams after our meetings are always of red darkness— the red of blood, the darkness of shelter. And all day afterward I am entangled in their web, and there is no escape, no exit, nothing to bring me out into the light.

She is fond of flowers—I noticed that—vivid ones. I know it from my eyes, which long for colors. And she cannot bear anything alive; the moment anyone enters the room, she's gone.

Nobody else has ever seen her. And it is seldom that she is not with me. I go into the kitchen to boil water, and there she is, silent as air, perched on a stool, or hiding in the corner behind the brooms.

And when she gnaws at her iron bread, I feel—it is a piece of my heart.

translated by Mirra Ginsburg

Khodasevich: irony and dislocation: a poet in exile
ROBERT P. HUGHES

The last of six children of already middle-aged parents—his mother was Jewish, his father Polish—he was a weak and sickly child. At first, he was not expected to live; when he did, he was coddled and indulged by his family. According to his own reminiscences,[1] the first eight years of his childhood were eventful and rich in useful impressions. They were years spent, to use his expression, in a "gynarchy" composed of mother, nurse, grandmother, and sister. As Roman Catholics, he and his family lived in a society that was almost completely Russian Orthodox. After completing his education at the university, he began his literary career in Moscow, but it was the year and a half that he spent in Petrograd, i.e. St. Petersburg, the eighteenth-century "window on the West," that was decisive in the formation of his aesthetic. He became one of the leading exponents of "Petersburg poetics," an evolution that was consummated just before and just after his emigration. Subject to the multifarious influences of Russsian decadence and symbol-

ABOVE PHOTO: Vladislav Khodasevich in the nineteen-twenties. All translations are mine. AUTHOR.

ism, he preferred a poetic method that had its origin, profoundly, in Pushkin. A distinguished representative of the Silver Age of Russian poetry (approximately the first three decades of the twentieth century), he spent his last seventeen years in poverty-stricken exile. A poet first and foremost, he eked out an existence in *émigré* journalism, producing a series of essays, articles, reviews, and books that have already become classics of Russian literary biography, criticism, and polemic. The end of his difficult life in the city of lights—Paris between the wars—came just one year before the beginning of the German occupation. He died on June 14, 1939.

Vladislav Khodasevich was born in Moscow at noon, May 16 (Julian calendar), 1886. The events, observations, and incidents of childhood reported in his autobiographical fragments reveal a good deal about the formation of his personality and its reflection in his poetry. The procedure may be doubtful, even illegitimate, but I should like to make use of the potential fallacy that an individual's childhood is reshaped in his memory through the experiences he has accumulated by middle age. More like Tolstoy and Proust, to cite only two examples of writers whose adult perceptions and predilections color their accounts of childhood, and less like Nabokov, whose recollections of his idyllic early years seem to arise out of the innocence and perceptions of a child, Khodasevich recalls and reflects, at times with love, and more often with bitterness and irony. He is more like Nabokov, however, in his sense of dislocation, which began early and lasted his lifetime.

Early in his reminiscences, he recounts a characteristic anecdote, preserved as family tradition:

My sister Zhenya, who was twelve at the time, was promenading me like a doll in a little wicker pram with wooden wheels. Just then a kitten came in. Seeing it, and popping my eyes, I stretched out my arms and pronounced distinctly: "Kithy, kithy!"

According to legend the first word spoken by Derzhavin was "God." This is of course incomparably more sublime. I can only be comforted because on the whole
there is a difference
Between Derzhavin and me,
and also because, in getting out my first word, I understood, after all, what I was saying, and Derzhavin did not.

Khodasevich tells the Derzhavin story in his excellent literary biography of the great eighteenth-century poet:

At birth he was exceedingly weak, tiny and puny. A severe cure was employed: according to the local custom of those places, the child was baked in bread. He did not die. A huge comet with a six-streamed tail appeared in the sky when he was about a year old. Amongst the local inhabitants there were ominous rumors, and they expected great calamities. When the comet was pointed out to the infant, he uttered his first word: "God!" [2]

Related to his subsequent interest in Derzhavin, the story from Khodasevich's childhood might introduce another important motif in his life: the reciprocal affection between the poet and cats. In the same memoir, he relates with pride an incident from his later life when he was picked up by a cat on the streets of Paris, how they drank together in a bistro, a cognac and a saucer of milk respectively, and how they went together to his place, although any further, more intimate acquaintanceship was out of the question because he lived in a respectable hotel.

Khodasevich does not indulge himself in a Disneyesque anthropomorphizing when he reviews the traits that he finds so admirable in cats: "they are not intelligent, they are wise"; "they are inclined to be dreamy and philosophical"; "they are impractical . . . , and their bravery is reckless"; "they are proud, independent, and they prefer to count only on themselves"; "their friendship is devoid of stormy manifestations, and there is not a hint of obsequiousness in it"; such friendship is displayed especially "when things are going bad for you, or when you have a heavy heart." More often than not, then, Khodasevich prefers the pleasure of cats' company to that of fellow human beings. Three of the poet's feline friends appear in the memoir: Nal (in whose eyes could be seen "the reflection of some other existence," when he awakened out of a "mysterious slumber"); Murr (whose sportive nature in games of hide-and-seek is fondly recalled); and Zaychunov (who cheered the poet on the saddest and dreariest occasions).

When Murr, a black cat named in Hoffmannesque allusion, died in 1931, Khodasevich was moved to write one of his finest poems, an elegy:

In play he was so wise and in his wisdom playful—
Comforting friend and my inspirer! Now
He's in those gardens, beyond the fiery river,
With Catullus and the sparrow, Derzhavin and his swallow.

O, lovely are the gardens beyond the fiery river,
Where there's no vulgar rabble, where in benefic rest
Belovèd shades of poets and of beasts
Enjoy the well-earned peace of all eternity.

And when shall I depart? I have no wish to hurry
My time, prescribed for travails on this earth,
But ever more I fly in ever-loyal dreams
To those removed by the mysterious net.

The Russian original of this poem, in iambic hexameter, with constant caesuras and alternating feminine and masculine rhymes, is an exquisitely realized example of elegiac verse.

A dirge on the death of a friend from the animal kingdom is a relatively rare item in Russian poetry, and it is not accidental that Khodasevich turned to the eighteenth-century poet he knew so well to find an appropriate predecessor. Derzhavin's poems on birds—from his metaphoric swallow, through the bullfinch who sings at the death of Suvorov, to his peacock, swan, nightingales, and little titmouse—are uncommon phenomena; and his whimsical four-line epitaph for a dog who fell to his death from his mistress' lap, on hearing the news of the death of Louis XVI, is delightful. In English, this awareness of the animal world is represented by such fine pieces as Christopher Smart's splendid "For I will consider my cat Geoffrey," the introduction to William Blake's "Auguries of Innocence," and Cowper's "Epitaph on a Hare," written on the death of a pet jackrabbit, which contains another expression of the kind of delight and pleasure Khodasevich took in cats: "I kept him for his humour's sake, / For he would oft beguile / My heart of thoughts that made it ache / And force me to a smile." The starling and the ass episodes in Sterne's *Sentimental Journey* are also an expression of this particular sensibility. To these examples there might even be added a poem of rather different character, Thomas Gray's droll "Ode on the

Death of a Favourite Cat, Drowned in a Tub of Gold Fishes," which concludes with a witty moral: "Not all that tempts your wand'ring eyes / And heedless hearts is lawful prize; / Nor all, that glisters, gold."

In many of these cases, however, and especially so in the instance of Khodasevich, such poems reveal a distrust of human relationships, a disgust, even, with human society (the "base rabble"); the company and example of animals is found to be preferable. But to return to the elegy on the death of Murr: the allusions to Catullus and Derzhavin refer to personae of love lyrics, who voice their regret at the passing of beauty, either a real woman or her surrogate, and thus ease their grief; while Khodasevich finds his consolation in dreaming of joining his beloved pet in the other, better world.

An intense passion that had its origin in his earliest years was Khodasevich's love of the ballet; he reports that he was a balletomane at the age of four. As a very small child he was tricked into going to the theater—after violent and tearful protest, he was told that he was to visit his nanny out in the country—and he attended his first ballet in the splendor of Moscow's Bolshoi Theater. If this supposed visit to "nanny's village" was nearly incomprehensible, the young boy was all the more bewitched by the experience. "The ballet had a decisive influence on my entire life, on the manner in which my tastes, predilections and interests were formed. In the final analysis, it was through ballet that I came to art in general and to poetry in particular. The Bolshoi Theater was my spiritual homeland." He describes the interior of the building in loving detail—the semicircular corridors, the polished steps of the flights of stairs, and the auditorium itself, filled with the odors of chocolate, perfume, and various fabrics. Ultimately, of course, the physical surroundings counted for little when compared with the captivating action on stage, which he would reproduce at home, as "monoballets," before a full-length mirror. He was partial to the role of the ballerina, which was always of greater prominence and effect.

His enthusiasm for the ballet, he declares, lasted into later life, but the only important poetic result seems to be the brief poem—the last he wrote in Russia—which he composed in Petrograd on May Day, 1922. In the commentary reproduced in the *Collected Verse* of 1961, he recalls the poem's composition: "May first, in the morning, in bed, sick, the deafening 'Internationale' of troops passing by on parade. I had been at 'Giselle' the evening before. . . . The day was extraordinarily bright and warm. It was very cozy in my room with its windows open on to the Moika."

Giselle

Yes, yes! In blind and tender passion
Live out your pain, burn out your fire,
And, like a letter, rend your heart,
Take leave of reason, and expire.

And then? The gravestone over you
Again you'll have to move away,
Again you'll love, and twitch your leg
Across the azure, moonlit stage.

The example of Pushkin (for subject matter alone, *Eugene Onegin,* Chapter 1, XX) comes almost involuntarily to mind: the paucity of metaphor (only one), the decisive verbs that carry so heavy a semantic load, the scudded but firm iambic tetrameter, the unobtrusive rhymes, and so forth. It is one of Khodasevich's most perfect little creations. However, what the poem also suggests is the angular grace and brilliance of the tightly constructed ballet music of Igor Stravinsky, his *Baiser de la Fée,* for example—in which the romantic music of Tchaikovsky is transformed and refined in a hard and clear twentieth-century sensibility—rather than Adolphe Adam's romantic music for the "classical" ballet that is the ostensible subject.

Another childhood experience that seems to haunt several later poems was a fall from his nanny's window, which was open onto a busy courtyard. "There was a parrot in a cage being carried out. I stretch out my neck, stand up—and suddenly the yard, that had been beneath me, is rising swiftly upwards, everything is tumbling head over heels, then something strikes me on the head, there's dirt being sprinkled down my back, and I, my eyes fixed on the blue sky, am sliding feet first down the roof." In a clatter of overturned flowerpots, he came to a stop with his heels set against the gutter that rimmed the edge of the tin roof. He was pulled back up and through the window by his nanny, nearly paralyzed with fright; and he was then and there bundled off to offer a prayer of thanksgiving. This happy conclusion is commemorated in one of the stanzas of his long poem about his nanny ("Not by my mother, but by the peasant woman out of Tula / Elena Kuzina was I reared . . ."):

> Only once, when I fell from the window,
> But arose alive (how I remember that day!),
> Did she, in the chapel of the Holy Virgin of Iveria,
> Light a penny candle for my miraculous escape.

Without suggesting a simple connection between this near fatal, obviously traumatic experience (intensified by the—undeserved, in his view—punishment he received from his parents) and the poetry of his later life, a kind of morbid fascination with windows, reflecting surfaces, and the nightmare of falling are continual features of his poetry. The verb "to fall" (*padat'/past'*), in its various grammatical guises and compounds, seems to be omnipresent in his poetry.

"From the Window" (1921) is a characteristic jaundiced view of the world. In the first "outlook," a small boy loses his kite, and a thief steals a chicken from a noseless old woman; all is set to rights in the second stanza, but then: "My quiet hell is put together again / In all its pristine harmony." In the second "outlook," the observer keeps waiting for a "crazed automobile" to crush someone, and he expects a violent, apocalyptic disturbance; and then: "The dreams that strangle my soul will be broken off. / All that I desire will begin, / And the angels will extinguish the sun, / A useless candle in the morning." If these poems were not so typical, the time, place, and circumstances of composition (hungry, the poet added the two lines of the first poem while he was walking through post-Revolutionary Petrograd to the marketplace to sell his ration of herrings, 23 July 1921; the second poem was written on the day he received the news of the death of Alexander Blok, 11 August 1921) might seem to be of greater importance. Another poem, written the following May, "I am gazing out the window—and feel scornful," presents an equally bleak picture of Khodasevich's very existence; he concludes by comparing himself with a worm chopped in two by a heavy spade and now writhing in a flowerbed. Sustaining the mood in his brief "The street was in semi-darkness" (1922), he observes a suicide from an open window just beneath the roof. The concluding couplet is a bitter epigram: "Happy is he who falls head downward: / The world is different for him, if only for a second."

In emigration, windows both reflect and frame for him the petty and the great horrors of existence. In "Berlin" (1923), he sits in a dimly lit cafe, warming himself; outside the polished plate-glass window (it seems to be enclosing an aquarium), many-eyed streetcars are swimming through the underwater linden trees. He is drawn into a double reflection: the table at which he sits is also reflected in the windows of the passing streetcars; and then, in a moment of understated but real horror, he recognizes his own severed head gazing back at him. The supposedly dispassionate and cynical observer the poet believed himself to be realizes that he, too, is confined and caught inside the "aquarium" of existence. The unposed question, then, is, "Who is really observing the entire scene?" In this, one of Khodasevich's strongest poems, the void of human existence is made frighteningly apparent.

Although Khodasevich did not choose to have his first two volumes of poetry preserved in his *Collected Verse* (published in Paris in 1927), the second volume, at least, was considered more than juvenilia by contemporary readers and critics. *Youth* was published in 1908, *The Happy Little House* in 1914, both in Moscow. The latter was favorably received by the influential Nikolai Gumilyov in one of his omnibus reviews in the Acmeist journal *Apollon* (published in St. Petersburg). Gumilyov praised Khodasevich's chary approach to writing (he thus does not wear out his welcome), and compares him in this respect to Tyutchev and

Annensky; he finds him a promising poet, but lacking a certain sureness and freedom of gesture. This is followed by an astute characterization that remains valid for the remainder of Khodasevich's poetic career: "European in his love for the details of beauty, he is nevertheless very much a Slav in his rather particular indifferent weariness and melancholic skepticism. Only hope or suffering is capable of bestirring such a soul, but Khodasevich voluntarily, even with a certain arrogance, renounces the one and the other." Gumilyov approves of his attention to technical aspects, even though he finds stylistically inexpressive passages. He concludes with a vague statement that would seem to relegate Khodasevich to the ranks of the Symbolists: ". . . he is for now only a ballet-master, but the dances he teaches are sacred dances." [3] *The Happy Little House* went through two more editions, in 1921 (in Petrograd) and in 1922 (in Berlin).

Khodasevich's third volume, *The Way of the Grain,* published in Moscow just before he departed for Petrograd in 1920, is the first set of poems the poet and most of his critics considered mature verse. Among the most effective and unusual of the pieces in this collection are the longer narrative poems in blank verse. In "Episode" (1918), he recalls a mystical event of three years before, when he was alone in his room on a dreary, wintry morning: he experiences a bifurcation of his self. For a brief moment he is simultaneously of the earth and beyond it, and he is able to see himself as if from the outside. Such a departure from his consciousness and the transformation of the ugly world became desirable to Khodasevich, and its attainment is also the subject of several short lyrics of this collection (e.g. "Smolensk Marketplace," 1916, and "Variation," 1919). There are other blank-verse narratives from this period. "November the Second" (1918), a view of revolutionary and civil war Moscow, concludes in restrained, prosaic sadness: "At home / I drank my tea, sorted out the papers / That had piled up on my desk during the week, / And sat down to work. But, for the first time in my life, / Neither 'Mozart and Salieri,' nor 'The Gypsies' / That day could slake my thirst." "Noon" (1918) depicts the poet as he daydreams about a visit to Venice until he is interrupted by someone asking the time of day. "An Encounter" (1918) is another recollection of Venice. "The House" (1919–1920) comprises reflections on the transitory nature of human existence as the poet observes a deserted, ruined building. "The Monkey" (1919), translated in the present volume by Vladimir Nabokov, recalls a moment of epiphany experienced by the poet on the day World War I began.

Immediately after the Revolution, Khodasevich did a brief stint as a functionary in various cultural organizations set up by the new Communist regime. His experiences are related with humor and foreboding in several sketches that were published in the nineteen-thirties and were later partially collected in his *Literary Essays and Memoirs* (New York, 1954). His bureaucratic career was short-lived, and toward the end of 1920 he moved to Petrograd. He soon took up residence in the House of Arts, a domicile established by Maxim Gorky in 1919 and inhabited by a large number of literary figures. (The house was closed by authorities in the autumn of 1922.) Khodasevich has left another valuable memoir describing his life on the "mad ship," the title of Olga Forsh's fascinating *roman à clef* about the denizens of this peculiar institution. It was here that Khodasevich lived in the "circular room" which is the setting for his famous "Ballad" (1921; "Orpheus" in Vladimir Nabokov's translation).

Here Khodasevich wrote the majority of the poems that appeared in his fourth volume of verse, *The Heavy Lyre,* published both in Petrograd in 1922 and, after his emigration, in Berlin in 1923. A great many of the poems discussed or mentioned above, those dating from 1920 to 1922, are from this collection. Taken in conjunction with the final two poems translated here by Nabokov (the closing poems of *The Heavy Lyre*), they present a portrait of the artist dislocated both physically and spiritually. The discrepancy between appearance and reality, the imprisonment of his soul in a despised environment, that was a major theme of his earlier poetry is here both more intense and vastly more mature.

One other poem will demonstrate the aesthetic of Khodasevich at this juncture in his life:

A burning star, the quivering ether—
In spans of arches night is hiding.
How is one not to love this world,
This whole unlikely gift of Yours?

You gave me five unsteady senses,
You gave me all of time and space,
At play in the mirage of arts
Is my poor soul's inconstancy.

And out of nothing I create
Your seas, Your deserts, and Your hills,
The total glory of Your sun,
That is so blinding to our eyes.

And suddenly at merest whim
I wreck this splendid senselessness
The way a tiny child pulls down
A fortress that he's built of cards.

A poem of great simplicity (in iambic tetrameter, with alternating masculine and feminine rhymes), it offers a typical Khodasevich construction: a scene of tranquil beauty is cut short by questioning; the poet's function is examined; he comes solipsistically to doubt the existence of the phenomenal world (is it all his own creation?), and then concludes with a pointed metaphor.

Khodasevich was at the height of his fame as a poet at the beginning of the twenties. In a retrospective poem written in 1926, "Petersburg," he reports that "They looked at me—and forgot / Their bubbling teapots; / Felt boots would be singed on the stoves, / As everyone listened to my poems." This would seem to be a scene set in the House of Arts, where literary readings and discussions were the order of every day. In the same poem he boasts of his influence on Soviet poetry: "I grafted, after all, the classical rose / Onto the Soviet wilding." The graft doesn't seem to have taken, for Khodasevich's poetry was studiously ignored and downgraded soon after he left Russia—as it is even today.[4]

The Heavy Lyre, however, was highly praised by numerous critics, and it remains the favorite volume of most readers. The famous Symbolist poet and novelist Andrei Belyi wrote a lengthy and glowing review-article whose title is partially self-explanatory: "The Heavy Lyre and Russian Lyric Poetry" (*Contemporary Annals,* 1923). He traces Khodasevich's poetic pedigree to the greatest nineteenth-century poets, Pushkin, Tyutchev, Baratynsky, and Fet, and considers him a worthy successor to the tradition. (This was Belyi's second article in praise of Khodasevich; the first appeared in Volume 5 of his own miscellany, *Notes of Dreamers,* in 1922.)

A more restrained appraisal, and perhaps one of the most interesting and accurate views of Khodasevich in this period, is the one given by Osip Mandelstam in 1923 in his article on the poets of that period, "Storm and Stress":

> Russian Symbolism had its Virgils and its Ovids, and it had its Catulluses, not so much in seniority as in the type of creative work. It is here that Kuzmin and Khodasevich should be mentioned. They are typical younger poets, with all the purity and charm of sound that is peculiar to younger poets. [...] Khodasevich cultivated Baratynsky's theme: "My gift is mean, and my voice not loud," and he played every possible variation on the theme of the stunted child. His junior lineage is traceable to the verse of the second-rank poets of the Pushkin and post-Pushkin period—amateur poets like the Countess Rostopchina, Vyazemsky, *et al.* Proceeding from the best period of Russian poetic dilettantism, from the family album, private verse epistles, workaday epigrams, Khodasevich brought right up into the twentieth century the intricacy and the tender coarseness of the folksy Moscow idiom that was in use in aristocratic literary circles of the last century. His verses are very folksy, very literary, and very elegant.[5]

Khodasevich left the Soviet Union, accompanied by Nina Berberova, in June 1922. They settled at first in Berlin, where he wrote some of his cruelest and most terrifying poems: the four-poem cycle "By the Sea," "Berlin," "From a Berlin Street," "An Mariechen," "No, no food shall I find today," "Summer Season," "Underground," "All is stone . . . ," "I arise enfeebled from my bed." Some of the titles themselves indicate the desperate and cynical mood that seems finally to have taken possession of the poet. He was close for a time to Andrei Belyi and Maxim Gorky, with whom he edited a journal, *Colloquy,* that was intended—vainly—for distribution in the Soviet Union. He left Berlin in November 1923. His pillar-to-post existence—from Berlin to Prague to Rome to Gorky's villa in Sorrento for two lengthy visits—finally ended when he and his companion settled in Paris in 1925. There he was to spend the rest of his life. These wanderings and his subsequent life and work in Paris are treated in fascinating and touching detail in Nina Berberova's *The Italics Are Mine.* Beyond a few notable exceptions, the sources of his poetry were gradually drying up. He found himself at a poetic dead-end. Berberova reports his anguished outcry: "I cannot, cannot, cannot live and write here, and I cannot, cannot, cannot live and write there."

One of the best poems he was able to produce in this period is his "Sorrento Photographs" (1926). It is comprised of a double set of superimposed recollections. The first is of the funeral of a poor janitor in Moscow and a Good Friday procession through the winding streets of Sorrento. The depiction of the entrance of the procession with the effigy of the Virgin into the cathedral, and the candles and singing within, is one of the few ecstatic moments in Khodasevich's poetry. The second set of overlapping recollections comprises a view of Naples through the early morning haze and one of the Peter-and-Paul citadel in St. Petersburg reflected in the river Neva. These memories are grouped around the controlling metaphor of a double-exposed snapshot taken by a careless amateur photographer. The portrayal of the play of memory and the interpenetrating depictions of Italian landscapes and Russian scenes is a remarkable achievement. This long poem is one of Khodasevich's most successful—if untypical—efforts.

"Sorrento Photographs" and the widely anthologized "Before the Mirror" are probably the poetic high points of Khodasevich's fifth and final collection, *European Night,* which was published in 1927 as the concluding section of his *Collected Verse.* After this date Khodasevich wrote very few poems. Perhaps the finest are the poems written "on occasion," such as the elegy on the death of Murr, the poem he dedicated to Katharine Hepburn after seeing her film performance as Mary Stuart (1936), and the magnificent fragment on the Russian iambic tetrameter (1938). An absolute master of this meter and deeply knowledgeable about the entire history of Russian poetry, the poet and his subject are a perfect match. For the final ten years of his life, Khodasevich devoted his best efforts to criticism and the study of literature.

He earned his livelihood in journalism, working for some of the major *émigré* publishing establishments in Paris. Only a few of the more than three hundred articles, essays, memoirs, and reviews that he wrote for *Days, Renaissance,* and *Contemporary Annals* have been collected. These few collections (the book on Derzhavin [1931], *On Pushkin* [1937], *Necropolis* [1939], and the *Literary Essays and Memoirs* [1954]) have long since gone out of print; only a handful of essays have appeared in English. In addition to working on the literary studies of which these volumes are examples, Khodasevich assumed a central position in the debates over the existence and the possibility of a Russian *émigré* literature.[6] Against Georgy Adamovich and Mark Slonim, the other leading critics of the emigration, Khodasevich maintained that an *émigré* literature was possible. What Russian literature abroad lacked, according to Khodasevich, was any real spirit, any real openness to experimentation and continuous renewal of themes and techniques. The younger writers, in his view, were too much under the thumb of older, established writers and critics, and they were at the mercy of a dwindling, uncritical readership. Although he insisted on the viability of Russian *émigré* literature, he was characteristically full of doubt and pessimism as to its future.

Khodasevich's death in 1939 marked the end of an era, both for European culture in general and for Russian *émigré* literature in particular. His passing was sadly observed with the posthumous publication of three poems and by two deeply felt appreciations of the man and his work by Nina Berberova and Vladimir Nabokov in *Contemporary Annals* (No. 69, 1939). Nabokov's contribution is a stirring defense against the poet's detractors, past, present, and future. Berberova's "In Memoriam Khodasevich" is also a valuable essay, not least in its intimate view of the poet and detailed knowledge of his life:

> ...Khodasevich belonged to that generation which did not manage to have its say before 1917 and to which immediately after 1917 almost no one knew how to listen, the generation crushed first by the war and revolution, and then by exile. His contemporaries either died young, or they stopped writing. A huge number of them committed suicide. He too stopped writing verse, because, despite all his "classicism," he could not continue when there was no one with whom and for whom he could continue. This would have been too much "in the anthological genre."
>
> He himself traced his genealogy from Derzhavin's prosaicisms, from a few of

the more harsh poems of Tyutchev, through the "very terrifying" lines of Sluchevsky about the old woman and the balalaika and through the "old man's intonation" of Annensky. There is much that is true in this, but the poison that is in Khodasevich's poetry, and what is the main thing—that precision and strength with which he poured this poison into his verse—is unique in Russian literature. Both Tyutchev and Annensky, if they had known his verse, would have come to meet him, because in their souls too there were those "holes burned by spilled acid" that were in Khodasevich's soul.

Notes

1. These "fragments from an autobiography" were published in 1933 in several issues of the *émigré* newspaper *Renaissance* (Paris), where the poet served as chief literary critic. They were reprinted in the miscellany *Aerial Ways,* IV (New York, 1965).

2. V. F. Khodasevich, *Derzhavin* (Paris, 1931), p. 10.

3. Nikolai Gumilyov, *Collected Works,* IV (Washington, 1968), pp. 343–44.

4. A flurry of interest a few years ago has subsided. Seven poems from *European Night* appeared in the journal *Moscow* in January (No. 1), 1963; the "By the Sea" cycle was published in truncated form. Vladimir Orlov's project to publish a collection of poetry by several important beginning-of-the-century poets (which was to include Khodasevich) has apparently been abandoned. The introduction for the projected volume, however, did appear in *Questions of Literature,* No. 10, 1966, pp. 111–43.

Nadezhda Mandelstam, in her second book of memoirs (Paris, 1972), indicates Khodasevich's position in the Soviet Union today and delivers the following judgment: "He was loved [in the twenties] and he is loved now. Today's young people know both the verse and the bilious prose of Khodasevich, but he has not broken into *samizdat;* on the other hand, his books bring a high price [on the black market]. The perplexity and pain of this poet are congenial to many, but his poetry brings no relief. There is in it a bitter deficiency, because his life was one of negation and nonacceptance. Only the genuinely tragic, based on an understanding of the nature of evil, brings catharsis."

5. Osip Mandelstam, *Collected Works,* II (Washington, 1971), pp. 345–46.

6. These and other matters and the polemics between Khodasevich and Adamovich are discussed in Gleb Struve's indispensable *Russian Literature in Exile* (New York, 1956).

VLADISLAV KHODASEVICH
translated by Vladimir Nabokov

The Monkey

The heat was fierce. Great forests were on fire.
Time dragged its feet in dust. A cock was crowing
in an adjacent lot.
          As I pushed open
my garden-gate I saw beside the road
a wandering Serb asleep upon a bench
his back against the palings. He was lean
and very black, and down his half-bared breast
there hung a heavy silver cross, diverting
the trickling sweat.
             Upon the fence above him,
clad in a crimson petticoat, his monkey
sat munching greedily the dusty leaves
of a syringa bush; a leathern collar
drawn backwards by its heavy chain bit deep
into her throat.

These poems were originally published in Khodasevich's *Sobranie stikhov* (*Collection of Poems,* Paris, 1927). Nabokov's translations, published a year after his arrival in America, appeared in James Laughlin's *New Directions 1941* (Norfolk, Conn., 1941), pp. 596–600. Professor Nabokov would distribute mimeographed copies of these translations to his students at Cornell University. It should be noted that they are verse renderings rather than the literal "ponies" Nabokov has insisted upon since undertaking and publishing his *Eugene Onegin* translation.

Hearing me pass, the man
stirred, wiped his face and asked me for some water.
He took one sip to see whether the drink
was not too cold, then placed a saucerful
upon the bench, and, instantly, the monkey
slipped down and clasped the saucer with both hands
dipping her thumbs; then, on all fours, she drank,
her elbows pressed against the bench, her chin
touching the boards, her backbone arching higher
than her bald head. Thus, surely, did Darius
bend to a puddle on the road when fleeing
from Alexander's thundering phalanges.
When the last drop was sucked the monkey swept
the saucer off the bench, and raised her head,
and offered me her black wet little hand.
Oh, I have pressed the fingers of great poets,
leaders of men, fair women, but no hand
had ever been so exquisitely shaped
nor had touched mine with such a thrill of kinship,
and no man's eyes had peered into my soul
with such deep wisdom . . . Legends of lost ages
awoke in me thanks to that dingy beast
and suddenly I saw life in its fullness
and with a rush of wind and wave and worlds
the organ music of the universe
boomed in my ears, as it had done before
in immemorial woodlands.
                           And the Serb
then went his way thumping his tambourine:
on his left shoulder, like an Indian prince
upon an elephant, his monkey swayed.
A huge incarnadine but sunless sun
hung in a milky haze. The sultry summer
flowed endlessly upon the wilting wheat.

That day the war broke out, that very day.

Poem

What is the use of time and rhyme?
We live in peril, paupers all.
The tailors sit, the builders climb,
but coats will tear and houses fall.

And only seldom with a sob
of tenderness I hear . . . oh, quite
a different existence throb
through this mortality and blight.

Thus does a wife, when days are dull,
place breathlessly, with loving care,
her hand upon her body, full
of the live burden swelling there.

Orpheus

Brightly lit from above I am sitting
in my circular room; this is I—
looking up at a sky made of stucco,
at a sixty-watt sun in that sky.

All around me, and also lit brightly,
all around me my furniture stands,
chair and table and bed—and I wonder
sitting there what to do with my hands.

Frost-engendered white feathery palmtrees
on the window-panes silently bloom;
loud and quick clicks the watch in my pocket
as I sit in my circular room.

Oh, the leaden, the beggarly bareness
of a life where no issue I see!
Whom on earth could I tell how I pity
my own self and the things around me?

And then clasping my knees I start slowly
to sway backwards and forwards, and soon
I am speaking in verse, I am crooning
to myself as I sway in a swoon.

What a vague, what a passionate murmur
lacking any intelligent plan;
but a sound may be truer than reason
and a word may be stronger than man.

And then melody, melody, melody
blends my accents and joins in their quest,
and a delicate, delicate, delicate
pointed blade seems to enter my breast.

High above my own spirit I tower,
high above mortal matter I grow:
subterranean flames lick my ankles,
past my brow the cool galaxies flow.

With big eyes—as my singing grows wilder—
with the eyes of a serpent maybe,
I keep watching the helpless expression
of the poor things that listen to me.

And the room and the furniture slowly,
slowly start in a circle to sail,
and a great heavy lyre is from nowhere
handed me by a ghost through the gale.

And the sixty-watt sun has now vanished,
and away the false heavens are blown:
on the smoothness of glossy black boulders
this is Orpheus standing alone.

Tolstoy's departure
VLADISLAV KHODASEVICH

"Tolstoy's *departure*" . . . "Tolstoy *departed* from Yasnaya Polyana . . ." In the autumn of 1910, when these words first appeared in newspaper headlines, they immediately acquired a particular nuance, alarming and fateful. He didn't *leave,* but *departed;* that is, he forsook something, broke with something, took a step which was important not only for him, but also for mankind.

The newspaper bulletins, which at first were unclear and contradictory, excited the imagination. He had departed for parts unknown; he had disappeared into space, had stolen away into an inclement night. Afterward, as though from a mist, fragmentary details began to emerge: Sofya Andreyevna, Chertkov, their rivalry, the testament.* Everyone understood that there were

---

* Vladimir Grigorievich Chertkov (1854–1936). Tolstoy's closest and most intransigent disciple, Chertkov was virtually a member of the Tolstoy household from the mid-1880's. Two decades of strife between Chertkov and Tolstoy's wife, Sofya Andreyevna, culminated in Tolstoy's final will and testament of 1909: copyrights to works published before 1881 were bequeathed to Sofya Andreyevna, rights to all published and unpublished works after 1881 were released into the public domain, and Chertkov was named executor of the literary estate. Chertkov's version of the acrimonious events of Tolstoy's final years can be read in his *O poslednikh dniakh L. N. Tolstogo* (1911; English translation, 1922) and *Ukhod Tolstogo* (1922) to which work the title of Khodasevich's article in part alludes. TRANSLATOR.

certain concrete reasons for this departure, that Tolstoy was set in motion by the mechanism of certain wholly commonplace events, and of course they wanted to know those reasons, to penetrate into those events. But at the same time, one guessed and sensed that the inner meaning of what had occurred outweighed the significance and force of all reasons, that now events would follow in which something far more important than all the Yasnaya Polyana squabbles taken together would be decided.

The news, which had acquired such an important and fateful meaning for all Russia, came directly from Yasnaya Polyana. But there it was assigned a far more ordinary, almost banal, meaning. People spoke and thought about Lev Nikolaevich's possible departure from Sofya Andreyevna almost exactly as they might think or speak of a certain husband *parting* from his wife, or a certain wife *parting* from her husband. And people there had become accustomed to pronouncing that word (aloud or to themselves) long before the inclement autumn night when it became a fact. As early as the summer of 1884, Tolstoy had already noted in one of his diaries, available to almost anyone who cared to read it: "It was terribly difficult . . . I should have left. It appears unavoidable." For the next twenty-six years, the possibility of a rupture hung constantly in the air at Yasnaya Polyana. One can say that people there not only reckoned with it, but even became accustomed to it. Relations between Tolstoy and his wife would improve, then became aggravated anew, at times being strained to the breaking point. Thus it was, for example, in June 1897 that Tolstoy wrote Sofya Andreyevna a farewell letter—and stayed. It is noteworthy, however, that evidently he did not particularly believe in the real possibility of his departure, because, after sealing the envelope, he wrote on it: "Unless I make a specific disposition of this letter, it is to be given to S. A. after my death." If he wrote that, then it means he did not really think he would ever leave her.

And then one day, after twenty-six years of constant suffering and indecision, the cup of his patience overflowed: he arose in the night, ordered the horses harnessed, shut the door to his wife's bedroom so that she wouldn't hear, and abandoned the house forever. Why, this time, could Tolstoy no longer bear it, and what gave rise to the departure?

The basic reason for Tolstoy's disagreement with his wife is clear to everyone: the point was that Sofya Andreyevna did not share the views which Tolstoy gradually had adopted over the period of their married life, and she could not and did not wish to subordinate herself and the structure of their family life to those views. Thence arose, for a multitude of the most varied reasons, a series of frequent conflicts. One need not be an opponent of Tolstoyan teaching to admit that in many respects Sofya Andreyevna was right. The Tolstoy she had married was not the later Tolstoy, and consequently she was not obliged to reorganize her life in accordance with the change that took place in him. One can blame her even less for not wanting to accept Tolstoyan teaching hypocritically, for the sake of appearances only, when inwardly she did not sympathize with it. In the same way, one needn't be a Tolstoyan in order to understand the extent to which Tolstoy found unbearable the life—contrary to the convictions he had achieved through much suffering—he had to lead at Sofya Andreyevna's side. Nothing separates people more deeply, more irremediably, than an idea. An ideological disagreement turned the Tolstoys' life together into a genuine tragedy, since each was right in his own way, and each in the eyes of the other was guilty although guiltless. Each could only be himself, and that caused both almost unbearable suffering.

The tragedy was complicated and deepened by the fact that the idea, which lay like an unbridgeable gulf between Tolstoy and Sofya Andreyevna, at the same time fettered him to her with a heavy chain. Tolstoy intended, sooner or later, to lead his wife to what he considered truth and salvation, and he did not feel that he had the right to give up this intention. The more agonizing the conflicts that arose, the more suffering Sofya Andreyevna's behavior caused him, behavior which at times was malicious or insultingly unbecoming (one can't deny that), and the more imperative the obligation not to abandon her seemed to him. He mentions this obligation more than once, in both his letters and his diaries. Even

Sofya Andreyevna's enemies, such as Chertkov, knew about it and acknowledged it. Ultimately, Tolstoy regarded the sufferings which Sofya Andreyevna caused him as a trial sent to him from on high and useful to him for his own moral improvement. Undoubtedly, from this point of view, a departure appeared to him a manifestation of moral weakness and not of strength. That is why he didn't depart sooner, but forgave Sofya Andreyevna for innumerable wrongs to himself, to his friends, and to all that was holy and dear to him.

The final confrontation, as everyone knows, was one of the most violent, and was played out not so much between Sofya Andreyevna and Tolstoy as between her and Chertkov. In essence, there was no conflict or anything particularly exceptional on this occasion which, in Tolstoy's eyes, could have justified his flight from Sofya Andreyevna. I mean, there was nothing to supply him with grounds for giving her up, renouncing forever the idea of "converting" her. What Tolstoy did was remove from his shoulders the cross which he had considered his moral and religious duty to carry. And if Tolstoy nonetheless departed, then something else freed him from his obligation to her, something which at the same time made him see his duty to himself in a different light. What was it?

When Alexandra Tolstaya came to her "departed" father in Shamordino and told him what was happening to Sofya Andreyevna, Tolstoy asked:

"So you say that the doctor doesn't find her mentally ill?"

"No, he doesn't."

"Well, anyway, what do they know?" he said with a wave of his hand.

The doctor's diagnosis vexed him. He considered Sofya Andreyevna mentally ill, and even wrote her about it: "I advise you to reconcile yourself to what has happened, to adjust yourself to your new situation for the time being, and, above all, to undergo treatment."

It would seem that had she been sick, even the simplest human decency, to say nothing of the lofty moral demands which Tolstoy made upon himself, should have suggested to him that now especially he had no right to abandon the wife with whom he had lived for forty-eight years. However, he not only abandoned her but even believed that he had no right to act otherwise, and—at first glance this might seem altogether monstrous—he left her precisely as a consequence of her illness. "I love you and pity you from the bottom of my heart," he wrote her, "but I can't act otherwise. . . . And it isn't a question of the fulfillment of any wishes or demands of mine, but only of your mental equilibrium, of a calm, reasonable attitude to life. But while that doesn't exist, life with you is unthinkable for me."

I pity you from the bottom of my heart, and nevertheless I'm leaving you. And I'm leaving you precisely because you're ill. One can explain this either as total baseness, which any man would have been ashamed to admit, or as the presence of some particular circumstance which abolished the former moral demands that Tolstoy had felt. Such a circumstance could not have been, and was not, Sofya Andreyevna's opposition to his teaching and his wishes: we have seen that Tolstoy had reconciled himself to such opposition for many years, and considered this his duty. And if now he felt that the commands of moral duty were rescinded, and if he made that abrogation directly dependent on her illness, then on that basis two conclusions can be drawn: first, that in the very nature of the illness there was evidently something unique, and second, that that uniqueness itself was of such an order that, because of it, moral duty to the ill woman had to give way to the demands of some other higher duty.

When Alexandra Tolstaya tells about the character traits which were always evident in Sofya Andreyevna, she is only truthfully describing the symptoms of her illness: hysteria. Sofya Andreyevna's struggle with Tolstoy (particularly toward the end) is explained not only by her lack of sympathy with his teaching, by her jealousy of Chertkov and others, and by worries about the family's material situation, but also by the fact that she couldn't withstand a pathological and passionate desire to degrade or kill the very soul in him—not only that which had made him the world-famous Lev Tolstoy, but that which as a whole made up his human individuality. He was compelled to depart, to flee, by an instinct of *spiritual* self-preservation. "To return to you when you are in such a condition would mean for me to renounce life," he wrote her, "and I don't consider that I have the right to do that." He didn't consider he had the right, for the moral duty to her was giving way to a religious duty to himself. Tolstoy had either to cure her, heal her, drive out the "demon," or depart, so as to save himself from contact with the demon. The power of healing and of driving out demons hadn't been given to him (although, perhaps, it could have been). There remained only flight, and he fled—in such fear, in such horror of her that the "unpleasantnesses" which she caused him do not alone explain that fear.

On the twenty-fourth of September, little more than a month before his departure, Tolstoy noted in his pocket diary: "A letter from Chertkov with reproaches and accusations. They are tearing me to pieces. Sometimes I have the thought of getting away from all of them." Afterward, Chertkov all but swore that on Tolstoy's part this was no more than "a passing mood" and that Tolstoy did not want, and could not have wanted, to rid himself of him, Chertkov. But five days before Tolstoy's departure, that same Chertkov wrote to the Bulgarian Tolstoyan, Dosev: "Should he depart from the house at Yasnaya Polyana, then in view of his advanced years and infirmities of age, he could no longer live by physical labor. Neither could he go off begging, staff in hand, and fall ill and die somewhere on the high road, or, as a wanderer, in a stranger's hut. However attractive such an end might be to him, and however theatrical and brilliant it might seem to the crowd which condemns him at the present time, simple love for the people who love him, for his daughters and the friends close to his heart and soul, would prevent him from taking such a course. Without being cruel, he could not refuse to settle somewhere on a modest property where they themselves, without the help of servants, could attend to his domestic needs. . . ."

However, Chertkov deluded himself in vain. Of course, the main reason for Tolstoy's departure from Yasnaya Polyana was Sofya Andreyevna: in her presence Tolstoy experienced genuine terror. But of Chertkov, too, and of all his other friends, he had had more than enough. He wasn't the least averse to ridding himself of them as well, and he proved to be just "cruel" enough not to dream of settling himself with them "on a modest property . . . without the help of servants."

As early as 1897 he had written: "Just as Hindus nearing the age of sixty go off into the forest, just as every elderly religious person wishes to devote the last years of his life to God and not to jokes, puns, gossip and tennis, so I too, entering upon my seventieth year, wish with all my heart for that tranquillity, for solitude. . . ." He expressed the same desire before his departure, when he wrote: "I am doing what old men of my age usually do. They depart worldly life in order to live the last days of their life in solitude and silence."

When he abandoned Yasnaya Polyana, Tolstoy had not yet prepared a future refuge for himself. In keeping with his habit, and a rule of his character, he tried not to guess about the future. And though we cannot guess at his final goal, because at that moment he did not have one, we can, judging from the direction he took, see quite clearly where he was being led—if not by a decision or an idea, then by an inclination, by the instinct of "an old, religious man."

He set out for the convent in Shamordino where his sister was a nun, and, naturally, such a choice was not accidental. Certainly it could not have been final. Tolstoy couldn't have helped realizing that Shamordino didn't suit him as a permanent residence, since he, a man excommunicated by the Church, would be the last person who could expect to find "tranquillity and solitude" in the vicinity of a convent. Thus, he could only have imagined Shamordino as the first halting place in his future wanderings. Why did he need this halting place? Evidently to speak with Sister Maria. But here a new question arises: Did he want to speak with her as his sister or as a nun? Of course it is extremely important that she was his sister, that is, someone personally and long since close to him; but the visit cannot be explained by family feelings alone, because at the time Tolstoy was not looking for family ties. The old family closeness must only have facilitated and simplified his contact with Sister Maria as a nun.

We know very little of what was said between Tolstoy and his sister, but we do know something. Before turning to this discussion, however, let us dwell on one episode which preceded Tolstoy's appearance in Shamordino.

Tolstoy and Dr. Dushan Makovitsky—whom he had taken with him not as a disciple and Tolstoyan, but as a doctor and kind person, a sort of attendant or guide—arrived at the Kozelsk station on the afternoon of October twenty-eighth. From there they had to go to Shamordino by horse. The route lay through the hermitage at Optino, which they reached by six in the evening. Another twelve versts to Shamordino remained; that is, two and a half hours of riding on a terrible road, in bad weather, at night. It was decided to stop in Optino and spend the night in the monastery hostel. But here is what is remarkable: the next day Tolstoy didn't arrive in Shamordino until six-thirty in the evening; that is, he left Optino at four in the afternoon, which means he spent most of the day, almost until twilight, in Optino, and not because he felt unwell: at that time he was still in good health. He was talking with Brother Mikhail, the "innkeeper" (that is, the monk who was in charge of the hostel). He inquired about the monks he knew and then went out, wandered over toward the hermits' quarters, twice went up to the house of the elder, Brother Varsonofy, stood at the garden gate, but didn't go in.*

Whereupon he set off from Optino. Brother Varsonofy later recounted how Brother Mikhail came to him, saying that Tolstoy wanted to see the elders. In response, Brother Varsonofy requested that Tolstoy be told that they would receive him joyfully and with

---

* Elders are men who have retired from secular life but have not taken monastic vows. They may live separate from the monastery, and are excused from regular monastic duties. TRANSLATOR.

respect. This account is usually disbelieved. Let us also leave it aside. But we have no reason not to believe what happened next.

A. Ksiunin, who visited Shamordino immediately after Tolstoy's death, reports Tolstoy's visit to Shamordino according to what Sister Maria told him. His book, recently republished, first appeared while Sister Maria was still living, at which time she refuted nothing. Ksiunin says that when Tolstoy "called upon his sister [in Shamordino he also stayed in the convent hostel], they sat together for a long time." They came out only for dinner, and invited the doctor and the nun who was constantly with Tolstoy's sister into the cell.

"Sister, I was in Optino. How fine it is there," Tolstoy remarked. "How joyfully I would live there, fulfilling the meanest and hardest tasks, but I would stipulate that I not be obliged to go to church."

"That's fine," his sister responded, "but they would make you promise to preach nothing and not to teach."

Lev Nikolaevich became pensive, bowed his head, and remained in that position for some time, until he was reminded that dinner was over.

"Did you meet with the elders?" asked his sister, resuming the conversation about Optino.

"No. . . . Did you really think that they would receive me? . . . You have forgotten that I am an excommunicate."

One shouldn't overestimate the significance of this record, but neither should it be underestimated. On the basis of what it contains, one cannot yet judge how future events would have developed, but the record holds much that is extremely important and significant. It testifies first to the impression Optino made on Tolstoy and, second, to his incipient idea of remaining, even on the condition that he not be required to go to church. But that's not all. It is very significant that, when Tolstoy's sister spoke to him about giving up the preaching of Tolstoyanism as a condition of his remaining in Optino, he made no objection, but lapsed into a pensiveness from which he didn't emerge for a long time.

We do not know what he was thinking. We also do not know how his discussions with his sister would have developed and where they would have led, for these discussions had just begun and Tolstoy by no means thought to avoid them, because it was precisely on their account that he had come to Shamordino. They were of course intended to be prolonged—Tolstoy had even chosen a house for himself to live in at Shamordino. Perhaps meetings between Tolstoy and the Optino elders would have taken place (later we shall see that there are grounds for such a supposition). It is not known, and no one can be so bold as to assert, that these discussions and meetings, these gropings, random ramblings around the Church, would necessarily have led to certain consequences as opposed to others. Perhaps Tolstoy would have stood his ground, or perhaps it all would have ended in a most tremendous event: Tolstoy's return to the Church. This event would hardly have passed without consequence, not only for himself but also for the whole of Russia, for all its religious, intellectual, and even, perhaps, political life. But all was wrecked and trampled upon at the very beginning. Tolstoy's final decision was not fated to ripen.

On the day after Tolstoy's conversation with his sister Maria, Alexandra Tolstaya arrived in Shamordino with news from Yasnaya Polyana: not only about Sofya Andreyevna's condition, but also about the most dreadful thing in the world for Tolstoy—that "his location, if not already discovered, was about to be discovered at any moment, and that he wouldn't be left in peace." In other words, not only would journalists and newsreel photographers from all over the world converge on him, but Sofya Andreyevna herself would overtake him. Read Alexandra Tolstaya's memoirs, and you will see what panic gripped Tolstoy. Had this news arrived a few days later, Sofya Andreyevna would perhaps no longer have terrified him, would have had no power over him; but now, in the face of her approach, his terror was such that he forgot everything, tore himself away without taking leave of his sister and without having come to an understanding with her about anything, and from Shamordino threw himself headlong, blindly, wherever his legs would carry him—again into the night, into the unknown.

"Let's look at a map," said Dushan Makovitsky. "If we're going, we have to know where."

Tolstoy's traveling companions bent over the map, and began to trace routes with their fingers. Place names swarmed and flashed by, places that sounded completely senseless under those circumstances, although the speakers supposed that their proposals were entirely reasonable: Novocherkassk, the Caucasus, abroad, Bulgaria. . . . Tolstoy took no part in this scurrying over the map. Where he fled was now a matter of indifference to him. He was fleeing for the sake of fleeing—that is, into space, into emptiness, into nowhere. This flight could only end as it did—in death. Only death could have provided a fitting end to that tragedy which, in the eyes of the whole world, threatened to turn into comedy (flight, pursuit, the wife catching up).

Sofya Andreyevna unwittingly rendered a supreme service to her sworn enemy Chertkov, and to the whole of Chertkovism in general: simply by the threat of her appearance, she cut off events which might not have occurred, but might well have occurred— the very events which for Chertkov would have meant supreme misfortune and catastrophe.

He was dying in unknown space, at the unknown station of Astapovo. On the very eve of his death, Brother Varsonofy, the elder from the Optino monastery, arrived in the company of another elder. Afterward, an invidious rumor circulated to the effect that Brother Varsonofy had arrived "on orders from Petersburg." In the atmosphere of that time, this sounded as if someone had said bluntly: "at the bidding of the department of police." The rumor gained credence; too many people took it on trust, without asking for proofs, which of course no one had.

It was a lie. Upon his arrival in Astapovo, Brother Varsonofy asked to be admitted to Tolstoy, was refused, and wrote Alexandra Tolstaya a letter which she cited in full in her memoirs. In part, Brother Varsonofy wrote: "I respectfully thank Your Excellency for your letter in which you write that your parent's will must be regarded as paramount by you and your whole family. But you are aware, Countess, that the Count told his sister, your aunt, the nun Sister Maria, of his desire to see us and speak with us." This reference to Sister Maria has a decisive significance. Had Tolstoy not expressed the desire to see the elders, Sister Maria would not have told Brother Varsonofy about it, and Brother Varsonofy could not have referred to her if she had not told him.

Alexandra Tolstaya did not admit the monks to her dying father. We have no right to blame her for that. She was concerned solely with prolonging the last minutes of Tolstoy's life, and a conversation with the elders, even the meeting itself, their appearance alone, would have disturbed Tolstoy profoundly.

We do not know how that meeting might have turned out had it taken place. We can judge only what was, and we hardly dare to surmise what might have been. But the Judge to whom all is manifest judged Lev Tolstoy by looking not upon what *was,* not upon what happened by the will of men, but solely according to what *might* have been had Tolstoy's final contact with the Church taken place.

That judgment we do not know.

November 21, 1935

translated by Elizabeth Shepard

On Khodasevich
VLADIMIR NABOKOV

This poet, the greatest Russian poet of our time, Pushkin's literary descendant in Tyutchev's line of succession, shall remain the pride of Russian poetry as long as its last memory lives. What makes his genius particularly striking is that it matured in the years of our literature's torpescence, when the Bolshevist era neatly divided poets into established optimists and demoted pessimists, endemic hearties and exiled hypochondriacs; a classification which, incidentally, leads to an instructive paradox: inside Russia the dictate acts from outside; outside Russia, it acts from within. The will of the government, which implicitly demands a writer's affectionate attention toward a parachute, a farm tractor, a Red Army soldier, or the participant in some polar venture (i.e. toward this or that externality of the world) is naturally considerably more powerful than the injunction of exile, addressed to man's inner world. The

This article, signed "V. Sirin," the pen name I used in the twenties and thirties in Berlin and Paris, appeared in the *émigré* literary magazine *Sovremennye zapiski,* LIX (1939), Paris. I have clung closely to my tortuous Russian text in the present translation into English. AUTHOR'S NOTE. (All subsequent notes are also by the author.)

latter precept is barely sensed by the weak and is scorned by the strong. In the nineteen-twenties it induced nostalgic rhymes about St. Petersburg's rostral columns, and now, in the late thirties, it has evolved rhymed religious concerns, not always deep but always honest. Art, authentic art, whose object lies next to art's source (that is, in lofty and desert places—and certainly not in the over-populated vale of soulful effusions) has degenerated in our midst to the level, alas, of remedial lyricism; and although one understands that private despair cannot help seeking a public path for its easement, poetry has nothing to do with it: the bosom of the Church or that of the Seine is more competent in these matters. The public path, whatever it looks like, is, artistically, always a paltry one, precisely because of its being public. If, however, one finds hard to imagine a poet, in the confines of Russia, refusing to bend under the yoke (such as, for example, declining to translate a Caucasian poetaster's jingles) and behaving rashly enough to put the muse's liberty above his own, one should expect to find more easily in *émigré* Russia plucky loners who would not wish to unite and pool their poetical preoccupations in a sort of communistery of the spirit.

Even genius does not save one in Russia; in exile, one is saved by genius alone. No matter how difficult Khodasevich's last years were, no matter how sorely the banality of an *émigré*'s lot irked him, no matter, too, how much the good old indifference of fellow mortals contributed to his mortal extinction, Khodasevich is safely enshrined in timeless Russia. Indeed, he himself was ready to admit, through the hiss of his bilious banter, through the "cold and murk" of the days predicted by Blok,* that he occupied a special position: the blissful solitude of a height others could not attain.

Here I have no intention of hitting bystanders with a swing of the thurible.† A few poets of the *émigré* generation are still on

---

* In verses written by Blok on the eve of our era:
"If only you knew, oh children you,
The cold and murk of the coming days . . ."
† The metaphor is borrowed from a poem by Baratynsky (1800–1844) accusing critics of lauding Lermontov (1814–1841) on the occasion of his death, with the unique object of disparaging living poets. Incidentally, the dry little notice accorded to Baratynsky in Pavlenkov's encyclopedia (St. Petersburg, 1913) ends with the marvelous misprint: "Complete Works, 1984."

their way up and, who knows, may reach the summits of art—if only they do not fritter away life in a second-rate Paris of their own, which sails by with a slight list in the mirrors of taverns without mingling in any way with the French Paris, a motionless and impenetrable town. Khodasevich seemed to have sensed in his very fingers the branching influence of the poetry he created in exile and therefore felt a certain responsibility for its destiny, a destiny which irritated him more than it saddened him. The glum notes of cheap verse struck him more as a parody than as the echo of his collection, *Evropeyskaya Noch'* (*European Night*), where bitterness, anger, angels, the gulf of adjacent vowels—everything, in short, was genuine, unique, and quite unrelated to the current moods which clouded the verse of many of those who were more or less his disciples.

To speak of his *masterstvo, Meisterschaft,* "mastery," i.e. "technique," would be meaningless and even blasphemous in relation to poetry in general, and to his own verse in a sharply specific sense, since the notion of "mastery," which automatically supplies its own quotation marks, turns thereby into an appendage, a shadow demanding logical compensation in the guise of any positive quantity, and this easily brings us to that peculiar, soulful attitude toward poetry in result of which nothing remains of squashed art but a damp spot or tear stain. This is condemnable not because even the most *purs sanglots* require a perfect knowledge of prosody, language, verbal equipoise; and this is also absurd not because the poetaster intimating in slatternly verse that art dwindles to nought in the face of human suffering is indulging in coy deceit (comparable, say, to an undertaker's murmuring against human life because of its brevity); no: the split perceived by the brain between the thing and its fashioning is condemnable and absurd because it vitiates the essence of what actually (whatever you call the thing—"art," "poetry," "beauty") is inseparable from all its mysteriously indispensable properties. In other words, the perfect poem (at least three hundred examples of which can be found in Russian literature) is capable of being examined from all angles by the reader in search of its idea or only its sentiment, or only the picture, or only the sound (many things of that kind can be thought up, from "instrumentation" to "imaginization"), but all this amounts to a random selection of an entity's facet, more of which would deserve, really, a moment of our attention (nor could it of course induce in us any thrill except, maybe, obliquely, in making us recall some other "entity," somebody's voice, a room, a night), had not the poem possessed that resplendent independence in respect of which the term "masterly technique" rings as insultingly as its antonym, "winning sincerity."

What I am saying here is far from being new; yet one is impelled to repeat it when speaking of Khodasevich. There exists not quite exact verse (whose very blurriness can have an appeal of its own like that of lovely nearsighted eyes) which makes a virtue of approximation by the poet's striving toward it with the same precision in selecting his words as would pass for "mastery" in more picturesque circumstances. Compared to those artful blurrings, the poetry of Khodasevich may strike the gentle reader as an overpolishing of form—I am deliberately using this unappetizing epithet. But the whole point is that his poetry—or indeed any authentic poetry—does not require any definition in terms of "form."

I find it most odd myself that in this article, in this rapid inventory of thoughts prompted by Khodasevich's death, I seem to imply a vague nonrecognition of his genius and engage in vague polemics with such phantoms as would question the enchantment and importance of his poetry. Fame, recognition—all that kind of thing is a phenomenon of rather dubious shape which death alone places in true perspective. I am ready to assume that there might have been quite a few people who, when reading with interest the weekly critique that Khodasevich wrote for *Vozrozhdenie* * (and it should be admitted that his reviews, with all their wit and *allure*, were not on the level of his poetry, for they lacked somehow its throb and magic), simply did not know that the reviewer was also a poet. I should not be surprised if this person or that finds Khodasevich's posthumous fame inexplicable at first blush. Furthermore, he published no poems lately—and

* An *émigré* daily in Paris before World War Two.

readers are forgetful, and our literary critics are too excited and preoccupied by evanescent topical themes to have the time or occasion to remind the public of important matters. Be it as it may, all is finished now: the bequeathed gold shines on a shelf in full view of the future, whilst the goldminer has left for the region from where, perhaps, a faint something reaches the ears of good poets, penetrating our being with the beyond's fresh breath and conferring upon art that mystery which more than anything characterizes its essence.

Well, so it goes, yet another plane of life has been slightly displaced; yet another habit—the habit (one's own) of (another person's) existence—has been broken. There is no consolation, if one starts to encourage the sense of loss by one's private recollections of a brief, brittle, human image that melts like a hailstone on a windowsill. Let us turn to the poems.

Marina Tsvetaeva
D. S. MIRSKY

After Marina Tsvetaeva's first books appeared in 1910 and 1912, she published nothing for ten years, and not until 1922 were several volumes of her poems—written during the war and the Revolution—published simultaneously. She then appeared before us in all her early strength. I say "early" because she has grown greatly since that time, and continues to grow, irrepressibly, like the fairy-tale Prince Guidon in his barrel. (*Sovremennye zapiski* first revealed Maria Tsvetaeva to *émigré* readers when it printed, in Nos. 7 and 8, a series of her poems that had been brought from Moscow by Balmont.) Thus, despite her early debut (she was still in school), Marina Tsvetaeva must be considered a poet of the postrevolutionary period.

And she is entitled to first place among postrevolutionary poets —or to one of the first two places; her only possible rival, Boris Pasternak, is a poet of a totally different stamp. Considering the unlikeness of the two, it is interesting to note the characteristics

ABOVE PHOTO: Marina Tsvetaeva
This essay was originally published in 1926 as a review of Tsvetaeva's verse tale "The Swain."

they have in common. Besides a clear, evident, unquestionable newness (I use this word in the strictest Bergsonian sense), a trait that seems inevitable and inescapable in a truly great contemporary poet, and besides an elevation common to both which really cannot be considered an individual trait in a lyric poet, the one thing we find in both Tsvetaeva and Pasternak is their major key: a buoyant vitality, an acceptance of life and the world. Those who are full of patriotic anxiety ought to rejoice that two of the foremost poets of our generation, so unlike one another in every other way, are united by precisely this quality. The fact is significant: all Russian literature of the preceding generation (with the exception of Gumilyov) was united by exactly the opposite qualities— hatred, rejection, and fear of life. This attitude, we now know, was prophetic, and after the obvious example of Blok, we have come to believe in the prophetic nature of poetry. May it not be that Tsvetaeva and Pasternak are presences just as prophetic as Chekhov and Blok? And at this moment in the West (I speak primarily of England, which I know, but it also seems true and relevant in France and Germany), poets of equal caliber are still imbued with our old mood of nostalgia and death.

But, I repeat, with the exception of these qualities, Pasternak and Marina Tsvetaeva are unlike, almost opposites. Pasternak is visual and material. His poetry is a mastering of the world by means of words. His words strive to depict, to transmit, to embrace the world of things. In this embrace and this mastery of real things lies all Pasternak's strength. He is a "naive realist." Marina Tsvetaeva is an idealist (not in the Wilsonian but in the Platonic sense). The material world is for her only an emanation of essence. Things live only in words; not *sunt*, but *percipiuntur*. Only their essences *sunt*. Her very perception, so sharp and persuasive, especially in her prose,* seems practically disembodied. The people in her reminiscences, so alive and inimitable, are not so much everyday, three-dimensional people as they are reductions of individuality and of inimitability almost to a point. The ability to see past and through the "visual tegument" to the nucleus of identity

* "The Hero of Labor" and "My Jobs." AUTHOR.

and, despite the boundlessness of personality, to convey the single-ness and the inimitability of that nucleus—this is the incomparable enchantment of Marina Tsvetaeva's prose. On the other hand, Pasternak in his novellas (*The Childhood of Lüvers*) gives only the teguments; his characters are not identities, but geometric spaces where exterior impressions intersect. (This is what people have in mind when they speak of Pasternak's congeniality to Proust.)

In poetry, the difference is revealed thus: for Pasternak the word is the sign of a thing. His language is neutral, international, fully translatable. For Tsvetaeva the word cannot be the sign of a thing, for the thing itself is only a sign. Words for her are more ontological than things; they bypass things and are directly con-nected with essences: absolute, self-contained, irreplaceable, un-translatable. Her poems are indissolubly Russian, the most indis-solubly Russian in all contemporary poetry. And rhythm, for Pasternak only a grid of length and breadth (which in no way detracts from its value in his poetry), is for Marina Tsvetaeva the essence of the poem; it is the poem itself, its soul, its source of life. Time in Pasternak's rhythm is Kantian; in Tsvetaeva's rhythm it is Bergsonian.

In Marina Tsvetaeva's reminiscences of Bryusov ("The Hero of Labor") we find these remarkable words: "The illimitable over-comes itself through a limit; but no one can overcome his own limits." She was illimitable from the very beginning. (I do not mean by this that her talent has no limits, but these limits are located to the sides and not in her path; her talent is an endlessly expanding angle, not a closed triangle; her field is limited, but not the range of her vision.) Judging by her earliest poems, one might have feared that she would never be able to overcome the limit of her illimitability—as in his time Balmont could not. In poems she wrote before 1919–1920 there was an excessive lightness, a want of restraint, that made it possible to speak of lack of control. The discipline of style was not in these poems. Beginning about 1920, she unswervingly and victoriously overcame her illimita-bility—and, like every master, she *zeigt sich erst in die Besch-*

*ränkung.** (Let me add that in her prose this process began later, and had not yet reached the same level). In the poems she wrote between 1916 and 1920 she achieves amazing, solitary, short-lived epiphanies, the God-given, unique "personal expression" that totally rescues even the worst lapses of taste (not infrequent in those years). But she had not yet fully mastered her demon. In her most recent work—"The Swain," "Poem of the End," "The Pied Piper," "Poem of the Hill," "Theseus"—it is precisely this full mastery, this complete technical success, that is so striking.

For a poet so romantic by nature (that is, so subjective and spontaneous) as Marina Tsvetaeva was, such a path is a rarity. The main role in overcoming her illimitability was played by her "verbality"—that is, her sensitivity (and for this reason her integrity) toward the word. A large role was played also by her involvement with folklore (beginning with "The Tsar-Maiden") and especially (beginning also with the same poem) by the discipline of a longer form, narrative and impersonal. It was thus she was able to overcome the empirical subjectivity of her early lyrics —that is, to change her poetry from a means for emotional outpouring into a tool of poetic construction. "The Tsar-Maiden" and "The Swain" are written upon themes imposed from without and are free from psychological information. But even as a lyric poet Marina Tsvetaeva has come forth transfigured from this school. Her most recent long lyric poems, "Poem of the Hill" and "Poem of the End" are completely non-"phonographic"; they are fully constructivist. These are not the lyrical jottings of experience, but poetic (*poetikos* means creator-ly, constructivist) constructions out of the material of experience.

The main thing that is new and unusual in the most recent work of Marina Tsvetaeva—and unexpected after her first poems—is the presence of style. Not stylization, but a real, personal, freely born style. In our time she is the only poet to have achieved style. Its presence assures the reader that he will be neither deceived nor offended by a false note. This judgment of mine probably surprises those readers who, to the contrary, find in Tsvetaeva's poems an

* [She] shows her talents through limiting herself. EDITOR.

insolent violation of all *their* canons of taste, and an unjustifiable (and incomprehensible) diversity. But her style must be understood from within, and for that, what Turgenev called "a sympathetic humor" is needed (and without it there seems no point in reading poetry at all).

"The Swain" is the first poem in which Marina Tsvetaeva attained her style. It is distinct from "The Tsar-Maiden" and from "Sidestreets" in this: there is no stylization in it. It is no longer an imitation of folk poetry, it does not resemble folk poetry, and yet it is as closely connected with folk poetry as a tree with the soil—not by likeness, but by root kinship. Tsvetaeva has long worked at freeing the Russian language from the fetters of Graeco-Latin and Romano-Germanic grammar and returning it to its natural freedom and natural forms of connection. (In this she is a brother-in-arms with Remizov.) In "The Swain" she has accomplished the task. Russian "verbless" syntax reigns totally in the poem (not in Balmont's sense, nor in Shikhmatov's, but in that she prefers to make do without verbs). And the direct consequence of this is the "broken" quality of her rhythm—just as the "fluidity" of Pushkin's iambic line was called forth directly by its connection with Lomonosov-Karamzinian verb-participle syntax. Marina Tsvetaeva is extraordinarily skillful in her ability to use monosyllabic words and contiguous stresses. The word, even the syllable, in her work receives a new freedom and importance, and intonation becomes a major grammatical force.

I see that I haven't room enough to give an exposition of the contents of "The Swain"; let me simply note that the subject is taken from the folktale "The Vampire." But the poet's own form of narrative offers neither difficulty nor incoherence. All that's needed is attention. But there is of course no point in reading anything without attention. True, a new style requires greater attention than one that is old and worn, but no greater than the attention needed by a child (or a grownup) who begins to read Russian poetry for the first time and who reads "Poltava" or "Demon." I mention these two poems precisely because I remember how I read them at the age of ten, astounded and exultant as

I discovered a new world—incomprehensible at first, then suddenly understandable—of a new system of relationships and values. I experienced that discovery again when I read the recent poems of Marina Tsvetaeva. And it is no ordinary experience, since the truly new is rare, and most of all a new style, "whole and integral."

"The Swain" was written in 1922 and published in 1924. Since that time (and with this I began my essay), Marina Tsvetaeva has not remained fixed in one place, but has grown—not daily, but hourly. "Poem of the End," published in the Prague miscellany *The Ark* (1926), "The Pied Piper" in *The Will of Russia,* "Poem of the Hill" and "Theseus," unfortunately still unpublished—all these are of an attainment still higher than "The Swain."

I realize that I have said nothing in this review about Marina Tsvetaeva and that I have convinced no one of anything. But a review about Marina Tsvetaeva is not enough; a book is needed (if indeed there's any point in non-poets writing about poets) and it ought to be written with pride, for she is our compatriot; and with rejoicing, for she is our contemporary.

translated by Paul Schmidt

> *Amidst the dust of bookshops, wide dispersed*
> *And never purchased there by anyone,*
> *Yet similar to precious wines, my verse*
> *Can wait: its turn shall come.*
> —Marina Tsvetaeva (*translated by*
> *Vladimir Nabokov, November 12, 1972*)

THREE POEMS BY MARINA TSVETAEVA
translated by Paul Schmidt

Poems grow like stars, like flowers,
Like the beauty a family never needs.
And there's only one answer possible
To praise, to apotheosis: Why to me?

We sleep—and then, between the paving stones,
The divine visitation, quatrefoil.
Understand me, world. The poet's dream reveals
The laws of stars, the formulas of flowers.

Psyche

1

I'm no impostor—I've come home at last,
And not a servant-girl—I need no bread.
I am your passion, and your Sunday rest,
Your seventh day, your seventh heaven.

There on earth they gave me alms,
Hung these millstones round my neck.
Sweetheart! Don't you recognize me?
I'm Psyche! Your swallow! I've come back.

2

Here, take these rags, my darling,
That once were tender flesh:
I've worn all out, torn all to pieces;
Two wings alone are left.

Clothe me in your splendor,
Have mercy, and pardon me.
And hang these tattered relics up
In the heart's sacristy.

1918

To Mayakovsky

1

The world's not the world
Without its wild ones . . .
Come back, baby—Vladimir,
Volodimir—*vladei mirom*—
World-owner, own the whole world!

2

The *Literary Gazette*—but that's not
The point, try and shed your own
Blood, *that's* the point—comes out
Once a week. His kind comes along

Once a hundred years. Your front-
Line fighter has fallen. Capital,
What other news do you want?
What sort of editorial?

Over here, my dears, we hear
(One petty *émigré* to another):
"Vladimir Mayakovsky? Oh, sure.
Deep voice, they say; used to wear

A funny shirt . . ." Your poor blood!
How can I love your New Order
When the blood of its first fighter's
On the second page of a paper called *Izvestia?*

3

In the coffin, in the conventional
dark suit, in sturdy, worn boots
with iron soles, lay the greatest
poet of the Revolution.
  —Special News Bulletin, *24 April 1930*

In boots with iron soles.
In boots in which he conquered a mountain—
It couldn't be climbed
By detours or evasions—

Worn down to a gleam
From that twenty-year climb.
The proletarian Mount Sinai,
Whose lawgiver was him.

In those boots—a two-foot-square apartment,
So he left the Housing Commission alone—
In boots in which, with a furrowed brow,
He carried and climbed and cursed that mountain—and sang.

In inexhaustible, flawless boots
Along the unplowed fields of October,
In boots—they were almost a deep-sea diver's—
The boots of a foot soldier, rather:

In the boots of a great campaigner,
Built, I'll bet, with Donbass nails.
The mountain of griefs of his own people,
Of the *One Hundred and Fifty* (state printed)

Million . . . And in a very real way
They *were* his own; he used to say:
"In my life I have nothing of my own!"
The mountain of griefs of us all—he had *that.*

It was in those—and they still talk of
Rolls-Royces they say he had!
As he lay dead he cried to the kids: On guard!
In those boots. They're the ultimate proof.

4

"The love-boat has wrecked on reality."

Who'd bet a penny
On a leader like that?
Kid, in what encyclopedia
Did you find your boat?

To end it all in a boat, and
A love-boat at that—scandal!
Stenka Razin—isn't he your equal?—
Dealt with reality better.

What a strange cure—open
Your faucet and the blood runs out.
Kid, this wasn't the proletarian
Way. Just like an aristocrat!

And all those dirty words you shouted
At us—for what? Blood, and not a new dawn!
You showed the white silk lining
Of your class in the end.

Like the nobleman who shot himself
At a performance of *Tosca*—sentimentality!
Kid! That wasn't the Mayakovsky
Way, that was fake nobility!

You should have set your cap at an angle
And tossed her over the side!
You lived like your own great-grandson;
You died as your ancestors died.

Look, when we get right down
To it—you ought to be ashamed.
A Soviet Russian Werther.
A tsarist Russian gesture.

Only then you'd have gone to jail.
Nowadays . . .
        Oh, my dearest enemy:
There aren't any love-boats left
Any more. None at all.

5

Shot—right in the soul.
The way you did your enemies in.
Today the God-fighter's
Torn his final temple down.

One last time—this time it worked.
Dead center—and he's dear departed.
Well, that's proof you have a heart:
You shoot it and it stops.

When we *émigrés* meet, over here:
"What a sensation! My, what a fuss!
You mean they have hearts over there
After all? On the same side as us?"

Shot—right on the mark.
Like at an amusement park.
Most people miss, nick their left ear lobe,
And wind up in bed with their wives.

Good for you! You didn't miss!
And all for a woman! What for?
If you think about it long enough
Even Helen of Troy was a whore.

With just a gesture—marvelous—
The Leftman amazed us—
Before, he could only hit targets
On the right—now he shoots left.

If he'd just shot right—you could operate
And your Big Boy would get well again.
But his shot went left—that's straight
To the heart—the Place the Poems come from.

6

A Soviet Potentate
Before the High Synod . . .
Hi, Seryozha.
Hi, Volodya.

Was it all too much? A little.
For general reasons? No, private ones.
You used a gun? That's the custom.
Did it hurt? It sure did.

So you're through with living?
Deal me out, you mean?
Stupid, Seryozha.
Real stupid, Volodya.

Do you remember how
You used to shout me down
At the top of your loud
Bass roar? Fine,

Only . . . Look at your love-boat
Now, your stupid sloop! What a mess!
Was it really because of a woman?
—If it was vodka, it's worse.

Your face was all puffy;
You must have been loaded.
Stupid, Seryozha.
Real stupid, Volodya.

Anyway—not with a razor.
At least that's neater.
So your last ace
Lost? . . . You're bleeding—

Put on a Band-aid.
Iodine helps.
Let's fix it, Seryozha.
Let's fix it, Volodya.

And what about Mother
Rusha? What? Where's
That? Back in the U.S.S.
R.? They're building? Sure.

Parents make babies,
Saboteurs make bombs.
Publishers play the same old games,
Poets write poems.

A new bridge was started,
Washed out in the spring flood . . .
The same, Seryozha.
As ever, Volodya.

And the birdhouse? The new poets?
They're pretty sharp;
While they weave us wreaths
They steal us blind, as if

We were dead. They've splashed
Old ROSTA with a cheap new shine.
—But they'll never get along
On Pasternak alone.

Shall we lend a hand,
Tear their dullness down?
Let's— (You want to, Seryozha?)
Let's fix it, Volodya!

Everyone sends his best . . .
What about old Alex
Alexandrovich Blok?
There! Alexander's an angel!

Sologub? Down along the canals,
Looking for his drowned wife's face
In the ice. Gumilyov, Nikolai?
Gone east—

(Wrapped in bloodstained burlap,
Thrown on a corpse-laden cart)
The same, Seryozha.
As ever, Volodya.

So it's still the same—well,
Volodya dear—dear friend—
Let's lay hands on ourselves,
Volodya, although your hands

Are gone. They're gone; well,
Seryozha dear—dear boy—
Let's light the fuse
That'll blow up Paradise!

And after we've shattered
Paradise to pieces,
Let's have one for the road!
Seryozha! Volodya!

7

Many great temples did he tear down,
But this was the fairest of all.
Eternal rest grant unto him, O Lord.
Let the soul of Thy enemy
Depart in peace.

Note on "To Mayakovsky"

When Vladimir Mayakovsky committed suicide in April 1930, Marina Tsvetaeva was disgusted by the efforts of her fellow *émigrés* in Paris and of the official Soviet press to make political and propagandistic capital of the tragic death of a great poet. This memorial cycle was the result.

Poem 1. The Old Russian form of the name Vladimir—Volodimir—is etymologically derived from the words that mean "to own the world."

Poem 2. "A funny shirt"—a reference to Mayakovsky's famous blouse of yellow necktie silk, which he used to wear in his prerevolutionary Futurist period.

Poem 4. The epigraph is a quotation from Mayakovsky's suicide note. Stenka Razin was a seventeenth-century Cossack rebel leader who, according to a popular song (composed at the end of the nineteenth century), threw a captive Persian princess he loved into the Volga when her presence caused friction among his followers.

Poem 5. "But his shot went left": Mayakovsky killed himself by shooting through his heart.

Poem 6 depicts an encounter in Heaven between the two Soviet suicide poets —Sergei Esenin (whose suicide Mayakovsky had denounced five years earlier in a poem and an essay) and Mayakovsky. "And what about Mother/Rusha . . .": The basic disagreement between the two poets was that Esenin loved the patriarchal and traditional old Russia, which Mayakovsky despised because his allegiance belonged to the future industrialized and collectivized U.S.S.R. "Old ROSTA": a government propaganda agency for which Mayakovsky had produced hundreds of posters and versified advertising slogans. Alexander Blok, Fyodor Sologub, Nikolai Gumilyov: three major poets who suffered death or personal tragedy in the aftermath of the October Revolution.

A poet on criticism
MARINA TSVETAEVA

*Souvienne vous de celuy à qui
comme on demandoit à quoi faire il
se peinoit si fort en un art qui ne
pouvoit venir à la cognoissance de
guère des gens—"J'en ay assez de
peu," répondit-il. "J'en ay assez
d'un. J'en ay assez de pas un."*
—Montaigne

Criticism: perfect pitch for the future.
—M. T.

1

He cannot be a critic ...

The primary responsibility of a critic of poetry is not to write bad poems himself. At least not to publish them.

How can I believe a voice—N's, let's say—when he doesn't see the mediocrity of his own poetry? The first virtue of a critic is the ability to see. This one, since he not only writes but publishes, is blind. Yet one can be blind to one's own work and see another's clearly. There are such cases. For instance, the mediocre lyrics of the tremendous critic Sainte-Beuve. But in the first place, Sainte-Beuve stopped writing; that is, he acted toward the poet in himself precisely as a great critic should: he evaluated, and passed judgment. In the second place, even had he kept on writing,

103

Sainte-Beuve the mediocre poet is redeemed by Sainte-Beuve the major critic, leader, and prophet for a whole generation. His poems were the foible of a great man—nothing more. They were a foible and they were an exception. What won't we forgive in a great man!

But let's return to certainties. Sainte-Beuve, with a tremendous creative achievement to his credit, stopped writing poems; that is, he rejected the poet within himself. N, with no such achievement to his credit, does not stop; that is, he persists in being a poet himself. A strong man, with a right to a weakness, disdains that right. A weak man, without that right, insists on it and thereby comes to grief.

—Judge, sentence yourself.

The verdict of the great critic Sainte-Beuve upon himself as a poet is a guarantee for me that he would not call what is bad in my work good (even apart from his authority, our evaluations correspond: what he thinks is bad, I do too). The judgment of Sainte-Beuve the critic upon Sainte-Beuve the poet is a guarantee of the critic's further infallibility and of his future immunity from prosecution.

The encouragement of the mediocre poet in himself by the mediocre critic N is a guarantee for me that he will call what is good in my work bad (even apart from my distrust of his voice, our evaluations don't correspond: if *that* is good, then mine, of course, is bad). Offer me Pushkin as an example and I will probably say nothing, and of course I will have to think it over. But don't offer me N as an example—I won't accept him and I'll only laugh. (How are we to take the poems of a verse-writing critic wise to the mistakes of others, if not as paragons? Surely not as rejects? Anyone who publishes something thereby declares, this is good. A critic who publishes thereby declares, this is a paragon. *Ergo:* the only poet not deserving of reprieve is the critic, just as the only defendant not deserving of reprieve is the judge. *I judge only judges.*)

The self-delusions of N-the-poet are affirmations of his fallibility and legal liability. Refusing to judge himself, he becomes a defendant, and turns us, the other defendants, into judges. I will not judge N as a merely bad poet. Criticism can do that. But N-the-judge, who is guilty of what he blames me for, that I will judge. A judge found guilty! Immediate retrial of all past cases!

And so: where no great achievement exists and where consequently we are not dealing with a great man, it follows, as a general rule, that bad poems by a critic of poetry are unpardonable. A bad critic—yet perhaps he writes good poems? No, the poems are bad too. (N *is* a critic.) Bad poems—but perhaps his criticism is good? No, the criticism is bad too. N-the-poet undermines the credibility of N-the-critic, and N-the-critic undermines the credibility of N-the-poet. You may approach it from whichever end you like.

Let me support this with a living example. Georgy Adamovich, who charged me with a disregard of elementary syntax, resorts, in the same review, a few lines before or after, to the following locution: ". . . in a dry, insolently-breaking voice."

The first thing I felt was—that doesn't make sense! A breaking voice is something involuntary, whereas insolence is an act of the will. The hyphen between "insolently" and "breaking" turns the word "insolently" into an attribute of "breaking"; that is, it raises the question: exactly *how* did it break? Not *why* did it break?

Can a voice break insolently? No. Out of insolence, yes. Suppose we change "insolently" to "impudently" and repeat the experiment. The answer is the same: out of impudence, yes; impudently, no. Because both insolence and impudence are conscious, active, and a breaking voice is something involuntary and passive. (A breaking voice. A sinking heart. The case is identical.) It sounds as if I had purposely, out of insolence, let my voice break. Conclusion: an absence of elementary syntax and a still more serious absence of logic. Sheer impressionism, whose roots, by the way, I understand perfectly, though I do not offend with similar violations. Georgy Adamovich wanted to give a simultaneous impression of insolence and a broken voice, to accelerate and strengthen this impression. Without thinking, he reached for a hyphen. He misused it. Now, to drive this lesson home:

Angrily-breaking, yes. Obviously-breaking, yes. Angrily, obviously, languidly, noticeably, wickedly, nervously, pitifully, humorously . . . Anything that contains no sense of intention, of active purpose is suitable, any word that will not clash with the passivity of a breaking voice.

In an insolent, breaking voice—yes. Breaking because of insolence—yes. Insolently-breaking—no.

Physician, heal thyself.

A series of enchanted changes in a beloved face . . .[1]

No one has a right to judge a poet unless he has read his every line. A body of creative work is all gradualness and succession. My 1915 explains my 1925. Chronology is the key to understanding.

"Why do you write so many different kinds of poems?"

"Because each year is different."

The ignorant reader mistakes for style something that is far simpler and also far more complicated—time. To expect from a poet identical poems in 1915 and in 1925 is the same as expecting him to look in 1925 as he did in 1915. "Why have you changed so much in the last ten years?" One never asks, for the answer is obvious. Instead of asking, one takes note, and having noted one adds: "Time has passed." It's the same with poetry. The parallel is so complete that I continue it. Time, as we know, does not improve one's appearance, except perhaps in childhood. And no one who knew me at twenty will say to me, at thirty: "How much prettier you've become." At thirty I may have become more defined, more striking, more distinctive, even more beautiful perhaps. But prettier—no. It's the same with poetry as it is with facial features. Poems don't become prettier with time. Freshness, spontaneity, accessibility, the *beauté du diable* of the poetic personality—all yield to clearly defined features. "You used to write better"—how often I've heard that! It means only that the reader prefers my *beauté du diable* to my essence. Prefers prettiness to true beauty.

Prettiness is an exterior criterion, beauty an interior one. A

106

pretty woman, a beautiful woman, a pretty landscape, beautiful music. With this difference, that a landscape may be beautiful as well as pretty (a strengthening, a transposition of the external to the internal) while music which is beautiful cannot also be pretty (a weakening, a regression from the internal to the external). Moreover, as soon as the phenomenon moves away from the region of the visible and the material, pretty is no longer fitting. A pretty painting by Leonardo da Vinci? We don't say that.

"Pretty music," "a pretty poem"—these testify to musical and poetic ignorance. Silly colloquialisms.

So then, chronology is the key to understanding. Two examples: love, and the process of the law. Every detective, as every lover, starts from a given moment and goes back to the source, to the first day. The detective follows his clues backward. There is no isolated act, but a chain of them: the first, and all that followed. The present moment is the sum of all preceding moments and the source of all that are to come. A person who has not read all my poems, from *Evening Album* (my childhood) to *The Pied Piper* (the present day), has no right to judge.

The critic: a detective and a lover.

Nor do I trust critics who are not quite critics and not quite poets. He didn't bring it off, he was a failure; he doesn't want to leave the world of letters, but his survival is a stunted one; he has not become wiser, he is still led into temptation by his own (unsuccessful) efforts. Since I couldn't do it, no one can; since there's no inspiration for me, then none exists. (If it did, I'd be the first to have it. . . .) "I know how it's done. . . ." You know how it's done, but you don't know how to do it. Consequently you still don't know how it's done. Poetry is only craft, the secret is technique, success comes from a greater or lesser degree of *Fingerfertigkeit*—it's all manual dexterity.

Hence the conclusion: *talent* does not exist. (If it did, I'd be the first to have it. . . .) From such failures we generally get theoretician-critics, critics of poetic technique, technical critics. At best they can be thorough. But technique as an end in itself is the worst possible end.

Someone who could not become a pianist (because of a muscular disorder) became a composer. When the lesser option became impossible, he chose the greater. A lovely exception to a sad rule: when the greater option is impossible (to be a creator) you choose the lesser one (to be a fellow-traveler).

It's the same as if a man, despairing of finding the Rheingold, declared that there was no gold in the Rhine and took up alchemy. Take a bit of this and a bit of that and you get gold. But then, since you know *how,* where is your *what?* Alchemist, where is your gold?

We are searching for the Rheingold and *we believe it exists.* And in the end, unlike the alchemists, we will find it.

(I chose the conjectural Rheingold on purpose, since only poets believe in it [*Rheingold: Dichtergold**]. Had I said the gold of Peru, the example might have been more convincing. This way, it's more honest.)

Stupidity is as heterogeneous and varied as intelligence, and the one, like the other, contains its opposite. And we recognize stupidity, like intelligence, by its tone.

Thus, for example, to the statement "There is no inspiration, there is only craft" (the Formalist method, a new variety of Bazarov-ism) comes an instant response from the same camp (stupidity): "There is no craft, there is only inspiration" ("pure poetry," the "divine spark," "true music"—all the commonplaces of philistinism). And a poet will never prefer the first statement to the second or the second to the first. A self-evident lie in an alien tongue.

2

He dares not be a critic ...

Be just, dear readers—and if you can't, at least use a little common sense!

In order to form a judgment about anything, you must live with it and love it.

Let us take a most obvious—that is, a most instructive—

---

* Literally, "poet's gold." EDITOR.

example. You buy yourself a pair of boots.* What do you know about them? That they suit you or they don't. That you like them or you don't. What else? That they were bought in a certain, let's say, a very fine shop. Your attitude to them and their brand name. (The brand name, in our case, is the author's name.) And that's all. Can you judge their durability? Their strength? Their quality? No. Why? Because you are not a bootmaker and not a tanner.

To judge quality, essence, anything that is not part of a thing's appearance, can only be done by someone who lives and works in that particular area. Your attitude is your own affair, but an evaluation is not your prerogative.

It is the same thing, dear readers, exactly the same, with art. Here is my poem. You like it or you don't, you grasp it or you don't, it is "pretty" (you think) or it isn't. But whether it is good or bad as a poem only an expert, a lover, or a master can say. You merely exceed your rights when you judge a world in which you do not live.

Why is it that I, a poet, do not give advice to bankers or politicians, not even *post factum,* after a bank failure or a governmental crisis? Because I know nothing about banks and governments, and I don't love them. The best I can do when talking to a banker or a politician is ask questions: "Why, in this given instance, did you act thus and so?" I ask; that is, I desire to hear, and possibly to form an opinion of, something I know nothing about. Not having an opinion, not pretending to one, I want to find out about something foreign to me. I allow myself to be instructed.

Why, then, don't you, bankers and politicians, talking in your turn to a bootmaker, ever offer him advice? Because any bootmaker would laugh in your face or behind your back, and say, "You don't know what you're talking about, Sir." And he'd be right.

* Tsvetaeva's extended comparison between boots and poetry refers to Alexander Pushkin's poem "The Bootmaker" in which the Greek painter Apelles advises a bootmaker to judge only the things he can understand. The final lines of the poem describe a friend of the poet who presumes to judge society but is unable to judge the quality of a pair of boots. EDITOR.

Why, then, do you, the same bankers and politicians, talking to me, a poet, give me advice? "Write like this," and "Don't write like *that*." And why—most amazing—have I, the poet, never yet, not once to one of you, laughed in your face like my hypothetical bootmaker: "You don't know what you're talking about, Sir."

There is a fine nuance here. When the bootmaker laughs he has no fear of insulting you. Your business, after all, "Sir," is on a higher level than his. His laughter is only a sign that he disagrees with you. But the poet's laughter will inevitably insult; the "poet"—in a philistine sense—is of course higher than a "banker." Our laughter, in the given instance, is not only an indication to another of his place, but an indication of a lower place. "Heaven" showing "earth" its place. So the philistine thinks, so he perceives it. And with that, though he doesn't know it, he deprives us of our last defense. There is nothing humiliating in not understanding anything about boots, but it is totally humiliating to know nothing about poetry. Our self-defense is another's humiliation. And much, much water must flow, many resentments build up, before the poet will overcome a false shame, and resolve to tell the lawyer, the politician, the banker to his face: "You are not my judge."

The matter is not a question of what is higher or lower, but simply of your ignorance of my field, and mine of yours. And I will make the same answer—I make it now—to a painter, a sculptor, a musician. Because I think them lower? No. Nor do I think you lower. My answer to you, a banker, and even to Igor Stravinsky, if he doesn't understand poetry, is the same: "You are not my judge."

To each his own.

All of which instantly dissolves under one condition: if we are able to enter each other's realm. Thus I have paid less attention to critics and poets than to the late F. F. Kokoshkin, who loved and understood poetry certainly not less than I. (He was a civic leader.) Thus I value the judgment of A. A. Podgaetsky-Chabrov (a man of the theater) more than that of critics and poets.

Read and love my work as you love your own. Then you may judge me.

Getting back to boots and poems. Which boots are bad? Those that will fall apart (the bootmaker). Those that have fallen apart (the purchaser). What kind of artistic productions are bad? Those that will not last (the critic). Those that have not lasted (the public). Neither the bootmaker nor the critic—experts in their fields—need to make tests. They know in advance. For the purchaser, whether of a pair of boots or a book of verse, time must be spent with the work; the test of time is needed. The whole difference is in the duration of that test. A bad boot is found out in a month; for a bad work of art you often need a century. Either the "bad" (the not-understood work that found no prophet) may turn out to be beautiful, or the beautiful (the work that found no judge) may turn out to be bad. Here we must deal with the quality of the material used in the boots and the poems, and all its consequences, with the palpability of matter and the impalpability of the human spirit. An average bootmaker can take one glance at a boot and say whether it's good or not. For this he needs no particular flair or feeling. But the critic, if he is to determine immediately whether a work is good or not *once and for all,* needs—besides all the requisite knowledge—flair, feeling, and the gift of second sight. The stuff a boot is made of, leather, is palpable and finite. The stuff of artistic production (neither sound, nor words, nor stone, nor canvas but the human spirit) is impalpable and infinite. There are no boots *once and for all.* But every lost line of Sappho is lost once and for all. For this reason (the palpability of the material) boots in the hands of the bootmaker fare better than poems in the hands of the critic. There are no misunderstood boots, but how many misunderstood poems!

And yet both boots and poems, from their very beginning, contain an absolute judgment of themselves: they are of good quality or not of good quality. And good quality is the same for both. Durability.

To perceive this internal judgment of a work upon itself, to possess an ear that is ahead of his contemporaries' by a hundred if not a thousand years—that is the critic's task, and it can be fulfilled only if there is a *gift.*

Anyone who writes criticism without the gift of second sight is an artisan—with the right to work, but not the right to judge.

To be a critic is to be able to see across three hundred years and to the ends of the earth.

All of which I would apply to the reader as well. The critic is an ideal reader who has taken up a pen.

3

Those I listen to ...

Among nonprofessionals (this doesn't mean that I listen to all professionals) I listen to every important poet and every important man. It's even better if both are one.

The criticism of an important poet, for the most part, is criticism based on a passion—for what is close and for what is alien. *Ergo,* it is a personal attitude and not evaluation; *ergo,* it is not criticism; and *ergo,* probably, that's why I listen to it. If an image of me does not arise out of his words, he himself is at least visible in them. A kind of confession, like the dreams we have about other people: the actions are yours, but I am the one who motivates them. The right of affirmation, the right of rejection—who disputes them? I am only against the right to judge.

An ideal example of just such loving self-sufficiency is Balmont's admirable book *Mountain Peaks,* the focused lens of all his ways of saying "yes." Why do I believe Balmont? Because he is an important poet. Because he speaks about something he loves. But cannot Balmont be mistaken? He can, and not long ago he was, seriously, about X. But whether X corresponds to Balmont's vision of him or not, Balmont's evaluation of him corresponds to Balmont; that is, Balmont, an important poet, is seen in it at his full stature. Looking at X, he sees himself. Looking past X, we see Balmont. And to look at Balmont, to see Balmont, is worthwhile. Consequently, even when he makes a mistake, the judgment of a poet on a poet (in this case a prose writer) is a good thing.

But besides this, might not his attitude be mistaken? For, surely, Balmont's entire evaluation of X is nothing but an attitude. Hearing and seeing such and such in him, he feels so and so. What's there to argue in that? It's so personal it can't be taken into consideration.

Evaluation defines the place of something in the world; an attitude defines its place in one's own heart. An attitude is not only not a judgment, it is itself beyond judgment.

Who would quarrel with a man who is attracted by his obviously ugly wife? All things are permitted to an attitude except one: to proclaim itself evaluation. Let the same man proclaim his ugly wife the foremost beauty in the world, or even in the neighborhood, and everyone would object and refute his proclamation. An attitude, the most extreme one, in whatever matter, is the prerogative of all—the important poet and any man in the street included—but with one condition: that it not exceed the bounds of the personal. "*I* think thus, *I* like this"—with a personal "I"—and I'll allow a bootmaker to reject my poems. Because that "I" bears no responsibility. But let that same bootmaker, omitting his "I," try to maintain that my work in general is worthless, what then? Same as always: I'll smile.

Are we to assume from the example of Balmont and X that a poet is in general no judge? Of course not. If a lyric poet, due to his own nature, exchanges a striving for judgment for the luxury of an attitude (a striving for impartiality for the luxury of preference), that still does not mean (1) that all poets are lyric poets; (2) that a lyric poet cannot be a judge. He merely does not want to be a judge, preferring (unlike the philistine) to love and not to judge. Not to want and not to be able: those are two different things. Someone who wants and who can: the lyric poet Khodasevich, in all his scholarly and critical activities.

When I hear people speak about some special "poetic nature" I don't believe it exists—and if it does, then it is not restricted to poets alone. A poet is one man multiplied a thousandfold, and particular poets differ among themselves just as human beings in general do. A "poet at heart" (it's a colloquial expression) is as vague a statement as a "human at heart." A poet, first of all, is someone who has escaped from the confines of his heart. A poet is outside the heart, not confined in it (his heart itself has escaped). In the second place, when he went beyond the confines of his heart he went into language. In the third place, this "poet at heart," which poet is he? Homer *or* Ronsard? Derzhavin *or*

Pasternak? Even—the difference is not in periods but in essences —Goethe *or* Schiller, Pushkin *or* Lermontov, Mayakovsky, finally, *or* Pasternak?

Equal gifts of heart and tongue: that describes the poet. Therefore, there are no nonwriting poets, or any nonfeeling poets. You feel but you don't write: you are not a poet (where are the words?). You write but you don't feel: you are not a poet (where is your heart?). Where is essence? Where is form? They are all one and the same. The indivisibility of form and essence: that describes the poet. Naturally I will always prefer someone who feels but doesn't write to someone who writes but doesn't feel. The first may be a poet tomorrow. Or a saint. Or a hero. The second (the versifier) cannot become anything at all. And his name is legion.

Thus, having established the existence of the poet-in-general, and the most essential sign of belonging to poetry, let us assert that "essence is form and form essence" is the only point of similarity that poets have in common. Poets are as various as planets.

One necessary observation. In the judgments of lyric poets (personal attitude), overestimation clearly prevails. (Glance through the German and French Romantics' reviews of one another.) In the judgment of epic poets (evaluation), underestimation. Consider the example of the dispassionate Goethe, who underrated Hölderin, underrated Heine, underrated Kleist. (This underestimation is highly indicative—precisely of his own contemporaries. And of his contemporaries, precisely of his compatriots. The same Goethe gave the young Byron his due and overrated Sir Walter Scott.) This example seems to refute my proclamation of the right of one poet to judge another. But only seems. The right to judge is still not the right to execute. More precisely: a verdict is still not an execution. Or: execution is not yet death. No one—not even Goethe—and no words—not even those of Goethe at eighty —were able to kill Heine: *sum!* Goethe underrated him, but Heine survived. But (comes the reply) after Goethe's unflattering opinion, had Heine been weaker, he might have put an end to himself, as a man or a poet. But had Heine been weaker he would not have been Heine. No, Heine is life, and *inextinguishable*. Goethe's opinion of Heine was only an additional stimulus to work. ("You've overlooked me, but you'll see me yet!") And for us, a hundred years later, a stimulus to thought. Goethe—and so wide of the mark! Why? We begin to think. First about Goethe and Heine, their essential dissimilarity; then about their ages, eighty and thirty; about age itself, what it is, does it exist, about Olympianism and demonism, about attraction and repulsion, about many things. . . .

Consequently, even in the cruel case of one poet's underestimation of another, the judgment of a poet on a poet is a good thing.

So much for the poets. Who else do I listen to? To any important voice, whosoever it may be. If an old rabbi, made wise by race, age, and the prophets, talks to me about my poetry, I listen. Does he love poetry? I don't know. He may never have read any. But he loves (he knows) all those things out of which poetry comes, the sources of life and being. He is wise. And his wisdom suffices for me and for what I write.

I listen to the rabbi, to Romain Rolland; I listen to a seven-year-old child, to all that is wisdom and nature. Their approach is cosmic, and if the cosmos is in my poetry, they will discern it and respond. I don't know whether Romain Rolland loves poetry; take the extreme possibility, that he doesn't. But in poems, beyond poetry (the poetic element), all the elements are yet present. These Rolland loves for certain. The presence of the poetic element in me will not impede him, its absence in him will not impede me; they cannot.

"I'll come right to the point. . . ." Which is all that I need.

When I mention a seven-year-old child, I also mean the people, the *folk,* the unspoiled, primal, savage ear.

And to whom do I listen besides the voice of nature and wisdom? The voices of all apprentices and of all masters.

When I recite a poem about the sea, and a sailor who knows nothing about poetry corrects me, I am grateful. The same for a woodsman, a blacksmith, a stonemason. Everything they give me from the world external to myself is a blessing, because in that world I am nothing. And I have need of that world hour after hour. One cannot discuss imponderables imponderably. My goal is to affirm, to give my work weight. And in order for my imponderable (my soul, let's say) to have weight, I need a vocabulary and a usage belonging to the here-and-now, some measure of weight already known to the world and accepted in it. The soul. The sea. If my sea simile is incorrect, the whole poem falls apart. (Only specifics are convincing: a certain hour upon the sea, its appearance, its habits. In love, you cannot get by with "I love . . ." alone.) A poet's most terrible, most persistent (and most honorable!) enemy is the visible world—an enemy he can conquer only by getting to know it. The poet's whole purpose is to put the visible in the service of the invisible. I take you, my enemy, with all your treasures, for my slave. And what an effort of inner vision is required to translate the invisible world into the visible! (This is what the creative process is all about.) How well we must know that visible world! More simply yet: a poet is one who must know everything exactly. He who knows everything already? But what he knows is different. He knows the invisible, he doesn't know the visible yet, and yet he needs the visible unceasingly for his symbols. *"Alles vergängliche ist nur ein Gleichnis."* * Yet I need to know this *vergängliche,* otherwise my likeness will be false. The visible is the cement, the legs on which a work of art stands. (In French, *"ça ne tient pas debout."*)

The formula of Théophile Gautier, which was and is so often abused (compare it with Goethe's!): *"Je suis de ceux pour qui le monde visible existe"* † is broken off at the most important point: *as a means,* and not as an end.

The self-sufficiency of the world is nonsense, as far as the poet is concerned. For a philosopher, this leads to questions; for a poet, to answers. (Never believe in a poet's questions. All his *whys* and *to what ends* are *becauses.*) But in his arguments (his similes) a poet must be wary. If I compare, let's say, the soul with the sea

* All that is transitory is only a symbol." EDITOR.
† "I am one of the people for whom the visible world exists." EDITOR.

and the mind with the chessboard, I must know both the ocean and chess, every moment of the ocean and each move on the board. A lifetime is not enough to learn everything. And so I turn to those with experience in their fields, to experts.

A poem is only convincing when it can be verified by a mathematical (or musical, which is the same) formula. I am not the one who will do the verifying.

For that reason I take a poem about the sea to a sailor, not to a lover of poetry. What will the first give me? Backbone—for my soul. What will the second give me? At best a weakened echo of my soul, of myself. In all that does not pertain to my soul, I need others.

Thus from professions, trades, to sciences. From the unknown world to the knowable. Thus from the sailor, the woodsman, the blacksmith, the locksmith, the baker to the historian, the geologist, the physicist, the geometrician, an ever-widening circle.

No poet was ever born with a knowledge of geological strata and historical dates. What was I born knowing? The souls of my heroes. Clothing, rites, dwellings, gestures, speech—everything, that is, that knowledge can yield I take from experts in the field—the historian and the archaeologist.

In a poem about Joan of Arc, for instance:

> The transcript of the trial is theirs.
> The pyre is mine.

4

Those I obey ...

> J' entends des voix, disait-elle,
> qui me commandent ...*

I obey something that sounds constantly within me but not uniformly, sometimes indicating, sometimes commanding. When it indicates, I argue; when it commands, I obey.

The thing that commands is a primal, invariable, unfailing and irreplaceable line, *essence appearing as a line of verse.* (Most usually as a final couplet, to which all the rest then accrues.) The

* "I hear voices," she would say, "that command me...." EDITOR.

thing that indicates is an aural path to a poem: I hear a melody, but not words. The words I have to find.

More to the left—more to the right, higher—lower, faster—slower, extend—break off: these are the exact indications of my ear, or of something *to* my ear. All my writing is only listening. Hence, in order to write further—constant rereading. Without rereading at least twenty lines I cannot write one more. It is as if the whole poem were there from the very beginning, some sort of melodic or rhythmic sketch of it; as if the poem, which in my present moment writes itself (I never know whether it will write itself to completion), were already, somewhere, written out quite precisely in full. All I do is reestablish it. Hence this constant watchfulness: Is this the way it is? Do I deviate from it? Do I give way to myself, to my willfulness?

My task is *to hear true.* I have no other.

5

Why I write . . .

Not for the millions, not for some one-and-only, not for myself. I write for the poem alone. The poem, through me, writes itself. Is this the time to be concerned with myself or with others?

Here we must distinguish two stages: the creative and the post-creative. The first has no *why;* it is all *how.* I would call the second the everyday, practical stage. The poem is written. What's to become of it? Who is it for? Who will buy it? Oh, I make no bones about it: when the poem is completed, that second question is the most important one for me.

Thus the poem is *given* twice: in the spirit and in the world. Who will take it?

A few words about money and fame. To write for money is base; to write for fame, virtuous. Here colloquial speech and colloquial thought are both wrong. To write for anything whatsoever except the poem is to doom it to transience. The only things written that way—and perhaps they should be—are editorials. Fame, money, the triumph of this or that idea, any extraneous goal—and the poem perishes. The poem, while it is being written, is its own goal.

Why do I write? I write because I can't help writing. Question me about goals and I answer about reasons, and it cannot be otherwise. . . .

Between 1917 and 1922, I produced an entire book of so-called civil war (White Guard) poems. Did I intend to write a book? No. The book happened, it came about. To extol the ideals of the White Guard? No. But White ideals triumphed in it. I was inspired originally by the thought of the White Guard, but I forgot about it from the first line on. I thought only of the line I was writing. I encountered it again only after the final full-stop: the White Guard, living, incarnated against my will. The guarantee of the effectiveness of these so-called civil war poems is precisely the absence of political considerations in the process of the writing, and in the unity of the purely poetic considerations. What is true of the ideology is true also of the practical stage. After these poems have been written, I can read them in public and be rewarded with either fame or death. But if I think about that when I undertake them, I will not write them, or will write them in a way that deserves neither fame nor death.

Considerations before completion and after completion. This was what Pushkin had in mind in his lines about the inspiration and the manuscript,[2] and colloquial thought will never be able to understand it.

Fame and money. Fame—how majestic, how spacious, how dignified, how harmonious. What grandeur. What peace.

Money—how petty, how pitiful, how inglorious, how vain. What meanness. What futility.

What, then, do I seek, when I have written something and submit it to someone or other?

Money, my dears. As much as I can get.

Money enables me to go on writing. Money is my tomorrow's poems. Money is my ransom from the hands of editors, publishers, landladies, shopkeepers, patrons; it is my freedom, and my writing desk. Money is more than my writing desk; it is the very *landscape* of my poems—that Greece I so much longed to see while I was writing *Theseus;* and the Palestine I will long for when I write *Saul;* ships and trains that go everywhere, to every seacoast and beyond every sea.

Money enables me to write not only more, but better, not to take advances, not to precipitate events, not to stop up gaps in my poems with incidental words, not to spend time with X and Y in hopes that they will publish or "arrange" something. The choice is mine, the selection is mine.

Money, finally—a third and most important point—enables me to write *less.* Not three pages a day, but thirty lines.*

My money, before all else, dear reader, is *your* gain!

Fame? *"Être salué d'un tas de gens que vous ne connaissez pas"* † (a phrase of the late Scriabin's, though I don't know whether it was his own or borrowed). An added daily burden. Fame is a result, not a goal. All the greatest glory seekers loved not fame, but power. Had Napoleon sought fame he would never have objected to St. Helena, that most perfect of pedestals. It was not fame Napoleon regretted on St. Helena, but power. Hence his longing, and his spyglass. Fame is passive; love of power is active. Fame reclines, "resting on its laurels." Power rides a horse, and quests for those laurels. "For the glory of France and the sake of my own power"—that, at the bottom of his heart, was Napoleon's motto. Let the world obey France, and France—me. The name of Napoleonic *gloire* is *pouvoir.* He, a man of action before all else, never cared about his reputation (an essentially literary phenomenon). To burn oneself at both ends for the roar of the crowd and

---

* The point is less applicable to me than to anyone. (1) If (like Onegin) I was "in haste to live and hied myself to feel," I was in no haste to publish. Thus between 1912 and 1922 I didn't publish a single book. (2) Haste of the spirit does not necessarily indicate haste of the pen. "The Swain," which, it was claimed, was written "at a single sitting," took three months—writing without a break, daily. "The Pied Piper" (six chapters) took half a year. (3) Every one of my lines contains "all I can do within the limits of a given hour."

Let my rough drafts bear witness to the supposed "facility" of my writing. AUTHOR.

† "To be greeted by a mass of people you don't know." EDITOR.

the babble of poets—he despised both crowd and poets too much for that. Napoleon's purpose was power; his fame was a consequence of its attainment.

I admit a poet's fame as publicity, for financial motives. Thus, though squeamish about publicity personally, I applaud Mayakovsky's sweep, boundless in this as in everything. When Mayakovsky needs money, he does something sensational once again ("a purge of poets, a slaughter of poetesses," his trip to America, etc.). People go to see the scandal and pay money. Mayakovsky, as a major poet, cares nothing about either praise or detraction. He himself knows what he is worth. But he does care about money, he cares a lot. And his self-advertisement, by its very vulgarity, is so much cleaner than the parrots, monkeys, and harems of Lord Byron. He, as we know, did not need money.

A necessary observation: Neither Byron nor Mayakovsky ever involved their art in matters of fame; both used the refuse of their personal lives. Byron wants fame? He gets himself a menagerie, lives in Raphael's house, *perhaps* goes to Greece. . . . Mayakovsky wants fame? He puts on a yellow blouse and poses in front of a fence.

The scandalous private lives of a good half of all poets are only a cleansing of *that other* life, so that they are clean *there*.

Life is messy, notebooks are clean. (For "clean," read "full of words, black." A clean notebook is black with words.) Life is noisy, notebooks are still. (The ocean gives an impression of stillness even during a storm. The ocean gives an impression of labor even during a calm. The first case is an observer in action; the second, a laborer at rest. In every force there is an incessant conjunction of stillness and labor. The peace that we sense in every force is our own confidence in it. The ocean is like that. And a forest. And a poet. Every poet is a *pacific* ocean.)

Thus, before our very eyes, a commonplace is overturned: in poetry, anything is permitted. No. Precisely in poetry, nothing is. In private life—everything . . .

Fame is parasitic. In the vegetable kingdom, power is an oak tree, fame is the ivy. In the animal kingdom, fame is a courtesan reposing on the warrior's laurels. A pleasant supplement, and it costs nothing.

Fame is a kind of Dionysian ear cocked at the world, a Homeric *qu'en dira-t-on?* The furtive backward glance, the misapprehending ear of the maniac. (A combination of two manias: delusions of grandeur and of persecution.)

Two examples of unalloyed love of fame: Nero and Herostratus. Both were *maniacs*.

Comparison with the poet. Herostratus, in order to glorify his name, set fire to a temple. The poet, in order to glorify a temple, sets himself afire.

The greatest fame (the epos), and the greatest power, is anonymous.

There is a dictum of Goethe: "One ought not write a single line that is not intended for a million readers."

Yes, but there's no need to hurry those readers, to expect them in this very decade or this very century.

"One ought not . . ." But clearly one had. It sounds more like a prescription intended for others than for himself. The dazzling example of that very same *Faust,* not understood by his contemporaries and still being deciphered for lo these hundred years. *"Ich, der in Jahrtausenden lebe . . ."* * (Goethe. Eckermann.)

What is beautiful about fame? The word itself.

6

Varieties of critics

Let us consider the professional critic. Here we distinguish three types.

The first one is common: the critic-*constateur,* the certifier, the temporizing critic, who certifies the work only after it has gained acceptance, the critic with a ten-year time lag. If a true critic is a prophet, this one is a prophet in reverse. A *post-factum* critic, frequent and honest, he is part of the thickest stratum of honest readers (for there is another kind). He never discovers

* "I who live in millennia." EDITOR.

America, never recognizes the genius in the child, never bets on an untried horse (no newcomers for him); he keeps clear of current trends, and never makes *gross* mistakes.

A cultured reader.

But there is another reader, uncultured. The mass reader, the reader who reads by hearsay, with a time lag so *post factum* that in 1925 he considers Nadson [3] a contemporary, and the sixty-year-old Balmont a promising youngster. The distinguishing feature of such a reader is his lack of discrimination, the absence of *Orientirungssinn*. Thus, speaking of "modernism," he throws Balmont, Vertinsky,[4] and Pasternak all in one pot, distinguishing neither chronology nor worth, nor the place created and occupied by each poet, and covers it all with a word he doesn't understand: "decadents." (I would derive decadent from decade. Every decade has its decadents. But then they'd be "decadists" or "decaders.") This sort of reader calls everything after Nadson decadence, and contrasts everyone after Nadson with Pushkin. Why doesn't he contrast Nadson with Pushkin? Because he knows Nadson and loves him. But why Pushkin? Apparently because there's a monument to Pushkin on Tverskoy Boulevard. For I maintain he doesn't know Pushkin. The reader by hearsay is true to himself even here.

Still—the anthologies, the F's, examinations, busts, death masks. "Pushkin's Duel" in display windows and "Pushkin's Death" on posters. Pushkin's cypress tree in Gurzuf and Pushkin's estate, Mikhailovskoe (where is it, exactly?). Hermann's aria and Lensky's aria (indeed, the Russian vulgarian knows his Pushkin mainly vocally!). The single-volume Sytin edition of *Pushkin* with Pushkin as a child, his cheek propped on his fist, and 500 illustrations in the text (the visual method of teaching poetry—poetry at a glance; indeed the Russian vulgarian knows his Pushkin mainly by sight!). And let's not forget the Repin picture in the living room (sometimes even in the dining room), with all those cloaks being dragged across a snowy field—it's all so respectable, overflowing with antiquity and jubilee celebrations. The Tverskoy Boulevard monument, finally, with its falsified Pushkin lines:

> And long will I be loved by my nation
> For waking the good within them by my song,
> For being useful by my delightful poems.[5]

Pushkin by hearsay (hearsong—all those tenors and baritones), Pushkin-at-a-glance (the aforementioned Sytin edition): they know him from opera librettos and anthologies—from the librettos better than from the anthologies. Thus the Russian vulgarian and his knowledge of Pushkin. And opposing it all, there stands Pushkin and the Russian language.

"What poem by Pushkin do you like?"

"Everything."

"Well, what do you like best?"

"Eugene Onegin."

"What about the lyric poems?"

(A pause. Occasionally an anthological reminiscence.) "Winter. The peasant rejoices." [6] (Occasionally a confusion by association.) " 'The Sail.' " [7]

(The vulgarian before Goethe's monument: *"Wer kennt Dich nicht, O grosser Goethe! Fest gemauert in der Erden! . . ."* *)

Pushkin's prose? Inevitably, *The Captain's Daughter*. Nobody ever reads Pushkin's Pugachov.[8]

For such a reader, Pushkin in general is something in the nature of a perpetual celebrant, who never did anything except die (his duel, his death, his last words to the tsar, his farewell to his wife, etc.).

The name of such a reader is rabble. Pushkin hated him, and wrote about him in *The Poet and the Rabble*. The rabble, the dark mass of dark forces, destroyer of thrones more important than royal ones. Such a reader is an enemy, and his crime is blasphemy against the Holy Ghost.

What is his crime? The crime is not in the darkness, but in refusal of the light; not in misunderstanding, but in opposing understanding, in intentional blindness and malicious prejudice. In ill-will toward the good. I include among the rabble-readers all

---

* "Who doesn't know you, great Goethe? Firmly embedded in the earth! . . ." The quotation is actually from Schiller's *The Bell*. EDITOR.

those who heard of Gumilyov for the first time the day he was shot and who now go around shamelessly proclaiming him the greatest poet of modern times. I include among them all those who hate Mayakovsky because he belongs to the Communist party. (I don't know if he is a party member. He's an anarchist, that I know.) Those who hear Pasternak's name and say: "Oh, the painter's son?" Those who know that Balmont drinks and that Blok "went over to the Bolsheviks." (An astounding intelligence of poets' private lives! Balmont drinks, commits bigamy, and has a great time. Esenin drinks too, married an old woman and then married an old man's granddaughter,* and then hanged himself. Belyi left his wife Asya, and he drinks too. Akhmatova fell in love with Blok and left Gumilyov and was then married to . . .—there's a whole series of versions. [I don't dispute the Blok-Akhmatova idyll, by the way; the reader knows best.] Blok doesn't live with his wife, and Mayakovsky lives with somebody else's. Vyacheslav Ivanov did such and such. Sologub did something or other. And that other one . . . have you heard?)

Thus, without getting beyond the titles, they feel qualified to be biographers.

Such a reader not only has no respect, he cannot even read. And without reading, he not only opines, but judges. About him, and him alone, is Pushkin's line: "And never argue with idiots!"

Don't argue. Just show them the door as soon as they open their mouths.

There are also rabble-critics. With a slight allowance for their level of illiteracy, what is true of the rabble-reader is true of the rabble-critic.

The rabble-critic is the same as the rabble-reader, but it's not enough that he doesn't read—he writes.

Now about two kinds of critics representative of the present. The first—the dilettante—of the emigration; the second—the handy reference man—of Soviet Russia.

* I.e., Isadora Duncan and Lev Tolstoy's granddaughter. EDITOR.

Who among the *émigrés* does not write criticism? "Do a book notice," "Write a review." (To do a book notice would seem to imply noticing a book. Alas, those who write them often notice nothing; they notice what is not in the book. They write about nothing.) Lawyers write, unprofessional young men write, older men who are professionals in other fields write, everybody writes, the public itself writes. So to the question: Who among the *émigrés* writes criticism? the answer is: Who doesn't? The article is passé; the "notice" now flourishes. Quotation is dead; unsubstantiated statement abounds. I read, let's say, about a totally new author, someone I've never read, that he's a hack. On whose authority? A name at the bottom of a column. But it's a name I never heard of. Or have heard of in some other field. Where is the substantiation that shows that author to be a hack or a prophet? Where is there any quotation? There is none. I am supposed to take it on faith.

The dilettante critic is the foam on the surface of a questionable kettle of fish—the public. What's cooking within? The liquid is dark. So is the foam.

The above is in reference to criticism by unknowns, which has yet to bring forth a single notable name. (A name means not nepotism, but talent.) But there is not much more cause for rejoicing to be found in criticism by people who are known, at times even famous.

The lamentable article by the academician Bunin, "Russia and Inonia," [9] which slanders Blok and Esenin and contains obviously garbled quotations (better write nothing at all, than this) that are meant to expose the godlessness of all contemporary poetry and the hoodlums who write it. (Bunin has forgotten his own novel, *The Village,* a wonderful piece, but full of vileness and obscenity.) The rosewater that trickles through the articles of Eichenwald. The feigned perplexity of Zinaida Gippius—an important poet, surely—over the syntax of a no less important poet, Boris Pasternak (not a lack of good will, but the presence of ill-will). I must qualify as truly indecent A. Yablonovsky's article on Remizov, A. Yablonovsky's article on my "Germany," and

A. Chyorny's article on Remizov. ("Remizov and *Émigré* Criticism" is an article yet to be written. If not by me, then by someone else. If not now, in a hundred years.)

A rare and delightful exception: someone whose judgment about poets is *not* based on political position (that way madness lies!): D. S. Mirsky. Among journals this applies to the entire critical sections of *The Will of Russia* and *In One's Own Way.*

Then there is a special case that I find puzzling. A critic (the most frequently read, well-reputed, and recognized critic) is writing about the anthology *The Ark,* published in Czechoslovakia:

". . . we'd prefer to point out the most interesting pages of the anthology. Unfortunately, in order to do so, we must bypass 'The Poem of the End' by M. T.—a long poem which this reader, at least, simply did not comprehend; it seems to him, however, that anyone else as well would have to decipher rather than read it, and even should he prove luckier and better at guessing than we are, he will yet purchase his pleasure at the price of great mental exertion." *

The first thing that struck me in the review was its meekness. The critic does not evaluate, he only expresses an attitude. ". . . did not comprehend"—what's that, an evaluation? No, a confession. Of what? Of his own lack of competence. "Incomprehensible" is one thing; "I did not comprehend" is another. That he read and disapproved is one thing; that he read and did not comprehend is another. "Why?" is the response to the first; "Oh, really?" the response to the second. The first is the voice of a critic, the second a voice from the audience. Someone or other read and did not comprehend, but allows the possibility—in another reader—of greater acumen and greater pleasure. Of course that pleasure will be purchased with "great mental exertion." The phrase is revealing. Make a little effort and you'll get it, but as for me, I don't want to be bothered. This is no longer meekness but, if not ill-will, at least a clear absence of good will. A reader can say that, but a critic shouldn't. Just as "I don't understand" is a renunciation of

* This is a quotation from an article by the venerable critic Yuli Eichenwald, whom Tsvetaeva discusses in the following pages. EDITOR.

your rights, so "I don't try to understand" is a rejection of your obligations. The first position is meek, the second inert. Encountering some difficulty, the critic simply bypasses the work itself. ". . . to decipher rather than read it . . ." But what is reading if not deciphering, interpretation, the extraction of a secret located within the lines, beyond the boundaries of the words? (To say nothing of difficulties of syntax.) Reading, before all else, is participation in creation. If the reader lacks imagination, not a single book will survive. Imagination and good will toward the work are required.

I have occasionally heard similar reactions from artists in other fields. "It's difficult. I want to relax, and here I have to search, to puzzle it out. . . ." To relax? From what? From *difficulty* in your own art. So you do recognize it where your own art is concerned. You just don't want to deal with it in mine. Well, maybe you're right, in your own way. Take care of your own business, I'll take care of mine. In such cases, by the way, the most effective reply has always been: "But suppose I say to you, a serious musician, that your sonata is too difficult and ask you for a waltz, what will you say? After all, I get tired from my own work and I want to relax too." (Pure pedagogy!)

They always understood and, if they didn't read my poems, at least they respected my difficulty and didn't ask for a little "light music."

But that was a musician, a worker in sound. What's to be said of a critic, a worker with words, who wants to avoid mental exertion and leaves it to *someone else to understand?* Of a servant of the word who asks me, a servant of the word, for "light verse"?

The formula exists, and it's an old one. The man I'm talking about can sign his name to it, with a clear conscience.

> **Poetry for you is pleasant,**
> **Lovely, sweet, and refreshing**
> **as lemonade in summertime.**[10]

Lemonade. It's lemonade this particular critic wants of me (and of poetry in general). Another one of his statements confirms this, a statement about another writer this time: ". . . if he had done this and that, he would not tire himself out, he would not tire his reader, but would on the contrary delight him here and there with *beautiful verbal splashes*." (My italics.)

To delight the reader with beautiful verbal splashes is not the purpose of literature. My purpose when I sit down to a poem is not to delight anybody, neither myself nor anyone else, but *to accomplish the poem as perfectly as possible*. Delight comes later, as a result of accomplishment. A commander about to give battle doesn't think of laurels, or of bouquets, or of crowds, only of the battle—and less of victory than of this or that position which must be taken. Delight comes later, and is real, but with it comes a great exhaustion. I have a great deal of respect for the exhaustion I feel after bringing my work to completion. It means that there was something to overcome and that my work was accomplished not without struggle. It means it was worth the battle. That same exhaustion I respect in the reader as well. Exhausted by my work? That means he read it well, and that he read something worth reading. The exhaustion of a reader is not devastating, but creative. Mutually creative. It honors the reader, and it honors me.

We will return to the *émigré* amateur critic (that one was hardly an amateur) with a striking example. But let us turn now to another kind of critic, firmly established in the Soviet Union, and naturally the reverse of the *émigré:* the handy reference critic. I would call such a critic a celebrant of the pseudo elect.

When, in response to my poem where form has been mastered and overcome by means of the rough drafts, I hear, "ten a's, eighteen o's, assonances" (I don't know all the professional terms), I realize that all my drafts were for naught, that they have come to light again, that everything I've created is again torn apart. Dissection—but the dissection of a living thing, not of a corpse. Murder.

"Mme. T, in order to achieve such and such an effect, was obliged to do this or that. . . ." First: how often they are wide of the mark! Second: who needs that "was obliged to" when the thing has been done? The reader? As an attentive and inquisitive reader, I say no. The writer? But once I've done the thing—and, let's assume, done it well—why should I hear from others what I already know from my own experience of working at it? At best this is repetition, confirmation. The verification of a problem already inarguably solved. In other words, a mere formality. Perhaps young poets need it? Recipes for producing certain effects? But name me just one major poet who writes according to someone else's (always private) recipes. (There are no public recipes for creative work.) Besides which, one man's meat is another's poison. A poet's theory is always *post factum,* conclusion drawn from his own working experience, a retracing of a path he has already traveled. I have accomplished something. How did I do it? And then, by means of an extremely painstaking examination of his drafts, by adding up vowels and consonants, by a study of stresses (I repeat, I'm unfamiliar with the terminology of the business), a poet arrives at a certain conclusion, which he later elaborates and publishes as this or that theory. But, I repeat, the basis of any new theory is one's own creative experience. Theory, in this case, represents a verification *of the ear by the intelligence;* it is simply a conceptualization of the sound. Theory is a kind of supplement to practice, free of charge. Can this theory be of use to someone else? Yes, it can, as a check. Belyi's sound system is confirmed by Belyi's already accomplished conclusions. Only the labor of conceptualization is avoided, all the rest is the same. In short, write on white pages and not according to Belyi.* Write on white pages, and if you must, verify it with Belyi. But that is all I can say in approval of schools of verse-making and methods of formal analysis as far as the literary marketplace is concerned. Either the labor of a scholar intended for a scholar (theories of versification), or the living word about living things intended for living people (criticism).

The handy reference critic, considering the poem from the formalist point of view, passing over the what and seeing only the

* A pun on the name Belyi, which means "white." EDITOR.

how, the critic who sees in the poem neither hero nor author (it is "made," not created) and stakes everything on the word "technique" is a phenomenon which, if not harmful, is at least useless. For important poets have no need of ready-made poetic theories, and *we* have no need of unimportant poets. I will say more: breeding minor poets is harmful and sinful. To breed mere artisans in poetry is like breeding deaf musicians. Once you proclaim poetry a craft, you drag into it whole circles of people not created for it, all those who lack the gift for it. "Well, if it's a craft, why not me?" The reader becomes a writer, and the true reader, confronted with endless names and trends (the less the value, the shinier the marquee), stops reading altogether, in despair.

Poetic schools (a sign of the times) are a vulgarization of poetry, and I would compare Formalist criticism to "Hints for the Young Housewife." * Hints to young housewives, hints to young poets. Art is a kitchen. All you need is the knack. But to complete the parallel, a cruel law of inequality rules both these areas. Just as a pauper cannot fold twelve dozen beaten egg yolks into a bucket of cream and flavor it with a quart of Jamaica rum, so too the poetic pauper cannot concoct out of himself the ingredient he hasn't got: talent. All he is left with are empty gestures over empty mixing bowls.

The only handbook is the poet's own ear, and, if it is absolutely necessary, Savodnik's [11] theory of literature: drama, tragedy, epic, satire, etc.

The only teacher is the poet's experience.

The only judge is the future.

7

The poet and the poem

Often, reading some review of my work and learning that "the formal aspects are beautifully solved," I think to myself, "Did I really have any formal aspects to solve?" Mme. T's intention was to give us a folktale, introducing into it elements of this, and of

---

* A variation of *The Gift to the Young Housewife by* Yelena Molokhovetz, the most popular Russian cookbook of all time. EDITOR.

that, etc." * Did *I* (the stress is on I) intend that? No. *That* was what I intended? No, not at all. I read a folktale, "The Vampire," in Afanasiev's folklore collection and I was puzzled. Why is it that Marusya, who is afraid of the vampire, so persistently refuses to admit what she has seen, knowing that deliverance lies in naming it? Why does she say no instead of yes? Fear? But fear can not only make us bury ourselves in a bed, it can make us jump out the window. No, not fear. Granted fear, but something else as well. Fear and what? When someone says to me, do this and you will be free, and I don't do it, that means I am not particularly interested in freedom; it means that my nonfreedom is more precious to me. And what is the precious nonfreedom that exists between individuals? Love. Marusya loved the vampire. That is why she never named him, and so lost, one after another, her mother, her brother, her life. Passion and crime, passion and sacrifice. . . .

That was *my* task, when I started working on "The Swain." To uncover the essence of the tale, already implicit in its skeleton. To release the poem from its spell. And not at all to invent a "new form" or a "folkloric form." The work wrote itself, I worked on it, listened to every word (not weighed—listened). The labor that went into the poem is confirmed by (1) the fact that the reader cannot perceive it, and (2) by my drafts. But all that is the poem's development, its realization, and not my initial conception.

How could I, a poet—that is, a person who deals with the essence of things, be attracted by mere form? If I am attracted by the essence, the form will come of its own accord. And it does come. And I have no doubt that it will keep coming. The form required by this particular essence, conjured up by me syllable by syllable. To cast the form, and then fill it with content? But what is this, making plaster casts? No, I have to be attracted by the essence; then I can realize it. That's what a poet does. And I will realize it (now it *is* a question of form) as *concretely* as possible. Essence is form: a child cannot be born different from what it is. The gradual revelation of features—thus a person grows, and a

* What follows is Tsvetaeva's reply to the critical reception of her folklore-based narrative poem "The Swain." EDITOR.

work of art as well. For that reason to approach the work "formally"—that is, to reconstruct for me (often completely incorrectly) my own rough drafts—is nonsense. Once the fair copy exists, the drafts (the form) are overcome.

Rather than tell me what I intended to accomplish in a given poem, show me what you were able to get out of it.

The folk, in folktales, interpret the dream of the elements; the poet, in the poem, interprets the dream of the folk; the critic (in a new poem) interprets the dream of the poet.

Criticism: the court of ultimate jurisdiction in dream interpretation.

The penultimate one.

8

What a critic ought to be

The god of highways and crossroads, the double-visaged god, who looks forward and back.

The critic is the sybil at the cradle:

> **The aged Derzhavin noticed us**
> **And blessed us as he went into the grave.**[12]

translated by Paul Schmidt

Notes

1. Quotation from a poem by Afanasy Fet.
2.   A manuscript is marketable;
   Inspiration is not for sale.

Alexander Pushkin, "Conversation
Between a Poet and a Bookseller"

3. Semyon Nadson (1862–1887), a civic-protest poet of the 1880's, whose sentimental doggerel enjoyed an enormous popularity at the turn of the century.

4. Alexander Vertinsky, the popular nightclub singer of the prerevolutionary times, who was also a favorite among the *émigrés* in Paris; after World War II, a Soviet film actor.

5. Lines 1–3 of the fourth stanza of Pushkin's poem *Exegi monumentum,* as originally written by the poet, went:
   And long will my nation love me
   For waking the good within them by my song,
   For glorifying freedom in my savage century.

The poem circulated only in manuscript during the poet's lifetime. After his death, Pushkin's friend, the poet Zhukovsky, doctored up the text to make it read as Tsvetaeva quotes it. It was from Zhukovsky's version that these lines were printed throughout most of the nineteenth century; and it was the passage altered by Zhukovsky that was chosen from the entire *oeuvre* of Pushkin to be engraved on the pedestal of the Pushkin monument erected in Moscow in 1880, which Tsvetaeva often visited as a child. Zhukovsky's version was finally replaced with Pushkin's own during the celebration of the centenary of his death in 1937.

Tsvetaeva's own note to this quotation reads: "An unerased and unerasable disgrace! This is what the Bolsheviks should have started with! What they should have put an end to! But the falsified lines are there in all their glory. The Tsar's lie that has now become the people's lie."

6. The first line on stanza 2 from Chapter 5 of *Eugene Onegin*, which was often printed in anthologies for children as a separate poem. The vulgarian misquotes the line and thinks it is the title of a poem.

7. A famous poem by Lermontov.

8. His *History of the Pugachov Rebellion*, which gives the factual historical background of *The Captain's Daughter*.

9. Inonia is a utopian country in a poem by Esenin.

10. A quotation from Derzhavin's ode to Catherine the Great, *Felitsa*. The "you" in the passage is the empress.

11. A literary reference book, widely used in prerevolutionary Russian secondary schools.

12. From Pushkin's *Eugene Onegin*.

A letter to Anna Tesková
MARINA TSVETAEVA

Clamart, November 24, 1933

Dear Anna Antonovna,

A letter at last!

I write in a breathing space between two manuscripts: "The House near Old St. Pimen's"—a chronicle of the Ilovaysky family (the historian Ilovaysky—I'm sure you know of him. His daughter was my father's first wife; I am not her daughter), very gloomy, but a true story: a house where everyone died except the old man —the piece may be published in *Contemporary Annals*. So I'm writing you during an interval between "Old Pimen" and "The Forest King" (*Erlkönig;* an attempt to decipher Goethe). I have little hope of placing the second piece: who today, among the *émigrés,* is interested in forest kings, or even in Goethe? I used to be badgered endlessly because of the "modernism" of my poems— now I hear nothing but reproaches for the "backwardness" of my

Anna Tesková was a Czech journalist who became Marina Tsvetaeva's friend in Prague in 1922–1925. Murr and Alya, mentioned in this letter, are Tsvetaeva's children, Georgy and Ariadna. "It would all be funny, if it weren't so sad..." is a quotation from a poem by Lermontov that has become a popular saying.

prose. (And when you realize that the former "modernism" and the present "backwardness" are both the same thing, namely, myself.)

I write almost no poems, and this is why: I cannot limit myself to one poem; they come to me in families, cycles, like whirlpools and even maelstroms in which I am inevitably *trapped*—and it's a question of *time*. I cannot write my current prose pieces and poems both at the same time; could not even if my time were my own. I am a concentric. And no one, anywhere—they forget I am a poet—will publish my poems. Not a line. "No one, anywhere" means *Latest News* and *Contemporary Annals*—there's nowhere else. The pretext is my incomprehensibility as a poet for the reader, but actually I'm incomprehensible for the editors, namely for Milyukov at *Latest News,* and at *Contemporary Annals* for Rudnyov, who is a physician by profession, a politician by avocation, and an editor (N. B., of the literary section!) by misunderstanding. "It would all be funny, if it weren't so sad . . ."

Emigration has made a prose writer out of me. It is *my* prose, and of course lyric prose is the best thing there is to write after poetry, but still and all—*after* poetry!

Of course I do write some occasionally, or rather I jot down passing lines of verse, but more often I don't even jot them down, I let them go again—*ins Blaue* (never *Graue,* even in Paris in November!).

There you have my "literary" affairs. When they award me the Nobel Prize (*they never will*), I shall write poetry. The way other people go on round-the-world cruises.

The Nobel Prize. On the 26th I am to sit on a platform and congratulate Bunin. To try to avoid it would be to protest. I make no protest, I simply disagree, for there is one writer incomparably greater than Bunin: greater, more humane, more original, and more needed—Gorky. Gorky is an era, and Bunin is the end of an era. But of course it's all politics, of course the King of Sweden couldn't pin a medal on Gorky the communist. . . . However there was also the third candidate, Merezhkovsky, and he too is without any doubt more deserving of the Nobel than Bunin. If Gorky is an era, and Bunin the end of an era, then Merezhkovsky is the era of *the end* of the era, and his influence both in Russia and abroad is far greater than Bunin's, who has clearly never had *any* influence, neither here nor there. And *Latest News,* comparing his style with Tolstoy's (as if it were only a question of style, i.e., of the pen one writes with), to Tolstoy's *detriment*—is being simply disgraceful. But of course we mustn't talk about all of that, must we?

Merezhkovsky and Gippius are furious. It's perhaps the first time in their lives that complicated pair has ever experienced a simple emotion.

They are both very old: he is about seventy-five, she is sixty-eight. Both are *hideous*. He is all bent over, like an old tree-root *Wurzelmännchen* (possessing neither charm nor forest, however). She is a painted *bone*—no, even more hideous than a bone: a cross between a skeleton and a wax doll.

Everyone now is terribly afraid of them; both of them, she especially, are evil. Like evil spirits.

I haven't seen Bunin yet. I *do not like* him: he is a cold, cruel, smug patrician. I do not like *him,* but his wife, yes—very much. She was a great help to me with my manuscript, for she is a friend of my elder sister (Ilovaysky's granddaughter) and remembers all that world very well. We corresponded for about half a year. They live in Grasse (Côte d'Azur), a region full of flowers (perfume manufactories), in the villa "Belvedere," on a high cliff. Now they will most likely find themselves a higher one.

Things are not so good with us. First of all, though no one is sick (seriously), no one is really well. Murr has a liver complaint, is on a diet, has gotten very thin—from the liver and also from this idiotic French school system: endless sitting and cramming! . . . [seven lines omitted]. Alya keeps on getting thinner, she's skinny and sluggish, it's evidently a severe anemia. Six years of study, in the meanwhile, are all for nothing, for she makes her living not by drawing but at odd jobs, like stuffing toy animals, or now (perhaps) she may get a job as an assistant to a dentist's assistant—for we have nothing to live on. She has changed a great deal inside as well . . . [23 lines omitted].

The apartment is dirty and cold (because of the coal, and because of its absence). It was dirty in Všenory too, but there was a big cozy stove and the woods outside the windows; it was the *coziness of poverty* and the spiritual consolation of *real* nature. I remember all those places, those long walks, those narrow little roads. I remember Czechoslovakia as something wonderful.

Many many thanks for the monthly packages, they always come to the rescue at the *last* minute!

You are the only person I have left.

translated by Paul Schmidt

Georgy Ivanov:
nihilist as light-bearer
VLADIMIR MARKOV

*Pogovori so mnoy o pustyakakh,
O vechnosti pogovori so mnoy*
—G. I.

Fifteen years after his death, Georgy [1] Ivanov (1894–1958) still "struggles through a fog of boredom and incomprehension" (70) [2] and remains probably the most neglected great Russian poet of our time. In the Western world, where, to quote the Russian proverb, every dog knows Yevtushenko and Voznesensky (two poetic midgets who behave like and/or are constantly presented as giants), such neglect is understandable. (1) The vacuum after Pasternak's death had to be filled with someone who was Soviet and alive. (2) *Émigrés* usually represent, politically, a lost cause, so it is automatically presumed that their poets are poetical losers, too. (3) We seldom try to discover yesterday and go, at the very least, to the day before yesterday to satisfy our spirit of adventure. The latter attitude is evidently valid for the Russian literati and press in exile, too, because there has not been an article about

ABOVE PHOTO: Georgy Ivanov on the steps of the flophouse in which he died.

139

Ivanov since his last obituary. Soviet Russians still do not appreciate him; they have no basis for such appreciation.[3] In books he is treated as a minor Acmeist (which he was before emigration). In 1961 specialists did not know that the poet had died in 1958 (see the index to the thirteen-volume complete Mayakovsky).

Of the great trio of Russian *émigré* poets, only Tsvetaeva has found a kind of niche in the Soviet pantheon, mainly because, first, she came back home (to commit suicide) and, second, she is an important component of another great twentieth-century triad— Mayakovsky-Pasternak-Tsvetaeva (deriving perhaps from Andrei Belyi). The second *émigré* giant, Vladislav Khodasevich, might be the next to be appreciated. His "classical heritage" style, the fact that he choked to poetical death outside Russia, his brief friendship with Gorky, and, to be sure, his scorn for the European bourgeoisie are definite assets to eventual recognition. Ivanov's time has not yet come, and he is, temporarily, only for limited consumption. There are hopeful signs, however. One can count at least three articles in English about the poet (by Irina Agushi, Katherine Filips, and Rod Patterson), one written by a native American and none by members of the literary elite of the Russian emigration. Thus, Ivanov's recognition seems to be coming from an unlikely corner.

It is difficult to write about Ivanov, and there is no coyness in saying so. The quasi-scholarly approaches, like counting alliterations, enumerating themes, or hunting influences, fail in his case even more than with many other poets. One cannot help feeling that the most important elements remain hidden behind the lines, to use a critical cliché.

Only four Russian critics have written about the mature Ivanov on what can be termed a "major scale" (i.e. not just reviewing his latest book); three treated the poet in a friendly way, and all four were at least aware that he was considered, at the time of their writing, the greatest living poet of the Russian emigration. Only Yuri Terapiano (*Literaturny Sovremennik,* Munich) deals in profound-sounding generalizations, which could, without change, be applied to dozens of other poets, i.e. that Ivanov revealed the disintegration of the modern soul and gave expression to the catastrophe that took place within it. Roman Goul (preface to Ivanov's *Poems*) is more concrete, though hardly more imaginative, and he does try to describe Ivanov's style. For Goul, Ivanov is a Russian existentialist and a poet of the St. Petersburg school, who wrote about the dying of art and the loneliness of modern man and whose "earthy" poems derive partly from Vasily Rozanov, the writer who also possessed the "gift of intimacy." Gleb Struve (in his book on Russian literature in exile) is a good example of a hostile critic who refuses to allot Ivanov a separate chapter in his sizable book and who, throughout his discussion, gives vent to his irritation at the poet's "nihilistic negation," murderous irony, cynicism, and coarseness. Ivanov's poetry is for Struve "a detailed analysis of a garbage can," and he gives Nikolai Otsup (a poet of modest abilities and achievement) a better chance of immortality.

Much more interesting is Georgy Adamovich's attempt (*Novyi Zhurnal,* #52) to cope with his enemy-friend's poetry. In his essay Adamovich, as always, digresses and often gives the impression he is speaking of everything except Ivanov, but with his customary sensitivity he drops little insights along the way [4] and for all practical purposes labels Ivanov's poetry "verses about everything going to hell," only to reverse himself by saying that this is poetry *ex profundis.* What makes Adamovich superior to his critical colleagues is his frank admission that he does not know what to do with Ivanov's poetry despite its surface simplicity and clear themes. He calls it "something complex, morbid, constantly contradictory and elusive" and unexpectedly concludes that Ivanov's poetry is permeated with light.

One can hardly expect unanimity from criticism written by contemporaries, but in Ivanov's case one does feel that a frontal attack has produced little but a series of clichés from the lesser critics or an admission of failure from the better ones.

Perhaps a comparison will produce more interesting results— and with whom can we compare Ivanov if not with Khodasevich, his only rival in Russian *émigré* poetry? [5] It is no secret that there is still an Ivanov "party" and a Khodasevich "party" and that the latter continues to be numerically stronger. Contemporaries like to choose, and perhaps have to, and it is only later that people begin to wonder why it was so necessary to choose between Nekrasov and Fet, Brahms and Bruckner, Tolstoy and Dostoevsky. One could quote Chekhov's Trigorin, who said, "Why jostle? There is enough room for everybody"—but in this case Ivanov does not get his due. Even his admirers avoid calling him the best at the expense of Khodasevich, whereas the Khodasevichites are often quite categorical in their preference. Vladimir Nabokov (who was praised by Khodasevich and murderously reviewed by Ivanov) considers Khodasevich "the greatest poet of our time." Andrew Field recently called Khodasevich "the foremost poet of the emigration." And there is no doubt on whose side Gleb Struve is in his book *Russian Literature in Exile*. So no harm will be done if the critical scale tips in Ivanov's favor, even if it means "teasing the geese" a little (Krylov, *Fables,* III, XV, 31). It is bound to hurt Khodasevich somewhat, because the contrast between the two poets is enormous; they are like darkness and light, war and peace, Mozart and Salieri. But we have to find out who is second in command. Before dealing in contrasts, however, we ought to state that these poets also have much in common. Both were "third generation" symbolists,[6] both belonged to the literary establishment of the Russian emigration, and both were, in a sense, "last poets" and were called such by critics. The poetry of each contains a great deal of acid, which means that both were essentially decadents [7]—a fact Ivanov admitted in his verse more than once. One can also find identical motifs in their poetry, such as dreams, violence, and suicide.

The comparison will be made on the basis of Khodasevich's *Collected Works* of 1927 and Ivanov's last book, *Poems,* which are comparable in the sense that each book sums up the respective poet's final and most mature period.[8] The statements in the following juxtaposition do appear overly simplified and therefore should be mentally modified to read "essentially" and "as a rule." One can always prove the opposite with another line from the same poet (*cf.,* for example, Khodasevich's "I hate going for a walk"

[76] and "I love solitary wanderings" [15]),[9] and there is the phenomenon which can be termed the futility of quotation. And yet those who respect Khodasevich for consistency have a point: he does belong to the breed of one-idea men (*odnodumy*). On the other hand, Gleb Struve blames Ivanov for inconsistencies with special gusto, and he seems to be right. It is enough to compare, e.g., such mutually exclusive poems on the "monarchist" theme as the deeply felt "Enameled cross in his buttonhole" and the sardonic poem on the double-headed eagle (72) (and either with the scathingly mocking "Here we are, more or less" [48]), to be inclined to agree with this. But the difficulty with Ivanov is not his "inconsistency" but the fact that he often says the opposite of what he really means, or that he deliberately omits the essential. On the surface, "And people? What use have I for people?" (26) is an excellent foil for Khodasevich's "I love people, I love nature" (76), but nothing could be more mistaken than a comparison of these two poems at face value. It is characteristic of the "nihilistic" Ivanov that he casually drops the line which could be used as a motto for his work, "I love life, my own as well as that of others," in a little-known poem not included in any of his collections (it is printed in *Novyi Zhurnal*, #44). His poetry is life affirming (which Khodasevich's certainly is not); it is about Man (*cf.* Khodasevich: "And Man? Isn't he there to be ignored by us?" [76]), about nature (not in Fet's sense, but who could forget Ivanov's branches and sunsets, among other nature images —whereas Khodasevich simply does not notice nature), and, above all, about Art (which did not interest Khodasevich very much).[10]

So let us begin our comparison (Khodasevich on the left, Ivanov on the right) with:

A hedgehog	A fox [1] *
Dualism of two worlds, strongly reminiscent of Tyutchev (with occasional sprinklings of Sologub). The world we all live in is ugly, vulgar,	This world with its colors, trees, weather, people. Ivanov belongs to human society and, though he claims to possess "the talent of

* This series of numbered notes immediately follows the comparison.

143

depressing (and on one occasion visibly infested with devils)—as observed by the poet through the window [2] of his ivory tower or "underground." But "through the coarse layer of earthly life" (24) one can sense the other world, in which Psyche already lives ("rodnoe, drevnee zhilyo" [105]), in which the spirit will—the world of primordial Night. To get there, one has to pierce the veil of Maya (impossible!) or to become spirit (possible, but a painful process, similar to teething). In the meantime, the impatient, sullen expectation for the Smolensk market to be transfigured. The transfiguration of the ugly world (which is *the* theme of Khodasevich) will be preceded by apocalyptic events—and may begin at any moment with a minor event, such as an automobile accident.

second sight," he is not preoccupied with metaphysics or mysticism. However, hopes and desires, presumably of a semi-otherworldly nature, sometimes—and for no apparent reason—drive one to a frenzy of expectation that in one second all will be "fulfilled." An unusually lighted or colored sky with clouds (similar to the one in Blok's poems) is apt to give birth to such promise, but this inevitably ends in exhaustion and depression.[3] Actually, the reader should read the section on aesthetics (below), because that is Ivanov's only metaphysics (and his main "content").

In view of the above, death is irrelevant, or identical with that highly desirable transition to the world of spirit—the "flowery path" (111). In practice, however, the images of death in Khodasevich's poetry are frequent, various, and contradictory (3, 27, 28, 32, 39, 42–43, 59, 79, 102, 104, 111).

To quote from Chekhov's "A Dreary Story," "I'm going to die soon, Katya."

It is not clear whether either of Khodasevich's worlds has anything to do with God, but he does speak with God occasionally (102, 178).

And so does Ivanov (92).

Little love poetry, if any.

Two noticeable examples of love poetry (in *Gardens* and in *Poems*).

The prevalent emotion seems to be an arrogant contempt—on one occasion, for himself (91), but mostly

Bored,[5] but not lonely (which Khodasevich is always); he even wants a dialogue with the Soviet

144

for others,[4] for whom that other world is hardly accessible. Also anger (*facit indignatio versum*—and Khodasevich *is* a sort of metaphysical Juvenal).

man. The emotional content of Ivanov's poetry is complex: contempt, yes, but also amusement, pity, admiration, indignation, tenderness, disgust—all of the "semi-" variety. The word "anger" (*zlost'*) appears often, but denotes various emotions from wrath to irritation and annoyance.

Toward the end of his life he erected for himself, in a poem, a Janus-like monument [6] at a crossroads in the future Russia (210). On a short-range scale, he was proud of having engrafted the "classical vine on the Soviet wilding" (123),[7] which brings us to

Did not build monuments.

his aesthetics: classical [8] ideals of clarity, brevity, tradition, truth.

Brevity, yes, by all means; but what is truth? And above all things, what is art? Isn't it meaningless, even absurd [9] (just like life), and yet [10] it exists, even performs miracles at times. Ivanov plays with poetic ideas; they are stronger than he is, and he is aware of this. The awareness of his own inadequacies is his strength.

(Omniscience and his own wisdom,[11] one of Khodasevich's favorite motifs.)

If Khodasevich overcomes the absurdity of this world by creating another one (which we have to believe in), Ivanov does it through his art, which is helpless, of questionable nature, and itself absurd, but is somehow capable, occasionally, of transforming reality.

As for "classicism," a sense of measure is the *sine qua non* of art (*not* novelty) (86), and here comes a touching moment where Ivanov and Khodasevich shake hands. But how beautiful, or rather how dear

Khodasevich wrote short poems: epigram-like, meaning-laden episodes or pictures. He was, however, a "major-form" poet: his mystical [13] experience is consistently described in blank verse on several pages. He tried cycles (the Cain-poems), long ballads, and others. He is a potential story writer.

to my heart, are those banalities [12] of life and especially of low forms of art (like Russian popular songs about chrysanthemums in autumnal gardens), which are customarily dismissed by severe judges.

Ivanov's consistently short poems (he wrote only two narrative ballads in his early years) are fragments, snapshots, ideas that have just occurred, diary jottings.[14]

Khodasevich tried to write in the "language bequeathed by centuries" (67),[15] i.e. he used the syntactical and phraseological clichés of Pushkin's time.[16] See also his deliberately obsolete stresses in *ravénstvo* and *otzýv,* which Pushkin did use at times but which must have been old-fashioned even for his time.

Ivanov's style is a mélange of colloquialisms,[17] "music," [18] and quotations.[19]

Khodasevich's favorite symbol: a fall.[20]

One of Ivanov's important motifs is upward flight, a sudden thrust of imagination to the verge of the no-more-imaginable.[21]

A clear example of Khodasevich's influence: Gleb Struve.

"O if only I could make a well-ordered [23] ode / Out of my death shout!" (124).

A clear example of Ivanov's influence: [22] Igor Chinnov.
"Before you die, you feel like having a chat" (*Roses*).

"How many more days before death? Three? Four?" (*Novyi Zhurnal,* #54).

Before the mirror: "I, I, I—what an absurd word" (158).

"Mirrors reflect one another/Mutually distorting their reflections" (22).

sharp	likable
calculated revelation	spontaneous control
dead-earnest	sense of humor
command	play
etc.	

Notes on preceding comparison

1. "Walking and thinking of *various* things" (64) ("Idu i dumayu o raznom");
cf. Khodasevich's "Smotryu v okno i prezirayu" (91).

2. "No, I cannot look through the window any more" (16).
"Through the dark window, I habitually looked into the basement" (42)
(here it is the other way, to be sure).
"He looks through the window" (57).
"Only once, when I fell from the window" (66).
"The wise one will come up to the window" (75).
Two poems (82–83) entitled "Through the window."
"I look through the window and I despise" (91).
"The view from our window" (109).
A poem entitled "Windows onto the Courtyard" (160–161).
And we could add the poem "Berlinskoe," which is about an unnamed restaurant window. Notice that Khodasevich's guest knocks at his window (19), not at his door. *Cf.* Nina Berberova's *The Italics Are Mine* (Russian ed., pp. 156–157). It is interesting to compare Khodasevich's "Windows onto the Courtyard" with Nekrasov's "Morning" (1874). In both poems the poets manage to observe through their windows at one glance more suffering and filth than other mortals have a chance to see in a year. Still Khodasevich is "windower" than Nekrasov: the latter looks through his window onto the street, Khodasevich into other people's windows.

3. *Cf.* Vasily Zhukovsky, "But the flight of the poor heart ends only in helpless languor."

4. The eternal conviction of a bohemian intellectual that his middle-class neighbor doesn't understand a thing. (Incidentally, Pushkin was free from this contempt for the average.) Not only does the poor neighbor never understand Khodasevich (the best examples: "Music," 64, "Evidence," 112), but his fellow literati are not much better: they seldom understand Khodasevich's poetry (see notes to "To Annie" (215), "Bacchus" (218).

5. "I love you, rain, for your rhythmical tediousness" (34).
"How dull it is to live in this world" (44) /quotation/.
"Even dreams are vertiginously dull" (48).
"Leave me! Ennui is making my bed for me" (56) /quotation/.
"I still cannot get used/To the boredom of this outrageous universe" (63).
"I walk through a fog of boredom . . ." (70).
"I'm so nauseatingly bored" (98).
"I'm bored to death" (104).
"The same invisible boredom hovers there" (104).
"I am bored by unfulfillable desires" (104).
In all these examples the Russian word is *skuka* or one of its derivatives. Ivanov uses other words synonymously—for instance, the Russian *Sehnsucht,* "that icy,

magic word" *toska* ("*toska* at any time of the year" [26]), which in its turn may appear as a synonym for happiness.

6. There is a whole book (not a terribly good one) on Pushkin's imitation of Horace's "monument" ode. A better idea would be to write a book on how Horace's poem fared in Russian poetry as a whole, up to our day. In the eighteenth century they simply translated it—from Lomonosov to Kapnist—but Derzhavin established a tradition of translation not just from Latin to Russian, but from Horace to oneself, summing up one's own poetic achievements on Russian soil. He was immediately followed by Pushkin and the mad Batyushkov; the last in this line seems to have been Bryusov (in 1912), who also did one "straight" translation of Horace's ode. Our century, however, developed the monument theme in a dozen diverse ways, all less direct than the double Lomonosov-Derzhavin heritage, and among the participants one finds such divergent poets as Anna Radlova, David Burliuk, Antonin Ladinsky, Velimir Khlebnikov, Vasily Kamensky (who has several to his credit), and Konstantin Olimpov (one easily notices that futurists were especially fond of this occupation). One can roughly divide these attempts into the "exegi monumentum" and the "non omnis moriar" varieties, the former being the most frequently and variously cultivated. For example, there is a group of conversations with the Pushkin monument ("Horace-twice-removed"): Mayakovsky, Esenin. There are subtly arrogant references to "the marble of my hand" (Nabokov), "negative" monuments ("I spit on the bronze..." in another Mayakovsky poem), pseudo-negative monuments (Akhmatova with her "Don't build me a monument there, build it here"), etc. Georgy Ivanov represents the much rarer "non omnis moriar" group ("It's true the poet in me may not die,/But the man in me is dying..." [22]).

7. "The Soviet wilding" probably refers to the physical energy and the dialectal infestation of some early Soviet, especially futurist-oriented, poetry (as well as of the prose of the likes of Pilnyak and some Serapions); things were to get worse before they got better if one recalls that Selvinsky's *Ulalaevshchina* was written after Khodasevich left Russia. It is more difficult to interpret Khodasevich's "engrafting." Did he mean his own poetry (thus thinking of himself as a Soviet poet), or did he have disciples in mind (which is unlikely)? The irony is that very soon it was officially, if not "back to classicism," at least "back to the classics," and Fadeyev's *Rout* was thus, in a way, a partial fulfillment of Khodasevich's dreams. In comparison, Ivanov never argues with Soviet aesthetics. He patronizingly praises the surface rightness of the naive "monks" of realism and recognizes too late that his own erstwhile involvement with "poisonous" decadence has led to retribution (the motif of *rasplata*).

8. The Russian classicists were roughly divided into the St. Petersburg and the Moscow varieties (usually, but not necessarily, connected with those cities). The former included Pushkin, Delvig, Baratynsky, Georgy Ivanov; the latter, Sumarokov, Shcherbina, A. Maikov, Bryusov, Khodasevich.

9. Ivanov was clearly aware that the decadent "end" was to be followed by the absurd, which he often (but not always) reproduced by primitivist means, especially in "Rayon de Rayonne." In his own way, he accepts (and misunderstands) the victorious avant garde, which, as "honest" baaing and mooing, is much preferable to the "poisonous air" and pretenses of the aesthetic atmosphere in which he grew up. Thus Ivanov contributes to the history of Russian literary primitivism, which began (strange as it may sound) in the eighteenth century with some of Trediakovsky's little songs (Vasily Kirillovich was unaware of it, to be sure, but reread his "Vesna katit" and "S odnoy strany grom") and was continued by Count D. I. Khvostov and Kozma Prutkov, before flowering in the twentieth century in Khlebnikov and Zabolotsky. Exile gave birth to a small pleiad of primitivists with a metaphysical touch such as Mamchenko, Odarchenko, and especially Ginger, who did speak "about the most important things" but not accord-

ing to Adamovich's prescriptions. Critics did not quite know what to do with such poets and sometimes chided them for lacking taste. They were a part of Ivanov's literary environment. As for Khodasevich, although occupying the position of a prominent critic in the 1920's and 1930's, he was singularly unreceptive to the avant garde, and he thoroughly misunderstood primitivism (see his review of Zabolotsky's "The Triumph of Agriculture"). In this he did not differ much from the orthodox Soviet critics.

10. "And yet" (*a vsyo-taki*) is a cornerstone of Ivanov's aesthetics, perhaps most clearly formulated in the poem "The conception is flawed, oddly" ("Byl zamysel stranno porochen"). Other examples:
"That pointless happiness . . . still possible" (34).
"and still I'll take you into this heart of mine, dear cloud" (59).
11. "Containing all the wisdom of the earth" (26).
"A wise man would come up to the window . . . / And gradually close / His sated eyes" (75).
"I see much, know much" (86).
"I know everything, see everything" (84).
"And omniscient like a serpent" (158).
12. Love of banality (which echoes Pushkin's respect for the average) is proclaimed by Ivanov in another of his manifestos, "I love the hopeless quiet," and, developing Adamovich's image, one can view much of Ivanov's poetry as "light shining through cliché." Ivanov would have appreciated the idea of Camp, were he alive today. This lovable banality creates a special flavor and makes Ivanov's verse utterly untranslatable. Khodasevich, like Chekhov, is translatable; it is "vsyo mysl' da mysl'" (Baratynsky).
13. Khodasevich constantly alludes to, or even technically describes (as in "Episode"), mystical experience, whose essence, however, is never properly revealed. (Daniel Bures.)
14. In addition to Ivanov's "Diaries," let us remember two other memorable émigré attempts: Vyacheslav Ivanov's "Roman Diary of 1944" and Nikolai Otsup's mammoth *Diary in Verse* (1950).
15. "Yazyk zaveshchannyi vekami." See Khodasevich's poem about his wet nurse (66–67), that sprawling and flabby exercise in immodesty which was hailed as a masterpiece by critics and, for some reason, impressed the poet's colleagues in the hungry Petrograd of 1922. Actually, this cliché-ridden solemnity is untypically imprecise for Khodasevich: what "centuries," for example? The scholarly Khodasevich ought to have known that he was using the language of the early nineteenth century.
16. Khodasevich revered, studied, and imitated Pushkin and (no doubt deliberately) never mentioned him in his poems (except indirect references in "November 2" and "Brenta"). Ivanov wrote three poems with Pushkin in them (none are in *Poems*).
17. Colloquialisms are an eternal problem and a source of enrichment in literary language. All great Russian poets (Derzhavin, Krylov, Griboedov, Zhukovsky, Pushkin, Tyutchev, Lermontov, Nekrasov) tried to include them or build on them in different ways. On the other hand, in the twentieth century the use of colloquialisms is often (and not quite correctly) considered the domain of the futurists (Khlebnikov, Mayakovsky, Pasternak). That is perhaps why Ivanov, who does build on colloquialisms extensively and uniquely, sounds at times like Mayakovsky (the conversation with Pushkin in *Novyi Zhurnal*, #54) or Nekrasov ("Chetvert' veka proshlo zagranitsey"). He could be described as evolving from painting (*Heather*) through music (*Roses*) to spoken language (late poetry)— and this is another reason for his untranslatability. How can one render precisely such lines as *Umeret'? Da vot ne umirayu* or *Nu i poteryayu dushu?*
18. A much abused word since Verlaine and Nietzsche. Poets and critics could

never agree as to whether it has to do with consonants and vowels, with word and phrase repetitions, or with outright mysticism (Blok's "Listen to the music of the Revolution!"). Whatever it means, "music" is always a metaphor for poetry (or for "poeticality") with many possibilities of double metaphor (Ivanov: "Music which burnt down my life"). Perhaps it is better to agree that "music" is that indefinable quality which we sometimes call poetic or verbal magic—and damn all structural analysis. It was a rare Russian poet at the beginning of our century who did not aspire to some kind of music. The first poem in Khodasevich's *Heavy Lyre* is entitled "Music," and in it the poet chops wood in the company of a poor wingless creature of a neighbor, who is utterly incapable of hearing the Music—which the poet claims to hear as it comes from above. We even know the orchestration: harps and celli (Berlioz? Debussy?). More revealing is the last poem in the book, the famous "Orpheus," in which the poet mechanically (by rocking) brings himself to a state of trance, in which he believes he hears the Music. Music is, however, absent from Khodasevich's own verse—heavy, creaky, bilious, devoid of charm. Ivanov, who confesses that in his heart "there is little reason, much music" (59), is a different matter. He seldom (and never ostentatiously) speaks about music; more often he complains that he does not hear it. It comes and goes, but it comes unexpectedly and is born out of nothing ("podvernulas' muzyka, eyo i zapishu," 117). Some of his typical "musical" pieces are those about Villon, about Ophelia, "Tikhim vecherom," "V dymu, v ogne . . ."

19. Which makes him quite "modern"; *cf*. the poetry of T. S. Eliot and the music of Stravinsky and Berio. Recently, an entire book of criticism was written in the form of a cento (Andrew Field, *Complection of Russian Literature*). On the other hand, perhaps there is a law: the last man in any series resorts to quotation.

20. "And if the acrobat falls" (18).
"And every night I fall, conquered" (20).
"Only once, when I fell from the window" (66).
"My heart . . . falls from the heights" (68).
"My dear soul, my light one, my fall-prone one" (68).
"Psyche falls under it" (71).
"The kite fell into the neighboring garden" (82).
"I fall into myself" (85).
"Psyche who falls into delirium" (86).
"The Angel of Fall" (95).
"Close your eyes and fall and fall" (114).
"Happy is he who falls head down" (140).

21. Although quantitatively the word "flight" does not appear in Ivanov's verse with the regularity of "fall" in Khodasevich's, it is nevertheless very characteristic of it. For example, in his lines "the lawless star flies into the darkness" (36) or "the music-poisoned arrow . . . flies into emptiness" (56), not only Khodasevich, but also many others, would probably have used the verb "to fall." Ivanov's specialty is not just flight, but what a Russian would call *vzlyot,* i.e. an upward flying movement. He flies with incredible ease and invariably reaches those frontier areas which he knows so intimately but which are not yet "another world." They are "on the border of melting and ice . . . of music and dream" (32), and it is impossible to say what begins beyond the border: catastrophe, "shining emptiness," eternity, the "fragile ice of non-being," or triumph. At any rate, it is a region where there is "radiance" (*siyan'e*) and where words, "touching on triumph and becoming triumph, disintegrate and lose their meaning" (*Roses*) (*cf*. Khodasevich, who in his Orpheus poem, unexpectedly and in contradiction to his aesthetics, admits that "sounds are truer than meaning" [119]). Those areas are suggested to Ivanov here below by the sky, whose colors and shapes give promise of a transfiguration which is not unlike that of

Khodasevich (see "At the entrance to the slaughterhouse" [37]). Transfiguration and metamorphosis are familiar to Ivanov's readers: day is transformed into music among other things (25), "melody becomes a flower" (57), Lermontov emerges with "silver spurs" (57), and Ivanov's own shabby overcoat "drowns in the stars" (36).

22. As Gleb Struve correctly states, Ivanov himself assimilated from everybody—from equals and from lessers: from Khodasevich, Steiger (especially dots at the beginning of a line or phrase, parentheses), Odarchenko (103), Elagin (92). Toward the end of his life, Ivanov was more and more attracted by his old friend Mandelstam. First he quoted him, then began imitating his late manner (100).

23. It is really strange that Khodasevich, the author of a book on Derzhavin and a poet who was aware of continuing what Lomonosov had begun in 1739 (206), did not know that the Russian eighteenth-century ode followed "the beautiful disorder" as its main principle and did not want to be "well-ordered" (unless under the pen of a Sumarokov, but this is hardly what Khodasevich meant). It is nevertheless significant that both Khodasevich and Ivanov had points of contact with eighteenth-century poetry, which had been so long ignored and neglected before their generation. Ivanov, in his earlier poems, showed a nostalgic liking for a vague sentimentalism which is not traceable to any definite literary figure. He also used some pre-Romantic imagery.

Postscript to notes

The reader has long since guessed that this rambling essay is heavily biased in favor of Ivanov at the expense of Khodasevich, and has come to the conclusion that the writer does not like the latter and is rooting for the former. This is not quite so. The writer did love Khodasevich once. It would be stupid to debunk him. He is a tragic poet, or, more precisely, the poet of the tragic impasse. Pushkin's Salieri (who, by the way, has more grandeur than his celestial counterpart) is tragic, too. Khodasevich fails as your life's companion; he is not for the desert island; his lyrical self is not attractive; his philosophy (but not his sensibility) is too dated; and his verse shows little grace (for which his laudable "classical" features are small compensation). Even his complexity is an old-fashioned split, rather than a more human interplay of tiny contradictions. D. S. Mirsky once called Khodasevich "the little Baratynsky from the underground, the favorite poet of all those who dislike poetry" and he is wrong only in his choice of epithet. Khodasevich did inhabit an underground of sorts, he does derive from Baratynsky, and he was *the* poet for newspaper critics and magazine publishers of the Russian emigration. Somehow he does satisfy the people who do not really love or understand poetry (as well as those who do, of course), but who approve of poetry if it contains "ideas." From their point of view, Khodasevich had the wrong kind of ideas, but ideas nevertheless (which one could never say of Ivanov). In short, the situation was not dissimilar to that of Apollon Maikov in the last century. Khodasevich's noble aversion to the avant garde played its part, too, and such deservedly respected critics as Weidlé and Terapiano could not but be attracted by him on these grounds also. After the onslaught of "mediocre" futurists who, at the beginning of the 1920's, appeared to constitute a possible literary establishment, it was a comfort to know someone who wrote "like Pushkin" and yet sounded contemporary. Khodasevich's "content" was appealingly profound and, at the same time, his "form" was so pleasingly "classical." The trouble, however, is that Khodasevich lacks charm, humanity, and freedom (just as Bryusov and Gumilyov do), and if one absolutely has to have these qualities in a favorite poet, there is no choice but Ivanov in the given context. After Khodasevich's scorn, reading Ivanov is a relief, and one accepts his "non-profound" old-age grumbling (so similar to that of another quoter, Prince Vyazemsky) as something dear and human. Even his poorer poems live, breathe, and are an indispensable part of the picture, whereas the best of Khodasevich is slightly dead and one wishes the worst had never been written—"Sumerki," for instance, most of his Berlin verse, and "Ballada." But the most important thing is that Ivanov sometimes tosses you behind the clouds with that rose (27), whereas Khodasevich is chained to this world in its most hateful aspects. This is why he wants another world so intensely—out of despair. In short, Ivanov may not be a greater or a better poet, but he is more of a poet (at least in this opinion).

Why Khodasevich the poet was choked to death by his exile while Ivanov blossomed is still an unanswered question. They both disliked being *émigrés,* and in his verse Ivanov complained more often about "choking" than did Khodasevich. Perhaps Ivanov was lucky to have found, like Bunin and Remizov, that "beautiful distance" from which an artist must contemplate his native land. Such distance is often a necessary precondition for poetry, and this is why the world-famous statements of present-day Russian writers that they cannot create outside Russia (the statements which move both Western intellectuals and Russian *émigrés* to tears) are in truth pathetic. Closeness to their roots is precisely the reason why Russians produce mediocre and provincial literature in alarmingly increasing quantities. If one is to believe Andrei Voznesensky, "Tvardovsky was singing in Florence." No matter how ridiculous it may seem to sing a Russian folksong and thus waste precious time while being surrounded by stones which could change your life, this singing has its deeper significance. Gogol's "beautiful distance" was obviously at work at that moment and Tvardovsky couldn't help singing. And if Tvardovsky had been a genuine poet (like Khodasevich and Ivanov), he would have returned to Russia with a masterpiece.

Appendix I: five masterpieces

"The melody becomes a flower" ("Melodiya stanovitsya tvetkom").

One of Ivanov's unbearably beautiful poems. The content (i.e. music equals nature equals poetry equals Lermontov) requires some explanation. The "unrealized" genius Lermontov had a particular meaning for some influential literati of Russian Paris. Bunin and Adamovich placed this "second greatest" Russian poet higher than Pushkin, which had something to do with the *émigré* contempt for success as symbolized in the figure of the impeccable Pushkin. The blind Remizov, when out for a walk with his white cane, used to tack a note on his door for eventual visitors: *Vykhozhu odin ya na dorogu.* Ivanov quotes from the same poem in the final distich of his strangely irregular sonnet with two five-line stanzas followed by two distichs. Each stanza contains a metamorphosis. In the longer ones, these transformations are presented through two sets of enumerations. In stanza one, music becomes nature in a series of deliberately banal poetic images; in stanza two, a string of prosaic synecdoches and metonymies describe Lermontov. In the distichs, the transformations take the form respectively of a pun (fog, *tuman,* becomes a town, Taman', in Lermontov's novel), and of a metamorphosis through epithet (silver spurs). We could add that the first line works like the first theme of a sonata allegro with its triple -o-; that Ivanov handles his polysyllabics unbelievably well; and that the second quotation makes a triumphal march out of the familiar melancholic adagio of the original Lermontov line (which is accomplished metrically through the assertive alexandrine of line 13, prepared by the only other, but indecisive, alexandrine in line 10 in the otherwise five-foot iambic poem—and Lermontov's original is in trochees).

"An enameled cross in his buttonhole" ("Èmalevy krestik v petlitse").

Whether one is a monarchist (how many are there left?) or a socialist, one cannot deny that these modest eight lines about the last Russian tsar and his family eclipse whole libraries of poems about Lenin (even Mayakovsky wrote on that worthy subject only competently). This glance-at-a-photograph poem could have been written even by a Communist for his desk drawer, it is so apolitical, human, and party-borders-transcending. Its three-stress amphibrach may suggest a ballad or what the Russians call "cruel romance" (banality again!), but its composition is perfect. Again a metonymical enumeration (this time of the details of the uniform of the unnamed monarch) at the beginning, and a simple listing of the rest of the photographees at the end. This "factual" frame of four lines embraces four middle, mildly exclamatory, and symmetrically placed lines and phrases, which suggest tragedy, nostalgia, and many other things. An almost unnoticeable sigh (or sob?) in the penultimate line is realized through the omission of a single syllable.

"I still find enchantment" ("Eshcho ya nakhozhu ocharovanye").

The charm of trifles (*auch kleine Dinge können uns entzücken*) attracted Ivanov throughout his poetic life, but this parable about a rose and a trash can is something special. Pushkin, Batyushkov, Vyacheslav Ivanov, and Rilke come to one's mind so far as the rose in poetry is concerned, but hardly any of their roses lives so intensely, and at the same time dies before our eyes, as does the rose in this poem. The description of raindrops on the petals is a marvel, though it is achieved through casual placement of near-cliché polysyllabics (and one "ego-futurist" mannerism). It is so memorable and beautiful (there is no other word, sorry) in its juxtaposition of r's and hissives and in its silvery sheen (a metamorphic symbol with Georgy Ivanov; the other Ivanov would have made it golden). That all roses land in trash cans is a banality hardly worth uttering, but isn't there a touch of tragedy about this? Old-fashioned, agreed, but concrete objects do become essences—again before our eyes.

"Little by little I have learned" ("Ya nauchilsya ponemnogu").

This brief but exhaustive study of twentieth-century conformism-out-of-despair (or anti-Utopia-come-true) seems to form a sequel to the previous poem: the same inevitability, but the mood is more somber, since here even trifles no longer enchant. This is also a jewel of "civic" poetry: doesn't the former aesthete now show quite a social consciousness (though the wrong kind, of course)? A masterpiece of sarcasm, too, demonstrating that Ivanov was not just a poet of the Russian emigration. The ending, with its surprising switch from everyday triviality to the universal "no exit," is accompanied by a sarcasm-increasing change from the colloquialism of the beginning to the insistent vocalism (three a's, three o's) of the end—which does not refute the fact that the conversational lines are also filled with vowel effects. The Hell at the end echoes Khodasevich ("Through the Window," I) and so do the stars ("Stars"), but Ivanov overwhelms us with a more crushing chord: the stars appear not just as a human distortion and a cheapening of the Lord's design (as in Khodasevich), but as the Devil's own ornament for the Universe.

"Sunset engulfing half the sky" ("Zakat v polneba zanesyon").

A terse masterpiece of concentration and abrupt transitions. Two "strong" lines surround the single "soft" one at both ends. One of Ivanov's many sunsets gets clothed in royal colors and fabrics (in fact, Ivanov must be the first Russian poet since Derzhavin to use the word *visson* /byssus/), swallows up beautiful Nice, and ends in a slight misquotation from Zhukovsky, which is immediately distorted further and negated ("Lenore does not dream a thing," *cf*. Ivanov's "Only dreams do not deceive" [94]). If Zhukovsky's translation of Bürger's *Lenore* (or rather its first Slavicized version, *Ludmila*) inaugurated Russian romanticism in 1809, Ivanov's poem is, in a sense, the end of this movement almost one hundred and fifty years later. If "Melody becomes a flower" combines music and quotation, here quotation complements painting.

Appendix II: Ivanov Book by Book

> *Pechatalis'? A gde? V kakom Giperboree?*
> —*G. I.*

The Embarkation for Cythera (Otplyt'e na o. Tsiteru. Poèzy. Kniga pervaya. "Ego." St. Petersburg, 1912).

Evidence of Ivanov's ego-futurist beginnings. His heart seems to be not with Severyanin, though, but with Kuzmin the aesthete. A typical book by a young decadent who follows the fashions of the day. It was hailed by Gumilyov, who for some reason read it with a "feeling of physical satisfaction." Watteau of the title will remain in Ivanov's poetry to the very end. Poems are mannered, ostentatiously refined in imagery, rhyme, and meter. Echoes of the young Pushkin; also of Blok, Vyacheslav Ivanov, Akhmatova, *et al*. In addition to the Cythera poems (parks with statues, Cupids, Venuses, doves), there are "aesthetic" landscapes and interiors, weary autumnal elegies, and quasi-religious poems about monks.

The Chamber (Gornitsa. Kniga stikhov. "Giperborey." St. Petersburg, 1914).

The title is explained in the introductory poem ("the sky like a sunlit chamber"). A firmer hand, but not much real promise. Mostly a continuation of the *Embarkation,* with the theme of weariness predominating (almost Apukhtin-like in its morning-after moods); Kuzmin the dandy is very noticeable (a homosexual note;

"I polish my nails with a brush"). A "World of Art" atmosphere and themes: some poems are poetic counterparts to the nostalgic old–St. Petersburg scenes of Alexander Benois and Yevgeny Lanceray. Acmeist detailed "painting," especially in still-life poems ("Vse ottushovany staratel'no otlivy, / Vse zhilki tonkie pod kozhitsey vidny"). Two subject matters stand out: old lithographs and the *saltimbanques,* the latter often with romantic knifings in taverns and intoxication with names of non-Russian people and ports. Part II—from now on a more or less regular feature of Ivanov's books—twenty-five earlier poems (twenty from the previous book), sometimes slightly retouched or provided with a title.

A Monument to Glory (Pamyatnik slavy. "Lukomor'e." Petrograd, 1915).

A bibliographical rarity, usually dismissed by people who never saw it (and by the poet himself) as so much patriotic trash, but actually not so bad after all. Not all poems are patriotic (i.e. poems for newspapers, praising Russian troops and their European allies, extolling Slavs in general, and condemning Germans for atrocities and cultural barbarity). There is a cycle of poems about St. Petersburg (but they are mostly about monuments to famous troop leaders), and there is a "Kuzminian" section. Ivanov seldom reprinted poems from this book (one in *Heather,* five in *The Icon-Lamp*).

The next two books helped to create a stable image of Ivanov as a poet, especially in Soviet literary-historical surveys. One of the reasons is that both had two editions, one Russian and one foreign.

Heather (Veresk. Vtoraya * kniga stikhov. "Al'tsiona." Moscow-Petrograd, 1916).

This marks the end of Ivanov's apprenticeship and sums up what could be labeled his "first period." In fact, there is not much

* This does raise the question of which of the preceding three books Ivanov considered his first.

difference in mood between this book and the *Embarkation* of 1912: the same aestheticism, dandyism, and "the charm of precious trifles" (and, speaking of Kuzmin, Ivanov even introduces Sir John Fairfax in person in one of the poems). The title derives again from the first poem in the book: a playboy, during a hunt in England, is suddenly visited by the idea of death on the moor heather. Otherwise all the familiar "World of Art" features: love for old lithographs and etchings (here Gumilyov served as a model), painting and painters (Watteau, Claude Lorrain, the Flemish school), a predilection for subdued, misty tones. "Pictures" predominate, often of sentimentalist ancestors (a smile and a sigh): for Ivanov, the eighteenth century is not Kantemir, but rather Dmitriev. Exactly one half of this book is old verse, almost all of it from *The Chamber*. In the second edition (Grzhebin, Berlin, 1923) Ivanov dropped quite a few poems and added a few (among them translations from the French).

Gardens (Sady. Tret'ya kniga stikhov. "Petropolis." Petrograd, 1921).

Ivanov remained a minor poet of the Kuzmin-Gumilyov school in this next book, especially in its second section (this book consists entirely of new poems, no reprints), but something had happened. A breeze, a stream, a lyrical movement, all so welcome after the static quality of his earlier poems. Perhaps Ivanov really had fallen in love for the first time (a prerequisite for writing poetry, according to Alexander Sumarokov). This new kind of poetry (and those who date it from Ivanov's later *Roses* are wrong) is concentrated in the first part of the book: musical, often about music and about love—and this is only slightly colored by Ivanov's old Ossianic pre-Romanticism as well as interspersed with Oriental stylizations which had briefly disappeared after the first *Embarkation*. *Gardens* is a farewell to a miniaturist's brush and to India ink. Parallelisms and repetitions clearly aim at a musical effect. The well-known "I am begging not for love" (with the familiar lines about snow and madness) is precisely in this vein. In *Heather* and *Gardens* (as well as in the following *Icon-Lamp*), there is also a characteristic preoccupation with technique. It is not mild experimenting, but rather occasional cultivation of rarities such as unrhymed *dol'niki,* interesting "choriambs," and attempts at heterotonic rhyme. Collecting rarities extends to epigraphs, which are a treat for quotation hunters: Ivanov invariably quotes from little-known works. In the second edition (Grzhebin, Berlin, 1922) five poems were added, three dropped, and a few lines were reworked.

The Icon-Lamp (Lampada. Sobranie stikhŏtvorenii. Kniga pervaya. "Mysl'." Petrograd, 1922).*

Ivanov's last Russian-published book marks an uncertain end to his biographical St. Petersburg period. It is his last Kuzmin-inspired book (with an added bit of Mandelstam, whose melody, it is true, almost broke through in *Gardens*). It is not merely a selection from his previously published work, as one might deduce from the subtitle: thirty-nine of the eighty-five poems are new, and the old ones sometimes appear in a reworked form. Still, in each of the five sections there is an admixture (or more than that) of earlier poetry from all of his previous volumes. The plan is as follows: (1) love and lyrical landscapes; (2) Kuzmin's "Russian Eden"; (3) "pictures"; (4) St. Petersburg; (5) "sins of youth," i.e. very early verse. Although Ivanov proclaims that he "loves the works of painters no longer," both painting (as poetic method) and painters (Turner, Gainsborough) make their last sizable appearance in his poetry. Uncertainty about where he is going comes to the fore very clearly in one poem ("Snow is yellow and melted"), where Ivanov first sounds like Esenin, then like Bunin.

Roses (Rozy. "Rodnik." Paris, 1931).

Ivanov's first book of poems written abroad appeared almost a decade later and was hailed as a great achievement even by his

* At the end of his *Poems,* Ivanov lists a second edition, which he dates 1923 (his date for the first volume is 1921), but I have not seen it. AUTHOR.

future detractors. It was hardly a "new Ivanov," however. Except for the poems about Russia, some "Paris" poems, and a number of "memory" poems (the themes of the "snows of yesteryear" and of the year 1913, the latter to be later heard in Akhmatova's poetry), the others would not really be out of place on the pages of *Gardens,* where Ivanov's "music" was launched. Only this time the music is not just present, it is proclaimed, it has become "ideology." On the other hand (and especially in trochaic poems), this music coexists with spoken intonation, which points the way to Ivanov's later poetry. Parallelisms and repetitions reign supreme, and Ivanov even resorts to "double-voice," invented by Balmont, and to pauses, often making the latter visible by such Parisian trademarks as dots beginning a sentence and parentheses. As for Parisian aesthetics, its best expression can be found in Ivanov's lines: "We are unable to find the right words, and we do not want to use the approximate ones any longer." Ivanov suddenly becomes a poet of momentous themes, rather than of *Kleinmalerei:* death, emptiness, cold, the nature of happiness. The combination of the first three earned him the label of a nihilist, especially after the publication of the poem "Thank god there is no tsar." There is an abundance and a steady movement of distinct motifs such as, of course, roses, then stars, blizzard, wind, light, and spring— the whole very reminiscent of Blok. But it is not a *sui generis* return to symbolism (characteristic of all Acmeists in their later phases); perhaps it is a late flowering of Romanticism in Russian poetry which is also noticeable in the switch from his earlier, Ossianic imagery to Byron and the sea, in the emergence of the idea of another world (a rarefied region of ideas, the frontier of the Universe), and the Zhukovsky-originated theme of the helplessness of art (which Ivanov has already developed into the theme of the meaninglessness of art). A touch of Heine is visible, too. Striking, on the other hand, is the lack of fear of banality, coming as it did after the pronounced snobbishness of his earlier books, and his birth as a "civic" poet who speaks, in his political miniatures, about history, the fate of Russia, and the problems of mankind.

The Embarkation for Cythera (the same title as his first book but with a slight difference in Russian: Otplytie na ostrov Tsiteru. Stikhi Georgiya Ivanova. "Petropolis." Berlin, 1937).

Another summing up, which offers in the first part only twenty new poems (differing little from those in *Roses*). The second part is taken up by *Roses* in its entirety (with four omissions), and the third presents a selection from *Heather* and *Gardens,* with minor reworkings.

A Portrait Without Likeness (Portret bez skhodstva. Stikhi. "Rifma." Paris, 1950).

The major poet Georgy Ivanov emerges, properly speaking, only after World War II with this slim, inconspicuous-looking volume of fifty-one poems, a miracle of poetic condensation and the last landmark in Ivanov's work. "People will be memorizing this book some day," wrote another Parisian poet, Smolensky. Several critics noticed what they termed "surrealism" and "the grotesque" in these poems, and some insisted that Ivanov entered into "a conflict with his own harmony" (Terapiano). Ivanov is no chameleon. He is, however, a sponge and a miser: when something new appears, look in the earlier books and you will find the beginnings of this novelty; for instance: the Oriental motifs, the embarkation for Cythera, roses. In *Portrait* there are echoes of Steiger, anticipations of Chinnov, and, more strangely, similarities with the two last "transrational" dramas of Iliazd (*cf.* the figure of a naive realist painter, the theme of the likeness of a portrait). Despite the poet's statement that he "looks at the present through his fingers," there are "civic" poems, to which his verse about his "incredible country" (i.e. Russia) also belongs. It is, however, the first time that an Ivanov book is so unified: its pervading theme is the nature of art, and its subtitle ought to have been "stikhi ob is-kusstve." Ten poems are singled out in a special section (which, incidentally, enraged many an *émigré* reader), entitled, absurdly, "Rayon de Rayonne," in which the same theme is treated in the manner of nonsense and primitivism (with the use of a quotational collage from such sources as Tchaikovsky's *Queen of Spades,* Gogol, and Gerhart Hauptmann). Also, in spite of the presence of such exercises in nineteenth-century Romanticism as "In smoke, in flame, in radiance, in lace," and the poem about Ophelia, there is a predominance of small talk and of diary. Ivanov's late poetry is a conversation with himself (and others) between "poetic" flights (*vzlyoty*). On the whole, a certain parallel with Pushkin suggests itself: he also developed from refined imitations of his school days through Romanticism to the "prosaic" idiom of his last years.

There is a temptation to include in this survey of Ivanov's books the twenty-poem cycle entitled "Poems of 1950" and published in *Novyi Zhurnal,* #25—not because the *émigré* theme sounds stronger here or the "Parisian note" finds its clearest expression in some of the poems ("Let's drink to nonsense, let's drink to failure!"), but because there is a greater assemblage of masterpieces here than anywhere else in Ivanov's work.

Poems of 1943–1958 (1943–1958: Stikhi. "Novyi Zhurnal." New York, 1958).

Ivanov's last book appeared only a short time before his death. It included "Portrait Without Likeness" (i.e. the first section of the book with the same title—with a few additions, omissions of poems as well as of stanzas, and "transplantings") and "Rayon de Rayonne" (increased by five), plus one more section, "Diary," which can be described as the grumbling talk of an old man who walks alone knowing he will die soon and who recalls Russia, complains, dreams, and talks sense and nonsense about the weather, poetry, the century, seasons, and how he slept the night before.

After Ivanov's death, a trickle of his poetry was published in Nos. 54 through 63 of *Novyi Zhurnal.* In these poems, the prevailing themes were his own dying "in full possession of talent" (not quite), insomnia, his own verse (which he quotes), and the dream "of returning to Russia as poetry." In one poem he says that he undertakes mental exercises—"to think of others, not of himself."

Notes

1. The poet's first name is one of the three modern Russian versions of "George." It is pronounced as Gay-OR-ghee, not as "Georgie."

2. The figures after quotes are page numbers in his last collection, *1943–1958: Stikhi* (New York, 1958).

3. The first poem in *The Icon-Lamp,* about an old Russian "church built of Olonets stone," might launch Ivanov's rediscovery in the U.S.S.R., where it has become fashionable to admire old churches now.

4. E.g., about "linking the personal and the common" in Ivanov's "Diary."

5. Let us disqualify Tsvetaeva on grounds of sex, standing apart from the mainstream, and having been "usurped" by the Soviets; one could think of a few dozen additional reasons.

6. Assuming there was no such thing as Acmeism (and was there?).

7. Decadents were the people who said to the preachers of the old ideals of truth, goodness, and beauty, "Yes, *my* truth; you can have your goodness; as for beauty, yes, by all means and first of all—but it is not what you think it is."

8. Khodasevich's book contains 112 poems and covers fourteen years (1913–1927); Ivanov's, 129 poems written during fifteen years (1943–1958). The former, however, has only thirty-two poems actually written in exile (it is often forgotten that his best book, *The Heavy Lyre,* with the exception of three poems, was written by the *Soviet* poet Khodasevich), largely in 1921–1922, whereas all of Ivanov's *Poems* (and much of his poetry before it) was written in emigration.

9. The figures in parentheses refer to the page numbers in *Sobranie stikhov* of 1961, which consists of the collection of 1927 plus a few uncollected poems.

10. One can find this theme only among his earlier poems, in the *Way of the Grain* ("Acrobat," perhaps "Brenta"); such later poems as "God is alive" are not about the nature of art but about Khodasevich's own contribution to poetry during his brief Soviet period.

Double vision
TWO AMERICAN POETS
TRANSLATE GEORGY IVANOV

I

Thank god there is no Tsar
Thank god there is no Russia
Thank god there is no God,

Only a jaundiced twilight
Only hoary stars
Only illimitable years.

Thank god there is no one
Thank god there is nothing
So dark, so dead
It could not be deader
Shall never be darker,
No one able to help us
And no need to help.

Theodore Weiss

II

Sleeping, he saw Ophelia in his dream
Swamp lights around her, nuptial mists

Like a musical spiral she drifted
Mirrors dreamlike reflecting her

Like a nimbus fireflies surrounded her
Like a forest cornflowers sprang up in her wake

How casual it is to suffer! You can surrender your soul
And still be unable to transmit a dream
And knowing that disaster stands at your back
To yearn for no one, to dream of nothing

Theodore Weiss

He slept, and in his dream he saw, amid
the swamp lights, in the mist of a wedding ceremony,

Ophelia, floating, floating like a spiral of music
in the slow-moving mirror that mirrored her like a dream.

A cloud of fireflies clothed her in light, and
a forest of cornflowers bloomed in her wake.

How simple it is to suffer! You can give up your soul and still
find no way to convey a dream across the waters of sleep,

and knowing that disaster lurks behind your back,
still, to yearn for no one; to dream, but to dream of nothing.

Ron Loewinsohn

III

The conception is flawed, oddly,
but just the same life opens
her misty eyes. Raising her head she sees only
the fog, yet she opens her wings like a swan,
testing the air.

Just the same shadows surge into life,
hovering. The candle continues to burn down, but
just the same the strings billow out into song.
Their happiness makes no sense, but they sing
just the same.

Ron Loewinsohn

The affair was badly flawed
Yet even so life opened
In the mist her misty eyes
Her double, swan-wide wings

And even so shadows flittered
While the candle spluttered
Even so strings twangled
Sounding their pointless happiness.

Theodore Weiss

IV

That pointless happiness, was it worth it?
It being, notwithstanding, possible? O certainly.
And it fluttered off into the emerald sky
Where the evening star is sparkling.

Be more gullible, frivolous, bold!
If you cannot sleep, contrive some dreams.
Be, if you can, one with the evening star:
Just as dazzling, just as cold.

Theodore Weiss

V

Floating, in thought, the daydream pervades the day
and lost there in your hand your fishing rod comes
suddenly into quivering life—and here, so quickly,
is the little golden fish on the hook.

It's all so quick, so charming:
The sun, the wind, the water.
Even the fish feels the crowding pressure
of its stream. Even the fish needs misfortune.

The fish needs the sky to fade suddenly into evening,
it needs the boat to stroke the water,
gently, like a wife needs the butter to start bubbling
gently in the frying pan.

Ron Loewinsohn

Losing yourself in thought, daydreaming,
Your rod begins to quiver in your hand
And here's the golden minnow
On the silver hook.

It's so spontaneous, so winsome:
The sun, the wind, the water.
Even the fish feels choked in its stream
Even it requires bad luck

The sky to be struck out,
The boat to fondle the water,
The butter to start sizzling
Gently in the frying pan

Theodore Weiss

VI

1

Mirrors, reflecting each other,
Mutually distort their reflections.

I've faith not in the invincibility of evil,
But only in the inevitability of defeat,

Not in the music that scorched my life,
But in the ashes the scorching left.

2

A game of fate. A game of good and evil.
A game of wits. Imagination's game.

"Mirrors, reflecting each other,
Mutually distort their reflections,"

They assure me: you've won the game!
It hardly matters, I no longer play.

It's true the poet in me may not die,
But the man in me is dying abundantly.

Theodore Weiss

from St. Petersburg Winters

Esenin's fate
GEORGY IVANOV

On December 27, 1925, Sergei Esenin committed suicide at the Hotel Angleterre, a decrepit, modestly elegant hotel on the St. Isaac Square that was known to everyone in Petersburg.

From the hotel windows, the Zubov residence, a mansion of black marble situated to the right of and behind St. Isaac's Cathedral, was visible. To the left, on the other side of the Moika Canal, towered the State Control building. In pre-Revolutionary days the pulse of Petersburg's literary and artistic life was felt in these two buildings, and Esenin was a frequent guest in both.

It's probable that more than once he looked through the plate-glass windows of Count Valentin Zubov's study to the other side of the square, where the two-story Angleterre took refuge. As he looked, he would recite his poetry, showing off as usual, with intentional coarseness, the incomprehensible peasant words:

> ... It smells of russet flapjacks,
> In the skeel by the door there's kvass.
> Above the little oven hatches
> Cockroaches shove themselves into cracks.

169

Lovely . . . Lovely . . . Applause, ingratiating smiles. "Sergei Aleksandrovich, Seriozha, recite some more or, even better, sing something. You sing so charmingly those . . . what do you call them? . . . *chastushki?"*

The rustle of silk, scent of perfumes, mixed Russo-Parisian chatter. Husky footmen in singlets and white stockings carry around trays of sweets, cherry brandy, and tea. And in the midst of all this, Esenin's resounding voice was like a premonition from another world, like an icy breeze in a sweet-smelling greenhouse:

> **I'm nursing a secret little daydream**
> **That I'm pure of heart,**
> **But under cover of the autumn winds**
> **I too will slice someone up.**

On the second floor of the State Control building the salon was not quite as opulent and the furniture not quite as antique as at Count Zubov's. But the social set was about the same. This was the apartment of the famed dignitary "X."

"X," by the way, never appeared at those receptions. The guests were the friends of his nephew Mikhail Kovalev, who published poetry under the name Riurik Ivnev and was Esenin's intimate friend and inseparable companion. He was a puny specimen with a pale, birdlike face and colorless, squinting eyes behind a ladies' tortoiseshell lorgnette. His clothing was exquisitely sloppy—an expensive suit with a stain on it; his elegant necktie was always askew and the heels of his patent leather shoes worn down. Riurik Ivnev was constantly twitching, fussing, turning this way and that. And after almost every word he would say, half questioningly and half distractedly: "What? What? Sergei Esenin? What? What? His verse is simply magic. What? Take a look at his hair. It's the color of ripe rye grain. What?"

The social set was about the same as in Zubov's mansion, and yet not quite. Here, interspersed among glossy suits, one found priests' cassocks, peasant "bowl" haircuts, and baggy trousers tucked into tall boots.

Esenin held the place of honor. A middle-aged man, dressed like a peasant coachman, conversed with Esenin in a singsong voice—or, more accurately, sermonized to him. A sugary smile played on his face, but his grey eyes looked intelligent and cold. He too was a peasant poet, "the minstrel from Olonets," as he would introduce himself, Nikolai Klyuev.

In a cooing voice Klyuev would say: "Soon, soon, my dear Seriozha, the fiery fountains will gush upward, the birds of paradise will begin to twitter, the font of tears will be uncovered and God's truth will be revealed." Esenin would listen respectfully, but a sly spark was concealed in his eyes. He was strongly influenced by Klyuev and liked him very much, but it seems he didn't really believe in the "fiery fountains."

"What? What?" Ivnev's lisping voice could be heard nearby. "Me? Me, a staunch pacifist! What? It's really better to call me a defeatist. Russia's only chance is to open the front lines and let the conquerors in with church bells ringing. It's the only way to save her. What?"

As it happened, both Klyuev and Ivnev were to play fateful roles in Esenin's life. Through them he was to meet those who would subsequently lead him to the Bolsheviks. The respective fates of these two men, so different from one another, also differed. The last I heard of Ivnev, in the late twenties or early thirties, he had been named ambassador to Persia, or Afghanistan, or some such place. Klyuev was sent to Siberia during the "dispossession of the kulaks" period. While in Siberia he addressed to Stalin a pathetic petition in verse which ended with the words: "Let me live or allow me to die!" The "Father of Peoples" magnanimously allowed him to die.

It so happened that Esenin made an unexpected visit to Klyuev late on the eve of his suicide. The relationship between them had long since gone sour, and they almost never saw each other. Esenin's appearance was frightening. Klyuev, scared stiff, babbled like on old man. "Go away, go away, Seriozha, I'm afraid of you . . ."—and he hastened to turn his former friend out into the December night. After leaving Klyuev's home, Esenin went straight to the Hotel Angleterre.

Esenin killed himself at dawn. He first made an unsuccessful attempt to open his veins. Then he hanged himself, having twice wound round his neck the strap from his suitcase, a souvenir from his honeymoon trip with Isadora Duncan. He made a shambles of the room before he died. Chairs were turned over, the mattress and sheets were yanked off the bed, the mirror smashed, and everything around was spattered with blood. He wrote his farewell letter, an eight-line verse, in blood. The letter begins:

"Good-bye, my friend, good-bye . . ."

Throughout his brief, romantic, reckless life Esenin aroused stormy and contradictory passions in the people around him. And he himself was tormented by passions just as stormy and contradictory. He lived by them and because of them he perished. Perhaps because his passions could find a total outlet neither in poetry nor in a life cut short by the abrupt spasm of suicide, a strange and magical thing has happened to him. Esenin has been dead now for a quarter of a century, but everything connected with him continues to live, as if exempt from the general law of death, cessation and oblivion. It's not only his verse that lives, but everything connected with him, with Esenin "in toto." All that surrounded him, upset him, tormented him, made him happy, all that in any way touched him, continues to breathe with the vibrant life of the present day.

This is approximately how I feel it. If, for example, Esenin's overcoat and hat were found still hanging on a coat rack somewhere, then they would be the coat and hat of a man who had just taken them off. They would still be warm from his body, and his being would still emanate from them. It doesn't make sense? Can't be proved? I agree, and I don't intend to try either to explain or prove. I am convinced, however, that among those for whom Esenin is precious, I'm not the only one who feels the unprovable-yet-irrefutable vitality of everything connected with him—including, even, his hat. And it's this unusual quality that gives all of Esenin's verse—even the unsuccessful, even the really weak lines—a particular power and significance. And, at the same time, it keeps us from judging his verse objectively. The people who will be able to give an impartial evaluation of Esenin's work will be those who have ceased to feel the effect of this sorcery. It is possible, even probable, that their evaluation will be more restrained than ours. But this won't happen for a good while yet. It won't happen until Russia frees herself, heals herself, both physically and spiritually. Here lies the exceptional quality, I would say the "genius," of Esenin's fate. For as long as his beloved homeland is fated to suffer, he is assured of, not a notorious "immortality," but a *temporary* (as temporary as Russian suffering and just as lasting) *life.*

It was in either the fall or winter of 1913, in the editorial offices of the magazine *The New Life,* that I first heard Esenin's name spoken. With a customary haughty-grumpy expression on his smoothly shaven white, stony face, Fyodor Sologub (the "brick in a frock coat," to quote Rozanov) was telling me about the young peasant poet who had been in to see him.

"He's a cute little fellow, blue-eyed, humble," Sologub described him disapprovingly. "He was sweating from obsequiousness; sat on the very edge of his chair, ready to jump up at any second. Toadied to beat hell: 'Ah, Fyodor Kuzmich!' 'Oh, Fyodor Kuzmich!' And it was all sham of the purest water! He flatters me, all along thinking to himself, 'I'll humor the old goat and he'll get me in print.' Well, you can't fool me. I took this Ryazan rube and showed him up for just what he is. I made him admit that he'd never read my poetry, and that before coming to me he had managed to lick the boots of both Blok and Merezhkovsky. And this business about teaching himself to read and write by the light of a burning wooden candle—that's rubbish too. It turns out that he graduated from a teacher's college. In short, I probed under his phony velvet hide and found his true essence: a boundless self-esteem and a desire to become famous at any cost. I found him out, gave him a good dressing down and the spanking he deserved. He'll remember this old goat!"

And then, without changing his disapproving, crotchety manner,

Sologub handed a notebook of Esenin's poetry to the editor, Arkhipov.

"Here. His work's not bad at all. There's a spark in it. I recommend you publish it—it'll enhance the magazine. And I think you should give him an advance. After all, the boy's fresh out of the country—he ought to have some change in his pocket. And he is a worthwhile boy: he has a will, passion, hot blood. Not at all like our little flits from *Apollo*."

Immediately afterward, people everywhere began talking about Esenin. We soon got acquainted and frequently saw each other here and there. Esenin's career had its start right before my eyes. But after the February Revolution, having become one of the Imagists, Esenin moved to Moscow, and except for a chance meeting in Berlin, I never saw him again.

After three or three and a half years in Petersburg, Esenin had become a well-known poet. He was surrounded by friends and female admirers. Many features that Sologub had first detected under Esenin's "velvet hide" came to the surface. He became arrogant, cocky, and boastful. But, oddly enough, his hide stayed on. Naiveté, trustfulness, and a sort of childish tenderness coexisted in his character with a mischievousness approaching rowdiness and a self-admiration that was almost boorish. There was a particular kind of charm in these contradictions. People loved him. They forgave him much that they wouldn't have forgiven another. And they pampered him, especially in left-liberal literary circles.

The Petersburg period of Esenin's career ended in an entirely unexpected way. In late autumn of 1916 a "monstrous rumor" suddenly broke out and was then confirmed: "Our" Esenin, "darling" Esenin, Esenin the "charming boy" had presented himself to the Empress Alexandra Fyodorovna in the palace at Tsarskoe Selo, read poetry to her, then asked for and received permission to dedicate a whole cycle of poems to her in his new book.

Nowadays it is difficult to imagine the indignation that gripped "progressive circles" when it was revealed that Esenin's "villainous act" was not a fabrication, not a "calumniation by the Black

Manuscript page by Ivanov.

Hundreds," but an indisputable fact. People rushed to Esenin for an explanation. At first he kept quiet. Then he confessed. Then he retracted his confession. Then he flew off somewhere—possibly to the front, possibly to the Ryazan countryside.

The resentment toward yesterday's darling was enormous. At times it was comical—for instance, in the case of the very rich and even more progressive lady, Sofya Chatskina, who in all seriousness called *Annals of the North,* the magazine she published, "the battering ram of art against tsarism." At a magnificent reception given in her hospitable apartment, she hysterically tore to pieces some of Esenin's manuscripts and letters, shrieking: "We've warmed a viper in our bosom! A new Rasputin! A second Protopopov!" In vain her more restrained spouse, Yakov Saker, tried to persuade the hysterical patroness not to ruin her health "on account of some renegade."

Esenin's book *Goluben'* didn't come out until after the February Revolution, so he had time to delete the dedication to Her Majesty. Several secondhand-book sellers in Petersburg and Moscow nevertheless managed to get their hands on a few proof sheets which bore the fatal: "With veneration I dedicate. . . ." In Solovyov's store on Liteiny Prospect, a proof copy was entered in a catalogue of rare books with the comment: "Extremely curious." Vladislav Khodasevich also had one of the proof sheets.

Had there not been a revolution, the doors of most Russian publishing houses (and the wealthiest and most influential among them) would have been forever closed to Esenin. Liberal opinion did not forgive a Russian writer such transgressions as monarchistic leanings. Esenin could not help knowing this and evidently was making a deliberate and conscious break. Which plans and aspirations led him to take such a daring step, no one can say. But, of course, Esenin would not take the risk for nothing. The Revolution disrupted his enigmatic calculations, and in a funny way also saved him from the inevitable antagonism of the liberals. An amusing metamorphosis took place: the all-powerful opposition, once having overthrown the monarchy and itself become the governing establishment, became suddenly powerless. The salt of the Russian earth suddenly lost its taste. Before the Revolution, two or three phone calls from "Pope" Miliukov in the editor's office of *Speech* were all that were required to expel a literary "apostate." From then on, the mechanism of public opinion worked under its own steam, automatically and mercilessly. But Esenin, as the saying goes, could "spit from a tall tree" on government Minister Miliukov and all the other former rulers of literary destinies who had now become high officials of the Great Bloodless Revolution. He knew perfectly well that the people who mattered didn't sit in the ministries of the provisional government, but at Durnovo's villa, Kshesinskaya's residence, and in the Council of Workers', Peasants', and Soldiers' deputies. Connections in those circles would open all doors and would eradicate the consequences of not merely a rash deed, but even of a criminal act. And through such people as Riurik Ivnev, Klyuev, Gorky, Ivanov-Razumnik and Bonch-Bruevich, Esenin's circle of acquaintances branched out and reached to the very top—Mamont Dalsky, Lunacharsky, Trotsky, right up to Lenin himself.

Immediately after the October Revolution, Esenin found himself not in the party (and he never did become a party member) but in the immediate proximity of the top Soviet hierarchy. There was nothing strange in this. On the contrary, it would have been surprising had things turned out otherwise.

It is psychologically impossible to imagine Esenin with Denikin or Kolchak, to say nothing of the first wave of *émigrés*. Everything, from his origins to his mental make-up, predisposed him to turn away from Kerensky's Russia and to give his sincere support to the "Russia of workers and peasants."

First of all, in Esenin's case, union with the Bolsheviks did not have that sinister stigma of betrayal that was inevitable for all Russian intellectuals. On the contrary, according to his way of thinking at the time, it was the provisional government that had betrayed the tsar and the people; but Lenin, having taken the power away from Kerensky, had fulfilled the people's will. That's how Esenin, in his instinctive peasant way, figured it out for himself. And that's the way his friends of the time—Klyuev, Pimen Karpov, and Klychkov—saw it.

In contrast, the Constitutional-Democrat and Social Revolutionary circles that Esenin had frequented before the Revolution had now become the February Government, and were organically alien to him. They had, in their turn, loved and pampered Esenin—and Esenin had let himself be loved and pampered. That was the limit of the relationship. The incident with the empress had exposed the deep mutual misunderstanding between Esenin and his intellectual patrons. For Lenin and his group, Esenin's "horrible deed" was simply an amusing trifle. "So the fellow made his way through the servants' entrance to the tsarina to curry a little favor. So what of it? If he's with us now and, what's more, if he's a talented person, we need him and that's that." "Who are you for? For us or against us? If you're against us—up against the wall. If you're for us, come over to us and work." These words, spoken by Lenin as far back as 1905, remained in full force in 1918. Esenin was "for," and his sincerity increased the value of that "for" just that much more.

Yes, sincerity. Most of the intellectuals who had joined the Bolsheviks were opportunists and self-seekers. Esenin joined for ideological reasons, so to speak. He was not an opportunist and he didn't sell himself. The same aspirations that a year and a half before had led him to walk into the palace at Tsarskoe Selo now drew him to Smolny. It's probable that he expected approximately the same thing from Lenin that he had from the tsarina. He expected the realization of a dream that is present in all his early verse—an age-old Russian dream which grew through the centuries into the soul of the common people, a dream of the ideal, just, holy peasant tsardom that the gentry wouldn't allow to come true.

Klyuev, who had influenced Esenin more than anyone else, sometimes called this dream the "New City" and sometimes the "Forest Truth." Esenin called it "Inonia." The poem with this title, written in 1918, is the key to understanding Esenin during the period of war communism. As poetry, this is probably the most perfect thing he ever created. As a document, it is graphic evidence of his strongly held, sincere revolutionary and godless feelings.

Stripped of its stylistic ornamentation and poetic allegories, Esenin's and Klyuev's "peasant dream" consisted of roughly the following: The ideal "Forest tsardom" would begin in Holy Russia when everything on her soil that was superficial, artificial, and alien to the people was destroyed—be it called empire, culture, intelligentsia, legal code, or whatever. It was necessary to let loose the red rooster, which would burn all that up. Only then would the "New City" rise from the ashes, like Kitezh from the bottom of the lake. It wouldn't particularly matter where exactly the red rooster was launched—from the left or the right, or what exactly would help the "Forest Truth" become a reality in Russia—the cudgels of the Archangel Michael Society or the bombs and bullet-proof vests of the terrorists.

Soon after the Bolsheviks seized control, Klyuev expressed this feeling in a remarkable poem. Unfortunately, I can remember only a few lines, but even they are expressive enough:

> **In Smolny * there's darkness of the woods,**
> **A taste of pine needles and brambles.**
> **There stands the austere wooden coffin,**
> **With the remains of Great Russia inside it.**
> **There is a spirit of Old-Believer dissidents in Lenin,**
> **A Father Superior tone in his decrees.**

The fact that Great Russia lies in a coffin at Smolny is by no means an expression of Klyuev's grief at her demise, or of indignation directed at her murderers at Smolny. Just the opposite. It is more accurately joy that the long-awaited beginning is coming. The former Russia, perhaps "Great," but belonging to the gentry, to the intelligentsia, not to "us," is finally dead—and high time. The place for the "New City" is now clear. And Lenin, murderer of the old Russia, is a fitting builder for the one to be. The lines of the poem point out the features in Lenin that gladdened Klyuev: the spirit of the Old Believers, i.e. the folk, peasant spirit; the

* Lenin's headquarters. TRANSLATOR.

Father Superior tone of his decrees is that of a rightful owner and is in the traditions of the church and the monasteries. Clearly, Lenin is a worthy, upright man of our own kind. And to help him is the true cause, the direct duty of every peasant. "O Lord, preserve the freedom / Of the commune's red sovereign!" was Klyuev's cry at that time. And in those days, for him, for Esenin, and for others close to them in spirit (and there were many of them) this didn't sound like the absurdity it seems today, but like a solemn "now lettest Thou Thy servant depart in peace."

In the Soviet Union, Esenin has been long dethroned and exposed.* Literature textbooks dedicate a few lines to him with the purpose of convincing Soviet school children that there's no reason to like Esenin and no point in reading his poetry, for he was a second-rate, "petty bourgeois" poet who was out of step with the times.

Esenin is never mentioned in print or on the radio. His books have been withdrawn from the libraries. In short, he has been officially shelved and forgotten.

But Esenin's popularity has been steadily growing. Handwritten copies of his verse circulate all over the country. His poems are learned by heart and sung as songs. In spite of the disapproval of the authorities, groups of Esenin's female followers call themselves by the romantic name "Brides of Esenin." In the relatively free atmosphere of refugee camps, displaced persons reprint his verse. And these little books, sloppily printed and selling for no mean sum, have a brisk circulation not only in the camps but also among the old *émigrés*—people, as is well known, singularly indifferent to poetry.

* The official attitude toward Esenin in the Soviet Union, described by Ivanov, was in effect from the time of the poet's suicide until about 1955. In Khrushchev's time, it was drastically revised, and Esenin was suddenly discovered to be a faithful son of the Revolution and a realistic poet after all. The revision was accomplished at the cost of deemphasizing some of the poet's most popular and representative lyrics, now seen as incidental and unimportant, and of suppressing certain portions of his biography. By now the pendulum has swung to the point where we can speak of an Esenin cult and an Esenin industry in the Soviet Union. EDITOR.

Just what is the secret of this steadily growing charisma of Esenin?

Esenin was undoubtedly a very gifted poet. But it is equally true that his talent cannot be considered of the highest order. Not only was he no Pushkin, he was not even a Nekrasov or a Fet. Furthermore, there was a whole set of circumstances—from a fame that came too easily and too soon to a real lack of culture—that kept his talent from developing evenly. Among the works he left there are more failures and misses than lucky discoveries and successes.

But it somehow happens that, in Esenin's case, formal analysis does not seem really necessary. Certainly his verse, like any verse, consists of various paeons, pyrrhics, and anacruses. Certainly his lines can be analyzed and measured out from this angle. But that sort of approach, tedious under most circumstances, is especially tedious when you have a book of Esenin in your hands. You can test and itemize the chemical composition of the spring air, too—but how much more natural simply to take a deep breath!

And for exactly the same reason one wouldn't want to approach Esenin's personality and biography with the ordinary criteria: moral-immoral, permissible–not permissible, white-red; with regard to Esenin this too is unimportant and pointless.

It's something else that is important. There is, for example, one surprising but irrefutable fact: a love for Esenin is common ground for both the sixteen-year-old "Bride of Esenin" who is a member of the Communist Youth, and the fifty-year-old, 100 percent irreconcilable "White Guard." The two poles of the Russian consciousness, distorted and dismembered by the Revolution, between which there is seemingly nothing in common, come together in Esenin—i.e. in Russian poetry. That is, in poetry in general. That is, in that essence which Zhukovsky so well defined: "Poetry is God in the holy dreams of earth. . . ." "God in holy dreams," i.e. an antidote for godlessness, dialectical materialism, slavery of the body, corruption of the soul, i.e in the final analysis—anti-Bolshevism.

The widespread explanation that Esenin fell from grace because he was a peasant poet is not at all satisfactory. Had Esenin, like

Klyuev, lived to see collectivization, it is probable that he too would have had to answer for "kulak tendencies." But Esenin was long dead by then. And as we know, the Bolshevism which is merciless toward the living is extremely indulgent toward the dead —especially if they were famous. That's understandable, since the attributes of the "Great October" that the present regime can safely maintain are becoming more few-and-far-between as time goes on. No matter how you look at it, Lenin's mummy by itself is not enough. So the deficit is successfully made up by various other celebrated corpses, various "cities of Gorky," "Mayakovsky squares," and so forth. I don't doubt that there would have been a square and all the rest for Esenin, too, if they had counted against him only the sins he committed during his lifetime. But Esenin committed another, unforgivable sin before the Soviet authorities—a posthumous sin. Esenin does from the grave what none of the living has succeeded in doing in thirty years: he brings Russian people together with the sounds of the Russian song, where the consciousness of mutual guilt and common brotherhood flow together into a common hope for liberation.

There, then, is the reason why the Bolsheviks try to convince Soviet citizens that there's no reason to like Esenin. This is why he has been declared "out of step with the times."

In pursuit of vanishing fame, Isadora Duncan arrived in Moscow late in 1921.

No longer young, she had filled out and put on weight. Of the onetime "barefoot goddess" there remained but little. Isadora could hardly dance any more, but this did not in the least keep her from enjoying the ovations in a packed-to-the-rafters Bolshoi Theater. Breathing heavily, she kept running out on the stage with a red flag in her hand. For those who had seen the former Isadora, the sight was rather saddening. But she was nevertheless Isadora, the world celebrity, and more important—she was dancing in the Red capital that was still unspoiled by foreign notables. And what's more, she was dancing with a red flag. The enraptured audience would not stop applauding. Surrounded by members of the Council of People's Commissars, Lenin himself was leading the ovations.

The famous dancer caught sight of Esenin at a banquet given in her honor after the first performance. Flushed with success, she felt as beautiful now as she once had been. And, as was her wont, she was looking over the banquet guests in search of someone worthy to share the day's triumph with her.

She glided over to Esenin and, hardly stopping to think, embraced him and kissed him on the mouth. She had no doubt that her kiss would make this modest bumpkin happy. But Esenin, having already managed to get quite drunk, was furious. He gave her a shove: "Get off, you old hag!" Not understanding, she gave him an even more passionate kiss. At this point he swung around and gave the world celebrity a resounding slap. Isadora gasped, then started wailing like a peasant woman.

Esenin, sobering immediately, rushed to kiss her hands, to calm her down, and to beg forgiveness. And so their love began. Isadora forgave him. With her diamond ring she scratched into the window pane: "Esenin is a hoodlum, / Esenin is an angel!"

The romance of the dancer and the peasant poet young enough to be her son soon resulted in lawful matrimony. Isadora and Esenin signed the papers in the Moscow civil registrar's office and went abroad—to Europe and America, then back to Europe. The marriage turned out to be unsuccessful and short-lived.

One spring evening in Berlin, in 1923, I was having dinner in Förster's restaurant on the Motzstrasse. I had finished eating, and was on my way to the door when someone called out to me in Russian from a crowded and noisy table. I turned around and saw Esenin. I wasn't surprised. Just a few days before, Maxim Gorky had told me that Esenin and Isadora were in Berlin.

I hadn't seen him for several years. At first glance he had hardly changed at all: the same cornflower-blue eyes and blond hair, the same boyish expression. He jumped up lightly, as if on springs, and held out his hand. "Hello! Long time no see. On your way through or are you an *émigré* now? If you're not in a hurry, let's get together and have a drink. No? Well, then let me go along with you a ways. . . ."

The doorman handed him his top hat and a black overcoat—short, but very wide. Having caught my surprised expression, he let out a self-satisfied chuckle: "I like extremes, you know. Bast peasant sandals or a topper and palmerston . . ." He jauntily tapped his hat down on his curls. "Remember when I appeared at Gorodetsky's that time in velvet plush pants and a gold belt? You haven't forgotten?"

"You remember, then?" he laughed. "Hilarious! What a clown I looked that night!" Yes, of course, a clown. But with a top hat and that overcoat, which for some reason he called a "palmerston," he looked something of a clown in Berlin, too. I didn't tell him that, understandably.

We walked along the quiet streets of Berlin-Westen. After a short silence he remarked: "Well, admit it, I was offensive to you Petersburg people, to you, Gumilyov, and that hornet Akhmatova. That's why they wouldn't print me in *Apollo*. But then, Blok recognized me right away. And he gave me some excellent advice: 'Swing harder on the swings of life. . . .' And I did! And I'm going to swing some more! What do you think he would say if he saw my swinging now?"

I said nothing, but it didn't seem Esenin was waiting for an answer. He kept on talking about Blok: "Ah, how I liked Alexander Alexandrovich. I was in love with him. I considered him the number-one poet. But now—" he paused for breath. "These days a lot of people—such as Lunacharsky and others—they're writing that I'm number one. Maybe you've heard? Not Blok, but me. What do you think of that? Maybe they're lying? Just hogwash?"

He stopped suddenly. "How'd you like to stop by our place in the Adlon? We'll wake up Isadora. She'll be glad. She'll make us some Turkish coffee. Please come. And it'll be easier for me with you there—no excuses and no explanations. As a matter of fact, that's why I had dinner alone tonight—we had another fight. We fight a lot these days. It's terrible, I know. She really aggravates me. She's a remarkable girl, a star, a brain—but something's missing, the most important thing. The thing we Russians call soul.

"Yes, let's go to the Adlon. You'd rather not? Well, some other time then. You should get acquainted with her sometime, anyway. And you should see how she dances with the scarf. Remarkable. The scarf comes alive in her hands. She holds it by the tail when she starts dancing. And it seems it's not a scarf in her hands, but a hoodlum. As if there were two people dancing, and not just her alone. You can't believe your eyes, there's such—how would you say—*expression* in it. The hoodlum embraces her, strangling and smothering her. But then, bang! The scarf's under her feet. She's torn him off and trampled him—and that's the end of him. There's no more hoodlum, just a crumpled rag lying on the floor. It's amazing how she does it all. Takes your breath away. I can't sit still through it. It's just as if it were me lying under her feet. Just as if it were the end of me."

I was in a hurry, people were waiting for me. The description of the scarf dance left me cold. I could picture Isadora, panting and puffing, jumping heavily across the Bolshoi stage with a red flag in her hand. The emotion in Esenin's voice didn't get through to me. I would feel emotion later, reading that he had hanged himself with a strap from one of the suitcases that were then lying in his room at the Adlon—the swankest hotel in Berlin. And again, some two years or so later, when I learned that on the Promenade des Anglais in Nice, Isadora Duncan had been strangled by her own scarf. . . . It's true that "Poets at times can strange prophets be. . . ." Who would possibly argue—they really can be.

I stopped at the entrance to the house where my friends were waiting. "What? Already?" Esenin was surprised. "And I was just opening up to you. Pity, pity—as the hare says in Afanasiev's fairy tales. Well, it's all the same. It's always like that with me, anyway. Just as soon as I start speaking frankly, something shuts me up. In life and in poetry, too—always. It's a dreary business. Lots of people envy me, but what is there to envy, since in fact

I'm so bored. I drink hard and raise hell—and all from being bored. It's true, what I once said of myself:

> I've danced and cried the spring day through,
> And the fire has gone out.
> Sergei Esenin, it's a bore for me
> To look you in the face.

"Ugh, how boring it all is! Just deadly. Well . . . good-bye. I'm bored again and I guess I'll just move along somewhere else. I'll let off a little steam. Swing a bit."

He waved his top hat, and I watched as the wide skirt of his "palmerston" disappeared into a taxi. . . .

Esenin lived for a little more than two years after this last meeting. But what he experienced and endured in that time was enough for a whole lifetime—and a long, stormy, very unhappy one at that. All sorts of things happened to Esenin before November 23, 1925.

There was the breakup with Isadora and a lonely trip back to Moscow. There was a new marriage and a new breakup. There were, along the way, many other romantic encounters and leave-takings. There was a trip to Persia and a forced rest—in a mental hospital. There was a final, melancholy trip to the countryside, where the poet was disillusioned by everything he saw. There were, finally, new sprees and drunken rows that differed from the previous ones in that they now ended invariably with anti-Soviet and anti-Semitic outbursts. Nearly every night a drunken Esenin would begin to yell in the middle of a restaurant (or in the middle of Red Square, for that matter), "Kill the Communists—save Russia" and other things in the same spirit. Any other person but Esenin would have been executed, of course, but the perplexed authorities simply didn't know how to deal with "the number-one peasant poet." They tried to shame him, but got no results. They tried to scare him with a "public tribunal" in the "House of the Press," but this didn't help either. As strange as it may seem, the final outcome was that the Bolsheviks gave up. The Moscow police force was ordered to put the brawling Esenin into the drunk tank to sober him up, bringing no charges against him. Before long, all Moscow's policemen knew Esenin on sight.

Esenin was a typical representative of his people and his time. Behind him stood millions of similar, but anonymous, Esenins—his brothers in spirit, the accomplice-victims of the Revolution. Like Esenin, they were caught up in its whirlwind and blinded by it. They had lost their criteria of good and evil, truth and falsehood, and, thinking that they were flying to the stars, they landed face down in the mud. They traded God for dialectical materialism, Russia for the Internationale, and finally came to their senses under the burst bubble of the Revolution. Esenin's fate was their fate, and their voices could be heard in his. It is for that reason that Esenin's lines strike Russian hearts with such mysterious force and that his name, for the Russia of our day, is beginning to shine like Pushkin's—enlightening and irreplaceable.

translated by Brant Bassett

Torpid smoke
VLADIMIR NABOKOV

Foreword

Tyazholy dym *appeared in the daily* Posledniya Novosti, *Paris, March 3, 1935, and was reprinted in my collection of short stories* Vesna v Fialte *by Chekhov Publishing House (New York, 1956). It has now been translated by my son and me into English with particular care. In two or three passages, brief phrases have been introduced to elucidate points of habitus and locale, unfamiliar today not only to foreign readers but to the incurious grandchildren of the Russians who fled to Western Europe in the first three or four years after the Bolshevist Revolution. Otherwise the translation is acrobatically faithful—beginning with the title, which in a coarse lexical rendering that did not take familiar associations into account would read "Heavy Smoke."*

The story belongs to that portion of my short fiction which

refers to émigré life in Berlin between 1920 and the late thirties. Seekers of biographical tidbits should be warned that my main delight in composing those things was to invent ruthlessly assortments of exiles who in character, class, exterior features, and so forth were utterly unlike any of the Nabokovs. The only two affinities here between author and hero are that both wrote Russian verse and that I had lived at one time or another in the same kind of lugubrious Berlin apartment as he. Only very poor readers (or perhaps some exceptionally good ones) will scold me for not letting them into its parlor.
Montreux, March 8, 1971

When the streetlamps hanging in the dusk came on, practically in unison, all the way to Bayerischer Platz, every object in the unlit room shifted slightly under the influence of the outdoor rays which started by taking a picture of the lace curtain's design. He had been lying supine (a long-limbed, flat-chested youth with a pince-nez glimmering in the semiobscurity) for about three hours, apart from a brief interval for supper, which had passed in merciful silence: his father and sister, after yet another quarrel, had kept reading at table. Drugged by the oppressive, protracted feeling so familiar to him, he lay and looked through his lashes, and every line, every rim, or shadow of a rim turned into a sea horizon or a strip of distant land. As soon as his eye got used to the mechanics of these metamorphoses, they began to occur of their own accord (thus small stones continue to come alive, quite uselessly, behind the wizard's back), and now, in this or that place of the room's cosmos, an illusionary perspective was formed, a remote mirage enchanting in its graphic transparency and isolation: a stretch of water, say, and a black promontory with the minuscule silhouette of an araucaria.

At intervals scraps of indistinct, laconic speech came from the adjacent parlor (the cavernal centerpiece of one of those bourgeois flats which Russian *émigré* families used to rent in Berlin at the time), separated from his room by sliding doors, through whose ripply mat glass the tall lamp beyond shone yellow, whilst lower down there showed through, as if in deep water, the fuzzy dark back of a chair placed in that position to foil the propensity of the door-leaves to crawl apart in a series of jerks. In that parlor (probably on the divan at its farthest end) his sister sat with her boy friend; and, to judge by the mysterious pauses, resolving at last in a slight cough or a tender questioning laugh, the two were kissing. Other sounds could be heard from the street: the noise of a car would curl up like a wispy column to be capitaled by a honk at the crossing; or, vice versa, the honk would come first, followed by an approaching rumble in which the shudder of the door-leaves participated as best it could.

And in the same way as the luminosity of the water and its every throb pass through a medusa, so everything traversed his inner being, and that sense of fluidity became transfigured into something like second sight. As he lay flat on his couch, he felt carried sideways by the flow of shadows, and, simultaneously, he escorted distant foot-passengers, and visualized now the sidewalk's surface right under his eyes (with the exhaustive accuracy of a dog's sight), now the design of bare branches against a sky still retaining some color, or else the alternation of shop windows: a hairdresser's dummy, hardly surpassing the queen of hearts in anatomic development; a picture framer's display, with purple heathscapes and the inevitable *Inconnue de la Seine,* so popular in the Reich, among numerous portraits of President Hindenburg; and then a lampshade shop with all bulbs aglow, so that one could not help wondering which of them was the workaday lamp belonging to the shop itself.

All at once it occurred to him, as he reclined mummy-like in the dark, that it was all rather awkward—his sister might think that he was not at home, or that he was eavesdropping. To move was, however, incredibly difficult; difficult because the very form of his being had now lost all distinctive marks, all fixed boundaries. For example, the lane on the other side of the house might be his own arm, whilst the long skeletal cloud that stretched across the whole sky with a chill of stars in the east might be his backbone. Neither the striped obscurity in his room, nor the glass of the parlor door which was transmuted into nighttime seas shining with golden undulations, offered him a dependable method of measuring and marking himself off; only then did he find that method when in a burst of agility the tactile tip of his tongue, performing a sudden twist in his mouth (as if dashing to check, half-awake, if all was well), palpated and started to worry a bit of soft foreign matter, a shred of boiled beef firmly lodged in his teeth; whereupon he reflected how many times, in some nineteen years, it had changed, that invisible but tangible householdry of teeth, which the tongue would get used to until a filling came out, leaving a great pit that presently would be refurnished.

He was now prompted to move, not so much by the shamelessly frank silence behind the door as by the urge to seek out a nice, pointed little tool, to aid the solitary blind toiler. He stretched, raised his head, and switched on the light near his couch, thus entirely restoring his corporeal image. He perceived himself (the pince-nez, the thin, dark mustache, the bad skin on his forehead) with that utter revulsion he always experienced on coming back to his body out of the languorous mist, promising—what? What shape would the force oppressing and teasing his spirit finally take? Where did it originate, this thing growing in me? Most of my day had been the same as usual—university, public library—but later, when I had to trudge to the Osipovs on Father's errand, there was that wet roof of some pub on the edge of a vacant lot, and the chimney smoke hugged the roof, creeping low, heavy with damp, sated with it, sleepy, refusing to rise, refusing to detach itself from beloved decay, and right then came that thrill—right then.

Under the table lamp gleamed an oilcloth-bound exercise book, and next to it, on the ink-mottled blotter, lay a razor blade, its apertures encircled with rust. The light also fell on a safety pin. He unbent it, and following his tongue's rather fussy directions, removed the mote of meat, swallowed it—better than any dainties; after which the contented organ calmed down.

Suddenly a mermaid's hand was applied from the outside to the ripply glass of the door; then the leaves parted spasmodically and his sister thrust in her shaggy head.

"Grisha dear," she said, "be an angel. Do get some cigarettes from Father."

He did not respond, and the bright slits of her furry eyes narrowed (she saw very poorly without her horn-rimmed glasses), as she-tried to make out whether or not he was asleep on the couch.

"Get them for me, Grishenka," she repeated, still more entreatingly. "Oh, please! I don't want to go to him after what happened yesterday."

"Maybe I don't want to either," he said.

"Hurry, hurry," tenderly uttered his sister. "Come on, Grisha dear!"

"All right, lay off," he said at last, and, carefully reuniting the two halves of the door, she dissolved in the glass.

He examined again his lamp-lit island, remembering hopefully that he had put somewhere a pack of cigarettes which one evening a friend had happened to leave behind. The shiny safety pin had disappeared, whilst the exercise book now lay otherwise and was half open (as a person changes position in sleep). Perhaps, between my books. The light just reached their spines on the shelves above the desk. Here were haphazard trash (predominantly) and manuals of political economy (I wanted something quite different, but Father won out); there were also some favorite books that at one time or another had done his heart good: Gumilyov's collection of poems *Shatyor* (tent), Pasternak's *Sestra moya zhizn'* (life, my sister), Gazdanov's *Vecher u Kler* (evening at Claire's), Radiguet's *Le Bal du Comte d'Orgel,* Sirin's *Zashchita Luzhina* (Luzhin's defense), Ilf and Petrov's *Dvenadtsat' Stul'ev* (twelve chairs), Hoffmann, Hölderlin, Baratynsky, and an old Russian guidebook. Again that gentle, mysterious shock. He listened. Would the thrill be repeated? His mind was in a state of extreme tension, logical thought was eclipsed, and when he came out of his trance, it took him some time to recall why he was standing near the shelves and fingering books. The blue-and-white package that he had stuck between Professor Sombart and Dostoevsky proved to be empty. Well, it had to be done, no getting out of it. There was, however, another possibility.

In worn bedroom slippers and sagging pants, listlessly, almost noiselessly, dragging his feet, he passed from his room to the hallway and groped for the switch. On the console under the looking glass, next to the guest's smart beige cap, there remained a crumpled piece of soft paper: the wrappings of liberated roses. He rummaged in his father's overcoat, penetrating with squeamish fingers into the insensate world of a strange pocket, but did not find there the spare pack he had hoped to obtain, knowing, as he did, his father's heavyish providence. Nothing to be done, I must go to him.

Here, that is at some indeterminate point in his somnambulic itinerary, he again stepped into a zone of mist, and this time the renewed vibration within him possessed such power, and especially was so much more vivid than all external perceptions, that he did not immediately identify, as his proper confines and countenance, the stoop-shouldered youth, with the pale, unshaven cheek and the red ear, who glided soundlessly by in the mirror. He overtook his own self and entered the dining room.

There, at the table which long since, before going to bed, the maid had laid for late-evening tea, sat his father: one finger was grating in his black, gray-streaked beard; between the finger and thumb of his other hand he held aloft a pince-nez by its springy clips; he sat studying a large plan of Berlin badly worn at the folds. A few days ago, at the house of some friends, there had been a passionate, Russian-style argument as to which was the shortest way to walk from a certain street to another, neither of which, incidentally, did any of the arguers ever frequent; and now, to judge by the expression of displeased astonishment on his father's inclined face, with those two pink figure eights on the sides of his nose, the old man had turned out to be wrong.

"What is it?" he asked, glancing up at his son (with the secret hope, perhaps, that I would sit down, divest the teapot of its cosey, pour a cup for him, for myself). "Cigarettes?" he went on in the same interrogatory tone, having noticed the direction in which his son gazed. The latter had started to go behind his father's back to reach for the box, which stood on the far side of the table, but his father was already handing it across, so that there ensued a moment of muddle.

"Is he gone?" came the third question.

"No," said the son, taking a silky handful of cigarettes.

On his way out of the dining room, he noticed his father turn his whole torso in his chair to face the wall clock as if it had said something, and then begin turning back—but here the door I was closing closed, and I did not see that bit to the end. I did not see it to the end, I had other things on my mind, yet that, too, and the distant seas of a moment ago, and my sister's flushed little face, and the indistinct rumble on the circular rim of the transparent night—everything, somehow or other, helped to form what now had at last taken shape. With terrifying clarity, as if my soul were lit up by a noiseless explosion, I glimpsed a future recollection; it dawned upon me that exactly as I recalled such images of the past as the way my dead mother had of making a weepy face and clutching her temples when mealtime squabbles became too loud, so one day I would have to recall, with merciless, irreparable sharpness, the hurt look of my father's shoulders as he leaned over that torn map, morose, wearing his warm indoor jacket powdered with ashes and dandruff; and all this mingled creatively with the recent vision of blue smoke clinging to dead leaves on a wet roof.

Through a chink between the door-leaves, unseen, avid fingers took away what he held, and now he was lying again on his couch, but the former languor had vanished. Enormous, alive, a metrical line extended and bent; at the bend a rhyme was coming deliciously and hotly alight, and as it glowed forth, there appeared, like a shadow on the wall when you climb upstairs with a candle, the mobile silhouette of another verse.

Drunk with the italianate music of Russian alliteration, with the longing to live, with the new temptation of obsolete words (modern *bereg* reverting to *breg,* a farther "shore," *holod* to *hlad,* a more classic "chill," *veter* to *vetr,* a better Boreas), puerile, perishable poems, which, by the time the next were printed, would have been certain to wither as had withered, one after the other, all the previous ones written down in the black exercise book; but no matter: at this moment I trust the ravishing promises of the still breathing, still revolving verse; my face is wet with tears, my heart is bursting with happiness, and I know that this happiness is the greatest thing existing on earth.

Berlin, early 1935
Montreux, early 1971 (trans.)

translated from the Russian by Dmitri Nabokov
in collaboration with the author

Nabokov's dark cinema: a diptych

ALFRED APPEL, JR.

Ten distinct Squares here seen apart,
Are joined in one by Cutter's Art.
—The Argument of the Frontispiece
Burton's The Anatomy of Melancholy

Hol·ly·wood [2] (*hŏlē'-wŏŏd'*) n. *The U.S. motion-picture industry or the somewhat meretriciously glamorous atmosphere often attributed to it.*
—The American Heritage Dictionary

1. Negative images

"The twilight before the Lumières," laments *Ada*'s (1969) Van Veen in regard to the dark, muddy tonalities of an old photograph ("a sumerograph," he calls it, invoking Sumer, the ancient region of Babylonia, and *sumerki,* a Russian word for "twilight").[1] Although Nabokov admires certain classic films (Dreyer's *La Passion de Jeanne d'Arc* [1928]) and loves the screen comedies of Keaton, Chaplin, Lloyd, Clair, Laurel and Hardy, and the Marx Brothers, Van's metaphor is paradoxical. In Nabokov's fiction the descendents of those pioneering French cinematographers, the Lumières, would seem to have produced a commercial product that obfuscates rather than illuminates its human subjects. *Laughter in the Dark* (1938) was originally titled *Camera Obscura*

(1932), and the root meaning of *obscura* survives and persists in Nabokov's vision of a popular cinema that is dark indeed.

Because Nabokov is, with Borges and Queneau, the most learned and mandarin of living writers, his numerous allusions to movies might also seem paradoxical. They are, in fact, consistent with an aesthetic which connects Nabokov with several other great writers. Though a fantast and artificer who believes in the fictiveness of fiction, the texture of his prose nevertheless incorporates an extraordinary amount of material drawn from "real life": tags from Italian opera and Russian popular songs; allusions if not *tableaux vivants* copied from Flemish Old Masters and old French comic strips; literary references from Catullus to Updike; gleanings and intrusions from Nabokov's recondite researches and pastimes, his passion for chess and lepidoptery. The latter vocation (Nabokov is a professional) helps to define his particular sensibility. No more isolated in Montreux than was Joyce in Trieste (whose Aunt Josephine kept him supplied with Dublin information), Nabokov the biologist regularly exercises a cool curiosity about all facets of life, and his walk to the well-stocked neighborhood news kiosk in Montreux is a daily ritual. *L'Erald Tribune* (as it's called in *Transparent Things* [1972]), *Le Monde, Time, Newsweek, The New Yorker, The Saturday Review, Playboy, Esquire, Encounter, The Listener, The Spectator, The New Statesman, Punch,* the London Sunday newspapers, the *TLS, The National Review, The New York Review of Books,* and an occasional *Life* provide a balanced diet and satisfy a literary anatomist's penchant for subliterary but culturally significant details, glittering additions to whatever mosaic the writer has in progress (or mind). As in his 1,086-page *Eugene Onegin* Commentary (1964), novelist Nabokov assembles the quirky, compendious materials one associates with the bedside library, the great literary anatomies such as Burton's *Anatomy of Melancholy* (1651) or those *sui generis* masterpieces such as *Gargantua and Pantagruel* (1564), *Moby-Dick* (1851), and *Ulysses* (1922), in which the writer makes fictive use of all kinds of learning and unpromising bits and pieces of trash and trivia, effecting verbal collages which give pleasure and vividly communicate a sense of what it was like to be alive at a given moment in space and time. Typical of Nabokov's method is the note to line 91 of *Pale Fire* (1962), which paraphrases rather than parodies two ads from 1937 and 1949 issues of *Life*, since their absurdity cannot be outdone. That note is titled "trivia," an allusion to the great age of literary anatomy—Sterne, Swift, Johnson—by way of John Gay's *Trivia, or the Art of Walking the Streets of London* (1716). *Transparent Things*, with its Swiss locale and international local color, succinctly demonstrates how Nabokov makes aesthetic capital of a browse in a souvenir shop for tourists, a walk to the kiosk and a quick perusal of unpurchased journals. Early in the novel, Nabokov notes a sign on a snapshot booth, and laments how "The masculine ending and the absence of an acute accent flawed the unintentional pun":

$$3 \; P^{hotos}_{oses}$$

is incorporated in the text. *Osé* is French for "bold," "risqué," and both the booth and that sign (crying out for corrective graffiti) exist—across the street from Nabokov's news kiosk. "Dennis the Menace doesn't look like his father. Could he be illegitimate?" wonders Nabokov, back at the hotel, looking up from the comics page of *The Herald Tribune*. "Shall I inquire in a letter to the editor?" asks *Onegin*'s scholiast. "I wish you wouldn't," says Véra Nabokov. "They never printed your letter complaining about the plot inconsistencies in *Rex Morgan*." Sweet Reason prevails, but Dennis (or his cuckolded father) may yet surface in a Nabokov work. He is not, as some friendly critics have suggested, totally hostile to the "actual world," and its fictions—large and small— clearly fascinate him. Except for his positive view of screen comedy, Nabokov's references to cinema are the product of an anatomist's tour of the contemporary world, rather than a *cinéaste*'s total recall, a film buff's enthusiasm. The result is a kind of cultural criticism.

The *émigré* narrator of "Spring in Fialta" (1938), Nabokov's own favorite among his many stories, is a representative for a

European film company and, his gentility notwithstanding, a representative figure. He is acquainted with a Nabokov-like "Franco-Hungarian writer," and subsequently "even turned out to be of some use to him: my firm acquired the film rights of one of his more intelligible stories, and then he had a good time pestering me with telegrams." Like Nabokov's own experience in the thirties with two film options on *Camera Obscura* (the great German actor Fritz Kortner, in exile in England, was to play Albinus), nothing comes of that project. Depressed by the prospect of an unexpected reunion with the writer, the narrator admits that "one thing, however, considerably cheered me up: the flop of his recent play." [2] (Nabokov's play, *Sobytie* [*The Event*], had a brief Parisian run in 1938.) His is the entrepreneur's hostility toward the artist, and Nabokov more than returns it in kind; it pervades his work, especially in his conception of cinematic *poshlost'*, to use one of the two words he has fixed in our language (if *Time* is grist for your lexicon).

Like Lolita, but no nymphet, Margot in *Laughter in the Dark* "was mad on the movies." [3] She daydreams of stardom while serving as an usherette at the Argus, named after the hundred-eyed monster of Greek mythology, who was set to watch Io, a maiden loved by Zeus. "Good name for a cinema," thinks Albinus (p. 22), whom Margot will destroy after he has been figuratively and then literally blinded, just as Argus is slain by Hermes, who transforms lovely Io into a cow—quite appropriate to Nabokov's attitude toward the popular cinema; our Attic illustration of poor Argus' downfall renders his eyes as a terminal case of measles. An ironic and surprisingly antic image of sightlessness, the Argus is Nabokov's movie emblem and stamp of disapproval, his answer to MGM's imposing Leo the Lion, 20th Century–Fox's crisscrossing beams of light, Columbia's torch-bearing American goddess.

Employing a Flaubertian shorthand of characterization, Nabokov continually uses movies, as well as novels, paintings, and magazines, to define the minds and souls of his creations, the total nature of their existence. "The [new] glasses he had got were very becoming. He looked like the actor Hess in *The Hindu Student*, a movie," thinks Martha of Franz, her provincial, unglamorous lover in *King, Queen, Knave* (1928).[4] Throughout the novel a "Cinépalace" is being erected which will premiere the film version of the stage play *King, Queen, Knave*, an infinite regress that comments on the trashiness of Franz's and Martha's murder plot, quite apart from the novelistic artistry which contains them ("From [the door's] threshold [Franz] would fire half a dozen times in quick succession, as they do in American movies" [p. 179], or they might kill her husband in the woods, after which Franz would shoot Martha through the hand—"Yes, that's necessary, darling, it is always done, it must look as if we had been attacked by robbers" [p. 180]). "Martha . . . would tell [her cuckolded husband] in breathless detail the entire foolish film as the preface and price of a submissive caress" (p. 92). Hermann, the fatuous chocolate manufacturer of *Despair* (1936), asks Felix, "What is the opinion you have formed of me?" "Maybe you're an actor," answers the tramp whom Hermann has murderously and mistakenly cast as his "Double." [5] "You've guessed. . . . Yes, I'm an actor," says Hermann. "A film actor, to be accurate," and Felix, no fool in at least one matter, "seem[s] . . . disappointed" (p. 88). At the end of the novel, Hermann, the cornered "arch-criminal," watches the gendarmes closing in, but his shouts out the window—added by Nabokov to the 1966 translation—are directions addressed to the film company he imagines to be assembled below: *"Attention! I want a clean getaway. That's all. Thank you,"* and he steps into the medium deemed appropriate to a self-styled "mystery story" as misconceived and muddled as Hermann's. In search of a definitive composite picture of *his* identity, the *émigré* narrator of *The Eye* (1930) indulges "the fantasy that directs life" [6] and performs a trick even more difficult than Hermann's self-perpetuating murder: suicide followed by a free-wheeling ghostly return that would allow him a calm outside view of himself and easy access to at least all the spoken and written versions of his self. "I walked homeward and on the way had a wonderful idea. I imagined a sleek movie villain reading a document he has found on someone else's desk True, my plan was very sketchy," and it is as doomed to inevitable failure as any movie villain's quest (p. 67). The *émigré* actor Lik [= Russian for "face" (especially the representation of a saint) and "appearance"], the title character in one of Nabokov's finest stories (1938), had "won some fame, thanks to a film in which he did an excellent job in the bit part of a stutterer." [7] Lik's is no mere *tour de force*. The cruel, unfortunate role and Lik's thespian mimicry are equivalent to the precariousness of his very being: poverty, hypersensitivity, a state of loneliness as incurable as his medically diagnosed heart ailment. In *The Defense* (1930), Grandmaster Luzhin's wife, a most ordinary woman, "made his acquaintance . . . the way they do in old novels or in motion pictures: she drops a handkerchief and he picks it up —with the sole difference that they interchanged roles." [8] After his nervous collapse, she takes Luzhin to the very first film he has ever seen, an awful production, and Nabokov carefully and wittily paraphrases its trite plot, which includes a chess game (pp. 191–92). By having him cry at the film (analogous to Bobby Fischer's love for Motown "sounds"), Nabokov telescopes Luzhin's provincial, regressive, vulnerable innocence and isolation—the toll of his genius and circumscribing obsession—and underscores once more his mate's commonplace turn of mind. " 'Very, very good—that picture,' " Luzhin says the next day. "He thought a bit more and added: 'But they don't know how to play [chess—A. A.].' 'What do you mean, they don't know?' said his wife with surprise. 'They were first-class actors' " (p. 192). Lachrymose Uncle Henry in *Glory* (1932) "even cried at the movies," [9] but Nabokov affectionately indulges all the "immemorial and tender banalities" which deeply stir Martin Edelweiss, the novel's young *émigré* hero. His hapless infatuation with flirtatious, dark-eyed Sonia ignites a series of banal nocturnal fantasies familiar to any man who was ever young, and its culmination—if not climax—fully demonstrates that Martin is as naively romantic as he is keenly sensitive:

But while the bond of [dancing] bodies is still unbroken, the outlines of a potential love affair begin to form, and the rough draft already comprises everything: the sudden silence between two people in some dimly lit room; the man carefully placing with trembling fingers on the edge of an ashtray the just-lit but impedient cigarette; the woman's eyes slowly closing as in a filmed scene; and the rapt darkness, and in it a point of light, a glossy limousine traveling fast through the rainy night, and suddenly, a white terrace and the dazzling ripple of the sea, and Martin softly saying to the girl he has carried off, "Your name—what's your name?" Leafy shadows play on her luminous dress. She gets up, she goes away. The rapacious croupier rakes in Martin's last chips, and he has nothing left but to thrust his hands into the empty pockets of his dinner jacket and descend slowly into the casino garden and, then, sign on as a longshoreman—and there she is again, aboard someone else's yacht, sparkling, laughing, flinging coins into the water.

"Funny thing," said Darwin [his more sophisticated friend—A. A.] one night, as he and Martin came out of a small Cambridge cinema, "it's all unquestionably poor, vulgar, and rather implausible, and yet there is something exciting about all that flying foam, the *femme fatale* on the yacht, the ruined and ragged he-man swallowing his tears."

"It's nice to travel," said Martin. "I'd like to travel a lot." (pp. 82–83)

Nabokov is less indulgent of well-traveled Pnin, who, unlike his creator, fails to respond properly to the most delightful and ageless cinema artistry. At the fortnightly college presentation of "rather high-brow music and unusual film offerings,"

three ancient movie shorts bored our friend: that cane, that bowler, that white face, those black, arched eyebrows, those twitchy nostrils meant nothing to him. Whether the incomparable comedian danced in the sun with chapleted nymphs near a waiting cactus, or was a prehistoric man (the supple cane now a supple club), or was glared at by burly Mack Swain at a hectic night club, old-fashioned, humorless Pnin remained indifferent.[10]

Pnin is as pedantic as he is stolid and earnest: "Even . . . Max Linder used to be more comical," he snorts, identifying Chaplin's French precursor and possible early influence (p. 81).*

Nabokov's cinematic means are often succinct indeed: one of the "burly comrades" of Margot's brother in *Laughter in the Dark* "had eyes like the film actor [Conrad] Veidt" (p. 27), an image of intensity and villainy that draws on several nightmarish German films,† and Paul Pahlovich's second wife in *The Real Life of Sebastian Knight* (1941) says that his first marriage to the mysteri-

* Pnin views, respectively, Chaplin's *Sunnyside* (1919), *His Prehistoric Past* (1914, with Mack Swain), and *The Immigrant* (1917), where, to strike my own pedantic note, Charlie is in fact glared at by Mack Swain's successor as "heavy," Eric Campbell.

† Veidt specialized in macabre roles: *Das Kabinett des Dr. Caligari* (1919); Ivan the Terrible in *Das Wachsfigurenkabinett* (*Waxworks*, 1924); *Der Student von Prag* (1926); and *Orlacs Hände* (*The Hands of Orlac*, 1925), which Nabokov recalls with great pleasure ("Wonderfully macabre and bizarre, though most of those Gothic films were awful"). In addition to his numerous German appearances was the American film *The Man Who Laughs* (1928), because his mouth has been sculpted into a permanent grin. Adapted from Victor Hugo's story, it in turn inspired the Joker in the *Batman* comic book, as its creator has admitted, thereby serving history.

ous Nina (alias Madame Lecerf) "was merely a bad dream after seeing a bad cinema film." [11] "I shouldn't be surprised if she turned out to be an international spy. Mata Hari! That's her type. Oh, absolutely," says her former husband (p. 145), possibly drawing upon a memory of Greta Garbo's slinky title performance in *Mata Hari* (1932). Nina was "shallow and glamorous," says the narrator, "for all I knew she might be in jail or in Los Angeles" (p. 163). She "went to movies, bicycle races and boxing matches," says Humbert Humbert of his first wife, Valeria, "his big-breasted and practically brainless *baba,*" and his contempt for her is projected in appropriate cinematic terms.[12] When he learns of Valeria's infidelity, Humbert alludes to "the backhand slap with which I ought to have hit her across the cheekbone according to the rules of the movies" (pp. 31–32). His next wife, the slimmer Charlotte Haze, is described as a diluted Marlene Dietrich (p. 39), and when she announces her plans for a trip to Europe, Humbert says, "I can well imagine the thrill that you, a healthy American gal, must experience at crossing the Atlantic on the same ocean liner with Lady Bumble—or Sam Bumble, the Frozen Meat King, or a Hollywood harlot" (p. 92).

However cruel Humbert's characterizations may be, Nabokov is equally unsparing of his own person. No longer the sylphish 140-pounder of Berlin *émigré* days nor the lean Wellesley lecturer of 1941–48, Nabokov savors his memory of the New York premiere of Stanley Kubrick's film version of *Lolita:* "Date: June 13, 1962. Setting: Loew's State, Broadway at 45th Street. Scene: Crowds awaiting the limousines that drew up one by one, and there I, too, ride, as eager and innocent as the fans who peer into my car hoping to glimpse James Mason but finding only the placid profile of a stand-in for Hitchcock." [13] And in *Transparent Things* (1972), the person of "R.," a famous and aging "Nabokovian" novelist, unpleasant in several ways, is reduced to a celluloid transparency by the authenticity of Hugh Person's infatuation with Armande, a girl he has recently met. "All sham and waxworks," Hugh's interview with R. *becomes* a movie, and, dressed like an old Hollywoodian mobster ("Wallabees [suede shoes—A. A.] of a velvety cocoa shade, a lemon shirt with a lilac neck scarf, and a rumpled gray suit"), R. is subjected to a summary cinematic comparison consistent with "the illusory quality" of the entire "stiffly written scene" staged in a "bogus bar" for "the benefit of an invisible audience":

> Baron R. had coarse features, a sallow complexion, a lumpy nose with enlarged pores, shaggy bellicose eyebrows, an unerring stare, and a bulldog mouth full of bad teeth. The streak of nasty inventiveness so conspicuous in his writings also appeared in the prepared parts of his speech, as when he did now, that far from "looking fit" he felt more and more a creeping resemblance to the cinema star Reubenson who once played old gangsters in Florida-staged films; but no such actor existed.[14]

The actor, of course, is Edward G. Robinson, the film is *Key Largo* (set in a Florida bar [1948]), and only in a figurative sense do they not exist.

Particularly appalling to Nabokov is the content of the fiction-film, as it is sometimes called, to distinguish it from the documentary form—fictions whose plots and players are equally cartoon-like. "An actress with a little black heart for lips and with eyelashes like the spokes of an umbrella was impersonating a rich heiress impersonating a poor office girl," writes Nabokov of a film which Franz views in *King, Queen, Knave* (p. 93). Jilted in *Laughter in the Dark* by Axel Rex, her initial lover, distressed Margot "went to a dance hall as abandoned damsels do in films." There she is accosted by "two Japanese gentlemen," stock erotic threats to Aryan girls in many German films of the twenties (p. 38); earlier, in Cecil B. DeMille's *The Cheat* (1915), the villain's (Sessue Hayakawa) "evil" sexuality was based on his Burmese nationality. "She was so pretty," Nabokov says of Garbo, "but except for *Ninotchka* [1939], the films themselves were always so awful, the stories so absurd." He could not remember which Garbo films they had seen in the twenties and early thirties, though his wife recalled *Flesh and the Devil* (1927), a perfect example of trashy content almost transcended by various kinds of technical perfection. After Margot has casually told Albinus that she has mailed a letter to his home (surely to be intercepted by his wife), she picks up a book "and turned her back to him. On the right-hand page was a photographic study of Greta Garbo. Albinus found himself thinking: 'How strange. A disaster occurs and still a man notices a picture' " (p. 79). That distractive allure and those extraordinary technical means make the fiction-film easily susceptible to *poshlost'*.

Poshlost', says Nabokov, discussing Gogol and defining one of his favorite Russian words, "is not only the obviously trashy but also the falsely important, the falsely beautiful, the falsely clever, the falsely attractive," [15] a blending of pretentiousness, vulgarity, and cliché, insidious and cruel when it unintentionally mocks or parodies human needs and desires. Coldly cataloguing American *poshlost'*, vintage 1943, observed in *Life* magazine, Nabokov noted how "kind people send our lonely soldiers silk hosed dummy legs modeled on those of Hollywood lovelies and stuffed with candies and safety razor blades." [16] Considerably less innocent are the variegated Soviet propaganda films, preeminent *poshlost'*, which Nabokov scorns in several books. In *The Gift* (1937–1938), Fyodor and his mother visit a Berlin cinema, circa 1925, "where a Russian film was being shown which conveyed with particular brio the globules of sweat rolling down the glistening faces of the factory workers—while the factory owner smoked a cigar all the time." [17] Asked for the source of that image, Nabokov replied, "One of the big boys—Pudovkin's . . . what *was* the title?—*Sister? Brother? MOTHER!* [1926]. From Gorky's novel." It's probably distilled from Eisenstein's *Strike* (1924). "Perhaps. But those caricatures are all the same," he continued, "and *Krokodil* [the Soviet 'satirical' magazine] picked them up." Manipulating life *and* literature in the most fundamental of ways, the totalitarian state in *Bend Sinister* (1947) tries to enlist the cooperation of philosopher Adam Krug by kidnapping his young son, David. Transported to the State's infamous experimental station, where David is imprisoned, Krug is shown an ineptly projected "scientific" film intended as further "persuasion." An inscription appears upside down, a nurse giggles, and finally

A trembling legend appeared on the screen: Test 656. This melted into a subtle subtitle: "A Night Lawn Party." Armed nurses were shown unlocking doors. Blinking, the inmates trooped out. "Frau Doktor von Wytwyl, Leader of the Experiment (No Whistling, Please!)" said the next inscription. In spite of the dreadful predicament he was in, even Dr. Hammecke could not restrain an appreciative ha-ha. The woman Wytwyl, a statuesque blonde, holding a whip in one hand and a chronometer in the other, swept haughtily across the screen. "Watch Those Curves": a curving line on a blackboard was shown and a pointer in a rubber-gloved hand pointed out the climactic points and other points of interest in the yarovization of the ego.[18]

The curvaceous teaching aid was probably modeled on an imaginative infantry instructor's variant of World War II's most famous pin-up pose, published in *Look,* a bottomless wellspring of *poshlost'*. It pictured Betty Grable in that swimsuit, coyly looking back over her shoulder, squared grid coordinates superimposed on her curves, the smiling sergeant indicating with his donnish pointer "How to Read a Map."

Following another filmed sequence, "The Little Person Appears" on the screen: a still healthy David, dispatched down "floodlit marble steps" by a nurse. "David had his warmest overcoat on, but his legs were bare and he wore his bedroom slippers. The whole thing lasted a moment: he turned his face up to the nurse, his eyelashes beat, his hair caught a gleam of lambent light. . . . His face became larger, dimmer, and vanished. . . . The nurse remained on the steps, a faint not untender smile playing on her dark lips. 'What a Treat,' said the legend, 'For a Little Person to be Out Walking in the Middle of the Night' . . ." (p. 223). A cinematic specter, Nabokov's Rudy Bloom,[19] David has vanished in more ways than one; the State has already murdered him, by mistake. "Your child will be given the most scrumptious burial a white man's child could dream up," one of the Elders tells Krug (p. 226). Torture is inflicted upon Pnin by the "impressive Soviet documentary film" which is exhibited as part of that highbrow evening program: "Handsome, unkempt girls marched in an immemorial Spring Festival with banners bearing snatches of old Russian ballads such as *'Ruki proch ot Korei'* ["Hands off Korea"—A. A.]. . . . In a mountain pasture somewhere in legendary Ossetia, a herdsman reported by portable radio to the local Republic's Ministry of Agriculture on the birth of a lamb. . . . Eight thousand citizens at Moscow's Electrical Equipment Plant unanimously nominated Stalin candidate from the Stalin Election District of Moscow" (p. 81). Pnin, a lone *émigré* seated amidst American faculty fellow travelers, is moved to tears. Post–World War II neo-realism briefly flickers in *Pnin* as international *poshlost'*. One of "the obvious sources of Victor's fantasies" is "an Italian film made in Berlin for American consumption, with a wild-eyed youngster in rumpled shorts, pursued through slums and ruins and a brothel or two by a multiple agent" (p. 86)—*The Bicycle Thief* (1949) in reverse gear, "social comment" as a new context and one more excuse for cheap thrills, or what Van Veen in *Ada* calls "the *fokus-pokus* of a social theme" (p. 426).

Classless and universal, *poshlost'* is as rampant in intellectual and arty discourse as in advertising copy. Aiming a double-edged barb, Humbert tells the Beardsley School that he will return as soon as he has completed his "Hollywood engagement," hinting he is to be "chief consultant in the production of a film dealing with 'existentialism,' still a hot thing at the time" (1949, and his "engagement" punningly embraces *engagé,* the existentialist requisite [p. 210]). When Victor Vitry, "a brilliant French director, bas[es] a completely unauthorized picture on [Van Veen's first book] *Letters from Terra*" (p. 579), written fifty years before (1891), its enormous popularity is in part due to the way in which "the lovely leading lady, . . . Gedda Vitry, after titillating the spectators with her skimpy skirts and sexy rags in the existential sequences, came out of her capsule on Antiterra stark naked . . ." (p. 582). At age fourteen, Ada abandons botany in favor of movie-acting. She studies with "Stan Slavsky (no relation, and not a stage name), [who] gave her private lessons of drama, despair, hope. Her debut was a quiet little disaster" (p. 426). Stan's "theories" burlesque "the Method" psychologizings of Lee Strasberg's Actor's Studio (New York and Hollywood branches), in its turn a popularization of Stanislavsky's procedures at the Moscow Art Theatre that is as bald as Nabokov's pun. "One's first love," Ada tells Van, "is one's first standing ovation, and *that* is what makes great artists—so Stan and his girl friend, who played Miss Spangle Triangle in *Flying Rings,* assured me" (p. 426). "Bosh!" answers Van, for Nabokov. "Precisely," continues Ada, "he too [Bosh = Hieronymus Bosch—A.A.] was hooted by hack hoods in much older Amsterdams, and look how three hundred years later every Poppy Group pup copies him!"—a reference to neo-Boschian psychedelic *poshlost'* as practiced by high counter-culture painters.

The cinema is most susceptible to *poshlost'* when first-rate works of literature are being tailored to fit the needs and demands of a commercial world. Mlle Larivière, "the grotesque governess" in *Ada* who grows rich by rewriting famous works, crafts a tale "about a town mayor's strangling a small girl called Rockette . . . who liked to frolic" (p. 142)—her version of Maupassant's *La Petite rocque* (1886), and an allusion that simultaneously embraces the pneumatic, high-kicking chorus line at Radio City Music Hall (the Art Deco high temple of American *poshlost'*), formulates a high-brow tourist's murderous fantasy, and choreographs the downward arc of adaptation. "Based on an idea from the Bible," reads the screenplay credit in Cecil B. DeMille's first *Ten Commandments* (1923), while the more exacting scenario of *A Midsummer Night's Dream* (1935) is "By William Shakespeare / With Additional Dialogue By . . ."—his name, alas, escapes this scholar, but he was a Professor of English, as one may be reassured to know. A government-financed film travesty of *Hamlet,* based on some ideas in Shakespeare, is produced under academic auspices in *Bend Sinister* (Chapter Seven). Its additional dialogue includes a "Freudian" interlude that prefigures Laurence Olivier's Vienna-oriented version (1948), but Nabokov's is not idle fun. Film Tsar Goebbels was a pre-McLuhan master of *poshlost',* and distorting *Hamlet* to serve the State, analogous to Communist/Nazi erasures and revisions of the past, recalls their cinematic glorifications of Ivan the Terrible (1944) and Frederick the Great (1942). *Transparent Things'* Mr. R. is more successful but less fortunate than Nabokov's "Spring in Fialta" stand-in, inasmuch as his wife is "having an affair with Christian Pines [= French slang epithet for the male member—A. A.], son of the well-known cinema man who had directed the film *Golden Windows* (precariously based on the best of our author's novels)" (p. 32). Because the title *Golden Windows* telescopes the climactic hotel fire in *Transparent Things* and frames Hugh Person in the flame-tipped window through which he fails to escape, Nabokov is referring to the book at hand and clearly predicting its fated, unhappy future as a film. *Ada's* "physics fiction" Time-warp works in the opposite direction, which allows Van's book [= an anagram of "Nabokov"] to be filmed within Nabokov's book.

Van's speculative *Letters from Terra,* totally ignored when first published, is transformed by Victor Vitry into a horrific science-fiction farce. *Ada* is an improbable if not impossible book to film, but the screen rights have been optioned to a producer, much to the surprise of many readers (CRITICS NIX "ADA" FLICK, as *Variety* might headline this news). *"Ada* will be enormously difficult to do," grants Nabokov: "the problem of having a suggestion of fantasy, continually, but never overdoing it." [20] Vitry's distortions formulate Nabokov's fears; the director's grandiose effects are blatant, to say the least: "some said [he used] more than a million [extras], others half a million men and as many mirrors. . . . The conception was controversial, the execution flawless" (p. 580). Finding the "historical background absurdly farfetched," Van and Ada consider "starting legal proceedings against Vitry" (p. 581). The disparity between the film's content and technical competence suggests that Vitry, "the greatest cinematic genius ever to direct a picture of such scope" (p. 580), is a blending of several men— Stanley Kubrick, famous for *2001: A Space Odyssey* (1968) and *Lolita* (1962), marshaling the troops of DeMille, D. W. Griffith, or Abel Gance, director of the monumental silent French film, *Napoléon* (1925): "Look at all those tiny soldiers scuttling along very fast across the trench-scarred wilderness, with explosions of mud and things going *pouf-pouf* in silent French now here, now there!" "Three circumstances contributed to the picture's exceptional success," writes Nabokov, taking his measure of contemporary directors and their audiences: "organized religion . . . attempted to have the thing banned"; "in a flashback to a revolution in former France, an unfortunate extra, who played one of the under-executioners, got accidentally decapitated while pulling the comedian Steller, who played a reluctant king, into a guillotinable position"; and "the third, and even more human reason," was the emergence from her "cosmic capsule" of Vitry's naked wife, "Norwegian-born Gedda" [= a literally "liberated" Hedda Gabler], "though, of course, in miniature, a millimeter of maddening femininity dancing in 'the charmed circle of the microscope' like some lewd elf, and revealing, in certain attitudes, I'll be damned, a pinpoint glint of pubic floss, gold-powdered!" (pp. 581–82). She joins a chorus line of sci-fi miniatures extending from *The Lost World* (1925), *The Bride of Frankenstein* (1935), and *The Devil Doll* (1936) to *Doctor Cyclops* (1940), *The Incredible Shrinking Man* (1957), and *Fantastic Voyage* (1966). In addition to suggesting a DeMillean Kubrick, the "brilliant" Victor Vitry [from the French *vitré:* "glazed; of glass"] seems especially to mirror the French director Roger Vadim, at one time (*ca.* 1960) engaged to make a film of *Laughter in the Dark,* who bared Bardot (Mrs. Vadim) in *Et Dieu Créa la Femme* (*And God Created Woman* [1956]) and later exposed Ms. Jane Fonda, his then-blonde wife of that moment, in the satirical space opera *Barbarella* (1967). The corruption of *Letters from Terra* is climaxed by an outpouring of consumer goods modeled on the Davy Crockett and Batman crazes of the nineteen-fifties and sixties: "L.F.T. tiny dolls, L.F.T. breloques of coral and ivory, appeared in souvenir shops. . . . L.F.T. clubs sprouted. L.F.T. girlies minced with mini-menus out of roadside snackettes shaped like spaceships" (p. 582).

"Real" works fare no better on Antiterran reels. Chekhov, says Nabokov, is the Russian writer whose works "I would take on a trip to another planet," but he does not survive the ride to Antiterra. Ada appears with her and Van's mother, Marina Durmanova, in Chekhov's *Four Sisters* (pp. 427–30), but "It was the (somewhat expanded) part of the nun [a stranger to Chekhov, of course—A. A.] that Marina acted in an elaborate film version of the play" (p. 427). Marina, writes Ada, "sticks to Stan's principle of having lore and role overflow into everyday life, insists on keeping it up at the hotel restaurant, drinks tea *v prikusku* ('biting sugar between sips'), and feigns to misunderstand every question in Varvarva's quaint way of feigning stupidity." The studio gives her "a special bungalow, labeled Marina Durmanova" (p. 333), and "the picture and she received a goodly amount of undeserved praise" (p. 427). Poised "at the most delicate moment of [her] career," the printed praise exasperates Ada (" 'Durmanova is superb as the neurotic nun, having transferred an essentially static and episodical part into *et cetera, et cetera, et cetera*' " [p. 427]). Ada appears briefly in a "for adults only" movie called *Don Juan's Last Fling* (pp. 488–89, almost as funny as Mary Astor's and John Barrymore's performances in an earthly *Don Juan* [1926]), directed by "the gifted Yuzlik" [= Russian for "little Hughes," no doubt after Howard himself, who, among other things, invented the cantilevered bra and propelled Jane Russell in *The Outlaw* (1943)]. Chateaubriand's *René* (1802), rewritten by Mlle Larivière as the best-selling Book of the Fortnight *Les Enfants Maudits* (1887 [p. 198]), finally reaches the screen as another "Painted Western," *The Young and the Doomed* (1890), starlet Ada's scene cut out, except for a distinct shadow of her elbow— the fate, it would seem, of all "californized" (p. 199) classics:

> [Mlle Larivière] had had two adolescents, in a French castle, poison their widowed mother who had seduced a young neighbor, the lover of one of her twins. The author had made many concessions to the freedom of the times, and the foul fancy of scriptwriters; but both she and the leading lady [Marina] disavowed the final result of multiple tamperings with the plot that had now become the story of a murder in Arizona, the victim being a widower about to marry an alcoholic prostitute, whom Marina, quite sensibly, refused to impersonate. (p. 424)

Marina has an affair with the film's director, G. A. Vronsky— named, of course, after the dashing officer in *Anna Karenina* (1876), though a good deal has been lost—and gained—in his transmutation. G. A., as he is always addressed, California mogul-style, is "elderly, baldheaded, with a spread of grizzled fur on his fat chest, [and] was alternately sipping his vodka-and-tonic and feeding Marina typewritten pages from a folder" (p. 197).

Tolstoy's shade has thrice been shaken by absurd film adaptations of *Anna* (1927 [as *Love*], 1935, and 1948), and Nabokov's *jeu* may be of some solace to "old Lyovin," as Van warmly calls him. Although Nabokov has not viewed any of those versions, several unintentionally humorous still-photos have sufficed, especially one of Vronsky (John Gilbert) *en profil,* an aquiline bust all but choking on its collar. "Tell me, have you read Tolstoy?" Axel Rex asks a film star in *Laughter in the Dark.* " 'Doll's Toy?' queried Dorianna Karenina. 'No, I'm afraid not. Why?' " (p. 191). "I would like my readers to brood over my singular power of prophecy," says Nabokov, "for the name of the leading lady (Dorianna Karenina) in the picture invented by me in 1931 prefigured that of the actress (Anna Karina) who was to play Margot [almost] forty years later in the film *Laughter in the Dark"* (directed by Tony Richardson, adapted by Edward Bond, and starring Nicol Williamson and Mlle Karina, the setting disastrously moved from old Berlin to Richardson's own mod London [1969]).[21] The cast of *Four Sisters* includes Dawn de Laire (p. 430) and the melancholy Irish actress Lenore Colline, who is named after a phrase in Chateaubriand's ballad, *Le Montagnard émigré* (1806), an "incestuous" allusion thematically appropriate to *Ada* (p. 428) and another joke that scores against filmdom's international propensity for silly and pretentious screen names. *Four Sisters* is filmed "in Universal City," the actual name of a huge Hollywood studio lot (p. 333), but its existence in *Ada*'s "1889" makes it something more than a realistic detail. *Ada*'s fantastic antiworld transmogrifies all American place names save two; Los Angeles and Hollywood remain "Los Angeles" (p. 332) and "Hollywood" (p. 425), deemed fantastic enough as they are by a novelist who spent six months there in 1960, adapting his *Lolita* for the screen.

Humbert dismisses the Hollywood musical as "an essentially grief-proof sphere of existence wherefrom death and truth were barred" (p. 172). Throughout his fiction Nabokov suggests how the deepest, most personal truths may be trivialized by a concurrence of movie conventions and Stan Slavsky's applied lessons in "drama, despair, hope." On the eve of his beloved father's scheduled duel, fearful young Nabokov "refought all the famous duels a Russian boy knew so well," * none of them resembling "the ludicrous back-to-back-march-face-about-bang-bang performance of movie and cartoon fame." [22] Luzhin is deserted by his "chess father," impresario Valentinov, who "disappeared [and found] fresh amusement in the movie business, that mysterious astrological business where they read scripts and look for stars" (p. 93). A perverter of the imagination, like Axel Rex in *Laughter in the Dark* and Clare Quilty in *Lolita,* his name a play on his heartlessness and the reigning movie idol of the twenties, he reenters Luzhin's life as Dr. [!] Valentinov of the Veritas [Latin for "truth"; "real life"] Film Company, who offers a befuddled Luzhin a part in a trashy film that would re-stage Luzhin's terminated game with Grandmaster Turati. Understanding the offer as a last illusion, a trap meant to inveigle him into playing tournament chess again, Luzhin's "next move" is clear, and he kills himself (pp. 248ff.). A similar counterpoint is effected in *Pale Fire* (1962). John and Sybil Shade are watching television the night of their ungainly daughter's disastrous blind date. Abandoned by her disappointed companion, distraught Hazel Shade throws herself into an icy lake, and the moment of her death is synchronized with the TV preview of *Remorse,* a movie:

> **The famous face flowed in, fair and inane:**
> **The parted lips, the swimming eyes, the grain**
> **Of beauty on the cheek, odd gallicism,**
> **And the soft form dissolving in the prism**
> **Of corporate desire**

writes John Shade in his poem *Pale Fire* (ll. 450–54),[23] the watery verbs describing his daughter's fate, the actress' "soft form" in sharp contrast to bedeviled Hazel's desperate search for

---

* In Nabokov's story, "An Affair of Honor" (1927), set in Germany, an unhappy, disoriented expatriate, Anton Petrovich, thinks about his imminent duel, and imagines how he would turn up his jacket collar against the chill of the early morning: "That's how they did it in that film I saw." Although he also alludes to diluted Pushkin ("What does Onegin do in the opera?"), his initial vision defines the absurd and pitiable incongruity manifest in his attempt to assert old codes in the strange new world of the emigration (*Nabokov's Quartet* [New York, 1966], pp. 31–32). This idea, all pity and pathos removed, is central to the story "The Assistant Producer" (1943).

1475-65

History as fiction: Marlene Dietrich as Catherine the Great (with Sam Jaffe as Grand Duke Peter, holding one of his toy soldiers) in Josef von Sternberg's *The Scarlet Empress* (1934, "Based on a diary of Catherine II"—only one point of view, tsarina as unreliable narrator or prejudiced witness). Sternberg's Russian music, art, costume, and decor are a carefully stylized, anachronistic historical mishmash—High Church Tchaikovsky and Wagner, eighteenth-century Art Deco, Byzantine Expressionism, Romanesque Art Nouveau, *Belle Epôque–Wizard of Oz* couture—which is one reason the film has become a Camp classic, though the cultists (along with the Marxist critics of the thirties) miss the point of its parody of "authentic" historiography, as do the purists who would dismiss it as *poshlost'*, or a product of the Germanic vision of barbaric, "oriental" Russia. Unlike the naive, kitschy anachronisms in many costume melodramas, the "mistakes" in style and iconography are intentional and thematically correct. Of course "it was not a replica," says Sternberg in his autobiography, and, like the clockwork toy in *Pale Fire*, Sam Jaffe's little soldier is emblematic; the creator's playfulness is serious indeed.

deathless, elusive truths (the actress, says Nabokov, is Marilyn Monroe, not yet a suicide). In *Laughter in the Dark,* Albert Albinus casts himself into what he had hoped would be a love story, but instead finds himself trapped in a fatal thriller, the blind victim, literally, of cheap romance and his own movie shoot-out.

Nothing less than history itself is trivialized and effaced by *Ada*'s entrepreneurs, from doll-makers to film directors. Although the Vitry-Veen *Letters from Terra* clearly rehearses the first half of twentieth-century history, that fact is completely lost on enthusiastic McLuhanesque audiences so inured to sci-fi conventions that all history, including their own, has ceased to exist (p. 582). Nabokov's is a telling perception, to which this writer can sadly attest, having recently endured a campus film showing that shrewdly paired *The March of Time*'s "The Battle for North Africa" (1942) and *Casablanca* (1943), almost everyone's favorite bad movie. The spectacle of real men dying on newsreel deserts elicted jeers and cheers from the audience ("Right on!"); Bogart's and Bergman's war, save for the obligatory "Play it, Sam" applause, enthralled them all. "Strangely enough, that vile script was enacted in reality," says the narrator of "The Assistant Producer" (1943), a White Army western and spies-and-intrigue thriller based on actual events, and a story that presents history as fiction.[24] If history isn't a nightmare, then it is an open-ended, anti-Aristotelian melodrama, each new terrible twist in the "plot" having already been anticipated by the popular forms that reflect or vulgarly refract modern realities. "Meaning?" asks the narrator-scenarist-impresario, opening the show. "Well, because life is merely that—an Assistant Producer. Tonight we shall go to the movies. Back to the Thirties, and down the Twenties, and round the corner to the old Europe Picture Palace" (p. 75), and throughout the tale, cinematic form and metaphor cohere in a brilliantly projected series of fields of vision, not without humor: "Perhaps he found a haven in Germany and was given there some small administrative job in the Baedecker Training School for Young Spies. Perhaps he returned to the land where he had taken towns singlehanded. Perhaps he did not. Perhaps he was summoned by whoever his arch-boss was and told with that slight foreign accent and special brand of blandness that we all know: 'I am afraid, my friend, you are nott nee–ded any more'—and as X turns to go Dr. Puppenmeister's delicate index presses a button at the edge of his impassive writing desk and a trap yawns under X, who plunges to his death (he who knows 'too much')," writes Nabokov at the end of the story, on a page accidentally omitted from all printings after its appearance in Nabokov's *Nine Stories* (1947). "Dmitri loved a series of thriller pictures when he was nine or so [1943, *The Falcon,* says Dmitri], and we would see them at a cinema in Harvard Square," says Nabokov. "The hero [Tom Conway] was a broad-shouldered, handsome American who was always walking into places where things were stacked and stored. They would inevitably crash down upon him, but he would emerge unscathed. The Master Spy had one line, which he used continually on his captives: 'Our methods are simple but *ver–ry* effective.' " Nothing, it seems, is wasted on the literary anatomist.

"The Assistant Producer" also renders personal history as fiction: one of Nabokov's most arresting phantasmagoric images of *émigré* life in Berlin is that of Russian film extras playing themselves, as it were, in German films. In *Mashenka,* Nabokov's first novel (1926, translated as *Mary*),

Nothing was beneath [*émigré* Ganin's] dignity; more than once he had even sold his shadow, as many of us have. In other words he went out to the [Berlin] suburbs to work as a movie extra on a set, in a fairground barn, where light seethed with a mystical hiss from the huge facets of lamps that were aimed, like cannon, at a crowd of extras, lit to a deathly brightness. They would fire a barrage of murderous brilliance, illuminating the painted wax of motionless faces, then expiring with a click—but for a long time yet there would glow, in those elaborate crystals, dying red sunsets—our human shame. The deal was clinched, and our anonymous shadows sent out all over the world.[25]

The figurative violence of that dark but well-lit scene is striking, and Nabokov's dying sunset is the right directorial (and historical) touch, defining the emigration's pervasive twilight mood. On a subsequent evening, Ganin takes his silly girlfriend to the cinema: "On the screen moved luminous, bluish-gray shapes. A prima donna, who had once in her life committed an involuntary murder, suddenly remembered it while playing the role of a murderess in opera. Rolling her improbably large eyes, she collapsed supine onto the stage. The auditorium swam slowly into view, the public applauded, the boxes and stalls rose in an ecstasy of approval. Suddenly Ganin sensed that he was watching something vaguely yet horribly familiar" (pp. 20–21), the film in which he had appeared as an extra, "acting in total ignorance of what the film was about. He remembered young men in threadbare but marvelously tailored clothes, women's faces smeared with mauve and yellow make-up, and those innocent exiles, old men and plain girls who were banished far to the rear simply to fill in the background. On the screen that cold barn was now transformed into a comfortable auditorium, sacking became velvet, and a mob of paupers a theatre audience" (p. 21). The reader will soon realize (as Ganin does not) that the young man's horror is compounded subliminally by the fact that the bogus musicale in the "cold barn" is a travesty of "a charity concert staged in a barn on the border of his parents' estate" in pre-Revolutionary Russia (p. 44), where, "Amid the hot yellow glare" and the sounds of an opera bass from St. Petersburg supported by the village school choir, Ganin had first glimpsed lovely Mary, his emblem of the past (pp. 45–46). Seated unhappily in a Berlin cinema, "Straining his eyes, with a deep shudder of shame he recognized himself among all those people clapping to order" on the screen (p. 21).

Ganin's doppelgänger also stood and clapped, over there, alongside the very striking-looking man with the black beard and the ribbon across his chest. Because of that beard and his starched shirt he had always landed in the front row; in the intervals he munched a sandwich and then, after the take, would put on a wretched old coat over his evening dress and return home to a distant part of Berlin, where he worked as a compositor in a printing plant.

And at the present moment Ganin felt not only shame but also a sense of the fleeting evanescence of human life. There on the screen his haggard image, his sharp uplifted face and clapping hands merged into the gray kaleidoscope of other figures; a moment later, swinging like a ship, the auditorium vanished and now the scene showed an aging, world-famous actress giving a very skillful representation of a dead young woman. (pp. 21–22)

Only when Mary is "buried" will Ganin come to life. Later that night, "when he went to bed and listened to the trains passing through that cheerless house in which lived seven Russian lost shades, the whole of life seemed like a piece of film-making where heedless extras knew nothing of the picture in which they were taking part" (p. 22). At the end of *Mary*, he stands by the deathbed of Podtyagin, the *émigré* poet who has lost his passport and all remaining hope: "Ganin, gripping the edge of the bed with a strong white hand, looked in the old man's face, and once again he remembered these flickering, shadowy doppelgängers, the casual Russian film extras, sold for ten marks apiece and still flitting, God knows where, across the white gleam of a screen" (p. 110), the animate and inanimate rendered in death's monochrome.

The terrible fate and shame of the *émigré* poet Marina Tsvetaeva were in their way "cinematic" too. *I Am a Fugitive from a Chain Gang* (1932, with Paul Muni) was her favorite film because it mirrored her life, she said—and her husband, who on the eve of World War II turned out to be a double-agent, also worked as a movie extra, underscoring the metaphoric possibilities of that precarious and surreal occupation. (Tsvetaeva followed him back to the Soviet Union, and committed suicide in 1941.) Nabokov's first spy thriller, *Chelovek iz SSSR* [*The Man from the USSR*], an untranslated five-act play which was produced in Berlin in 1926, again evokes the shadowy trade in extras: an elderly, studio-bound ex-Baron, now a waiter, is the Soviet agent's "contact" in Act One's basement night club scene, and still wears his movie eye make-up (to save time between jobs and thus gain tips?). Marianna, the play's young *émigré* heroine, is a full-time film actress; role-playing and survival cohere. "You certainly are an unbelievable character," she says to the bold undercover agent. Marianna is "terribly tired" from that day's filming; the star, Pia Mora (the kind of satirical touch which will be extended in *Laughter in the Dark, Lolita,* and *Ada*), has acted and behaved badly, requiring eighteen takes for a single scene [Mora = "love" and "death" by way of Theda Bara, her name an anagram of "Arab Death," as everyone in the twenties knew]. "My role is the most crucial one in the whole movie, the role of a Communist. A hellishly difficult part," Marianna complains, unaware that she is about to become involved with a real Communist, and that her fiction will now be activated and unreeled.[26] Seventeen years later, in "The Assistant Producer," Nabokov once more records how "German film companies, which kept sprouting like poisonous mushrooms in those days (just before the child of light learned to talk), found cheap labor in hiring those among the Russian *émigrés* whose only hope and profession was their past —that is, a set of totally unreal people—to represent 'real' audiences in pictures," and Nabokov's "mushroom" image is not fanciful; in 1925 German film companies produced 228 features, as opposed to France's 77 and Britain's 44. "The dovetailing of one phantasm into another produced upon a sensitive person the impression of living in a Hall of Mirrors, or rather a prison of mirrors, and not even knowing which was the glass and which was yourself" (p. 83), he concludes, compressing *Mary's* dominant metaphor. "Yes," said Nabokov in 1971, "I have been a tuxedoed extra as Ganin had been (and a threadbare extra officer, too), and that passage in *Mashenka* is a rather raw bit of 'real life.' No, I don't remember the names of those films," and one can imagine a demented biographer, his eye on a definitive volume, squinting at grainy old German movies for a fleeting glimpse of Nabokov.

Reel life, to recycle an old pun, has at least twice developed that "Hall of Mirrors" image of *émigré* existence. *Surrender* (1927) represents the only American appearance of the famous Russian actor Ivan Mosjoukine (*né* Mozzhukin, 1889–1939), whose romantic swashbuckler roles were much admired by adolescent Nabokov (1912–1916). Mosjoukine made his own miraged appearance in the first stage of young Nabokov's life as exile. After the Revolution his family moved to the Crimea, where Nabokov senior became Minister of Justice in the hopeful Regional Government. One morning in the summer of 1918, with real battles raging in the north (the Civil War), Nabokov suddenly met on a mountain trail

a strange cavalier, clad in a Circassian costume, with a tense, perspiring face painted a fantastic yellow. He kept furiously tugging at his horse, which, without heeding him, proceeded down the steep path at a curiously purposeful walk, like that of an offended person leaving a party. I had seen runaway horses, but I had never seen a walkaway one before, and my astonishment was given a still more pleasurable edge when I recognized the unfortunate rider as Mozzhuhin [Mosjoukine—A. A.], whom Tamara [his first love, the model for Mary—A. A.] and I had so often admired on the screen. The film *Hajji Murad* (after Tolstoy's tale of that gallant, rough-riding mountain chief) was being rehearsed on the mountain pastures of the range. "Stop that brute [*Derzhite proklyatoe zhivotnoe*]," he said through his teeth as he saw me, but at the same moment, with a mighty sound of crunching and crashing stones, two authentic Tatars came running down to the rescue, and I trudged on, with my butterfly net, toward the upper crags where the Euxine race of the Hippolyte Grayling was expecting me. (*Speak, Memory*, p. 247)

All rehearsals concluded, the party over, both actor and carefree lepist would soon become permanent *émigrés; Surrender* starred Mosjoukine as a White Army officer who loses everything in the Civil War that had provided a backdrop for the actor's unreal meeting with Nabokov. A publicity photograph poses Mosjoukine with Edward Sloman, *Surrender*'s director, and some of those dazed Russian *émigré* extras "whose only hope and profession was their past." The theme is memorably orchestrated in Josef von Sternberg's *The Last Command* (1928), in which the great German actor Emil Jannings plays an ex-tsarist general who, now a poor old man in Hollywood, applies for work as an extra and is cast to replay his glorious former self in the film-within-the-film. The cruel, dizzying commission and that film's Communist director (William Powell) combine to drive Jannings insane. (Sternberg's scenario was inspired by a "true story" rather than, say, Pirandello's play *Henry IV* [1922].) Still-photos often fail to communicate the essence of a tragic performance or, even worse, freeze what seems to be an overblown expression, always a possibility in the context of the more stylized "theatrical" acting of the silent cinema. The haunting quality of *The Last Command,* however, is preserved in several stills: Jannings about to don his "costume" in the extras' common dressing room; Jannings being inspected like a young recruit by the assistant director and prop man, ready with a box of authentic medals; or the spectacle of Grand Duke Jannings, imprisoned by mirrors and carried away by his re-creation of the past as he bravely confronts a mob of revolutionaries or arrogantly reviews the troops of his last command, many of them played by actual Russian *émigrés*. "I had fortified my image of the Russian Revolution by including in my cast of extra players an assortment of Russian ex-admirals and generals, a dozen Cossacks, and two former members of the Duma, all victims of the Bolsheviks, and, in particular, an expert on borscht by the name of Kobliansky. These men, especially one Cossack general who insisted on keeping my car spotless, viewed Jannings' effort to be Russian with such disdain that I had to order them to conceal it," writes Field Marshal von Sternberg in his autobiography, *Fun in a Chinese Laundry* (1965).[27]

The most literally terrible version of Nabokov's prison trope was achieved by the Nazis. Interned in Theresienstadt, the "showplace" concentration camp maintained for inspection teams from the International Red Cross, Kurt Gerron (*né* Gerson) was forced to direct the anti-Semitic propaganda film *Der Führer schenkt den Juden eine Stadt* [*The Führer Gives the Jews a City*, 1944], which cast Jews as Jews. When the filming was completed, Gerron, his technical crew and actors were shipped to Auschwitz and killed. *Transport z raje* [*Transport from Paradise,* 1961], a Czech film, is based on that specific infamy.

Shame, rather than terror, and a vertiginous sense of illusion were experienced by many of Hollywood's more successful *émigré* directors, musicians, and performers, and it must have hurt less if one possessed a mordant sense of humor; unable to obtain work as a director, Otto Preminger had to play monocled Nazi generals, a fate preferable to Gerron's, however. Many other Austrian and German refugees (most of them Jewish) were cast as Nazi spies or leaders: Conrad Veidt and Hans von Twardowski (two of *Dr. Caligari*'s alumni), Peter Lorre, Fritz Kortner, and resolute Martin Kosleck (*né* Nikolai Yoshkin in 1907), a veteran of both the Russian and German stage who impersonated Josef Goebbels in five films, including *The Hitler Gang* (1944), with its all-star cast of German, Russian, and Polish exiles playing the men who had oppressed them. Kosleck also played the evil doctor who mortally drains the blood of blond Russian children in *The*

North Star (1943), one of several contemporary tributes to beleaguered, bucolic Mother Russia, the sort of films which contributed to Nabokov's cinematic vision in "The Assistant Producer." Red Army victories warmed and softened several *émigré* hearts and minds; thus director Gregory Ratoff's (1897–1961) saccharine *Song of Russia* (1944), an embarrassing companion to the pro-Stalin, fellow-traveling *Mission to Moscow* (1943), whose portrait of kindly Uncle Joe and his justifiable purge trials, his reasonable 1939 pact with Germany, and his fair-minded invasion of Finland (recent history as instant fiction) would surely have moved moviegoer Pnin to tears.

Because of their heavy accents, gifted Russians were usually cast, humiliatingly, as stereotyped Comic Russians (Decadent ex-Count or Countess, Compulsive Gambler, Gabby Bartender, Aristocratic Cabdriver—the *émigré* equivalents of the black actor's Uncle Tom roles) or, when not being asked to parody their past, limited to character parts (Akim Tamiroff [1899–1972], the Mexican *bandido*). Alla Nazimova (1879–1945), an early expatriate, played the Stoic Peasant in several World War II films; Olga Baclanova (1899–), a well-known singer and actress in Russia, became a hen-woman in *Freaks* (1932); and Maria Ouspenskaya (1876–1949), an exile from the Moscow Art Theatre who would die horribly in her bed from a cigarette-ignited fire, appeared as Mother Gin Sling's aged, silent Chinese amah in Sternberg's *Shanghai Gesture* (1941), and as the gypsy fortuneteller in *The Wolf Man* (1941) and *Frankenstein Meets the Wolf Man* (1943). Her role as the queen of the hidden valley of women under the Apeman's protection in *Tarzan and the Amazons* (1945) was a far (jungle) cry from *The Three Sisters*.

One generation's trash (and individual pain) is another's Camp. Since younger readers do not remember or cannot imagine a time when pop music went uncelebrated and motion pictures were not respected, if not revered, it is worth remarking that Nabokov's overridingly negative (no pun is intended) attitude is quite in keeping with his generation's opinions about mass culture in general—opinions which extend all the way back to Plato's

Gorgias, where Socrates, the premier critic of kitsch, makes the basic Platonic distinction between the enlightening, rational arts and the pleasureful, rhetorical, and hence counterfeit non-arts (or "knacks"). Nabokov's contemporaries Kurt Weill (1900–1950) and Bertolt Brecht (1898–1956), very active in Berlin during Nabokov's residence there, offer interesting points of reference, particularly since Brecht's Marxism, however anarchistic and unorthodox, is of course repugnant to Nabokov, and also because Nabokov, circa 1924, contributed cabaret sketches and song lyrics to "a quite fashionable Russian *émigré* night club called *'Sinyaya ptitsa'* ["The Blue Bird"], named after Maeterlinck's play," one of the Berlin *émigré* equivalents of the cabarets which fed the imaginations of Weill and Brecht. (Nabokov did it solely for money, and saw perhaps one performance.) *Happy End,* Weill's and Brecht's 1929 musical play, is about Chicago gangsters and Salvation Army girls; the head criminal, called the Governor, was played by Peter Lorre. Weill and Brecht had not yet visited America. Drawing upon more popular materials than had Brecht's earlier play, *Im Dickicht der Städte (In the Jungle of the Cities,* subtitled "A Match Between Two Men in the Giant City of Chicago" [1923]), or Franz Kafka's fabular, unfinished *Amerika* (1927), Weill's and Brecht's imaginary land had as its données newspaper stories, pulp fiction (*Black Mask* magazine), Dos Passos' *Manhattan Transfer* (1925), Hemingway's "The Killers" (1927), and Hollywood's romantic, pre-Depression period gangster films (*Underworld* [1927] and *The Docks of New York* [1928], both directed by Josef von Sternberg, soon to arrive in Berlin to direct *Der Blaue Engel [The Blue Angel]*). The title, *Happy End,* was in English, an explicitly ironic and mordant reference; America, not Germany in 1928, was the land of "Happy Endings," as they are (or were) willed by the conventions of popular culture and historical circumstances. The gusty *"Das Lied von der Harten Nuss"* ["The Song of the Hard Nut" (= head— A. A.)], a musical caprice in the manner of Chicago jazz, is addressed to hard-boiled American writing and behavior, as it was stylized in the popular arts and in Hemingway and Dos Passos

The Death of Argus.

"One of them had eyes like the film actor Veidt" (*Laughter in the Dark*): Conrad Veidt's horrific, heavily mascaraed eyes were featured in *The Cabinet of Dr. Caligari* (1919), in which he played Cesare, the closeted somnambulist. Here they appear in the same director's *The Hands of Orlac* (1925), Nabokov's favorite German film.

Cinematic *poshlost'*: Garbo and Gilbert as Anna Karenina and Vronsky in *Love*.

"Because of that beard and his starched shirt he had always landed in the front row . . . after the take [he] would put on a wretched old coat over his evening dress and return home" (*Mary*): the German actor Emil Jannings as an extra in *The Last Command;* the other man is a genuine Russian *émigré* extra.

I Am a Fugitive from a Chain Gang, the *émigré* condition according to Marina Tsvetaeva.

Personal history as fiction: *Surrender* (Mosjoukine and director Sloman at the center), and its *émigré* extras. "I wore such a uniform in one film," said Nabokov when shown this still, and he pointed to the officer on the right. "Am I here? No."

A prison of mirrors: Jannings faces the extras in *The Last Command*'s film-within-the film, the Reds played by extra Whites.

Personal history as fiction (continued): One of the Russian monarchist assassins who had murdered V. D. Nabokov in 1922 was later released from his Berlin jail by the Nazis and put in charge of the Gestapo's efficient *émigré* section. Countless Russian Jews thus passed through Theresienstadt (Terezin), the "showplace" concentration camp. The propaganda film made there cast Jews of many nationalities as "Jews." "We are happy here in Theresienstadt," they said,

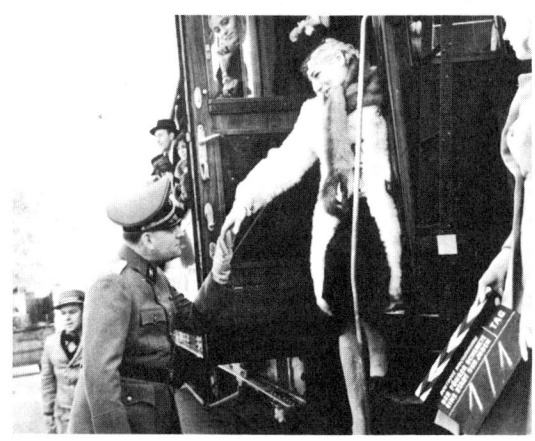

smiling over the sumptuous meals which, off-camera, they were not permitted to eat. *Transport from Paradise,* a Czech film, commemorates them as no gravestone ever can. Center: "Welcome to Theresienstadt!" A guest arrives in the film-within-the-film. Bottom: the transport from paradise departs for Auschwitz.

Walter Huston, a Russian peasant in *The North Star,* flanked by Nazi doctors Martin Kosleck, an *émigré* from Soviet Russia and a refugee from Nazi Germany, and (on the right) Austrian-born Erich von Stroheim, who played Field Marshal Rommel in the same year's *Five Graves to Cairo.*

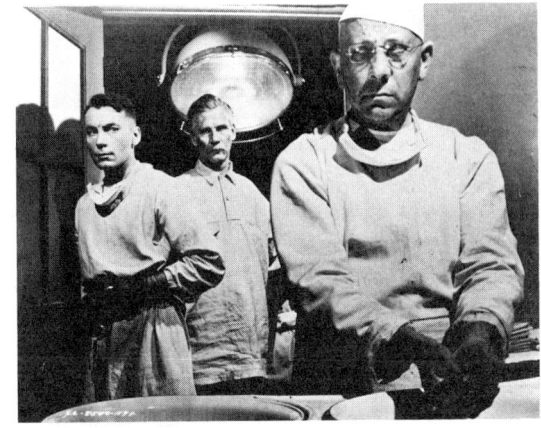

Hitler (Robert Watson) and Goebbels (Martin Kosleck) in *The Hitler Gang,* a veritable Madame Tussaud's Wax Works of Nazi leaders impersonated by refugee and *émigré* actors. The Reichstag burns behind them.

Mothers Russia: Ann Harding, Anne Baxter, and Ann Carter, Russian peasants awaiting the German army in *The North Star.* Their humble wall is graced by a portrait of Pushkin, curtained by a towel. This publicity-still is by the distinguished photographer Margaret Bourke-White, who had covered the Russian front in 1941–42, and was flown back from North Africa (courtesy of Samuel Goldwyn) to document Hollywood's front.

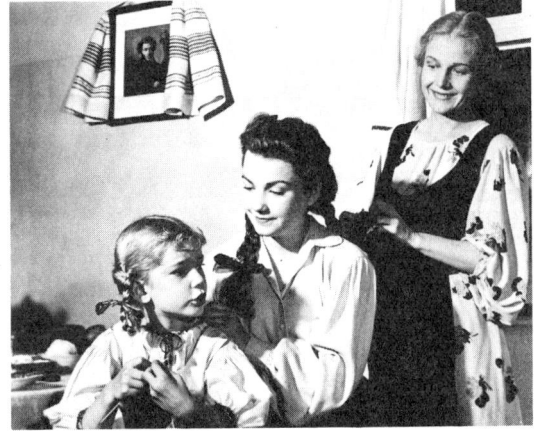

Celluloid Stalinism: left to right, U.S. Ambassador Davies (Walter Huston), Stalin (Manart Kippen), and *émigré* Vladimir Sokoloff in *Mission to Moscow.* An actor in Moscow, Sokoloff continued to perform in Berlin, Paris, and Hollywood, where he would return to "Moscow" and preside benevolently as Kalinin, president of the U.S.S.R. A propaganda exhibit maintained today at the Nabokovs' summer estate asserts that V. N. returned there in 1943 as a Nazi officer (played by Conrad Veidt?).

Two publicity stills from *Song of Russia,* a musical tribute to Russia's fighting spirit. The story, as reviewer Bosley Crowther capsuled it, is about "a young American caught in Russia by love and war." Before the war Robert Taylor, as a symphonic conductor, meets and marries a musical Russian girl. The war separates them. Reunited at the end of the film they are dispatched to America by plane "to state the spirit of Russia through their art."

The film's musical score is adapted from Tchaikovsky; an additional number, "Russia Is Her Name," was provided by Jerome Kern and E. Y. Harburg, and performed by a chorus of villagers. The *émigrés* in the cast included Vladimir Sokoloff and Michael Chekhov (1891–1955), the founder of actors' schools in London and New York, who had his Hollywood debut in *North Star.*

Emigré Leonid Kinsky (1905–   ) played a Soviet revolutionary in *Trouble in Paradise* (1932), sang "I'm an Old Cowpoke" in *Rhythm on the Range* (1936), and was Sasha the *émigré* bartender in *Casablanca* (right).

Stravinsky (center) visits Hollywood, 1937. Movie executive Boris Morros, an *émigré* and a U.S. agent (see his *Ten Years a Counterspy, 1957*), is on the left, next to Claire Trevor. By I. S.'s side is Akim Tamiroff, whose long Hollywood career and range of caricature and mimicry—Arab trader, American Indian, Italian gangster, Chinese warlord, Corsican killer, Spanish guerrilla, Mexican *bandido* or bodyguard— begs an unhappy question.

Tamiroff's performance in *Touch of Evil* (1958) as a grotesque Tijuana racketeer (about to be killed here by Orson Welles) is typically skillful, but the patent-leather toupee, pencil-line moustache, and dusky make-up cannot mask the intelligent eyes that belong to an actor who more than once must have pondered (if not lamented) the straight dramatic roles that many aging American "heavies" were allowed to play (e.g., Edward G. Robinson).

Olga Baclanova in *Freaks.*

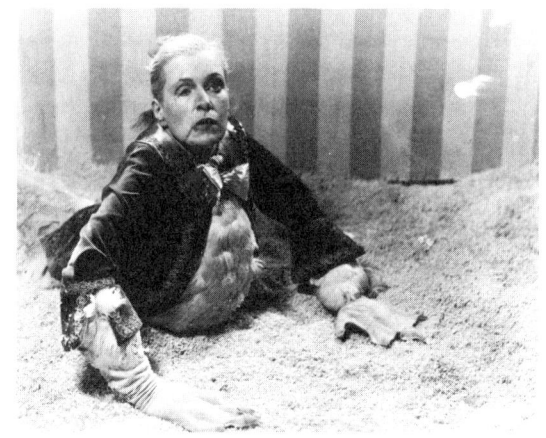

Emigré Mischa Auer (*né* Ounskowsky, 1905–1967), having played small Hollywood roles for years, successfully impersonated a gorilla in *My Man Godfrey* (1936), thereby convincing producers he could play idiotic, popeyed ex-noblemen and gloomy ballet masters ("Confidentially, eet steenks!" he says of everything in *You Can't Take It With You* [1938, right], from the Bolshevik Revolution to the dancing of pupil Ann Miller, who aspires to be a Pavlova).

"Think of all your countrymen who have made it big in the movies," says Groucho Marx to Sasha the Comic Russian Waiter in *Room Service* (1938), trying to cadge a free meal with a bogus offer of stardom. *"Who?"* asks the innocent Sasha (and Russian waiters and barmen are invariably Sashas). "Gregory Ratoff!" "Nazimova!" "Ginger Rogerovich!!" answer Chico and Groucho in rapid-fire succession. Right: Johnny Weismuller, Shirley O'Hara (prone), and inscrutable *émigrée* Maria Ouspenskaya in *Tarzan and the Amazons.*

Harold Lloyd in *Safety Last*, the model for Luzhin's suicide in *The Defense*.

"No wonder one peers over the parapet into an inviting abyss," writes Kinbote. Right: Buster Keaton.

Laurel and Hardy test Shirin's *Hoary Abyss* in *Liberty*.

Brats enjoy the natural province of play.

A Night at the Opera.

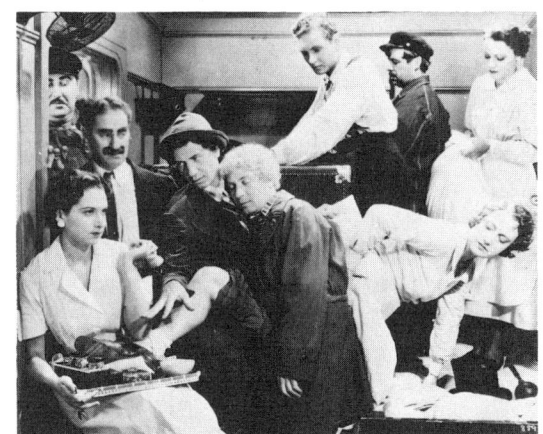

M'sieur Pierre's sartorial elegance: Laurel and Hardy and Dennis King in *Fra Diavolo,* an invitation to a hanging.

The comic rhythm and velocity of *Invitation to a Beheading*'s end: Chico, Groucho, and Harpo *Go West* (1940).

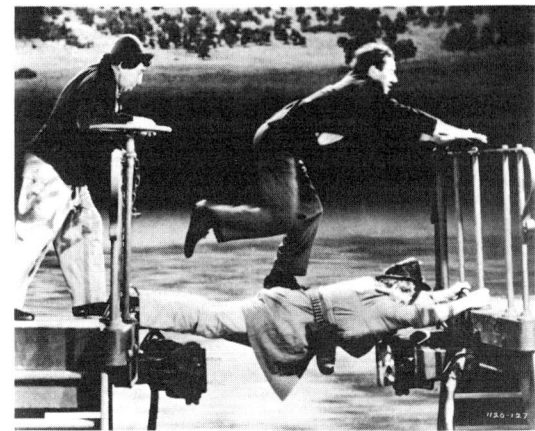

The apotheosis of a weakling: Harold Lloyd in *The Freshman*.

Laughter in the Dark, a 1939 necessity: Garbo and Douglas in *Ninotchka*.

(at the end of *Manhattan Transfer,* Jimmy Herf's hero is a man in Philadelphia who was hit on the head with a lead pipe for wearing a straw hat too early in the season). The effect of the song, however, is ambiguous; Brecht's lyrics are bitter, but Weill's music is an *hommage,* akin to Debussy's *Cakewalk* (1908) and *Minstrels* (1910), Satie's *"Ragtime du paquebot"* (from his *Parade,* first performed in Paris by Diaghilev's Ballets Russes [1917]), or, to contrast Nabokov with another grandly allusive Russian *émigré* master of parody and pastiche, Stravinsky's ragtime-influenced *L'Histoire du soldat* (1918), *Ragtime for Eleven Instruments* (1918), *Piano-Rag Music* (1919), and, in America, *Preludium for Jazz Ensemble* (1937), its satirical "dance band" finale notwithstanding. Stravinsky's stirring orchestration of *The Star-Spangled Banner* (1941), never the catchiest of American tunes, is the ultimate *hommage,* an *émigré's* expression of gratitude. Charles Ives and Aaron Copland are among the "serious" American composers who have utilized popular lore and song; the latter's *Dance Symphony* (1925) was excerpted from his *Grohg,* an unproduced ballet inspired by Diaghilev's extravaganzas and the German vampire film *Nosferatu* (1922). Brecht and Weill curiously anticipate the French film directors Jean-Pierre Melville (*né* Jean-Pierre Grumbach!), François Truffaut, and Jean-Luc Godard, who, thirty years later—also distanced by geographical remove— would absorb American popular materials, but in a totally positive spirit, and transform them into myth and an apolitical *paysage moralisé.* Weill's and Brecht's greatest work, *Aufstieg und Fall Der Stadt Mahagonny* (*Rise and Fall of the City of Mahagonny* [1930]), is set in another American fantasia, a lawless frontier town that also embodies Berlin. Weill parodies and quotes from many trashy German popular melodies ("That is eternal art," says one of the men of Mahagonny, listening to a maudlin piano solo [scene nine]), while Brecht's lyrics for the haunting "Alabama Song" are Tin Pan Alley by way of a kind of pidgin English: "Oh! Moon of Alabama / We now must say good-bye / We've lost our good old mama / And must have whiskey / Oh, you know why!" (the song's title and lyrics are in English). Similarly absurd are the lyrics and rhymes of Lolita's favorite song, "Little Carmen" ("And the stars, and the cars, and the bars and the barmen . . ." [p. 63])— Mérimée updated as movie melodrama:

> **And the something town where so gaily, arm in Arm, we went, and our final row, And the gun I killed you with, O my Carmen, The gun I am holding now.   (p. 64)**

Brecht believed that pidgin English would become the first international language, and it very nearly has, spoken by bar girls in Saigon, rock-'n'-roll singers in Tokyo, patois-infected teenagers throughout America, and their inarticulate *imagos* on the screen (*Easy Rider* [1969], *McCabe and Mrs. Miller* [1971]). "No sweat, man," said a South Vietnamese army deserter to a *New York Times* reporter as they retreated through inflamed Hue in the debacle of 1972. The witless lingo of Lolita and her friends is well recorded, a true finding that demonstrates the contagious banality of ads, bad movies, and hit songs worthy (if that is the word) of Weill and Brecht.

The commercial American cinema of the past has been rescued and redeemed in recent years (and rightly so), but it took too long; as with jazz and the hard-boiled writers in the thirties, French critics led the way in the fifties (André Bazin). Critical overpraise of "popular culture" has now created a retrograde mandarin backlash reminiscent of the thirties, when, except for an acknowledged trove of silent cinema classics (mainly Soviet), and perhaps the Marx Brothers (didn't T. S. Eliot admire Groucho?), most intellectuals on both sides of the Atlantic regarded movies with a hostility, or at best an indifference, based on aesthetic and socio-political principles.[28] Rudolf Arnheim's *Film* (1933), first published in Germany (expanded and reprinted as *Film as Art* [1957]), argued that the arrival of sound and color represented a decline in artistic form, while the sociological and anthropological poles of opinion were defined by such books as Leo Rosten's *Hollywood: The Movie Colony, The Movie Makers* (1941) and Hortense Powdermaker's *Hollywood, the*

Dream Factory (1950). With the exception of Hemingway, who sold his novels (rather than himself) to Hollywood, all the major and a good many minor American writers worked in California as screenwriters during the nineteen-thirties. Filthy lucre and artistic exhaustion were not the only forces that sent them westward. By failing to buy novels or attend plays, the American public could sentence a dedicated writer to a season in hell (as life "out there" was deemed); the writer, in turn, could revile the entire enterprise, audience included. The writers, most of them leftist, set the tone of the anti-Hollywood bias, their bitterness compounded by the fact that in Hollywood's social and creative hierarchies, screenwriters were near the bottom. (An ugly, rarely acknowledged aspect of the bias was articulated by Spencer Tracy when he said, "Out here the Kellys are working for the Cohens." [29] "You're doing pretty well for a 'Heeb,' " said Hemingway to MGM producer Bernard Hyman when his employee, scenarist F. Scott Fitzgerald, proudly brought his famous friend into Hyman's office in the Thalberg Building at Metro.[30] "Must you talk to me? This is a Gentile's house, you know," says screenwriter Clare Quilty to gun-toting refugee Humbert Humbert [p. 299].) Donations to Loyalist Spain aside, anecdotes told at the expense of illiterate, immigrant producers were the principal, immediate solace for the slumming, "successful" novelist or playwright who was down on his luck or as greedy as any mogul (see S. N. Behrman's charming memoir, *People in a Diary* [1972]). The Hollywood novel (there are more than one hundred) was supposed to even all sorts of scores; like the anti-academic "satires" of later decades, however, it usually shot down easy targets and collapsed in self-pity. And cynical, guilt-ridden old Hollywood hands, writing their memoirs at poolside, downgraded their own real achievements, however few, and told everyone what they wanted to hear about life in a Babylonian brothel (see Ben Hecht's *A Child of the Century* [1955]). Stravinsky sustained his early enthusiasm for jazz while a resident of Hollywood. (His jazz-tinged *Scènes de Ballet* [1944] was commissioned for Billy Rose's Broadway show *The Seven Lively Arts,* and the *Ebony Concerto* [1945] was composed for

Woody Herman's band.) He outdid Kurt Weill with *his* witty pop number *Tango* (1940), and actually accepted a commission from the Ringling Brothers for an elephant ballet—thus the even funnier *Circus Polka* ("for a young elephant" [1942]). Yet when writer Paul Horgan asked the maestro, whose best friends out there (among the famous, that is) were expatriate novelist-screenwriters Aldous Huxley and Christopher Isherwood, if his acquaintances in the film world gave amusing parties, Stravinsky replied that they were intolerably boring, the most recent having been populated by "forty-five pederasts and seventy-six miscellaneous idiots." [31] Idiotic indeed had been Walt Disney's dismaying bowdlerization of *Le Sacre du Printemps* (1913) in *Fantasia* (1940), his "tribute" to the great composers (Bach, Beethoven, Tchaikovsky, Schubert) —a work firmly ensconced in the pantheon of *poshlost'* and an *émigré* master's unhappy American *rite de passage.** The *Circus Polka,* with its climactic quotation of Schubert's *Marche Militaire,* might be called Igor's Revenge, for George Balanchine choreographed it as a Camp version of Disney's *Dumbo* (1941), and it was performed more than four hundred times by the Barnum and Bailey *corps des éléphants,* appropriately attired in tutus. Stravinsky's own forays into film scoring were frustrating if not wasted experiences. When studio arrangers wanted to alter his music for a movie about the German invasion of Norway (probably *Edge of Darkness* [1943], though Stravinsky forgot the title), the composer withdrew the score and transformed it into *Four Norwegian Moods* (1942). Another abandoned score, intended for a hunting scene in *Jane Eyre* (1944), resulted in the second movement of his *Ode* (1943). Commenting in retrospect on a sequence in *Scènes de Ballet,* Stravinsky said, "The recapitulation of the *pas de deux* with the full orchestra now sounds to me like—pardon the pleonasm—bad movie music: the happy homesteaders, having massacred the Indians, begin to plant their CORN." [32] Marxist critics were not alone in viewing movies as a sop for the masses.

---

* "STRAVINSKY HAD TO SACRIFICE A YOUNG VIRGIN TO REVOLUTIONIZE MUSIC" reads a recent youth-oriented advertisement for a new recording of *Le Sacre,* a bit of promotion beyond *poshlost'*.

Nabokov's opinions about movies are at once those of a "classicist" (after Plato—and Arnheim, whom he has never read) and, loosely speaking, a Marxist, as he will be happy to learn. In *Laughter in the Dark,* Albinus is at first "delighted in [Margot's] interest in the cinema and began to unfold a certain favorite theory of his regarding the comparative merits of the silent film and the talkie: 'sound,' he said, 'will kill the cinema straightaway' " (p. 122). "The verbal part of the cinema," continues Nabokov thirty years later, "is such a hodge-podge of contributions, beginning with the script, that it really has no style of its own. On the other hand, the viewer of a silent film has the opportunity of adding a good deal of his own inner verbal treasure to the silence of the picture. . . . I don't even remember if the best Laurel and Hardy are talkies or not. On the whole, I think what I love about the silent film is what comes through the mask of the talkies and, vice versa, talkies are mute in my memory." [33] "And having departed to the sphere of jaunty, quick-talking, self-important con-men with their patter about the philosophy of the screen, the tastes of the masses and the intimacy of the movie camera, and with pretty good incomes at the same time, [Valentinov] dropped out of Luzhin's world," writes Nabokov in *The Defense* (p. 93). Mrs. Luzhin is properly depressed when the guests at a Berlin dance ignore her celebrated husband, an artist in his own right, in favor of the Grosz-like movie producers (p. 195), and Dr. Valentinov's movie offer proves fatal. The cultural implications are clear.

While Humbert's denunciation of Hollywood musicals is not unfair to Ruby Keeler or Alice Faye, it does not exactly allow for the joy communicated by a Fred Astaire or a Bill (Bojangles) Robinson. Nabokov, however, doesn't pretend to be a film critic or historian, and the explicit "criticism" in his novels is always an artistic, thematic necessity. "I'm no *cinéaste,"* he admits; as Ada holds forth on the Nature of Film ("of course, the cinema has no language problems"), "Van swallowed, rather than stifled, a yawn" (p. 427). Asked about the films of Josef von Sternberg, Nabokov said, "the name of Sternberg means nothing to me," failing to connect that director with *Shanghai Express* (1932) and other Dietrich vehicles which he had enjoyed very much. While scripting *Lolita* in Hollywood, the Nabokovs attended a dinner party at David Selznick's luxurious house. Billy Wilder was there, and Gina Lollobrigida, too. "She speaks excellent French," says Nabokov. "It wasn't that good," interrupts Mrs. Nabokov. They were also introduced to a tall, rugged fellow. "And what do you do?" inquired Nabokov. "I'm in pictures," answered John Wayne, smiling through what must have been the worst moment in his long career. Like Stravinsky, Wittgenstein, and other average moviegoers who relax best at the cinema (Betty Hutton and Carmen Miranda musicals were the philosopher's favorite narcotic), Nabokov has seen more films than he is able or cares to remember. Yet the *catalogue raisonné* of negative images which opened this essay demonstrates that movies have made an indelible impression where names, titles, and some faces have escaped him. M. H. Abrams, Nabokov's colleague at Cornell for a decade (1948–58), recalls how Nabokov entered a living room where a faculty child was watching an old western on television. Immediately engaged by the program, Nabokov was soon quaking with laughter over the furiously climactic fight scene in a bar. Just such idle moments, if not literally this one, inform the burlesque of the comparable "obligatory scene" in *Lolita,* the tussle of Humbert and Quilty which leaves them "panting as the cowman and the sheepman never do after their battle" (p. 301). "More recently, on French TV I saw a Laurel and Hardy short in which the 'dubbers' had the atrocious taste to have the two men speak fluent French with an English accent," notes Nabokov,[34] and that idle moment may well have inspired the parodies of dubbing in *Ada:* the cast's "macedoine of accents—English, French, Italian" in *Four Sisters* (pp. 427–28), and a "madhouse" of bilingual babble that is rendered in scenario form (pp. 516–18). Professor Abrams' reminiscence suggests that nothing is lost on a certain kind of comic writer—the literary anatomist who, while remaining outside of "popular culture," nevertheless absorbs and utilizes both "high" and "low" materials.

239

The Nabokovs rarely go to the cinema any more ("I retire too early at night"), though they have seen Fellini's "wonderful *8½,* and *La Strada,* too. Excellent, excellent! The film of *Death in Venice,* a mediocre story, was visually most pleasant; the luggage was especially handsome. We detested [Buñuel's] *Viridiana,* a grotesque compote of private parts and Goyaesque borrowings. Why is it so admired?" A voracious reader of magazines and newspapers in three languages, Nabokov manages to remain *au courant*—disarmingly so, given his imperious attitude toward so many facets of what he deems to be contemporary nonsense. But because Nabokov the literary anatomist is often bemused by odd or Campy trivia, his wide-ranging inclusiveness is easily misunderstood. "No, I loathe popular pulp," he told an interviewer who pressed him on the matter of his references to popular culture. "I loathe go-go gangs, I loathe jungle music, I loathe science fiction with its gals and goons, suspense and suspensories [thus Vitry's *Letters from Terra*—A. A.]. I especially loathe vulgar movies—cripples raping nuns under tables [a mini-burlesque of Buñuel—A. A.], or naked-girl breasts squeezing against the tanned torsos of repulsive young males. And, really, I don't think I mock popular trash more often than do other authors who believe with me that a good laugh is the best pesticide." [35] Drawing upon Gogol's delineation of *poshlost'* in *Dead Souls* (1842) and realizing Flaubert's dream of a vast *Encyclopédie des idees reçues* (*Dictionary of Accepted Ideas*), Nabokov does mock "popular trash" more often and more consistently than any other modern author, and some of the best, darkest, and certainly most "moral" laughter in *Lolita* is achieved at the expense of the movies, expressed in terms uniform with the vision of his *émigré* fiction.

American movies abound in *Lolita* (I will publish on this subject elsewhere), and the novel represents a culmination of negative images. Except for Humbert, a scholarly European refugee, the main characters in *Lolita* are clearly a product or reflection of the films they have seen—or made. Whatever Clare Quilty may be in the disputable realm of "interpretation" (*Doppelgänger* and/or mock-Double), he is very definitely a hack screenwriter and pornographic filmmaker, a hateful corrupter of words and images as well as a kidnapper of little girls. He lures Lolita away with an offer of stardom in his Hollywood tennis opus, *Golden Guts,* and his protracted death scene—a parody of horror films, gangster thrillers, westerns, and the American masculine ethic (pp. 295–307)—comically upends the scenario that Quilty himself might have written. Quilty is deftly executed, in both senses of the word, and Nabokov stages his movie violence with an almost balletic grace. The scene is as "serious" as it is funny: with Quilty's death, a bad artist has bit the dust.

2. Positive images: several fine messes

There is surely implicit in Quilty's death scene a lesson for recent film and TV directors who, in the wake of the James Bond movies (in *their* turn a vulgarization of Hitchcock's excellent *North by Northwest* [1959]), would hope to spoof violence but instead end by demeaning and dehumanizing their audiences. If it is unfair to ask of visual modes what verbal structures can of course stage or suggest more easily, then at least scenarists and directors might submit themselves to one of the principal wellsprings of twentieth-century comedy. That lesson *can* be learned in the anarchic school of earlier American screen comedy, and Nabokov the moviegoer and youthful gagwriter has absorbed its curriculum, as has Stanley Kubrick, or at least the Kubrick who directed *Lolita* (1962) and *Dr. Strangelove* (1963).

"In Europe," Nabokov says, "I went to the corner cinema about once in a fortnight and the only kind of picture I liked, and still like, was and is comedy of the Laurel and Hardy type. I enjoyed tremendously American comedy—Buster Keaton, Harold Lloyd, and Chaplin. . . . However, today's Little Man appeal has somewhat spoiled Chaplin's attraction for me. The Marx Brothers were wonderful . . . [and] Laurel and Hardy are always funny; there are subtle, artistic touches in even their most mediocre films. Laurel is so wonderfully inept, yet so very kind. There is a film in which they are at Oxford [*A Chump at Oxford,* 1940]. In one scene the two of them are sitting on a park bench in a labyrinthine garden and the subsequent happenings conform to the labyrinth. A casual villain puts his hand through the back of the bench and Laurel, who is clasping his hands in an idiotic reverie, mistakes the stranger's hand for one of his own hands, with all kinds of complications because his own hand is also there. He has to choose. The choice of a hand. . . . My favorites by Chaplin are *The Gold Rush* [1925], *The Circus* [1928], and *The Great Dictator* [1940]—especially the parachute inventor who jumps out of the window and ends in a messy fall which we only see in the expression on the dictator's face." [36] Chaplin's poetry, celebrated elsewhere by Hart Crane and e. e. cummings, informs young Fyodor's own prose-poetry in *The Gift* (1937–1938): "in the flower beds around them rippled pale, black-blotched pansies (somewhat similar facially to Charlie Chaplin)" (p. 326). Earlier in the novel, set in Berlin circa 1925, Fyodor had observed that, "Over the entrance to a cinema a black giant cut out of cardboard had been erected, with turned-out feet, the blotch of a mustache on his white face beneath a bowler hat, and a bent cane in his hand" (p. 174)—only a local color detail, but emblematic in its scale, recalling the tribute to Chaplin in *Pnin* (p. 80).

It is not by chance that Nabokov should single out Laurel and Hardy's labyrinth or the parachute inventor's fall. "One likes to recall," he writes in *Gogol,* "that the difference between the comic side of things, and their cosmic side, depends upon one sibilant" (p. 142), and the inventor's "messy" disappearance complements fifty years of Nabokov's own creative researches, his unflinching contemplation of the void. "In the early twenties in Berlin—1924, perhaps, since I was not yet married—I got well paid for cabaret sketches for the *émigré* night club 'Sinyaya ptitsa,' or 'Bluebird,' " says Nabokov, recalling the period before he had written any novels and was turning from lyric poetry to short fiction and verse drama. He had recently composed *Smert' [Death]*, a short two-act "Byronic" play set in 1806 at Cambridge University, and *Dedushka [The Grandfather]*, another untranslated play of 1923, which also confronts the nature of death. The five-act "historical" verse drama of 1924, *Tragediya gospodina Morna [The Tragedy* *of Mister Morn*], extends the theme of death,[37] but none of these plays are comic, and that sibilant marks a wide gap. One sees it narrowed in Nabokov's commercial sketches. "There were a number of things I had entitled 'Locomotion,' " he says. "One sketch was a little on the *Candid Camera* lines, long before *Candid Camera*, of course (a program I loved, incidentally). It was situated on a railway platform. You saw a porter with a red nose trundling his luggage cart containing a very large trunk, very badly closed. At one point the trunk flew open and a skeleton half flopped out of the trunk but he merely pushed it back with his foot and went on his way. Then there was the sketch in which a wildly hirsute man visited a barber. The actor portraying the customer was a small chap, whose real head, concealed inside his collar, was topped by a dummy head, its face partially concealed by thick long whiskers and very long hair. The barber cut and cut, and when the man was finally shaved and shorn, only a tiny head remained, like the knob of a post with very big ears. In 'The Chinese Dragon' [title in English = a pun on '*chai*,' the Russian word for 'tea'—A. A.], a sequence of Chinese disappeared in a dragon's open mouth.* Another Bluebird 'Locomotion' had a Venetian background and presented a blind man going along the bank of a canal, taptapping with his cane. Visible were the edge of the canal and the moon reflected in the water. The blind man got nearer and nearer and at the very last moment, when he was practically at the brink, his foot already raised, he took out a

---

* As comic archetypes, these sketches bring to mind Samuel Beckett's works and the athletics of a play such as Jerzy Grotowski's recent *Akropolis,* whose concentration camp inmates disappear one by one into a box, the reverse of the stream of circus midgets who tumble out of a little car. Nabokov's reduced hairy man also recalls *The Barbershop* (1934), one of W. C. Fields's four Mack Sennett shorts—especially the scene in which a monstrously fat man (padded, of course) with a long beard comes into the shop to use the steam room. The barber, Fields, forgets about him, and when he finally rescues him from the locked steam bath, and the great clouds of steam have cleared away, we see that the fat man has shrunk, has melted into a little fellow, suspended inside huge, blimplike trousers. "For some reason," says Nabokov, "the films of Fields did not play in Europe and I never saw any in the States, either." Fields's comedy is more eminently American in subject and plot than that of Keaton, Chaplin, *et al.,* and perhaps less exportable. In any event, one likes to think of young Fields picking up pointers in Berlin *émigré* cabarets of the nineteen-twenties, a field for future study.

handkerchief, blew his nose, turned and went back, taptapping. (No, no, Alfred, don't say it; that tapping is not a reference to the blind stripling's leitmotif in Joyce's *Ulysses*.) These 'Locomotions' took about five minutes, there was music and songs explaining and commenting on the action. I wrote the lyrics of the songs, too. I think I saw only one performance. As I said, they paid well. But all this is not really very interesting, is it?" It *is* interesting, of course, and one is struck by how the Bluebird "Locomotions" anticipate, in manner and theme, works Nabokov would write years later: the various farcical elements of *Invitation to a Beheading* (1938), *The Waltz Invention* (1938), and *Ada* (1969); Quilty's death scene and the most darkly comical aspects of *Pale Fire* (1962).

One of the central themes, or actions, of *Pale Fire* is a kind of fully orchestrated "Locomotion": the activities of the Shadows, that regicidal organization of stooges, whose antics recall the Keystone Cops, and the Shadows' loathsome, bumbling, but lethal agent, assassin Gradus—Death as the common, rigid vulgarian (see pp. 151–54). Always dressed in brown and blessed with a "chimpanzee slouch" (p. 277), excremental Gradus is a failed "Jack of small trades" and everything else. "Mere springs and coils produced the inward movements of our clockwork man. He might be termed a Puritan" (p. 152). "He was not interested in sightseeing or seasiding. He had long stopped drinking. He did not go to concerts. . . . Sexual impulses had greatly bothered him at one time but that was over. After his wife . . . had left him (with a gypsy lover), he had lived in sin with his mother-in-law until she was removed, blind and dropsical, to an asylum for decayed widows." His attempts to castrate himself only lead to a "severe infection" (pp. 252–53). "Our 'automatic man'" (p. 279) "worship[s] general ideas and [does] so with pedantic aplomb" (p. 152), lynches the wrong people (p. 112), moves his lips "like wrestling worms" while he pores over newspaper ads (pp. 274–75), speaks "mediocre French" and "worse English" (p. 199), gets lost on the road to Lex [= "law" (p. 198)], and at the end of *Pale Fire* fights to control the diarrheal "liquid hell inside of him" (p. 282) as he rushes to relieve his gun on an unintended victim. When he writes out "their client's alias," Gradus' Shadow superior "shak[es] with laughter (death is hilarious)" (p. 256). Agent Gradus, an anti–James Bond Super-Op figure, evokes the image of the inept, dumb hoodlum who voraciously consumes candy bars and comic books when he's not bumping off the wrong guy, getting himself locked in bank vaults, or failing with the girls—a role played for laughs in many grade-B gangster films of the forties. Most strikingly visualized as a vaudevillian bat- or birdman villain from an old movie or animated cartoon (the Penguin in *Batman*), Gradus is a "grotesque . . . cross between bat and crab" (p. 150), a jet-age Angel of Death "avail[ing] himself of all varieties of locomotion—rented cars, local trains, escalators, airplanes—[though] somehow the eye of the mind sees him, and the muscles of the mind feel him, as always streaking across the sky with black traveling bag in one hand and loosely folded umbrella in the other, in a sustained glide high over sea and land" (pp. 135–36)—"rising, soaring, desecrating the sky" (p. 264). "I was the shadow of the waxwing slain," writes John Shade in the opening line of that veritable aviary, *Pale Fire*. ". . . Infinite foretime and / Infinite aftertime: above your head / They close like giant wings, and you are dead" (ll. 122–24). Akin also to the birdlike harbingers of doom that fly through the hellish skies of Bosch, Brueghel, Callot, Goya, Blake, Fuseli, Meryon, Ensor, and Baskin, Nabokov's iconographic personification of Death casts its vast shadow across the entire novel—its creations, creator, and readers—extends forward over *Ada* and *Transparent Things,* and reaches back to include *Speak, Memory, Invitation to a Beheading, Despair, The Eye, Bluebird,* and the three verse dramas. *The Tragedy of Mister Morn* introduces in turn a king who has been exiled from an imaginary land, a figure who will appear again in several of Nabokov's Russian works, emerging with final, mad tragicomic splendor in *Pale Fire.*

Death, the untranslated drama, is well titled, but Nabokov's is no morbid preoccupation. Student Van Veen achieves "a brilliant ascendancy" among his peers by mastering the "knack of topsy-turvy locomotion on his hands" (p. 81), bettered only by Nabokov, whose *Ada* reverses Time and rearranges geography. Early in the novel, Van describes the phases of Aqua Veen's disintegration, "every one more racking than the last; for the human brain can become the best torture house of all those it has invented, established and used in millions of years, in millions of lands, on millions of howling creatures" (p. 22). Those howls are audible throughout *Ada,* even in Ardis, since death exists in Arcady too. But it is fourteen-year-old Van's hazardous equipoise that best expresses the spirit of Nabokov's most transcendent performances: "Not the faintest flush showed on his face or neck! Now and then, when he detached his organs of locomotion from the lenient ground, and seemed actually to clap his hands in mid-air, in a miraculous parody of a ballet jump, one wondered if this dreamy indolence of levitation was not a result of the earth's canceling its pull in a fit of absentminded benevolence" (p. 82). Van's is the brio of gravity-defiant Oliver Hardy in *Hog Wild* (1930). Remaining atop a ladder as he and it are swept away by hapless Laurel's rampaging car, Ollie braves the underpasses and traffic and doffs his bowler to the startled passengers in an open-topped bus.

Nabokov's less daringly locomoted blind man of 1924 partakes of perhaps the most compelling of cosmic sight gags, a balancing act that is as funny as it is bracing, performed again and again by the masters of American screen comedy: Chester Conklin, his eyes widened by terror, as the Keystone Cops' auto teeters on the brink of a canyon (*ca.* 1918); blindfolded Charlie Chaplin skating around the rim of a balcony in *Modern Times* (1936), his gasp and retreat when he removes the cloth, a moment perfected earlier in *The Gold Rush* (1925), when he starts out the door and realizes that the storm-driven cabin is tottering over a cliff; nonplussed Buster Keaton suspended in various fearful postures—at an oblique angle in the ship's rigging of *The Love Nest* (1923), over the edge of a waterfall in *Our Hospitality* (1923), from a window in *College* (1927)—or perched high in a thin cyclone-torn tree in *Steamboat Bill, Jr.* (1928), what Nabokov in *Trans-*

parent Things calls "the silhouette of human panic" (p. 28); or Oliver Hardy on top of a leaning, wavering tower of piled chairs in *Fra Diavolo* (1933); Laurel and Hardy encased in cylinders of cement in *Our Relations* (1936), seesawing furiously on the edge of a wharf like two crazed metronomes, or contending with a gorilla as they haul a piano across a crumbling Alpine suspension bridge in *Swiss Miss* (1938), a scene that ends with Hardy dangling by his hands above the gorge. Their perilous scrambling on the superstructure of a new skyscraper in *Liberty* (1929) was a patent imitation of the most famous of such scenes, in Harold Lloyd's *High and Dizzy* (1920) or *Safety Last* (1923, repeated by him in *Feet First* [1930]), and in *The Defense* (1930), a still-photo from one of those Lloyd films, lying on Valentinov's table amid other shots of "frightened women and ferociously squinting men," suggests to ex-Grandmaster Luzhin his means of suicide: "a white-faced man with lifeless features and big American glasses [was] hanging by his hands from the ledge of a skyscraper —just about to fall off into the abyss" (p. 247). Reading a Soviet chess book in *The Gift,* Fyodor "began to enjoy quietly a study in which the few white pieces seemed to be hanging over an abyss and yet won the day" (p. 187), a forecast of the outcome of "Lik" (1938), composed immediately after Nabokov's completion of *The Gift.* Although the ailing actor appears in "a play of the nineteen-twenties called *L'Abîme* ('*The Abyss*')," it is his enemy who suffers that plunge and commits suicide on the story's last page. "No wonder one peers over the parapet into an inviting abyss," writes distraught Kinbote in *Pale Fire;* he will survive only long enough to complete his edition (p. 220). Fyodor meets the respected *émigré* novelist Shirin [= Russian for "breadth" or "width," *not* Sirin], author of *The Hoary Abyss,* who is "blind like Milton, deaf like Beethoven, and a blockhead to boot" (p. 327). In search of treacherous Margot in *Laughter in the Dark,* blind and doomed Albinus got out of the elevator and "moved forward and stepped with one foot into an abyss—no, it was nothing, only the step leading downstairs. He had to keep still for a moment, he was quivering so" (p. 287). Asked in 1970 to characterize his memory, Nabokov answered, "I am an ardent memorist with a rotten memory; a drowsy king's absent-minded remembrancer. With absolute lucidity I recall landscapes, gestures, intonations, a million sensuous details, but names and numbers topple into oblivion with absurd abandon like little blind men in file from a pier." [38] Cincinnatus in *Invitation to a Beheading* ends a chapter by writing (in the book-within-the-book) how he stepped from his windowsill onto the elastic air, and Nabokov literally leaves him transfixed in mid-air, a moment which not only telescopes the novel's main theme, its confrontation of death and dying, but is also strikingly similar to the way the blind man in Nabokov's "Locomotion" tests the void and teases the viewer.[39] "Yes, yes. A family group. I had not made those connections," said Nabokov, when several of these parallels were pointed out to him.

Nabokov's locomotive comedy is most free-wheeling in *Invitation to a Beheading,* the anti-utopian fantasia written in Berlin in 1935, an atypical refraction of contemporary German and Russian realities, the mammoth prison-society of Stalinist spies, informers, and interrogators best documented in Robert Conquest's *The Great Terror* (1968) and Nadezhda Mandelstam's deeply moving and sardonic memoir of the thirties, *Hope Against Hope* (1970). Like many of Nabokov's works (*Ada* most recently), *Invitation to a Beheading* revivifies several of the conventions and themes of science-fiction. "A writer for whom I have the deepest admiration is H. G. Wells," says Nabokov. "I could talk *endlessly* about Wells, especially his romances: *The Time Machine* [1895], *The Invisible Man* [1897], *The War of the Worlds* [1898], and *The Country of the Blind* [1904, expanded in 1939]," which is about the travails of the only man with sight (= spiritual isolation) in a land of sightless people. Cincinnatus is Nabokov's version of this by now stock figure who has undergone countless sci-fi permutations: The Last Man in the World; Cincinnatus even calls himself this (p. 95). That he is not permitted the full companionship of the Last Woman, a familiar twist in the trashiest of sci-fi (prose and film), is thematically important and consistent with his very human fears, which include sexual inadequacy and failure. Where allegorist Wells employs blindness, fabulist Nabokov divides his population, unevenly enough, between opaque (= sentient) and transparent (dehumanized) people. The futuristic world beyond Cincinnatus' prison is mapped with care. "Progress" has been made in transportation, city planning, child care, education, library science, literature, and, of course, in the relationship between executioner and victim. As in all anti-utopian fiction, the culture of the past is obsolete; Cincinnatus had once worked in a doll workshop making figurines of Pushkin and Tolstoy, those shams from "poetical antiquity," "the mythical Nineteenth Century" (p. 27). The novel's commentators subdue their natural, professional inclination to relate *Invitation* to Huxley's *Brave New World* (1932), Warner's *The Aerodrome* (1941), or Orwell's *1984* (1949), but the generic (though not aesthetic) kinship is strong and clear. It may not be apparent immediately because Nabokov eschews the reportorial exposition (see Vonnegut's *Player Piano,* 1952) and tendentious moralizing (see Heinlein's *Stranger in a Strange Land,* 1961) one often finds in admonitory utopias, and *Invitation*'s farcical action and tone make it unique. Its "map" is filled in gradually, through an accretion of vivid touches and precise, painterly details—a futuristic, Dürerlike landscape glimpsed through a partially opened window. Dystopia, moreover, is only part of the story, as it were, in *Invitation to a Beheading* (and *Bend Sinister,* its brother). It is also a novel of consciousness (old-fashioned as that may sound), which should suggest why Nabokov, in his Foreword to the American edition, does not welcome any comparisons with "G. H. Orwell or other popular purveyors of illustrated ideas and publicistic fiction" (p. 6). The Penguin paperback edition of *Invitation,* thanks to an extraordinary coincidence, is number "1984" in their series.

Véra Nabokov witnessed the first nocturnal book-burnings in the streets of Berlin, and while her husband wrote the first draft— "in one fortnight of wonderful excitement and sustained inspiration," a "spectacular exception" to his usual snail's pace—the searchlights from Nazi *fêtes* illuminated the wintry sky, stage lighting for the Nabokovs' second *Götterdämmerung*. "At Véra's cousin's flat," recalls Nabokov, "we heard Hitler's voice from rooftop loudspeakers," but in Cincinnatus' prison world, great dictators are figuratively and literally reduced in size; "Who is Mussolini?" asks the "Nabokovian" novelist Udo Conrad in *Laughter in the Dark* (p. 215), and Nabokov's untranslated story *Istreblenie Tiranov* ["Tyrants Destroyed"], written in Berlin in 1936, provides a Swiftian coda to *Invitation* by suggesting that derision is the best weapon. "When we left Berlin for good in '37, I was worried that the German authorities would discover that manuscript in our baggage," says Nabokov. " 'It's about Stalin,' I would have told them, but they didn't find it. They had their translators—the Nazis couldn't read Russian, of course, and perhaps not German, either."

Sentenced to die because he alone has retained his sentience, or opacity, Cincinnatus must contend with the omnipresent M'sieur Pierre, his executioner. "Life is a long lesson in death and dying," said Socrates, and near the end of *Invitation to a Beheading,* "the deputy city director" jumps up on the execution platform to announce to the townspeople a new furniture exhibit: "I also remind you that tonight, there will be given with sensational success the new comic opera *Socrates Must Decrease,*" a précis of the novel and the State's intentions (p. 220). Some of the other comic operas of the period are the Marx Brothers' *A Night at the Opera* (1935); the Ritz Brothers' *The Firefly* (1938, from Rudolf Friml's opus); and Laurel and Hardy's *Fra Diavolo* (*The Devil's Brother,* 1933, a burlesque of Frank Auber's operetta), *Babes in Toyland* (1934, based on Victor Herbert's operetta), and *The Bohemian Girl* (1936, a take-off on Michael Balfe). René Clair's futuristic *A Nous la Liberté* (1931) has its own "operatic" flourishes: the guards wear anachronistic royal costumes and, like Cincinnatus in the past, Clair's forlorn little prisoner is employed as a toymaker; he gradually joins the other prisoners, who sing with surprising joy. "I loved the French films of René Clair," says

Nabokov, "a new world, a new trend in cinema," [40] and *Invitation to a Beheading* is a whirling, slapstick extension of it—*The Shape of Things to Come* (H. G. Wells's formulations of 1933) submitted to a comic sensibility—a prototypical dystopia, such as Zamiatin's *We* (1920), worked over by Laurel and Hardy, the Marx Brothers, Lloyd, Langdon, or Keaton.

Whether or not film comedy has influenced Nabokov (and to what degree) is not the issue here. "Influence," of course, is a troublesome, controversial, and mysterious business. To see Nabokov's affinities with Laurel and Hardy *et al.* is perhaps to read *Invitation to a Beheading* less solemnly, to find new pleasure; except for Robert Alter's brilliant essay on Nabokov's conjunction of art and politics (*TriQuarterly* 17, Winter 1970), its critics have offered little help. "Spiritual affinities have no place in my concept of literary criticism," declares Nabokov in the Foreword to the American *Invitation to a Beheading* (p. 6), but the present occasion provides at least one instance where, "for better or worse, it is the commentator who has the last word," as Kinbote writes in *his* Foreword (p. 29).

Although Laurel and Hardy frequently share the same bed (*Their First Mistake* [1932]) and don women's clothing (*Another Fine Mess* [1930]), who would be so obtuse as to term them homosexual or transvestite? Their asexual or pre-sexual comedy recalls child-man Harry Langdon's earlier pantomime, *The Soldier Man* (1926), who is distracted by the udders of a cow, and Laurel and Hardy's own lactic slapstick is developed fully in *Their First Mistake*. The boys adopt a baby for Mrs. Hardy (Mae Busch), who has meanwhile left Ollie to file for divorce. They take care of the child, and the film ends with Stan draining the delicious bottle that has been handed to him by an equally somnolent Ollie; a year later they made a brief, unbilled appearance as guest babies in *Our Gang's Wild Poses* (1933). When they appear as their own children in *Brats* (1930) and behave very much like their "adult" selves, Ollie and Stan are defining the essentially childlike (as opposed to childish) nature of their comic world. The childlike exploration of being and nonbeing that is so touching in *Invitation to a Beheading* is also present in many Laurel and Hardy films, and its deep appeal is not lost on children. In *Saps at Sea* (1940), Stan picks a banana from a fruit bowl, sits down, and casually peels it, only to find another unpeeled banana beneath the skin. He flips the peel away, strips the banana again, and the same thing happens: another somewhat smaller unpeeled banana. After patiently performing this operation a few more times, with the same results, Stan peels it for what will be the last time, for it turns out there is no fruit there; his hand is now empty. He blinks his eyes and, shrugging his shoulders, blithely tosses the nonexistent banana away. My son watched it with me on television, when he was four, and found this scene hilarious. "What did he have, Richard?" I asked him. "He had a wonderful nothing," he answered. Maurice Sendak was quite right to transport his dreamy child to a wondrous kitchen staffed by three Oliver Hardys, who whip up a fine doughy mess (*In the Night Kitchen* [1970]). Cincinnatus is of their party. On the opening page, unsteady Cincinnatus is "like a child who has just learned to walk." A jailer embraces him like a baby and easily lifts him down from his table (p. 29), and at the execution M'sieur Pierre treats him like a child at bath- or bedtime: "We shall first of all remove our little shirt" (p. 221). Fittingly enough, young Emmie, the ballerina, is the first to take Cincinnatus backstage, enabling him to perceive that he is part of an artifice, someone else's grand design, a "game" whose outcome is difficult to foresee; "Terra Incognita" is the title of a 1931 Nabokov tale. "Let them be. . . . After all, they are both children," says M'sieur Pierre, unable to recognize childhood as the natural province of the most profound kinds of play (p. 166). All the characters are clearly shams, waxen dummies, animated authorial toys. " 'I know that the horror of death is nothing really, a harmless convulsion—perhaps even healthful for the soul—the choking wail of a newborn child or a furious refusal to release a toy,' " (p. 193), writes Cincinnatus in the book he is rushing to complete.

"We play, we die," exclaims the desperate narrator of " 'That in Aleppo Once . . .' " (1943),[41] and *Invitation to a Beheading,* staged on one of Huizinga's playfields of the mind, poetically investigates the possibilities. "The fortress must have suffered a mild stroke," writes Nabokov at the beginning of the last chapter (p. 213). M'sieur Pierre brings Cincinnatus a checkerboard, a box, and a punchinello doll, signal authorial gifts no less than the child-like, rhythmic prose that seems to scan—Death as an iamb:

> "You've had company?" [Pierre] inquired politely of Cincinnatus when the director had left them alone in the cell. "Your mama visited you? That's fine, that's fine. And now I, poor, weak little M'sieur Pierre, have come to amuse you and amuse myself for a while. Just see how my Punch looks at you. Say hello to uncle. Isn't he a scream? Sit up, there, chum. Look, I've brought you lots of entertaining things. Would you like a game of chess first? Or cards? Do you play anchors? Splendid game! Come, I'll teach you!" (p. 137)

Music and mime, circus stunts and stage props, and playthings too numerous to mention prevail throughout the novel. Recalling one of Harpo Marx's enchanting, impromptu harp recitals (*A Night at the Opera, A Day at the Races* [1937]) or Laurel and Hardy in several films (*Pardon Us* [1931, as escaped convicts], *The Music Box* [1932], *Bonnie Scotland* [1935], *Way Out West* [1937]), the cast of *Invitation to a Beheading* occasionally forgets the furious business at hand and breaks into a spontaneous dance: "Rodion the jailer came in and offered to dance a waltz with him. Cincinnatus agreed. They began to whirl. The keys on Rodion's leather belt jangled; he smelled of sweat, tobacco and garlic; he hummed, puffing into his red beard; and his rusty joints creaked. . . . The dance carried them into the corridor. Cincinnatus was much smaller than his partner. Cincinnatus was light as a leaf. The wind of the waltz made the tips of his long but thin mustache flutter, and his big limpid eyes looked askance, as is always the case with timorous dancers. . . . At the bend in the corridor stood another guard, nameless, with a rifle and wearing a doglike mask. . . . They described a circle near him and glided back into the cell, and now Cincinnatus regretted that the swoon's friendly embrace had been so brief" (pp. 13–14). Nabokov acknowledges that his title alludes to Weber's *L'Invitation à la Valse* (as well as Baude-laire's *L'Invitation au voyage* [see p. 94]), and the entire cast's subsequent, more frenzied prancing (p. 156) anticipates the grand finale of Fellini's *8½* (1963). In order to escape the ship's crew in *Monkey Business* (1931), another animated Punchinello, Harpo by name, takes refuge in a children's Punch and Judy show. Harpo thrusts his head through the little theater's curtain, clips a puppet's body to his collar, and "freezes." The captain cannot determine which of the three puppets is real. Along with Harpo's autistic, soundless aria in *A Night at the Opera,* that brilliant sequence best recapitulates Nabokov's dreamlike mode, his operatic puppet show; the beautifully controlled, accelerating rhythms of the action are also akin to *Petrushka* (1911), another playful Russian's positively resolved puppet show. "We shall all dance, we shall all die," says Marthe on her deathbed in *King, Queen, Knave* (p. 271). *The Waltz Invention* is doomsday.

Recalling *A Night at the Opera,* Nabokov dwelled on "the opera, the crowded cabin, which is pure genius. I must have seen that film three times!" [42] He lovingly rehearsed the cabin scene in detail, the stream of people piling in, delighting particularly in the arrival of the manicurist. Nabokov's first, no doubt unconscious, tribute to the scene occurs in *Invitation to a Beheading.* Cincinnatus' wife, Marthe, crams her entire family into his cell for a visit, including all their furniture:

> **How they lumbered in! Marthe's aged father, with his huge bald head, and bags under his eyes, and the rubbery tap of his black cane; Marthe's brothers, identical twins except that one had a golden mustache and the other a pitch-black one; Marthe's maternal grandparents, so old that one could already see through them; three vivacious female cousins, who, however, were not admitted for some reason at the last minute; Marthe's children—lame Diomedon and obese little Pauline; at last Marthe herself, wearing her best black dress, with a velvet ribbon around her cold white neck, and holding a hand mirror; a very proper young man with a flawless profile was constantly at her side. (pp. 98–99)**

More furniture, household utensils, a tricycle, "even individual sections of walls continued to arrive," as do a lawyer, a cat, M'sieur Pierre, and "the director" (p. 104). Responding to the now cozy environment, one of Marthe's brothers, a distinguished singer, bursts into song as "everybody began talking simultaneously. *'Mali é trano t'amesti!'* Marthe's brother sang full voice," in corrupt, Marxian Italian (p. 103). Nabokov mocks the stilted Italian of *Il Trovatore,* the Marx Brothers' main target. Although the phrase is a syntactical mishmash, there is sense in Nabokov's nonsense. *Mali* is the masculine plural for "evil," *é trano* a re-created *é strano* ("it's bewildering"), and *t'amesti* a non-existent form that approximates the imperfect subjunctive "you loved you"—parodic evocations of overused operatic tags and a summary of Cincinnatus' isolation. The packed Zemblan jail in *Pale Fire* (p. 144) outdoes both this scene and its *Night at the Opera* precursor (repeated by the Marxes in *Room Service* [1938]).

Assisted by the jailers Rodion, Rodrig, and Roman (Nabokov's Three Stooges), M'sieur Pierre, the lethal "operatic woodman" (p. 171), has all the sartorial panache of Laurel and Hardy in *Fra Diavolo.* Dressed for the execution "in a pea-green hunting habit," the pea-green hat graced with a pheasant feather, "Attractively rouged M'sieur Pierre bowed, bringing together his patent-leather boot tops, and said in a comic falsetto: 'the carriage is waiting, if you please sir. . . . Off to do chop chop' " (p. 207). But their farce comes apart at the execution, and Pierre fares even worse than the impresario of *A Night at the Opera,* who, briefly locked in a closet, is spared the early sounds and sights of the opening night debacle: the orchestra's segue from *Il Trovatore* to "Take Me Out to the Ball Game," Harpo's Tarzan-like swoops through the scenery, and so forth. An equestrian match for the Marx Brothers' game-winning gladiatorial horse-drawn garbage cart in *Horse Feathers* (1932, a burlesque of *Ben-Hur* [1926]), the skinny old nag pulling the ancient "scarred carriage" breaks into a miraculous gallop and flies by the eager crowds (p. 217). Like Harpo Marx amuck, Stan Laurel as his target, "A person in Turkish trousers came running out of a cafe with a pail of confetti, but, missing, sent his vari-colored blizzard into the face of a cropped fellow who had just come running from the opposite sidewalk with a bienvenue platter of 'bread and salt' " (pp. 217–18). As vulnerable as Chaplin and as innocent or pre-sexual a "lover" as Harry Langdon, or Laurel and Hardy, or Keaton in *Sherlock, Jr.*

(1924),* cuckolded and threatened Cincinnatus nevertheless resists the circus they would make of death and all life. At the last possible moment at least one Cincinnatus refuses to play his part in *Socrates Must Decrease,* and—like the Showman in *Petrushka* or Gradus in *Pale Fire*—impotent, unlucky M'sieur Pierre is mocked and defeated.

Journeying to the execution, Cincinnatus copes with his "implacable fear," "even though he knows perfectly well that the entire masquerade is staged in his own brain" (p. 213), that he is playing out his part in an authorial dream, the psychological phenomenon that allows a creative sleeper to perceive his nightmare as an "unreal" drama and calmly confront and control it on a new dream-level. The head of "one Cincinnatus" is on the chopping block, counting loudly as Pierre's ax begins its arc, when suddenly "the other Cincinnatus" (spirit, soul?) joyfully gets up and looks around (p. 222), like ghostly Petrushka's triumphant appearance above his limp straw body (definitively performed by Nijinsky), or Buster Keaton roused from the nightmare that has placed him on a hangman's scaffold in *Convict 13* (1920), or the moment in *Sherlock, Jr.,* when movie projectionist Keaton, falling asleep on the job, divides himself and departs from his body by means of a technical trick (a superimposition on a double exposure). Buster's dream double leaves the projection booth, scrambles over the orchestra pit, and climbs into the film-within-the-film to rescue the heroine. Cincinnatus moves in the opposite direction, toward the author and his readers, easily achieved in a verbal infinite regress. As the creaking set and setting of Nabokov's most limpidly structured artifice come unglued, Cincinnatus slowly descends from the platform, "a spinning wind" whipping all sorts of debris and falling scenery past him (pp. 222–23), recalling the most extraordinary and moving scene in all Keaton: Buster standing alone in the street while a cyclone rips apart the town of *Steamboat Bill,*

* In *Sherlock, Jr.*'s final moments, Buster turns to the film-within-the-film for amatory instructions. The hero kisses his girl, and Buster does the same, but when hero and heroine next appear with babies, perplexed Buster can only shrug his shoulders.

Jr. With no warning, the wind-loosened front wall of the two-story building behind him collapses on its unseeing victim, and Buster, playing Everyman as stationary target, disappears from view. The settled timber reveals Buster, still on his feet, motionless, unmoved, facing the camera, standing in the fallen wall's lifesaving open window. He walks away, but after a glance over his shoulder and a classic double-take, he races away in terror, the gale in pursuit. Cincinnatus, however, has outdistanced fear—"By myself," he had said, several times, as the awful moment drew near—and his triumph is akin to Harold Lloyd's apotheosis of a weakling in *The Freshman* (1925), who zigzags his way through crashing tacklers to score the game-winning points, leaving in his wake a field littered with bodies. Pierre has been dispatched and grotesquely reduced by crushing debris and authorial magic, just as Stravinsky's Showman is chased off by the two trumpets' dissonant fanfare (a bitonal combination of C and F-sharp). Cincinnatus is finally as indominable as a Marx (Groucho, not Karl), and at "the end" of the novel (a renewal and in the best sense a beginning), he strides through the chaos "in that direction where, to judge by the voices, stood beings akin to him" (p. 223), gathered by Nabokov into Yeats's "artifice of eternity."

The diminution of the hairy man in Nabokov's Bluebird "Locomotion" not only anticipates Field's *The Barbershop;* it pinpoints one of the most nightmarish of sight gags: physical dismemberment, displacement, or metamorphosis, the human equivalent of the "empty" banana routine in *Saps at Sea,* which offers a succinct paradigm. *Going Bye Bye* (1934) ends with Laurel and Hardy having had their legs twisted around their necks by a vengeful criminal, while another figurative threat is literally achieved by the ship captain in *The Live Ghost* (1934), who twists Laurel's and Hardy's heads back to front, as in one of Marc Chagall's early Russian painterly caprices. The Three Stooges (vulgarized Laurel and Hardy) suffer similar indignities, their bones or savagely tweaked noses creaking and crackling like stripped engine gears, gross textbook examples of Bergson's definition of comedy ("the mechanical encrusted upon the living"). Occasionally the boys will bark like dogs, a Darwinian descent reversed in the *Speaking of Animals* shorts of the forties, in which crudely cartooned lips are superimposed on "talking" creatures ("Animals is de cwaziest peoples!" was always narrator Lew Lehr's closing tag in Fox Movietone News's *Dribble Puss Parade,* a dreadful imitation of that series). Fear may be at the center of the universal fascination with freak shows ("Move along, kid," said four-hundred-pound Baby Irene in 1944 after my chubby friend had stared for fifteen minutes), the human oddities offered for view in Ripley's *Believe It or Not* and its movie short version, *Strange As It Seems*—the perverse appeal, too, of the popular German children's book *Ströllpeter, The Plastic Man* comic books, horror film metamorphoses and sci-fi miniaturism, and the amusement park funhouse mirrors which allow us to transform ourselves temporarily into monstrous sight gags and to view our safe return to "normalcy." How fortunate we are! "A metamorphosis is a thing always exciting to watch," writes Nabokov in *Gogol* (p. 43).

Authenticity and existence are also at stake in the best involuted *Bugs Bunny* animated cartoons of the nineteen-forties and fifties, which, according to their chief animator, Chuck Jones, often drew their inspiration from Keaton, Laurel and Hardy, and the Marx Brothers. "I loved that Bunny," says Nabokov, "he was so different from those sentimental Disney *poshlyáchkis* [= the feminine plural], except for the Duck, who endured real trouble. Was the Bunny Disney's?" Scholars may recall a *Bugs Bunny* cartoon (Warner Brothers, *ca.* 1943) in which there is a running battle between the rabbit and the artist, whose visible hand alternately wields a large gum eraser and a drawing pencil, terrible weapons which at one moment remove the rabbit's feet so that he cannot escape, and at another give him a duck's bill so that he cannot talk back,[43] not unlike the lot of the characters in *Invitation to a Beheading,* where the creator (if not *the* Creator) is ultimately more sympathetic. On the way to "do chop-chop," dreamer and dream (or Yeats's inseparable dancer and dance) grow more distinct, and lucidly self-conscious Cincinnatus "suddenly understood that everything had in fact been written already." He only needs time to finish writing *his* book: "I ask three minutes—go away for that time or at least be quiet—yes, a three-minute intermission—after that, so be it, I'll act to the end my role in your idiotic production" (p. 209). "You can't kill me. You ain't got time. This is the end of the picture," says the helpless sheep to the knife-wielding wolf that has strapped him to a platter in the animated film *No Mutton fer Nuttin'* (1944).[44] Earlier in the novel, "cartooned" Cincinnatus had been taken apart and reassembled at will, and his rusty-jointed jailers have interchangeable parts, in both senses of the phrase.[45] Literal-minded source hunters, seeking links in the chain, should be told that Professor Nabokov, lecturing at Cornell, delighted in a similar resolve in *Ulysses* (1922): * Bloom's vision of ghostly Virag, his suicide father, metamorphosed into a garrulous birdman, the grotesque Nighttown equivalent of his son's morbid and crippling diurnal mourning. Virag unscrews his head, tucks it under his arm, and exits: "Quack!" is the disembodied bird-head's first and final word.[46] The epilogue to *Freaks* (1932) reveals that the aroused denizens of the sideshow have demonically transformed Cleopatra, the trapeze *artiste* and instigator of their local miseries, into a hen-woman who is exhibited in her own sideshow box, squawking unintelligibly. That denouement is given a somewhat lighter treatment in the following year's *Dirty Work* (1933), which finds chimney sweeps Laurel and Hardy serving a mad scientist who has just discovered a youth-rejuvenating formula and turned a duck back into an egg. Helpmate Laurel accidentally knocks Hardy into a vat containing the elixir. A chimpanzee shortly emerges, wearing Hardy's bowler hat; "I have *nothing* to say," states the indignant chimp. Badly beaten up by his wife in *Thicker than Water* (1935), Hardy is taken to the hospital. Laurel is forced to donate blood, but too much is taken and the transfusion process is reversed. The incredibly complicated comic business ends with Laurel and Hardy

---

* Prior to his three class-weeks on Joyce, Nabokov would lecture on "three tales of transformation": Gogol's *The Overcoat,* Stevenson's *Dr. Jekyll and Mr. Hyde,* and Kafka's *The Metamorphosis,* "a supreme, perfect masterpiece." He might also have included Gogol's *The Nose,* a lengthy and bona fide sight gag which Nabokov loves.

having exchanged roles (by virtue of make-up, dubbing, and clothes), Stan playing the "shrunken" Ollie. "Here's *another* fine mess you've gotten me into!" he says, borrowing Hardy's most famous line. Sweet vengeance is similar, in Nabokov and Lewis Carroll as well as Laurel and Hardy and *Freaks.* In the course of their escape from prison in *Liberty,* Laurel and Hardy crush a burly, pursuing policeman in an elevator, reducing him to a midget. At the end of Queen Alice's riotous party in Chapter Nine of *Through the Looking-Glass* (1872), "the Red Queen, whom she considered as the cause of all the mischief . . . had suddenly dwindled down to the size of a little doll, and was now on the table, merrily running round and round after her own shawl. . . . 'I'll shake you into a kitten,' " says Alice, and she does (Tenniel's drawings for the very brief Chapters Ten and Eleven illustrate the metamorphosis beautifully). When last seen in *Invitation to a Beheading,* Pierre is in the care of "a woman in a black shawl," who is "carrying the tiny executioner like a larva in her arms" (p. 223). "Death be not proud, though some have called thee / Mighty and dreadful, for, thou are not so," wrote Donne in an earlier address to the executioner, higher toned than Nabokov's, but no less serious. " 'The thought, when written down, becomes less oppressive,' " states Cincinnatus in his book-within-the-book (p. 194).

Priglashenie na kazn' (its Russian title) was serialized in 1935–1936 in three issues of the most distinguished *émigré* journal, the Paris-based *Sovremennye zapiski* [*Contemporary Annals*], and in 1938 was published in book form by Berlin and Paris *émigré* presses. After *Lolita*'s success (1958) created a market for Nabokov's hidden *oeuvre, Invitation to a Beheading* was the first book to be translated (1959, dateline "Oak Creek Canyon, Arizona"). By 1971, with the publication of *Glory* [*Podvig,* 1931], Nabokov had completed the Englishing of his nine *émigré* novels, but he opens his Foreword (dateline Montreux) with a bibliographical catalog that is more somber than triumphant. "He who cares to scan the list [of novels] given below should mark the dramatic gap between 1938 and 1959," declares Nabokov, referring to the *émigré* and American editions of *Invitation*. The gap is dramatic in several ways, not all of them happy.

Having moved to Paris the previous year, 1938 represents the apogee of Nabokov's "Russian career." He had recently completed *The Gift, The Waltz Invention, The Event,* and several of his best stories (datelines Paris, Cap d'Antibes, Mentone, and Marienbad), and published *Soglyadatay [The Eye]*, a collection of fictions. Never insensitive to auguries of the future, Nabokov had already begun to exercise a polyglot author's options, though *writing* in your second or third language is no blithe experience, especially in early middle age. At the end of 1936, he had translated *Despair* for a London publisher—"This was my first serious attempt," he says, "to use English for what may be loosely termed an artistic purpose"—and in Paris he wrote in French as well as Russian: "Mademoiselle O" (now Chapter Five in *Speak, Memory*) and what he calls "a very difficult" critical article on Pushkin for the prestigious *Nouvelle Revue Française.* "Paulhan [Jean Paulhan, its editor] wanted to know who had helped me," says Nabokov, with justifiable pride. Contemplating Hitler's rapid adjustments of the map of Europe and the fact that his wife Véra is Jewish, Nabokov chose to compose his next novel in English. *The Real Life of Sebastian Knight* was written in their 1938 apartment "on rue Saigon, between the Etoile and the Bois . . . in a large sunny bathroom [which] doubled as my study," and was published three years later in America. In 1939 he traveled to England to seek an academic position, but there were no offers; later that year, Nabokov's mother died in Nazi-occupied Prague (his father, murdered by Russian Monarchist assassins in 1922, is buried in what is now East Berlin). Refusing to surrender an *émigré* writer's sole legacy, his language, he began composing another Russian novel, *Solus Rex* ["The King Alone," the title in Roman, not Cyrillic, type]. A long section from it was the lead contribution in the last issue of *Sovremennye zapiski* (1940), whose editor, Ilya Fondaminsky—"a saintly and heroic soul who did more for Russian *émigré* literature than any other man," eulogizes Nabokov in *Speak, Memory* (pp. 286–87)—would soon perish in a German death camp, as did Nabokov's brother in 1945. On May 28, 1940, Nabokov, his wife, and young son sailed for America and a new life in English (that bibliographical gap), leaving behind *Solus Rex* * and the German and French chapters of the Russian emigration.

> **Beyond the seas where I have lost a sceptre,**
> **I hear the neighing of my dappled nouns,**
> **soft participles coming down the steps,**
> **treading on leaves, trailing their rustling gowns**

Nabokov would write in "An Evening of Russian Poetry" (1945), commemorating a loss that choreographers, composers, and musicians in exile did not have to overcome, since they had at their fingertips an international language and a ready audience (Balanchine; Stravinsky; and Rachmaninov, who kindly offered Nabokov an ancient cutaway to wear for his first lecture at Stanford University's 1941 Summer Session; and Dmitri Tiomkin, whose Oscar-winning scores, concurrent with Nabokov's Americanization through *Lolita* [1955], would include *High Noon* [1952] and *The High and the Mighty* [1954], mordant titles in the context of the plight of the *émigré* writers). At the end of *Pale Fire,* Kinbote says of Shade and his poem, "I even suggested to him a good title—the title of the book in me whose pages he was to cut: *Solus Rex;* instead of which I saw *Pale Fire,* which meant nothing to me" (p. 296).

With German armies circumscribing France, the winter and spring of 1940 was a fearful time. Anyone who has negotiated and survived the bureaucratic labyrinth of Nansen passports and exit visas knows that *émigré* confusions, anxieties, and terrors are well recorded in Nabokov's epistolary tale " 'That in Aleppo Once . . .' " (1943, dateline Boston), the "Refugee Blues" W. H. Auden attempted to express in *Another Time* (1940); Nabokov's title, a tag from *Othello* supplied by the narrator, suggests that one more

---

* "Ultima Thule," another section of the abandoned book, would be published in 1942 in the "American" *émigré* journal *Novy Zhurnal* [*New Review*]; finally translated, it now appears in Nabokov's *A Russian Beauty and Other Stories* (New York, 1973).

despairing *émigré* will soon take his own life. A brief respite was offered the Nabokovs by a Parisian showing of *Ninotchka*—the only Garbo film, according to Nabokov, that is not doomed by "its corny scenarios and overwrought players." Her first American comedy cast Garbo as an inhumanly humorless and glacially business-like Soviet agent dispatched to luxurious Paris (the plot, familiar to most readers, need not be rehearsed). *Ninotchka* contains several biting sequences analogous to the blended Communazi phenomena of *Invitation to a Beheading* and *Bend Sinister,* not surprising when one notices that its director was Ernst Lubitsch and its scenarists included a Viennese Jewish refugee named Billy Wilder. When the three male Soviet agents go to the station to meet Garbo (they don't expect a woman), one spies a bearded fellow with a proletarian knapsack. "That must be the one!" "Yes," says another, "he looks like a comrade!" They follow him, but before they can greet the "comrade," he is met by a German girl. The two exchange the Nazi salute: "Heil Hitler!" Nabokov recalls with a not entirely apolitical delight the ways in which the three Soviet agents, ensconced in their hotel's Royal Suite, quickly succumb to "capitalistic" pleasures. The scene he remembers most vividly, the film's most famous interlude, is the thawing of Garbo by Melvyn Douglas. Seated together in a carefully chosen "working-class" restaurant (a cozy atmosphere for seduction), suave Douglas tries to force Garbo to laugh by telling a series of stupid jokes. She remains unmoved until, in his frustration and fury ("You have no sense of humor! *None!* No humor!"), he leans excitedly on his flimsy table, which topples over, sending him and everything else crashing to the floor. The restaurant quakes with classless mirth. Garbo struggles to maintain her composure, but suddenly a laugh bursts through the stolid mask, and she too roars with uncontrollable laughter. It is a wondrous moment. Remembering the scene thirty years later, Nabokov also rocks with laughter, as he must have done in 1940, when laughter in the dark, to borrow a phrase, was as rare as it was necessary. Joyous as well as haunting, *Invitation to a Beheading* offered its contemporary

263

audience the same opportunity, though its form and affirmative tone seem to have confused almost as many readers as were sustained.

Whether baffled or impressed by the novel, *émigré* critics were correct in their complaints that the "Kafkaesque" *Invitation to a Beheading* was "un-Russian" and belonged to some "foreign" tradition; their heated remarks curiously echo the previous decade's attacks on the "neoclassical" Stravinsky's "traitorous" departure from *âme slave* [the Slavonic spirit]. Prattle about "influences" and "traditions" aside (English C-41, "Modern Comedy: Aristophanes to————," MWF 2:00), the novel's affinities with screen comedy seem clear, and they constitute a brightly lit exit sign, or beam of light, in Nabokov's dark cinema. "A wonderful movie could be made of *Invitation to a Beheading,"* says Nabokov, and, in a sense, it has been done.

Quilty's long death scene represents a return to earlier movie madness, and its violent pratfalls and verbal vaudeville have countless visual analogues in Laurel and Hardy's theater of cruelty. In *County Hospital* (1932), immobilized Hardy is abruptly hoisted from his bed and suspended by his broken leg when the doctor falls out the window and clings to the pulleys of Ollie's traction. Far more savage is the climax to *Them Thar Hills* (1934), which builds slowly toward the inevitable orgy of destruction. "Bend down," says Hardy's tormentor, who then proceeds to douse his trousers with gasoline. Hardy retains his composure and gazes plaintively at the camera, as if to say, "Bad form to resist or run," an example of "grace under pressure" never imagined by Hemingway. "Got a match?" the man asks Laurel, who sweetly obliges, and flaming, gout-afflicted Hardy hops about wildly, finally jumping into a well that contains liquor discarded earlier by hastily departing bootleggers. The terrible explosion catapults Ollie into the air, "higher and higher, like old, gray, mad Nijinski, like Old Faithful, like some old nightmare of mine, to a phenomenal altitude," as Humbert says of Quilty (p. 304), whose gravity-defying acrobatics also evoke images of Keaton's amazing, Veen-like feats in films such as *Sherlock, Jr.:* pole-vaulting from a roof into the back seat of the villain's speeding car, or being propelled through an open window after a ride on the handlebars of a motorcycle—or, if only to insist upon the persistence of a certain kind of comic mechanism, the image of the Three Stooges and a gorilla trapped together at the end of *Idle Roomers* (1944) in an elevator that wildly hurtles up, up, and away, but not, unfortunately, into orbit. At certain moments Humbert's own violent action would seem to have been choreographed by the Buster Keaton who outruns the entire metropolitan police force in *Cops* (1922), or the anti-Sisyphus who runs, leaps, and dodges down a hillside to escape an avalanche of one thousand rocks in *Seven Chances* (1925), or the aging Keaton whose acrobatics dazzled Parisian music-hall audiences in 1953: "I see myself following [wounded Quilty] through the hall, with a kind of double, triple, kangaroo jump, remaining quite straight on straight legs while bouncing up twice in his wake, and then bouncing between him and the front door in a ballet-like stiff bounce, with the purpose of heading him off, since the door was not properly closed" (p. 305). Their violent *pas de deux* is executed with precision as well as gusto; the accelerating velocity of the chase, its zaniness, its realization of a range of dreamlike impossibilities all further suggest that, "underworlder" burlesques and other targets aside, the entire scene is also staged in the style and spirit of the unsentimental film masters whom Nabokov admires most—Keaton, of course; the Marx Brothers; and Nabokov's "favorites," Laurel and Hardy.

The comedy of Humbert's erratic marksmanship is exceeded only by the magical resiliency of Quilty, who, like Oliver Hardy *in extremis,* accepts with uncommon gentlemanly grace the violence performed upon his ample person:

> Suddenly dignified, and somewhat morose, he started to walk up the broad stairs, and, shifting my position, but not actually following him up the steps, I fired three or four times in quick succession, wounding him at every blaze; and every time I did it to him, that horrible thing to him, his face would twitch in an absurd clownish manner, as if he were exaggerating the pain; he slowed down, rolled his eyes half closing them and made a feminine 'ah!' and he shivered every time a bullet hit him as if I were tickling him, and every time I got him with those slow, clumsy, blind bullets of mine, he would say under his breath, with a phoney British accent—all the while dreadfully twitching, shiver-

ing, smirking, but withal talking in a curiously detached and even amiable manner: 'Ah, that hurts sir, enough! Ah, that hurts atrociously, my dear fellow. I pray you, desist. Ah—very painful, very painful, indeed . . . God! Hah! This is abominable, you should really not—' His voice trailed off as he reached the landing, but he steadily walked on despite all the lead I had lodged in his bloated body—and in distress, in dismay, I understood that far from killing him I was injecting spurts of energy into the poor fellow, as if the bullets had been capsules wherein a heady elixir danced. (p. 305)

Growing larger before Humbert's eyes, as in another one of Laurel and Hardy's sight gags involving grotesque physical distortion (*They Go Boom* [1929], in which cold-sufferer Ollie is inflated further by an inhalator), "bloated" Quilty trudges through Pavor Manor, "bleeding majestically," as invincible as Rasputin. " 'Get out of here, get out of here,' he said coughing and spitting; and in a nightmare of wonder, I saw this blood-spattered but still buoyant person get into his bed and wrap himself up in the chaotic bedclothes," regressive Laurel and Hardy's unsafe haven in numerous films. Humbert "hit[s] him at very close range through the blankets, and then he lay back and a big pink bubble with juvenile connotations [= the Lolita they have both "consumed"] formed on his lips, grew to the size of a toy balloon, and vanished" (p. 306), not unlike the explosive interlude in *Saps at Sea*, when Dr. Finlayson attempts to cure bedridden Hardy, suffering from a nervous collapse, by having him inflate a large toy balloon. Minutes later "Quilty of all people had managed to crawl out onto the landing, and there we could see him, flapping and heaving" (p. 307)—Nabokov's version of a death scene performed by Oliver Hardy, exuberant Quilty's resiliency recalling Laurel and Hardy's lovely "Locomotion" at the end of *Hog Wild*. Crushed between two streetcars, their miraculous car still runs, if only in a circle, like some crazed infernal machine. Even Quilty's slow death, its thematic "meaning" aside (the persistence of evil, however banal), is consistent with the spirit that is underscored by the last syllable in Ada's name when it is pronounced correctly in the Russian way —"*da*"! Yes, an echo of Molly Bloom's cascade of musical *yeses*, comedy's soaring, affirmative note, sustaining us above the hoary abyss contemplated by Keaton and Lloyd, Kinbote and Luzhin, Shirin and Nabokov. "The [Alpine] gondola [containing Hugh

Person and Armande] would have gone on gliding forever in a blue haze sufficient for paradise had not a robust attendant stopped it before it turned to reascend for good," writes the author of *Transparent Things* (p. 54), bringing to mind the closing moments of *The Balloonatic* (1923), when the canoe bearing Buster Keaton and his girl sails over the edge of a waterfall and floats through the air, suspended by love and (as the camera moves back, visual surprise) the more literally supportive balloon—which deflates our sentimental metaphor.

The Nabokovs' arrival in America in June 1940, on a ship peopled mainly by Jewish refugees, was of course a joyous occasion. Their most vivid memory of the event is characteristic of Nabokov's art: two Immigration Service officials (formidable to any traveler, but especially to *émigrés*), discovered young Dmitri Nabokov's boxing gloves in the family's baggage. The inspectors grabbed the gloves, each donned one, and they began to spar together—a Laurel and Hardy introduction to the promised land. "Velcome to Amer–r–rika!" said a friend-of-a-friend, in a thick, unintentionally comical German accent, greeting the Nabokovs after they had passed through Immigration's portals. Five years later, in Boston, Nabokov would become an American citizen. On their way to the citizenship exam and ceremony, Nabokov's sponsor, Mihel Karpovich, a staid Harvard professor and former consular official, told the apprentice American, "No joking, *no* joking, *please!*" "Oh, a *professor!*" said the Immigration official upon meeting the candidate. A solemn Nabokov began the oral exam. "Name the American presidents," which Nabokov did, unerringly. He was next told to read aloud from a standard text which began, "The child is bold." *"The child is bald,"* declaimed Nabokov, soon to purchase new eyeglasses. "You can't read English," said the official, "he is *bold.*" "No, no," argued Nabokov. "Why should the poor little child be 'bold'? He is very young. It should read '*bald.*' " "You're right, I never thought of that," said the official and, save for the mortified Karpovich, everyone laughed. Nabokov would teach for almost two decades in America, where he quietly launched several books composed in English, causing only minor ripples. With no fanfare whatsoever, the Paris-based Olympia Press brought out *Lolita* in 1955. Three years later it was published in America and, as John Shade writes in *Pale Fire,* "Hurricane Lolita / Swept from Florida to Maine." "A painful birth, a difficult baby, but a kind daughter," *Lolita* enabled Nabokov, at sixty, to resign his professorship. Part of the fortune lost in 1919 had been restored exactly forty years later, the rubles miraculously converted to dollars, and the Nabokovs would soon move again, first to Hollywood to script *Lolita,* and then to Switzerland in 1960. His last public appearance at Cornell was as featured speaker at the 1959 Festival of Contemporary Arts, before an audience of four or five hundred, which included Deane W. Malott, president of Cornell. The subject: "On Censorship." Lecturing on recent Soviet Literature, rather than *Lolita,* Nabokov constructed socialist realism's ideal love scene, Boy Meets Girl at the Factory (or was it a farm? witnesses disagree, legends grow)—the boy and girl standing next to each other but never touching since they are manning their machines and have a work quota. Their dialogue a parody of Party jargon, Nabokov played both roles, his entire body vibrating violently as he delivered, in a terrible machine-induced stutter and stammer, their banal and hapless endearments. All witnesses agree that Nabokov made his exit from academe over a tumultuous sea of laughter.

"If you want to make a movie out of my book, have one of these [criminal] faces gently melt into my own, while I look," says Humbert, studying the "Wanted" posters in the post office at Wace (p. 224). It seemed incredible to Nabokov in 1955 that such a film might be made, but it is not surprising that Quilty's "cinematic" death scene would eventually be the most memorable interlude in Kubrick's *Lolita.* Nabokov's unpublished screenplay contains several other screen comedy set pieces which Keaton would have relished and no doubt happily realized. In the novel, young Humbert's mother accidentally dies in a parenthetical throwaway phrase ("picnic, lightning" [p. 12]), but screenwriter Nabokov visualizes "A MOUNTAIN MEADOW—THUNDERHEAD ADVANCING

ABOVE SHARP CLIFFS": "Several people scramble for shelter, and the first big drops of rain strike the zink of a lunch box. As the poor lady in white runs toward the pavilion of a lookout, a blast of livid light fells her. Her graceful specter floats up above the black cliffs holding a parasol and blowing kisses to her husband and child who stand below, looking up, hand in hand." [17] In another sequence, Clare Quilty discovers Lolita seated in his uncle's dentist's chair. Quilty "pumps the chair up and backwards with his foot. . . . There should be a fantastic blend of an Amusement Park wobblecar and a flying machine. Summer clouds and sun stripes glide by. Lolita soars, Lolita solos," says the scenarist, and the interlude recalls the wonderful barbershop scene in *The Great Dictator,* in which the competitive, megalomaniacal despots (Chaplin and Jack Oakie) have their chairs cranked up skyward. Although Kubrick dropped these "visuals" from his vastly revised shooting script, he did include his own *hommage* to earlier screen comedy. Chaplin's tussle with the wall-bed in *One A.M.* (1916) informs Humbert's and the night porter's equally funny struggle with the collapsible cot at the Enchanted Hunters, but the slapstick is distractive—a sop for the censors?—and the tone is wrong; for all its ironies, the crucial seduction scene is ultimately no laughing matter, no "Honeymoon Hotel." As excellent as James Mason is as Humbert, the scenario and director (if not the medium itself) fail to communicate Humbert's delicately balanced tonal oscillations, the original scene's splicing of lust and despair, its verbalization of the pain at the center of all the playfulness and parody:

Every now and then, immediately east of my left ear (always assuming I lay on my back, not daring to direct my viler side toward the nebulous haunch of my bed-mate), the corridor would brim with cheerful, resonant and inept exclamations ending in a volley of good-nights. When *that* stopped, a toilet immediately north of my cerebellum took over. It was a manly, energetic, deep-throated toilet, and it was used many times. Its gurgle and gush and long afterflow shook the wall behind me. Then someone in a southern direction was extravagantly sick, almost coughing out his life with his liquor, and his toilet descended like a veritable Niagara, immediately beyond our bathroom [Quilty—A. A.]. And when finally all the waterfalls had stopped, and the enchanted

269

Dark Cinema: Returning from a walk (November 1972), Nabokov and I entered the dimly lit bar of the Montreux Palace Hotel. Standing at the bar, he ordered a scotch, and I asked for a well-known aperitif which was not in stock. "Good!" said Nabokov, "that's no drink for a man." Our rather tight-fitting overcoats still on (mine dark blue, his olive brown), we began a three-way badinage with the barman on the nonavailability of that aperitif. "We're like Hemingway's killers," observed Nabokov, speaking out of the corner of his mouth in mock-gangster fashion. Pointing to his wide-brimmed gray fedora, placed in gentlemanly fashion on a bar stool, Nabokov said, "I should return it to my head, no?, and heighten the realism. I loved 'The Killers' and the film version, too [1946, directed by Robert Siodmak]: the first scene in the diner was superb, each detail so exact [above, Charles McGraw and William Conrad], the unappetizing kitchen in which the killers, working with frightening dispatch, truss together those innocent men. The scene in which the fellow [Burt Lancaster] awaits his fate in a tawdry, shadowy rented room was excellent, too. But the remainder of the film added a good deal to Hemingway, didn't it? Gangster stuff . . . [Nabokov grimaces] . . . more conventional, but very well done." The killing of Quilty parodies that "stuff," but the acute observation of roadside America, the Germanic *Stimmung* ("mood") of *film noir* is everywhere in *Lolita*.

hunters were sound asleep, the avenue under the window of my insomnia, to the west of my wake—a staid, eminently residential, dignified alley of huge trees—degenerated into the despicable haunt of gigantic trucks roaring through the wet and windy night.

And less than six inches from me and my burning life, was nebulous Lolita! After a long stirless vigil, my tentacles moved towards her again, and this time the creak of the mattress did not awake her. I managed to bring my ravenous bulk so close to her that I felt the aura of her bare shoulder like a warm breath upon my cheek. And then, she sat up, gasped, muttered with insane rapidity something about boats, tugged at the sheets and lapsed back into her rich, dark, young unconsciousness. As she tossed, within that abundant flow of sleep, recently auburn, at present lunar, her arm struck me across the face. For a second I held her. She freed herself from the shadow of my embrace—doing this not consciously, not violently, not with any personal distaste, but with the neutral plaintive murmur of a child demanding its natural rest. And again the situation remained the same: Lolita with her curved spine to Humbert, Humbert resting his head on his hand and burning with desire and dyspepsia. (p. 132)

Hovering Humbert's "ravenous bulk" recalls countless Sleeping Beauty horror tales and films, and Nabokov's *mise-en-scène* creates a veritable dark cinema here, for his most evocative aural and visual descriptions are in the manner of classic nineteen-forties *films noirs,* with their oppressive, rain-washed nightscapes and their desperate, driven men—seemingly decent people who have irreparably committed themselves to their obsessions or passions, and are suddenly criminals (*vide* the American work of refugee directors Fritz Lang, Otto Preminger, Billy Wilder, Max Ophuls, Robert Siodmak, and Curt Bernhardt whose *Possessed* [1947] is remarked by Humbert [p. 264]). No naturalistic camera, however, could capture the image of his "tentacles," "the warm breath" of Lolita's shoulder, or, short of narration, the sound of Humbert's voice. Tough-minded members of the jury might argue that Humbert is dissembling, but the passage is instructive. What, then, asks Kinbote in *Pale Fire,* is the "password"? "Pity," answers John Shade (p. 225). Nabokov's best comedy, like that of his screen colleagues, blends farce and terror, and humanizes us through laughter.

Notes

1. Vladimir Nabokov, *Ada* (New York, 1969), p. 399. Subsequent parenthetical page references are to this edition. Hardcover first editions are always the rule.

271

2. Vladimir Nabokov, "Spring in Fialta," in *Nabokov's Dozen* (New York, 1958), p. 18.

3. Vladimir Nabokov, *Laughter in the Dark* (New York, 1938), p. 26. Textual references are to this edition.

4. Vladimir Nabokov, *King, Queen, Knave* (New York, 1968), p. 50. Textual references are to this edition. See also pp. 52, 61, 87, 115, and 117–18.

5. Vladimir Nabokov, *Despair* (New York, 1966), p. 87. Textual references are to this edition. See also pp. 54, 83, 218.

6. Vladimir Nabokov, *The Eye* (New York, 1965), p. 39. Textual references are to this edition.

7. Vladimir Nabokov, "Lik," in *Nabokov's Quartet* (New York, 1966), p. 49.

8. Vladimir Nabokov, *The Defense* (New York, 1964), p. 86. Textual references are to this edition.

9. Vladimir Nabokov, *Glory* (New York, 1971), p. 35. Textual references are to this edition.

10. Vladimir Nabokov, *Pnin* (New York, 1957), p. 80. Textual references are to this edition.

11. Vladimir Nabokov, *The Real Life of Sebastian Knight* (New York, 1941), p. 147. Textual references are to this edition.

12. Vladimir Nabokov, *Lolita* (New York, 1958), p. 28. Textual references are to this edition and my own edition, *The Annotated Lolita* (New York, 1970), which has the same pagination.

13. Unless otherwise noted, such quotations are drawn from informal conversations with Nabokov in Montreux, Switzerland (January 1968, August 1970, September 1971, and November 1972).

14. Vladimir Nabokov, *Transparent Things* (New York, 1972), p. 30. Textual references are to this edition.

15. Vladimir Nabokov, *Nikolai Gogol* (Greenwich, Conn., 1944), p. 70. Also see pp. 63–69. Nabokov keeps his definition of *poshlost'* up to date; see any of several interviews, especially *Paris Review*, No. 41 (Summer–Fall 1967), 103–4, where *poshlost'* ranges from airline stewardesses to Mann's *Death in Venice*.

16. *Ibid.*, p. 67.

17. Vladimir Nabokov, *The Gift* (New York, 1963), p. 102. Textual references are to this edition.

18. Vladimir Nabokov, *Bend Sinister* (New York, 1947), p. 222. Textual references are to this edition.

19. See James Joyce, *Ulysses* (New York, 1961), p. 609, and compare with Nabokov's description: "The murdered child had a crimson and gold turban around its head; its face was skilfully painted and powdered: a mauve blanket, exquisitely smooth, came up to its chin" (*Bend Sinister*, p. 224).

20. Alfred Appel, Jr., "Conversations with Nabokov," *Novel: A Forum on Fiction*, IV, 3 (Spring 1971), 213.

21. *Ibid.*, 212.

22. Vladimir Nabokov, *Speak, Memory* (New York, 1966), p. 191. Textual references are to this edition.

23. Vladimir Nabokov, *Pale Fire* (New York, 1962), p. 49. Textual references are to this edition.

24. Vladimir Nabokov, "The Assistant Producer," in *Nabokov's Dozen*, p. 77.

25. Vladimir Nabokov, *Mary* (New York, 1970), p. 9. Textual references are to this edition.

26. Act One is the only part of the play ever to appear in print, in *Rul'* [*The Rudder*], January 1, 1927.

27. Josef von Sternberg, *Fun in a Chinese Laundry* (New York, 1965), p. 132.

28. Notable exceptions in the nineteen-thirties include Graham Greene in England and Otis Ferguson and William Troy in America.

272

29. Larry Swindell, *Spencer Tracy* (Cleveland and New York, 1969), p. 139.

30. Aaron Latham, *Crazy Sundays: F. Scott Fitzgerald in Hollywood* (New York, 1971), p. 178.

31. Paul Horgan, *Encounters with Stravinsky: A Personal Record* (New York, 1972), p. 99.

32. Igor Stravinsky, album liner notes, *Stravinsky Conducts Ballet Music* (Columbia LP MS 6649). Since "Hollywood" serves as a negative touchstone in all artistic areas, Stravinsky's brilliant associate, Robert Craft, says of Schoenberg: "The ending [of *A Survivor from Warsaw,* Op. 46], I think, is the most moving he ever wrote—compare it with the MGM ending of the *Genesis* prelude where he has no words to inspire him and where he even forgets his own *Satire* on composers who end in C major after wandering about traversing all the keys" (album notes, *The Music of Arnold Schoenberg,* Vol. 1, *Robert Craft Conducting* [Columbia LP M2S 679]). Creon's first aria in Stravinsky's *Oedipus Rex* (1927) wittily *begins* in C major, another satire of exhausted artistic means akin to Nabokov's parodies of high and low materials. "The music? I love it, *all* of it, even the Messenger's fanfares, which remind me of the now badly tarnished trumpets of early 20th Century–Fox," wrote Stravinsky in 1963 (album notes, *Oedipus Rex* [Columbia LP M31129]).

33. "Conversations with Nabokov," *op. cit.,* 214–15.

34. *Ibid.,* 213–14.

35. "The Strong Opinions of Vladimir Nabokov—As Imparted to Nicholas Garnham," *The Listener* (10 October 1968), p. 463.

36. "Conversations with Nabokov," *op. cit.,* 213.

37. For a paraphrase of these untranslated works, see Andrew Field, *Nabokov: His Life in Art* (Boston, 1967), pp. 75–78.

38. "Conversations with Nabokov," *op. cit.,* 214.

39. Vladimir Nabokov, *Invitation to a Beheading* (New York, 1959), p. 97. Textual references are to this edition.

40. "Conversations with Nabokov," *op. cit.,* 214.

41. *Nabokov's Dozen, op. cit.,* p. 141.

42. "Conversations with Nabokov," *op. cit.,* 213.

43. These devices are done to death, figuratively speaking, in the most violent *Tom and Jerry* cartoons, which are to *Bugs Bunny* what the helicopter assault scene in *From Russia with Love* (1963) is to the famous cropduster chase sequence in *North by Northwest* (1959).

44. I've not seen this cartoon, and am drawing upon Barbara Deming's recollection of it in *Running Away from Myself* (New York, 1969), p. 190. She offers several other good examples of the ways in which comedies of the nineteen-forties "demolish before our eyes . . . all that has stood there the moment before" (p. 191).

45. The anti-hero of Nathanael West's parodistic *A Cool Million* (subtitled "The Dismantling of Lemuel Pitkin" [1934]) suffers in similar fashion. Over the course of the novel he loses several working parts, and, as the stooge in a vaudeville finale, is divested of his remaining good eye, toupee, and wooden leg (which is knocked into the audience)—a scene that Nabokov's Cornell student Thomas Pynchon seems to have drawn upon in *V.* (1963) when the gang of Maltese urchins unhinges the prefabricated and helpless transvestite priest.

46. *Ulysses, op. cit.,* p. 523.

47. The screenplay will be published within a year. Quotations copyright © 1973 by McGraw-Hill International, all rights reserved.

Poplavsky: the heir presumptive of Montparnasse
ANTHONY OLCOTT

Boris Poplavsky was one of those relatively rare artists about whom no one was equivocal; his admirers, largely contemporaries, took him for a leader, an inspiration, and were almost fanatically devoted to him, while his detractors, for the most part people who had fled Russia as adults, were puzzled and disturbed by his apparent idleness, his strange poetry, his use of drugs, and his love of *épatage*. This wide divergence of opinion reflects the conditions of the literary scene in the first emigration and may be, at least in part, explained as a manifestation of the *émigré* "generation gap." These first *émigrés,* who left Russia in the period between the two world wars, may be divided roughly into those who fled the Revolution as adults and those who weren't yet fully grown. In literature, the adults already had established reputations, had readers in Russia, and came naturally to dominate the literary scene in exile. At first, authors like Bunin, Kuprin, and the Merezhkovskys only reprinted their pre-Revolutionary works, but by the mid-twenties and early thirties they were again turning out new material, keeping the *émigré* publishing houses busy. It was this generation which edited the journals, controlled the writers' funds, and, for the most part, bought the books. The group was still emotionally tied to Russia, dedicated to trying in some way to make sense of what had become of their former lives and to continuing the political struggle. Of course, as Soviet power consolidated itself, this last concern faded, but apparently never died out, for as late as 1953 the editor of the New York journal *Opyty* (*Experiments*) felt it necessary to publish in the first issue a disclaimer which announced that, despite the solidly anti-Bolshevik feelings of everyone concerned, the magazine would be concerned solely with literary matters.

The second group in the emigration consisted of those who had been born in Russia but while still young had been taken away and planted in new countries, where they finished their schooling and established their lives. The members of this generation were undeniably Russian, but they also knew the language and literature of their new homeland, as well as those of Russia. In certain cases, they became artists in the new culture rather than the old. The most famous writer of this generation, Vladimir Nabokov, is an obvious example, though even better ones are writers like Henri Troyat, Zoé Oldenbourg, and Nathalie Sarraute, who write exclusively in French. Poplavsky, though he wrote in Russian, was well aware of this difference in backgrounds, as he noted:

The homeland [of the young generation] is neither Russia nor France, but rather Paris (or Prague, Tallinn, etc.), with only a certain remote projection into a Russian infinity, as Athens or Ios was the homeland of the writing Greek, with a secondary projection into the enormous ancient world.[1]

Poplavsky, by the unhappy fact of his death at thirty-two, is something of a symbol of this younger generation, for he lived exactly one-half his life in Russia (to the age of sixteen). The other half, minus time spent in Constantinople and in transit, he lived in Paris, where he died in 1935. Thus he was at least half French, a fact rather oddly underscored by certain passages from his diaries, where identical entries were made first in Russian, then in French.

Obviously such a difference in the backgrounds of the *émigrés* led inevitably to a difference in literary influences, concerns, and ambitions. But for the artists of the younger generation, this difference had abnormally severe consequences, which were the product of other basic facts of the first emigration: its small size, its widely dispersed membership, and its relative poverty. Though there was a fantastic proliferation of journals, newspapers, and publishing houses during the emigration, most of them folded quickly, leaving the young writer who was fortunate enough to be published little time to establish a following. Almost all the publishing ventures were owned by members of the older generation, who were naturally wary of young new artists, particularly artists like Poplavsky, who wrote poems like "A Sentimental Demonology," which begins:

> Day descended, infinitely withered,
> And a finger of rain twirled a transparent globe.
> God called me, but I didn't answer.
> We were embarrassed, and cursed our shyness.[2]

Though the poverty of *émigré* life did favor poets more than prose writers (poetry can be printed more cheaply, as it fits into the empty crannies of newspapers and journals) even the life of the poet who achieved some fame was far from plush, as the poet Koncheyev says in Nabokov's *The Gift:*

"Fame? ... Don't make me laugh. Who knows my poems? A thousand? A thousand five hundred, at the very outside two thousand intelligent expatriates, of whom again ninety percent don't understand them. Two thousand out of three million refugees! That's provincial success, but not fame." [3]

Thus poverty, indifference, derision, and silence were the lot of many of the young writers of the first emigration. Even Poplavsky, who was among the best known and most widely printed of these writers, had by his death succeeded in publishing only about sixty poems and nine chapters of the novel *Apollon Bezobrazov* (the title of which in Russian is paradoxical—*The Formless Apollo*), in eight different journals. The publication of the one volume of verse which appeared during his lifetime, *Flagi* (*Flags*), was due not to its purchase by any publishing house, but to the largesse of the widow of a wealthy Rigan, one Lydia Kharlampievna

Pumpyanskaya, who financed its printing. In other words, the writers of this younger generation were, by the grim economic facts of their lives, all but barred from literature.

These conditions existed for all young writers, and as such provide a partial explanation for Poplavsky's small body of work. However, these conditions say little of Poplavsky, for he was more than merely one of a multitude of impoverished artists. Though it is impossible to exaggerate the poverty in which he lived, too much can be made of it, as the great critic and poet Vladislav Khodasevich may have done in his obituary to Poplavsky:

A man who has not slept enough because he has no shelter, a man who is tormented by hunger, a man who has not even a corner in which to be alone simply cannot write, though he be a genius a hundred times over. One must be a complete ignoramus or have no conscience to compare the poverty of Montparnasse [the bohemian quarter of Paris where many of these writers lived] with the poverty of former writers. Poplavsky's daily budget averaged seven francs, three of which he gave to a friend. Next to Poplavsky, Dostoevsky was what Rockefeller is next to me.[4]

All of the above is true, yet there is also a certain element of truth in Gleb Struve's remark that "Poplavsky, a healthy fellow, a boxer, a 'strong and agile athlete,' didn't know how to work and didn't want to work." [5] Though it was doubtless difficult for a young *émigré* to find a job in Paris during the thirties, it is almost certainly true that Poplavsky did not particularly want to be employed. It is simply not true, however, that he neither wished nor knew how to work; he would lock himself away for days on end, doing nothing but writing. He was very widely read, and had ambitions to be even more so. As he wrote:

Often I withdraw into the library ... because a long time ago the idea of a deep responsibility regarding the dead writers of all ages was formed in me, to read them through. For, I think, they lived not for themselves and not for their contemporaries, but precisely for me. It is as though they beseech me from the shelves, let them fulfill their purpose, save their lives, otherwise so pointless.[6]

The size of Poplavsky's body of work can also be underestimated: three additional volumes of verse were published after his death,[7] as well as a selection of observations from his diaries,[8] four additional chapters of *Apollon Bezobrazov*, and the beginning of another novel, *Domoy s nebes* (*Homeward from Heaven*). Even during his lifetime, he published more than it would seem; he wrote a number of reviews and articles for the magazine *Chisla* (*Numbers*), including critiques of art exhibits, general evaluations and explanations of postcubist painting techniques, and two articles on boxing (Poplavsky was a fan of Primo Carnera). Further, there is a large amount of material which was never published, including the rest of his diaries, other parts of both novels, and, almost certainly, more poems, for Poplavsky began to write when he was sixteen and seems to have composed nearly every day after that. Thus, despite the importance of the general conditions of his life as an *émigré,* the real uniqueness of Boris Poplavsky lies somewhere outside those conditions.

More important is his own view of his life and his understanding of his environment. At least part of the answer to Professor Struve's observation is that Poplavsky failed to see the point of a job which merely provided material sustenance; he was concerned with problems he felt were more fundamental, such as his spiritual existence, his relationship with God, and the meaning of life and art. As he put it, "The emigration is a tragic, impoverished paradise for poets, for dreamers and romantics." [9] It is a dangerous exercise to try to pinpoint the Poplavsky philosophy, for he was a follower of Krishnamurti, Rozanov, the Orthodox Church, the Catholic Church, Hinduism, and any number of other thinkers and sects, both in succession and in conjunction. As Georgy Adamovich put it:

> **I met him fairly often. There never was any way of knowing or foreseeing what Poplavsky would arrive with today, who he would be this evening: a monarchist, a communist, a mystic, a rationalist, a Nietzschean, a Marxist, a Christian, a Buddhist, or simply an athletic young man who detested all abstract wisdom and thought one need only sleep well, eat up, and do exercises to build up the muscles.[10]**

Further, Poplavsky was a devoted and accomplished talker, able to think quickly and acutely and to defend any position he cared to take—for an entire night, if he so desired. Something of the flavor of such conversations is conveyed by one of the chapters of *Apollon Bezobrazov,* where Poplavsky says of his character:

> He especially loved to talk about repetition, about the beauty of infinitely long attention and the deepening of attention, about the saintliness of Oriental ascetics. He talked about how the sound E is the beginning, O the environment and sum of everything, U the will and the sound of the trumpet ending the world, A the plenitude of affirmation and eternity, I the force penetrating the surroundings, the beginning of every personality and sadness. In the same way he talked long about the meaning of ancient names, such as Ozakhoo, Indra, Ioann, Anna. Then he would talk of quantity and quality, of the divided and the whole, of freedom and necessity.[11]

Adamovich wrote that he had encountered minds like Poplavsky's in but a few men, among them Velimir Khlebnikov and Osip Mandelstam.[12]

Poplavsky's abilities as a talker, combined with his more unfortunate habit of *épatage,* have been confused by some people as a tendency to lie;[13] a more accurate evaluation would be that he avoided the truth, or perhaps even that he saw a number of truths, each of equal validity—which would also explain his mélange of philosophies, further compounded by his voracious reading. He seems to have discerned patterns in widely separate thinkers, which he synthesized and made over to his own requirements, often without the slightest chance that such synthesis would be apparent to others.

The problem of determining Poplavsky's view of the world is complicated, too, by his age. He began publishing in 1928 and published for just seven years. Much of what appeared in print seems to be the record of a man experiencing rapid spiritual change, so that probably any philosophy he expounded may be applied only to the Poplavsky of a certain period, rather than to the whole man. For example, *Flags* contains poems written between the poet's sixteenth and twenty-fourth years,[14] which largely explains the undeniable weaknesses of the book. Also responsible is the poor editing the manuscripts received. Not only were many poems printed with superfluous stanzas which a good editor would have advised the poet to drop, but serious misprints crept in as well—including, in one place, the printing of the last stanzas of one poem at the end of another, obviously mangling both. In subsequent volumes, not only are the editing and the printing far more carefully done, but the poems are primarily those of the last five years of his life. In other words, these are the poems of what maturity was accorded him, and they show him, as in fact do parts of *Flags,* to have been on his way to developing into a major talent and influence. It is not sufficient to counter the assertion of Poplavsky's future development, as some critics have done, with the cases of Blok, who had published many of his major poems by age thirty-two, or of Lermontov, who died five years younger than that. Tyutchev, on the other hand, published his first poetry when he was thirty-three and didn't become well known until he was in his fifties; and Annensky was first published when he was forty-eight.

During his lifetime Poplavsky was not often mentioned in print, and even more rarely discussed enthusiastically. After his death, however, there appeared a number of laudatory articles and statements, surprising not only for what was written, but also because of who wrote them. Merezhkovsky is said to have considered that the fact that the emigration had produced Poplavsky was more than enough to justify it to all future judgments.[15] And Yuri Terapiano, writing in 1953, said that had Poplavsky had an editor, had he rewritten or eliminated a few poems, then *Flags* would have been the best book of poetry the emigration had yet produced.[16] Even cooler heads had extraordinarily high opinions of Poplavsky. Adamovich wrote that Poplavsky's poetic gift was much stronger, freer, and more abundant than that of Belyi;[17] while Khodasevich, probably the strictest and most sternly classical of all critics and poets in the first emigration, praised Poplavsky with almost as little reservation as did Merezhkovsky, writing that "As a lyrical poet, Poplavsky was doubtless one of the most talented in the emigration, even, perhaps, the most talented."[18] The obituary from which that remark is taken is interesting in its entirety, for Khodasevich took the view that the emigration was killing its younger writers and, in a sense, insuring its own doom by refusing to support a developing literary culture. Thus the death of Poplavsky was not only a tragedy because he was so senselessly murdered,[19] but also, and more importantly, because the emigration had lost a major poet, who could have developed into an artist of real significance. If the poems of *Snezhnyi chas* (*Snowy Hour*), which date from the period 1931–1935, are true indicators, Poplavsky, in his last years, was in fact moving away from the murky mishmash of Blok and surrealism, which had in places marred *Flags,* toward a real mastery of eidological poetic composition. As Nikolai Tatishchev, Poplavsky's close friend, wrote:

Poplavsky used words as a musician uses sounds; the sound gives an image, but an undefined one, and it speeds immediately to die away, making way for another, similar but different.[20]

This type of composition is obviously fraught with the danger of obscurity, but when it is successful, the result is beautiful lyric poetry. Nabokov quite accurately describes its sounds as "plangent tonality,"[21] but fails to convey the startling visual qualities of Poplavsky's verse. Poplavsky had the eye of a painter (he in fact studied to become a painter for a time), and his poems combine color and image in visual patterns as fleeting and vivid as his aural patterns. Had his developing mastery continued unchecked, then Poplavsky would without dispute be now considered a major poet. Obviously this heightens the tragedy of his death.

It must be noted that all the men quoted above refer to Poplavsky as a poet, and indeed the larger part of his published work is poetry. However, he also wrote a great deal of prose, most of which belongs to his last years. Indeed, there is some evidence that he was turning increasingly to prose as he grew older, which means that, far from pushing on to perfect eidological composition, he might instead have been setting off in a totally new direction at the time of his death. The year before he died he published three apparently discrete short prose works, and the first section of *Homeward from Heaven* appeared the year after, with subsequent sections somewhat later; all of his published prose works postdate 1930. Adamovich suggested, in fact, that poetry may not have been Poplavsky's milieu at all, writing that "Neither Belyi nor Poplavsky were people who would find themselves fully in poetry, would grow up, bloom, only in it be able to express themselves." [22] If Adamovich's comparison was meant to stand, then this implies that Poplavsky was turning to prose; for Belyi is probably best known today for his prose.

Poplavsky's prose involves a small set of characters, said to be drawn from life. Notable among them are Bezobrazov; Therese, a part-Russian girl who has been raised in a Swiss convent and knows how to talk with rocks and plants; and an "I" who seems at times to be Poplavsky, at times to be an admirer invented to describe and praise his inventor (Poplavsky used Apollon Bezobrazov as a pen name). In *Apollon Bezobrazov* it is Bezobrazov who is the center about whom all the other characters revolve. As Poplavsky wrote:

Apollon Bezobrazov was entirely in the present. It was like a golden wheel, with neither top nor bottom, which the perfection of the world spins pointlessly ... on which someone invisible stood, ravished from the world by his horrifying happiness.
In his presence, everything turned to stone, as though he were Medusa.[23]

By contrast, in *Homeward from Heaven* Bezobrazov is barely mentioned, and Oleg, who is described from the third person but who closely resembles the "I" of the first novel, is the center. Similar in both works are not only the shared characters, but also the style in which the pieces are written. Poplavsky's prose is a distinctive blend of conventional narrative techniques, lyrical free-association, normal rhymed verse printed as prose, street songs, and others, each succeeding the other in kaleidoscopic fashion. This is not to suggest that his prose works are identical in style, for they are not; in fact, Poplavsky had a broad range of narrative techniques under his control. In each work some techniques dominate, as in the Therese chapters of *Apollon Bezobrazov* where the tone is mystical lyricism, somehow Zen-like, while the last chapters of the same book form a journal which records the pole-ward drifting of a boat, in a manner closely similar to the end of Poe's *The Narrative of Arthur Gordon Pym of Nantucket*. A short story, *Bal* (*The Ball*), which looks suspiciously like a chapter from *Apollon Bezobrazov,* is by contrast a welter of viewpoints and styles, alternating incoherent chatter with cafe songs, lyrical outbursts, and rhymed verse to imitate, and masterfully, the mind of a drunken poet at a public dance.

The great pity of Poplavsky's prose is that it was published only in fragments; this makes his writing seem both formless and pointless, beauty with no purpose, to which Poplavsky was vehemently opposed. Despite the sloppy spontaneity which his works seem at times to convey, he was a meticulously exact worker. As Tatishchev wrote:

> One might think that questions of form didn't interest him at all. Each of his poems seems to be an improvisation. In fact, he occasionally rewrote a single poem as many as forty times, correcting not only separate words and lines, but the whole thing, from beginning to end.[24]

Poplavsky himself wrote of the need for form in the apparent chaos of postcubist paintings, noting that "a painting must have compositional axes and symmetries";[25] probably he recognized a similar principle in prose. He definitely was opposed to useless art, to beauty for its own sake, and at times seems to have considered all beauty in art to be a lie, a falsification of the world. The purpose of art was to him the true representation of life, aided by artistic insight; as he put it, "The artist attempts to help nature complete itself, to bring out its exhausted tendencies."[26] Since the life Poplavsky and his contemporaries knew was in many ways ugly, obviously purely beautiful art seemed false, and the artist who practiced it "dries himself up," as Tatishchev expressed it,[27] citing the example of the Romantic poet Zhukovsky. The example is probably Poplavsky's, for *Flags* contains a poem entitled "Imitation of Zhukovsky," which begins, "A naked virgin arrives and drowns / An impossible tree dressed in a tunic sighs."[28] Needless to say, Zhukovsky would never have written such lines.

Whatever "axes and symmetries" Poplavsky's works now contain is difficult to say, not simply because his novels exist only in fragments, but also because his innovative style was part of a form, the whole of which is difficult to reconstruct from its shards. As his hatred for "Beautiful Art" would imply, Poplavsky was opposed to literature as a discrete activity and wished to merge it with private correspondence and other writing done without thought of an audience. This idea was bound up in his preoccupation with spiritual existence, with the specific fact of each human life. Literature can express only that fact, and everything outside it is sham beauty or hackwork. In Poplavsky's words: "The artist describes only himself and that which he could become, his potential. . . . Every artist who creates from the void the new, and that which never was, relative to his past, his memory, lies and invents"; [29] and "Literary hackwork of all kinds, every concession to the public, is a betrayal of spiritual torment, the wages of which are petrification and cabalistic death." [30]

It was on the basis of this opposition that Poplavsky was attempting to build a new literary form, one which would represent his own existence and the spiritual fact of the emigration, and he was seeking it in the form of the diary. As early as 1930 he wrote that "The private letter, the diary, and the transcript of a psychoanalysis are the best methods of its [i.e. the fact of the spiritual life] expression"; [31] and by the last issue of *Numbers,* in 1934, he wrote of this new literary form as an accomplished fact:

The new subjective diary-like literature teaches a man, as much as possible, greater respect for himself, his eternal love, eternal separation, eternal loyalty, eternal betrayal, entirely personal, of God. This new literature is saving man from Russian self-abasement, fatal to every life.[32]

Thus the diary was the ideal form toward which Poplavsky was working, and his attempts to achieve it led him into a contradiction which he never resolved: the artist who writes for an audience is a liar, while the artist who writes only for himself doesn't really exist, as he can save no one. He effected something of a compromise when he wrote that writers "write neither for themselves nor for the public. They write for friends," [33] but this was ambiguous and unsatisfying, for by emphasizing the importance of the person, Poplavsky lowered the significance of what is written. He said almost as much when he wrote:

The good poet can never write anything bad, and a bad poem by a good poet is many times preferable to a good poem by a bad poet. In fact, in general poems aren't important. It is much more important to be acquainted with the poet, to drink tea with him, to go to the movies with him, for poetry is in general a surrogate, for those who can't converse face to face.[34]

Poplavsky made no mention of prose in those remarks, and it is unclear whether he did so deliberately or because he intended "poetry" to mean literature in general. Quite possibly it is the latter, for in another article he wrote:

There is no art and none is necessary. Love of art is cheapness (*poshlost'*), re-sembling the cheapness of seekers of the pretty life, and to every famous writer is to be preferred another unknown genius who ironically flexes a big athletic hand before himself and says under his breath, "They'll never find out." [35]

In either case, Poplavsky's ideas had an obvious anti-literary bent, which suggests the third possible course his development might have followed—that of concentrating upon his personality and either leaving literature entirely, or, like the athletic genius above, writing for himself alone. It is thus fitting that Poplavsky seems to be remembered now primarily as a personality rather than as an artist. Even Yuri Terapiano, who wrote sympathetically of him, said he was a personality, not a talent, whose significance for the emigration was his enormous breadth of character.[36] It was on the basis of personality as well that people's opinions were usually split: the bohemian set of Montparnasse adored his guru-like pronouncements, and the societal pillars were outraged and aghast at each new Poplavsky escapade—without much attention paid to his art by either side.

Of course, it is precisely his personality which is most difficult to determine, both because he was the center of partisan warfare, making it hard to accept completely statements from either side, and because a writer's personality is in general a most difficult thing to deduce from his writings. This is trebly true of a writer like Poplavsky, who was given to hyperbole and lightning reversals of opinion and was capable of chatter so persuasive that one suspects he periodically converted himself. Thus, while it is obviously unfair to simply dismiss him as a drug-crazed decadent, there is also something suspiciously saccharine about Tatishchev's statement:

Deepening with the years, Poplavsky's break with the world was transformed into another even more difficult trial, that of eternal doubt whether there exists on earth true love and friendship, whether even they aren't illusions, whether

Doubtless the truth lies somewhere between the two positions, but exactly where is still to be determined. Until more of Poplavsky's own materials are published, his personality can be sketched only in the broadest of terms. One may draw from his poetry, his prose, and the statements of his friends only that certain air which Poplavsky called *esprit:*

The *esprit* of an artist is the tangible expression of all his ideas, of all his dreams and beliefs, and, in a very large measure, of his life, but most important, a greater or lesser relationship to art, as to something holy and prayerfully important.[38]

In other words, it must for now be sufficient to generalize about Poplavsky's personality, to say that he ardently sought God, and just as ardently warred with him; that he enjoyed shocking the sensibilities of others; that he was profoundly sympathetic to the suffering he saw about him; and that he was an artist of accomplishment and untapped skills.

The fact that he was an artist is ultimately the most important, not simply because his writing is the only concrete evidence of him which exists, but also, and more importantly, because he wrote well. At times he wrote very well indeed, giving us insights not only into the emigration, though his vision of it is vividly preserved in his poems, not only into his own emotions and thoughts, though they are interesting in their own right, but also into the physical world about us. Like a painter, Poplavsky was acutely sensitive to visual detail, and his poetry, through startling imagery and colors utterly divorced from convention, records the harsh beauties of the urban landscape—of skies filled by night glows of red, purple, green; of dusty trees in the parks, beaten down by heat; of sidewalks colored by the dawn of a night through which one hasn't slept. As Poplavsky said, "Half his life the artist learns, after which he tries perhaps, long and tortuously, to unlearn, to find anew his lost naiveté and the freshness of perception of children and primitives." [39] Reading Poplavsky, one feels what those all-night cafe conversations must have been like —Poplavsky talking, scattering a shower of ideas, images, rhythms, some successful, some poor, all half-formed, hinted at, synthesized from the most disparate of life's experiences, and all of it forcing his listeners to see the world through new and fresher eyes. At his best, Poplavsky is exhilarating, for clearly visible in his works are both the pain and the great joy of creation. Perhaps he was, as Tatishchev wrote, approaching "that region where aesthetics are replaced by ethics, service to beauty by pity toward people, and where one must stop writing poetry . . . and this gift must be overcome," [40] and perhaps he was at the edge of a new creativity which would have encompassed his multitude of ideas and emotions. In either case, his death was a great loss. What he left is important and needs to be read, for Boris Poplavsky is a poet, and a personality, unfairly and too long forgotten.

Notes

1. B. Iu. Poplavsky, "Vokrug 'Chisel,' " *Chisla,* 10 (1934), 204.

2. Poplavsky, *Flagi* (Paris: Chisla, 1931), p. 15.

3. Vladimir Nabokov, *The Gift* (New York: Capricorn, 1970), p. 353. It should be pointed out that Koncheyev actually was only imagined to have said this by the hero, Fyodor. The basic point, however, still stands.

4. V. F. Khodasevich, *Literaturnye stat'i i vospominaniia* (New York: Chekhov, 1954), pp. 238–239.

5. G. P. Struve, *Russkaia literatura v izgnanii* (New York: Chekhov, 1956), p. 314.

6. Poplavsky, "Sredi somnenii i ochevidnostei," *Utverzhdeniia,* 3 (1932), 103.

7. They are *Snezhnyi chas* (Paris: n.p., 1936); *V venke iz voska* (Paris: Dom Knigi, 1938); and *Dirizhabl' neizvestnogo napravleniia* (Paris: n.p., 1965).

8. *Iz dnevnikov: 1928–1935* (Paris: OIzd, 1938).

9. Poplavsky, "O misticheskoi atmosfere molodoi literatury v èmigratsii," *Chisla,* 2/3 (1930), 311.

10. G. V. Adamovich, *Odinochestvo i svoboda* (New York: Chekhov, 1955), p. 280.

11. Poplavsky, "Apollon Bezobrazov," *Opyty,* 1 (1953), 72.

12. Adamovich, *op. cit.,* p. 280.

13. Iu. K. Terapiano, *Vstrechi* (New York: Chekhov, 1953), p. 113.

14. *Ibid.,* p. 115.

15. Adamovich, *op. cit.,* p. 275.

16. Terapiano, *op. cit.,* p. 115.

17. Adamovich, *op. cit.,* p. 276.

18. Khodasevich, *op. cit.,* p. 241.

19. At the time it was widely supposed that Poplavsky had either overdosed himself or had committed suicide by poison. In fact, he was murdered by a

deranged friend; the circumstances of his death are rehearsed by Simon Karlinsky, "In Search of Boris Poplavsky: A Collage"; see pages 311–333 of this issue.

20. N. Tatishchev, "Poet v izgnanii," *Novyi Zhurnal,* 15 (1947), 200.

21. Vladimir Nabokov, *Speak, Memory* (New York: Putnam, 1966), p. 287.

22. Adamovich, *op. cit.,* p. 276.

23. Poplavsky, "Apollon Bezobrazov," *Chisla,* 2/3 (1930), 89.

24. Tatishchev, "Boris Poplavsky—poet samopoznanaiia," *Vozrozhdenie,* 165 (1965), 26.

25. Poplavsky, "Okolo zhivopisi," *Chisla,* 5 (1931), 192.

26. *Ibid.,* p. 192.

27. Tatishchev, "Poet samopoznaniia," *op. cit.,* p. 28.

28. Poplavsky, *Flagi, op. cit.,* p. 19.

29. Poplavsky, "Sredi somnennii," *op. cit.,* p. 97.

30. Poplavsky, "Otvet na anketu o svoem tvorchestve," *Chisla,* 5 (1931), 287.

31. Poplavsky, "O misticheskoi atmosfere," *op. cit.,* p. 309.

32. Poplavsky, "Vokrug 'Chisel,' " *op. cit.,* p. 207.

33. Poplavsky, "Sredi somnennii," *op. cit.,* p. 98.

34. Poplavsky, "Po povodu . . . ," *Chisla,* 4 (1930/1931), 166.

35. Poplavsky, "O misticheskoi atmosfere," *op. cit.,* p. 308. For a detailed explanation of *poshlost',* see Vladimir Nabokov, *Nikolai Gogol* (New York: New Directions, 1944), pp. 63–74.

36. Terapiano, *op. cit.,* pp. 113–14.

37. Tatishchev, "Poet v izgnanii," *op. cit.,* p. 201.

38. Poplavsky, "Okolo zhivopisi," *op. cit.,* p. 195.

39. *Ibid.,* p. 194.

40. Tatishchev, "Poèt v izgnanii," *op. cit.,* p. 205.

In the distance

It was quiet in the world, it was late.
The angel was dirty and hungry, but forgot his hunger
And lay down to sleep under the starry banner
That spread itself over the city like a blanket.

While the palms made a black fan over the casino
Where sunset, a bonfire of sadness, burned itself down,
The sky quietly opened its rooms
And the ghosts on the tower celebrated the arrival of night.

Their voices were untroubled.
All the past slept before them on the
Sacred, snow-white plain.
All the future floated there, barely visible.

On the edge of the sky, on the brink of night,
Stars awoke and eyes were dreamt of,
While, far below them, the moon was rising
And a night bird made a soft moan.

On the tower time sang. The tower dimmed
And the moon crept wearing only a nightgown.
The dirty angel slept in the beams of its light
While from the heavens there floated to him a comet.

translated by Ron Loewinsohn

The rose of death

to Georgy Ivanov

In a black park we were celebrating the arrival of Spring.
A dime-store violin was quietly telling its lies.
Death descended in a balloon
Tapping the shoulders of those in love.

Rosy the evening air, roses carried in the wind.
On the margin the poet sketched his patterns.
Rosy the evening air, roses smelling of death
While green snow falls on all the branches.

The dark air sheds its stars like petals,
Nightingales sound exactly like motors, singing,
And in the pavilion over the green sea
Tubercular gas is glowing.

Under the spangled sky ships leave port,
Spirits wave handkerchiefs from the bridge,
And sparkling in the dark air
A locomotive chants on the viaduct.

In the darkness the lit city runs up the hill.
Night is noisy by the dance hall
And soldiers prepare to leave the city,
Drink thick beer at the station.

Low, very low, so low it touches their souls,
The balloon of the moon floats over the sideshow
And from the boulevard, to rickety calliope music,
The merry-go-round waves its hands at the ladies.

And Springtime, the rosy Springtime, boundlessly
Rosy and smiling, retreats, draws off into
The firmament, unfurling a dark blue fan.
The inscription written on it is vivid: Death.

translated by Ron Loewinsohn

Rondeau Mystique III

The cats feel cold. They yawn.
Yes, Yes.
While over the tower of the world
The years are flying. Butterflies. Years.

Angels are carrying white bricks,
They are building a house
While the others sleep in the woods, doing nothing,
The golden woods.

Lady Autumn put a spell on them
With blue.
She kissed them on their tender, childlike foreheads
By the hill.

Who's this walking in the abyss, humming?
It's time to sleep.
In the blue two kings pour sand
Back and forth.

The King of Day is fragile, sickly and tender,
He watches
The sand falling white as snow
Onto the balcony.

He searches for sacred sounds in a book.
But the book is asleep,
It has folded its pages like arms
Across its chest.

Meanwhile the King of Night walks on the sun
With a dead head.
He is catching butterflies in a fine net,
A fine, pale blue net.

It is then that the time of life flows down,
Flows down like water
To carry Ophelia to her homeland
Forever.

translated by Ron Loewinsohn

Biography of a clerk

A scribe's profession is mysterious:
he loafs incredibly.
When he's happy, he bleats (that sly sheep)
and he hopes untiringly, and free of charge.

He surrenders patiently to sleep
(to all traitors he is the closest friend).
He sleeps and dreams: the devil stole springtime
and hocked it—which made everybody nervous.

Then he gets up and moves like the moon,
walks through the city on his depraved legs,
bathes in a stream, and like an idiot
sits in a streetcar, surrounded by enemies.

And quietly, quietly he moves his hand
—pink claw, blue splotches—
while under the mill-wheel, under the bridge, under his foot
the river flows, carefree—and free of charge.

And again he weeps insolently. How dare he
exist, he the most offensive of crayfish?
slowly chewing the chalky air,
how dare he rustle like paper money?

And he buzzes, he squeals greedily,
he dances like a pampered dog,
while all around, with questions in their hands,
his enemies sit wearing terrifying dunce caps.

translated by Emmett Jarrett and Dick Lourie

Another planet
to Jules Laforgue

With our monocles, our frayed pants,
our various diseases of the heart,
we slyly think that planets and the moon
have been left to us by Laforgue.

So we scramble meowing up the drainpipe.
The roofs are asleep, looking like scaly carp.
And a long-tailed devil, wrapped in a thundercloud,
struts around like a draftsman's compass on a map.

Sleepwalkers promenade.
House-ghosts with sideburns lounge sedately.
Winged dogs bark quietly;
we fly off softly, mounted on dogs.

Below, milky land glistens.
A train belching sparks is clearly visible.
A pattern of rivers ornaments the fields,
And over there is the sea, its waters waist-deep.

Raising their tails like aeroplanes,
our pilots are gaining altitude,
and we fly off to Venus—but not the one
that wrecks the charts of our life.

A motionless blue mountain, like a nose.
Glassy lakes in the shadow of mountains.
Joy, like a tray, shakes us.
We head for a landing, our lights fading out.

Why are these fires burning on the bright sun's surface?
No, already they fly and crawl and whisper—
They are dragonfly people, they are butterflies
as light as tears and no stronger than a flower.

Toads like fat mushrooms come galloping,
carrots buck and rear and quiver,
and along with them toothed plants
that cast no shadows are reaching for us.

And they start to buzz, they start to crackle and squeak,
they kiss, they bite—why, this is hell!
Grasses whistle like pink serpents
and the cats! I won't even try to describe them.

We're trapped. We weep. We fall silent.
And suddenly it gets dark with terrifying speed.
Frozen rain, the snowy smoke of an avalanche,
our dirigible no longer dares to fly.

The insects' angry host has vanished.
And as for us, we have stretched out to die.
Mountains close us in, a deep blue morgue shuts over us.
Ice and eternity enchain us.

translated by Emmett Jarrett and Dick Lourie

Rembrandt

Voices of flowers shouted in the field.
Time turned the windmill quietly.
At the table a warrior was reading a book,
while at the bottom of the stream, in a transparent flock,
clouds floated, always towards the east.
In the heat, fishes were not jumping,
the factories below were idle.
The golden summer clock
ticked with soft ringing over the dead sea:
that's the warrior, still reading in his book.
Its letters weep and sing
and the clock of the universe is running slow.
Warrior, tell the noontime souls
what you're reading there about the future.
The warrior has turned around—he is laughing.
The voices of the flowers in the field fall silent
while softly from the bottom of the universe
flows the ringing of that first eternal pain.

translated by Emmett Jarrett and Dick Lourie

How awful, getting tired

How awful, getting tired.
All of life rushing at you
And you haven't strength to live.
Go back to your little hole.

Hide, be secretive,
And listen all night
To little leaves shaken
By a drop of rain.

Quiet light in the window,
The leaves barely move,
The long day darkens,
The street sounds die,

This world lacks something—
Not the glitter of proud truths,
They're only shadows of shadows—
And thinking's worn you out.

Through pale blue twilight
Sick people hurry home,
Their best years hidden
In a dark swarm of cares.

Stay still, listen to the rain.
Your God's a god of pity,
Not of truths or miracles—
The rest is only lies.

Nobody likes you.
You're alone and poor.
Of course, she's with you and
What's happiness without her.

But still, with her, why rest
Or even dream of heaven . . .
Streaky sunset.
Rainy night.

translated by Paul Schmidt

a chapter from
Homeward from Heaven
BORIS POPLAVSKY

Jumping from boulder to boulder, Tanya and Oleg made their way down toward the water. She led the way, playful and delighted with her own fearlessness, the precision of her movements, and the strength of her sun-browned legs; he followed, stumbling clumsily, frequently falling down and scraping his hands, over-excited, dumb with love, diffidence, and the summer heat. Any other time he would have gladly taken part in the race, he would have made a show of his desperation, but now the blood was pounding so hard in his ears that he could hardly keep up with her. Finally, after scaring off a whole colony of nudists who, like skinny red crayfish, scuttled off behind the rocks, the exhausted couple crawled down onto the flat boulders of the rocky promontory and sat down where each breaking wave covered them with a fan of fresh sea spray. The wind was picking up; on the horizon lay a thin white strip; from beyond the horizon a gale was sending tall columns of waves which from time to time lost their seething whitecaps in their haste.

As it came in toward shore, each wave would dig before itself a dark blue pit, at the bottom of which glittering stones were noisily tossed about; the wave would rise up in a towering blue wall, and just at the point of breaking it would shoot up and crash against the rocks. Then the foam would rise up over their heads, and in the cracks between the boulders the frothing blueness surged forward, but as the wave would retreat whole waterfalls came gurgling back out to sea.

Bored at just sitting there, Tanya moved up closer and threw off her shoes; the wide cuffs of her faded beach pajamas turned dark from the water, but that did not stop her—crazed with excitement she would clamber out onto the wet rocks. Like a fussy old man, Oleg was afraid for her, because under the dazzling sky the sea and the wind were becoming satanically fierce right before his eyes; now a wave which looked to him as high as a house would approach, and in mock terror Tanya would dash back, shouting inaudibly into the wind. With wild freshness water would pour down from the sky and cover their faces and chests. Their clothes and hair clung to their faces; squinting, they would dry themselves off, laugh and snort, and in answer the crystalline waves would advance one after another, thundering theatrically down and drenching them from head to foot. One especially powerful wave all but dragged Oleg out to sea, so that clinging to the sand with his hands and feet he could barely hold his ground and was thoroughly frightened. The spectacle before them was now grandiose and the danger was considerable, since in a caldron like that the ability to swim would be useless, and anyway Tanya, as is often the case with people who are strong by nature, understood nothing of sports and was a poor swimmer.

Amidst the endless fountains and the constant, joyous roar, they were now laughing uncontrollably; emboldened to the point of rashness, they were climbing out between two waves into the very heart of the caldron. Tanya would fling back her arms and, squinting, she would hold her face up to the water, and with all her rowdiness and exuberance she finally got through to Oleg and reassured him once and for all.

Finally, having enjoyed themselves to the full, worn out, happily tired, wet as puppies, they climbed back, found their shoes, and clumsily set about putting them on their wet, seashell-pink feet; they ran their fingers cursorily through their hair and set off homeward along the mountain footpath. Soon emerging from the rocky chaos, they stumbled upon a pale-faced group of bored Russian vacationers who sat with their cigarettes and their *Latest News,* and gazed at them with a sort of superstitious bewilderment.

Again Tanya's wide yellow back, no longer as frightening and hostile as before, swayed before Oleg, and he was almost happy— there was still a month of these wonders to go. But soon they reached the garden gate and had to part, as it was time for Tanya to crawl through the window into her room, since the bourgeois society of the old folks had long since been assembled at the table on the garden patio. And Oleg, left alone in the woods, fell back into his lower class habits and set off wandering wherever his legs would carry him, looking for Bezobrazov so that the two of them could slip like Indians into the kitchen, where they would munch their everlasting rice with oil and tomatoes which they now cooked for four days in advance on the brazier; but they had appetites like wolves, and eating after being at the seashore is a great pleasure.

After dinner Tanya would shut herself up in her room to study, but no sooner would the blinds close than she would fall asleep in the oppressive heat, her face and shoulder always resting on the same page which was worn by the weight of her slumber. In the noonday wilderness, Oleg wandered wild and solitary, his sun-bleached hair appearing here and there on the rocks. As he waited, time moved slowly, and everything around him seemed uninteresting—too insistently bright, too threatening, alien, in- imically, dazzlingly impersonal. Just as slowly as ever, the waves fell softly on the sand, and it seemed that the water dozed there for half a minute before it again stirred, not in the least quickening its usual rhythm just because Oleg, frowning malevolently into the blue expanse, was sitting on the sand, waiting. He would have liked for everything to speed up as it sometimes does in the movies, and rush headlong toward six o'clock. And at six, in the dead silence, listening to the crunch of his own footsteps across the gravel, he would approach the cottage as if it were a lion's cage, and knock on the window. Receiving no answer he would cautiously open the shutter, and Tanya, awakened by the bright light, embarrassed, with her face red like a baker-woman's and sated with sleep, would jump up and set about combing her hair.

Soon Nadya, a wide-faced girl of unusually doll-like, athletic beauty, also entered the room through the window. In contrast to Tanya, she laughed a lot in her spontaneous and naively coquettish manner, looking at everything with her huge, defiant blue eyes, although like Tanya she also had a beastlike instinct for silence and reserve. After Nadya, her gangster-bodyguard barged in—a tall, gloomy, handsome fellow with political convictions, who spoke a strange Parisian-Russian jargon, a mixture of gallicisms and Soviet-style slang. Nadya and Tanya always remained silent when they were together—Tanya maliciously, intelligently, tensely awaiting, seizing, utilizing, condemning every word; Nadya naively, crudely, laughing deep down, opening her huge, protruding, completely vacant sky-blue eyes. Pliant as a beast, elusive, she was a magnificent specimen of Russian sexual creativity.

It was a beautiful gathering of young, athletic bodies that were piled into a small, whitewashed room whose window had neither frames nor glass, but only a single green Italian antique shutter. But floating, hanging above them was that eternal torment, that hereditary prudish Russian boredom of Chekhov's grandiloquent heroes, which frowns upon speaking of anything earthly or dear, and does not know how to speak of anything exalted without boredom: the spirit wrestling with the body. A rather crude, affected camaraderie on the outside and on the inside a tense, severe battle of love. The eternal, joyless, painfully familiar atmosphere of a Russian *gymnasium*.

The ape-man would come too (sometimes even walking on his hands)—a taciturn, deep brown statue composed entirely of muscles, with the beautiful, remarkable, thick-lipped face of a Spanish criminal-artist-aristocrat. And finally, out of nowhere

Apollon Bezobrazov would enter (through the door, like the old folks), met by a somber, significant look from Tanya's suddenly darkened eyes, and with him a Georgian-looking young lady who was thoroughly exhausted by the heat.

But their conversation didn't pan out, because inwardly Oleg, as the oldest, felt himself above them all just as outwardly he clumsily groveled, wanting desperately to be accepted because of Tanya; he compromised his sincerity and dignity and castigated himself for that, maliciously mimicking to himself their semi-Russian turns of phrase.

Therefore everyone liked to dance. For one thing, it put an end to conversation, and for another it was sexual liberation, a secret, sexually aesthetic release from the boredom that was aging their young hearts. They liked to have a drink too, but they were afraid, for somewhere nearby lived and walked the terrible bearded creator who supported them—the glitter-eyed, gold-spectacled former revolutionary, now a learned chemist and a big businessman.

The mechanical voice of the gramophone resounded strangely in the sun-baked silence of the garden on the rocky promontory. It was sad, cracked as if coming from afar, from Paris, as if heard by telephone but audible. Outside, the dazzling noonday heat was now replaced by the motionless, glittering heat of evening. The cicadas were shouting louder than ever, but already the garden was permeated with the orange-pink light of the clouds at sunset, and beyond them the sea below was already taking on that strange, heavy, leaden, oily shine which immediately made everything threatening and somewhat unreal, so it seemed that any second now, between two branches, there would appear in the distance, strangely dreamlike and with astral clarity, a black Aegean ship, its brownish-red sail hanging motionless over the glassy expanse.

Serenely slow, dolefully insistent, like a bee, the gramophone rang out, and everything continued to be bathed in the reflected reddish brilliance of the sky.

Suddenly understanding, suddenly seeing something new, alien, and inescapably tormenting in Tanya, Oleg could no longer believe it was she who just a few hours ago had spent all morning wandering and horsing around with him. Sullenly flirting with Bezobrazov, Tanya was again her majestic, stony, somewhat oppressive, arrogant self.

Several times already Oleg had tried to get up and ask Tanya to dance, but his heart would begin to beat so agonizingly, and suddenly he would seem to himself so awkward, so ugly and narrow-shouldered that out of psychopathic fear of a refusal he could not make up his mind, but finally got up anyway. And barely conscious, barely touching Tanya, he put his arms around her. The gramophone struck up "Jalousie," a slow, eternally memorable gypsy tango of that summer; and so, barely brushing against her, hardly daring to move, he floated across the room with her, and the room floated before them in the sultry pinkish twilight of a motionless August evening. They were dancing, and suddenly Oleg's heart was discovering, realizing, comprehending that they were floating together into one endlessly long abyss of pain, humiliation, defeat, injury, parting, but the force of floating off, breaking away, pushing off from earth and the old life was so overpowering, so new, so compelling that Oleg, beside himself, did not defend himself, but laid himself painfully open, and proceeded inexorably toward that force as if marching off to battle— melting, irrevocably perishing, selling himself into slavery in that hot, pink, motionless evening air.

Ringing softly, coming softly to life, the muffled sounds slowly made their way through the heavy air, and were now destroying Oleg, literally tearing him apart; sweetly painful, painfully sweet, they were entering, floating into, slicing into his heart. It seemed as if huge distances, frescoes, mountains, fabulous accounts of cities and voyages were opening up somewhere outside the window, and he did not dare touch, not even with the tips of his fingers, did not dare feel the extraordinary, formidable body of this deity that was dancing with him. The dance ended, but Oleg now knew that his heart had opened up, awakened for a long time to come. He also knew that Tanya did not love him and maybe never would. Inside him the twilight thickened until it was suffocatingly palpable; something threatening, like a summer thunderstorm, something forever unique tortured him and cut voluptuously into his heart. And for a long time afterward he and Bezobrazov, like escaped convicts, sat in their forest facing each other by two tree stumps, munching their insipid rice with tomatoes and topping it off with sweet, unpeeled cucumbers, calmed down by the distinct presence of something irreparable.

The endlessly long summer day finally came to an end. The fainthearted, hysterical housekeeper was setting the dinner table. In her strangely sullen way, Tanya agreed to meet Oleg after seeing off Ivan Gerasimovich, who was staying in the next cottage. Both girls by agreement were supposed to return home, but right then beyond the wicker fence they silently parted, disappearing in the darkness to go about their dark affairs. Sitting by the road in an uncomfortable pose on a pile of pine branches, Oleg waited. In the woods the gloom was impenetrable. On weekdays music did not play in Saint-Tropez, and somewhere way out there beyond the mountains the motors of military aircraft were humming as they made their night flights. Sometimes a huge star would start to move between the black branches, or sometimes two or three would move symmetrically at once. But having crossed the sky, they would disappear amidst the even rumble, and again the night would be beautiful, impenetrable, hostile. Enveloped by the night, Oleg was like a prehistoric hunter—lost, tense, all ears. For him, a city youth, a young man of the cafes, a young *émigré* who had grown up in the rain, everything was still so extraordinary, and the silence was so powerful, so frightening, so complete, that he was constantly conscious of the blood roaring in his ears. Far, far off, from the distance, he could hear Tanya's steps; he heard the last words which she laughingly flung after Nadya, "You watch out with him," and the soft, clear, gradually approaching crunch of the gravel under her firm feet, of her firm feet on the dry branches. And then finally, glimmering dim and white between the trees, there appeared the quiet, wordless, fairy-tale circle of light from a flashlight. Concealing himself in the darkness, Oleg remained silent and the white beam kept coming closer, completely concealing its holder, and suddenly Oleg felt himself fixed in the focus of an electric eye, and, like a captured beast, stared wildly into it.

On that star-filled night, saturated with the heavy odor of pine needles, among the rocks that were still warm in the darkness with their memory of the sun, they quarreled for the first time, and in a crazed burst of bravado, Oleg tore away from Tanya and went wandering along the shore in the ominous light of the late-rising crescent moon, humming to himself his favorite crude strains of the Wedding March from *Lohengrin;* and then suddenly all at once his excitement dissolved, his heart physically contracted with a presentiment of the irreparable, and he rushed off to search for her and did not find her. Oh horror, horror, cosmic bewilderment of the ancients, primeval despair of one surrounded by the giants of fate and nature! In a state of wild torment, Oleg ran back toward the cottages and stopped in confusion at the intersection of several roads. By now the moon had risen higher and the entire forest was sliced into pieces by white strips of light—but where among them was Tanya? Where had she gone? She wasn't at home—Oleg had already managed to look in her window. . . . Where, whither, in what direction had she set off in this threatening chaos of trees, moon, and rock? Despair, despair . . . I'll never see her again, everything is lost—and above him, carved out in black silhouettes against the theatrically blue-tinted sky, huge needle-clothed monsters hovered, as if their swaying branches were reaching out in the motionless storm of the moon, the soundless storm of moonlight, like the black hair of a giant, lashed by the silent winds. And at their feet Oleg literally wrung and gnawed at his hands with uncertainty and anxiety, and again everything seemed to be a theater: it was all only pretending to be the sky, the trees, and the moon so as better to exterminate and destroy him. To destroy his soul, which had risen up in its solitude, which had soared too high and therefore, like a mad dog, was condemned by all of nature.

On that star-filled night, they kissed for the first time, completely losing for several hours all sense of reality in a frenzy of sensuality. But it was not with peace, not with sweet reconciliation and new life that their lips met, but with something fiercely and mercilessly hostile. Twisted all awry in his powerful paws, Tanya lay freezing on the ground as if in a cataleptic fit; and he, joylessly crazed, kneaded, wrung, and kissed that hot, resilient flesh in an uneasy, painful delirium of unexpected good luck and expectation of foul play. Finally, worn out with excitement, sated with suffering and pleasure, seized by some kind of repentance, she said, "No, I can't love you. There's a man I'm bound to, to whom I'm obligated. . . . I'm tired, I'm sick of lying, and I don't have it in me now to strain my spiritual muscles and lay open my heart to you." "So you don't want to play clean—you're just tossing me small change, well, I can do without your filthy small change. . . . I wish you luck. . . ." All in a flush, all agitated by Tanya's animal-like caresses, Oleg broke away from her and, suddenly growing rabid, suddenly turning hard and bitter with all the passion of his love, consumed, convulsed by the militant madness of his mortification, disappeared into the darkness. Thinking he would come back, Tanya buttoned up her clothes and waited; gloomily, disdainfully, bitterly she got up, made her surefooted way down the slope through the underbrush, and quickly reached the sleeping Saint-Tropez. Like some athletic ghost, she wandered through the streets and suddenly met the whole semi-adult gang of Oleg's enemies. She drank and danced with them until morning, while all that night Oleg searched for her, wandering about in a flood of tears, watching for her, terrified, repentant, even naively thinking she might have fallen off a cliff somewhere. He himself had visions of throwing himself from somewhere even higher than that, until the blue of morning began to shine and Oleg, wincing as if from a blow and shielding his face from the blueness, collapsed into heavy, sweet nonexistence, because from that day, from that night, Oleg's life of torment began.

And another dazzling August day arose over Saint-Tropez. Perhaps it was even more flawless, more radiant, more peaceful than usual because the cicadas, having droned out their sunrise service, suddenly slackened, faded off, and fell altogether silent as if they had never been there at all. Opening his eyes, Oleg, not instantly but only a pulse-beat later, remembered what had happened. At first when he again saw the brilliant, exquisitely fresh branches in the blue expanse above him, Oleg felt like bursting out laughing and shaking Bezobrazov out of his slumber, but in exactly one second the consciousness of something urgent and irreparable jolted, squeezed his heart so that first he opened his eyes morbidly wide and then immediately winced, and it was at that very moment that the irreparable began to come true and Oleg's hell began.

That morning Tanya had gone off to the market with the housekeeper; to run after them and search for her would have been senseless and silly, because in front of other people Tanya could control herself beautifully, she could speak through clenched teeth with particular stoniness to people with whom she'd had intimate conversations in private. In peaceful times this actually made his happiness more acute, for it inserted something like a patch of nonlove into the fabric of love, pointing out, underlining the distance they had covered, or a patch of love's beginning into its continuation. Sometimes it can be so pleasant at a dance to exchange formal greetings with the person one loves, as if from a distance, when, wearing her nicest dress and in full radiance of her charm, she appears to us in that same enigmatic aura of temporary ceremoniousness or embarrassment or deliberate primness which once surrounded her when she first appeared before our wonder-struck eyes. But in times of quarrel this feigned alienation seemed so real that Oleg actually suffered from Tanya's politeness.

And so there was nothing to do but kill time until after dinner, and in Oleg's tortured, anxious state of mind that was hellishly difficult. Again Oleg swam out almost beyond the horizon, and coming back with no small difficulty onto a completely empty beach from which all the Franco-Russian young men walked off on their slender legs to their respective cottages, he suddenly stumbled upon the object of his age-old and futile longing—a white canoe which belonged to a certain aristocrat with a toupee who always looked at Oleg with particular hostility.

That morning for the last time the sea shone for Oleg with its dazzling blue calm. He still did not know it was the last time, he still did not believe in separation—just as for a long time a living being does not believe, cannot believe, in death, in spite of all its obviousness. Rocking clumsily, the boat was moving quickly away from shore. Here was the place to which Oleg would usually swim just to spite the vacationers. Don't you think you'd better go back? You're all tired out from your swim and the oar hurts your hands. No, farther on into the deep-blue, out toward where the deserted lighthouse appears and disappears in the distance, like a white hillock, or a barge, a buoy, a shooting target—hard to say what.

Once more Oleg turned his back on the shore, nearly overturning the canoe. The boundlessly blue, infinite azure again opened up before him. Further and further onward. Now, after he came around the promontory, the waves turned into long, tall, deep, uniform blue mountains. Moving toward shore, they slowed the boat, which no longer seemed to be moving. The scorching sun was blazing over his head, but in spite of his worry that he was now far away both from the shore and the island, Oleg now and then forgot everything, put down his oar, stared into the water, and immersed himself in the chaste pleasure of contemplation. Especially down there in the great depths it was miraculously beautiful. Through the dark violet crystal, some sort of black stripes were still visible against the lighter colored sandy bottom. Behind him, the towns from Saint-Tropez to Sainte Maxime disappeared and everything contracted into a narrow strip of sand beneath a green strip of pines. But the distant mountains, on the contrary, shot up and moved closer, and above them tall billows of white clouds made them still higher. To the right and left appeared an unfamiliar shoreline; the sea's violent rocking forced Oleg to come to his senses and, disregarding his worn and blistered hands, to row with all his might. Suddenly an island emerged out of the water—big, rocky, and covered with a solid layer of bird droppings—and as Oleg came closer the waves on the open sea were pounding so hard and raising the boat up so high that it filled almost to the top with water, but it did not sink because its whole covered bow and stern were made to float. But the hardest part was climbing out. Without any transition, the rocks dropped off into the depths.

Water and foam were seething between the rocks and everything all around was covered with sharp-shelled mussels. Oleg looked back in fear, but to return without resting was completely impossible. Finally making up his mind, he threw the oar out onto the rocks, jumped in the water, pushed and dragged the boat out to a secure spot, and then, covered with scratches, with a terrible pain in his back, swaying with fatigue, excitement, and exultation, he climbed out onto the hot boulders amidst a cloud of startled birds. How far away from everything he was. His heart was bursting with loneliness and fear of the blue expanse of the sea. Going back was torture. For two hours he drifted, weak with exhaustion and carried along by the waves, and finally he moored half a mile down from where he had set off. And then, with the pitiful, exhausted look of someone expecting to be congratulated, he walked back along the shore to the beach and immediately caught sight of Tanya, who was squinting and watching him with idle malevolence as she talked in a slow undertone with his enemies; he had already gathered his courage to go up to her when a narrow-shouldered Arab-like young man as skinny as a skeleton went right up to them, and from the way Tanya jumped abruptly to her feet and the two of them, without saying good-bye to anyone, went right off into the woods at the other end of the beach, Oleg understood that this was Tanya's fiancé.

The sun set over the black shoreline; this is how I've imagined the rocks where the shackled Siberian convict wrestles with his fate. My love, promise that you will not leave me, let me bid you good-bye just one more time. The sun set and again the day blazed forth, the mountains disguised themselves in wings of stone, the green plumage of the hills burned in the sunlight. High, high above, the primordial being, the eternally new, unique azure was repeated in the water. And far off in the waters, barely visible in the noonday silence, motionless in the same constant pose, lay the islands toward which once a day the dark brown launch set off from Le Lavandou, in the white-hot silence; its antediluvian motor would knock and rattle endlessly on, until finally it would die down, and the cicadas would resume their clamoring, although their voices were softer.

The white air, a burning white liquid fire, filled and isolated all objects; everything was hidden, consumed, united by it as if by the real presence of some all-permeating indifferent deity.

Oh molten happiness, summertime, world without happiness, how beautiful, merciless, dazzlingly perfect you are over my world of torment; for it is over the desert, over the cyclopean fortresses where prisoners suffocate, over the stone quarries filled with the dry, hollow thud of convicts' hammers, over Rio de Janeiro, over Caledonia, over Guiana that such a dazzlingly flawless sun hangs suspended.

Oleg's torments had begun. Tanya was now nowhere to be found, and only at dinner time when he, like a homeless waif, would hang around outside the kitchen would he get a glimpse of her faded blue slacks, and she would again disappear until nighttime with her curly-haired gypsy-boy fiancé, with his so delicate, so painfully refined, never sunburned, biblical face. And just as Oleg had once smugly marveled at the boldness with which, regardless of everything and without giving herself away, she could leave the group and go off with him to wander, swim, clamber about on the rocks, so now also, with that same perfect, animal-like grace she would disappear with her narrow-shouldered victim; and Oleg, in spite of his tireless surveillance, did not once meet them, not once did he catch a glimpse of them, neither on the beach by the sluggish water, nor in the woods where her degenerate friend's tent looked totally uninhabited, nor in the mountains, nor on the road. She disappeared, she ceased to be. Oleg tried to read; he had brought so many books with him that he had hardly been able to lift his suitcase, but so far he had not read a single page—it all seemed like smug, dead nonsense. Sometimes he would fly into a black rage, and, straining his muscles, he would search for them, wandering along the rocks in hopes of finding them, but that too was futile, for they had apparently left La Favière.

Black from the sun, muscular, disheveled, wearing the close-fitting sweaters that were the uniform of his exile, he would wander about Le Lavandou, met and followed by surprised and hostile looks. He would sit on a jetty by which no ships passed, or in a church where there were no worshippers. He had come to like the dirty water in the port, the bottles and cans on the bottom, the newsstand. Mortally humiliated, in a humiliating rage of jealousy he would appear here and there; he stopped swimming and did not even do his calisthenics. As for the mountain wastelands, the rocks, the clouds, the sea vistas, he did not even think about all that any more; it all now seemed to him a stupid stage setting, a crudely painted backdrop in a ballet. It's all so crude, crude, crude, Oleg repeated spitefully to himself, the Creator really does have such primitive tastes in art; and only occasionally, as he came around a bend in the path, a microscopic inlet would come into view between two boulders and he would be struck by its useless perfection, invisible to the world. There he would lie down, his stomach against the sand and his face to the water, humming wordlessly, thoughtlessly, lifelessly, examining the stones and gravel on the bottom. Yellow, sun-heated stone walls surrounded him on all sides; everything lost proportion and the multicolored gravel on the bottom seemed a totally independent, motionlessly happy world. Microscopic waves would rush up, warming his hands. . . . The pain would die down. . . . Face in the sand, he would fall asleep and, gone to the world, sleep for an hour or two, and suddenly he would jump up, look around with bloodshot eyes, and, wringing his hands, set off again on his futile search.

Oh, torment, prison of jealousy, under the blinding sky, why did he come here, give in, yield to temptation, renounce Apollon's way of life—securely, haughtily athletic, without happiness, without nature, without destiny? And now all the ardor accumulated over the years in this loner, who had climbed higher than he should have, had been liberated by the earth and rushed toward Tanya.

He did not see her, yet constantly saw her before him, and she seemed to him even more beautiful. Her soft and evil face, with its amazingly tender, evil, and fine lips, her furrowed brows and such perfect, animal-like, and exact movements pierced him right to the heart. In the noonday silence she was everywhere, she was nowhere.

Everything was now repugnant to Oleg: the sea did not beckon him to swim, the mountains did not beckon him to tramp about, walking on the sand was as hard as walking through glue, he did not feel like eating, but at night the consoling sleep at least did not flee from his eyes. After dinner, everyone but Tanya and her insolent brute would now get together, and sunk in a deep melancholy—the gloominess of an unsuccessful summer—they would sit on a blanket under a tree and play cards, or on a straw mat in the tent which, saturated with sunlight, was like a pinkish yellow striped Arabian tent-dwelling. Nadya and her athletic Slavophile quarreled; and crudely, as if she belonged to him, he railed at her for her mistakes at cards. "What do you know, anyway? . . . Well, all right, go ahead and deal . . . all right." The orthodox young lady could not bear the heat and, getting ready to leave, she looked at everything with her huge exorbitant eyes which brimmed with bewildered sadness. The ape-man was engrossed in his inexplicable Spanish thoughts; he now pulled his hair back with an Indian-style headband and wrapped some sort of braid on his wrists, thereby showing a savage, primordial elegance in adorning his completely naked body. Apollon Bezobrazov, wizened and with an overgrowth of beard, was competing in immobility with the rocks: sitting on a rock he would turn to rock; he was always away, and to everyone's surprise he was reading the books which Oleg had so painstakingly and so pointlessly brought on his back.

And where had all Oleg's thought-laden books disappeared without a trace, all his thick notebooks crisscrossed with notes and comments? Oleg had left them all in Paris. For a whole month now, he had read nothing, written nothing, and he had not prayed. A wild freedom from God and a fear of God accompanied him everywhere. That way, it seemed, things were more spontaneous; he would meet the unknown life face to face—peacefully, defenselessly, and without consolation—but life, like the unbearable sun, sparing him nothing, was striking him full in the face.

translated by Charty Bassett

In search of
Poplavsky: a collage
SIMON KARLINSKY

An introductory digression

I first ran into Boris Poplavsky's name in 1940 or 1941, and it was a case of mistaken identity. I was in Beverly Hills, California, at the home of a remarkable woman named Anna Semyonovna Meller, who in the days of my childhood was Madame Antoinette, the best known and most elegant *couturière* in Harbin. My mother's dressmaking establishment, Levitina-Karlinskaya, was not even a close second, but theirs was a friendly rivalry. Anna Semyonovna's adopted son Alex, six years my senior, was the idol and the despair of my Manchurian childhood: a champion ice skater, a concertizing pianist at the age of twelve, and a stoic who, during a hike in Chalantung, went on talking with a smile after a sharp rock had opened a bleeding gash on his knee. (I was half his age at the time and I remember screaming my head off at the mere sight.) Now, in California, he was a surrealist painter, had been awarded a Guggenheim grant, and had spent a summer in New York, where he had met Pavel Tchelitchew and the son of Max Ernst and a number of other persons of equally supernatural

311

stature. Staying as a boarder at Anna Semyonovna's was Alex's friend Eddie, a young man of similar origins and background (his parents owned a dress shop on the Bubbling Well Road in Shanghai, and my mother had worked for them in her early youth), a former Berkeley architecture major who was now studying costume design at an art school somewhere near Westlake Park. Eddie's sketches usually took first prize at school competitions, with the second prize going to his principal rival and fellow student, a melancholy-looking German refugee boy named Rudi Gernreich.

Waves of pure happiness would wash over me every time I waited for the Wilshire bus to take me for a day or a weekend to the Meller home in Beverly Hills, away from everything that made my life in Los Angeles glum and barely endurable: the incomprehensible courses in civics and physics (even their names seemed interchangeable) at Belmont High; the hopelessly boring afternoon job at the grocery store; and the pointless weekly exchange of mutual insults between Jack Benny and Rochester on the living room radio. ("It is all probably very funny and subtle, if we could only truly understand it," my father would assure me after denying me permission to turn the dial to some concert music. But I *did* understand it all and it was *not* funny.) At the Mellers', things were altogether different. To begin with, it was perfectly all right to speak Russian and to have been born in China without having everyone exclaim, as they did at school, "How did you ever manage *that?*" or "Were your parents missionaries?" Instead of Jack Benny on the radio, there were real live stars to be encountered in Beverly Hills. Once I had to jump back when a long black car swung into a driveway with George Raft at the wheel and Rita Hayworth next to him. Another time, Eddie and I were walking past the John Frederics millinery shop on Beverly Drive and were stopped dead in our tracks by the sight of the most unbelievably beautiful woman either of us had ever seen. She was selecting a hat inside. We stood there staring, exchanging whispered conjectures as to who this magical creature might be; then a saleslady came out, not to ask us to move, but to announce, "Miss del Rio would like to know which of the two models you gentlemen consider more becoming." None of the Dolores del Rio films I saw later even began to do justice to the unforgettable radiance of her beauty.

Many years later, I felt a shudder of recognition as I watched that same scene reenacted (transposed into a comical key) in Billy Wilder's film *Witness for the Prosecution.* Could Eddie have recounted it to someone during his brief career at the film studios? He was designing costumes for Gene Tierney and Maria Montez at Universal—or was it United Artists?—when he was run over and killed by a drunken driver. It happened as he was crossing Beverly Drive one evening in 1945, about half a block from where he and I had once stood admiring Dolores del Rio. Eddie also had connections in the world of burlesque. Rose La Rose wanted a new kind of stage costume and he came up with one that featured a quivering pink lobster over the G-string. One night he sneaked me backstage at the burlesque house on Main Street (I was too young to purchase a ticket), and I watched from the wings a performance of a tassle-twirler named Ermaine Parker. Afterward we went out for coffee with her and her tall, handsome husband, the straight man for the foul-mouthed, baggy-pants comedian in the show. The talk was mostly about the couple's infant son, who had developed a liking for classical music before he learned to speak.

There were art exhibits of new painters, to which Alex or Eddie would take me: Salvador Dali at the Ambassador Hotel, Eugene Berman and Christian Bérard at little galleries on Sunset Strip. But above all, books and poems were a part of daily life at the Mellers'. It was there that I was introduced to, or urged to read, *Look Homeward, Angel; To the Lighthouse* (which I couldn't get through on the first try); *Portrait of the Artist as a Young Dog* (the book that provided the model for the title came later); a volume of short stories by Noel Coward (which I still think quite good); and collections of poems by Wallace Stevens, Dylan Thomas, and (whatever happened to him?) George Barker. While everyone at home and at school kept urging me to forget about those useless Russian books I was forever dragging about, Alex

313

and Eddie, older and wiser, never considered giving up their cultural heritage. Alex had his cult of the "three fellow-Alexanders"—Pushkin, Blok, and Scriabin; he had given up playing the piano when he decided that, compared to the later period of Scriabin, all music was primitive and dull. The three of us used to get high reciting Blok to each other, mostly from "The Mask of Snow" and "The Nightingale Garden" cycles. But here I could contribute as well as receive. One day, after leafing through a *Synthetic History of the Arts,* by a Soviet scholar named Ioffe, at the Los Angeles public library, I learned of the existence of Boris Pasternak and Velimir Khlebnikov. There was no Khlebnikov at the library, but I immediately copied out his poem about the grasshopper which Ioffe had cited to illustrate some principle of modern painting or other. They did have *My Sister Life* and *Themes and Variations.* I took these over to the Mellers' the next weekend, and while the older generation (Alex's parents and his aunt Madame Olga) pronounced Pasternak incomprehensible, Alex and Eddie both agreed that here was a major discovery.

I also introduced them to my favorite modern Russian novelist, a man I knew only as V. Sirin, with whose work I had become involved several years earlier. When I brought over my copy of *Invitation to a Beheading,* Eddie tried reading it out loud, but his long sojourns in Shanghai and Berkeley had done something to his Russian stress. (This was not noticeable when he spoke, only when he read aloud.) I took the book away from him and began to read slowly, getting all the stresses right, but after three pages I had to stop: Eddie was on the floor, his legs kicking in the air, a beatific smile on his face. "Stop it, I can't stand it, it's too beautiful," he was moaning. Alex's reaction was a little more reserved. He kept the book for several days and when he returned it, he remarked, "If I were a writer, this is how I would want to write." And a little later: "I had the damnedest feeling I wrote some of it myself." Sirin then joined Pushkin, Blok, Pasternak, Thomas Wolfe, and Dylan Thomas in our literary pantheon.

It was on one such enchanted Sunday afternoon, leafing through the New York Russian newspaper *Novoye Russkoye Slovo* (still extant and thriving), to which Anna Semyonovna subscribed, that I came upon Poplavsky's name—and this is where the mistaken identity part comes in. A memoirist (Yuri Terapiano? Vladimir Varshavsky?) was reminiscing about the Russian Montparnasse of the 1920's. He could vividly remember the poet Boris Poplavsky, drunkenly declaiming:

And the nightingale in the Sanskrit tongue
Shouts "More wine! More wine!" over the yellow rose.

The name was unfamiliar, but there was something about those two lines that made me resolve to look up their author. As a matter of plain fact, however, the lines were not by Poplavsky. I could never find them in any of his books, and after years of fruitless searching I finally, through sheer accident, discovered the awkward truth. The lines are a quotation from the *Rubaiyat* translated into Russian by Ivan Tkhorzhevsky. In connection with that translation Vladislav Khodasevich, when asked one morning why he looked so poorly, quipped: "I had a terrible nightmare. I dreamed that I was a Persian poet and that Tkhorzhevsky was translating me." But never mind. These two lines of Tkhorzhevsky's pseudo-Omar did direct me to Poplavsky.[1]

The discovery

The strange Aztec-Mayan pyramid that houses the main public library in downtown Los Angeles will always remain for me one of the endearing spots in Southern California. Its dark tile walls that kept the air comfortably cool on the muggiest days; the long, Alhambra-like vistas that opened from one room to another; the purling fountains in the inner yards (if I'm making it sound garish and eclectic, it no doubt was) I still find unforgettable. There was a Russian lady in the Foreign Books Room, whose name I never learned, who made it a point to purchase everything worthwhile in contemporary Soviet and Russian *émigré* literature. The library's collection of volumes on Russian painters and painting and on the Soviet theater of the 1920's was nothing short of opulent.

Yes, of course they had Poplavsky at that library. There were two slim volumes: a selection from his journals and a volume of verse called *Flags*. I got *Flags*, opened it in the middle, and immediately felt as though I were falling through a hole in the ice. Nikolai Tatishchev described his first impression of reading *Flags* thus: "A pure and piercing sound. Hardly anything can be made out. Now and then something breaks through and stings you. 'O Morella, come back, it will all be different one day.' Alarm, apprehension. The barometer needle quiveringly indicates a storm. A degree of agitation that can be expressed only in deliberately approximate terms." [2] This was how a mature person, a close friend of the poet and the publisher of his posthumous books, reacted to *Flags*. My own impression (and it remains one of the most vivid of my entire life) was somewhat different. I was struck first of all by the bright colors, the swirling images, the authenticity of the dreamlike states the poems conveyed: *

> **In the emerald waters of the night**
> **Sleep lovely faces of virgins**
> **And in the shadow of blue pillars**
> **A stone Apollo slumbers.**
>
> **Orchards blossom forth in the fire,**
> **White castles rise like smoke**
> **And beyond the dark blue grove**
> **Vividly dark sand is ablaze.**
>
> **Flowers in the garden hum,**
> **Statues of souls come to life**
> **And like butterflies from the fire**
> **Words reach me:**
>
> **Believe me, angel, the moon is high,**
> **Musical clouds**
> **Surround her, fires**
> **Are sonorous there and days are radiant.**

My English cannot reproduce the pulsating music that emanates from these lines in Russian, nor does it convey the artful and often startling rhymes. There are pages and pages in this little book that project this blend of color and music, but there are also other things:

---

* The translations of the Poplavsky poems are mine. AUTHOR.

> We shelter our caressing leisure
> And unquestioningly hide from hope.
> Naked trees sing in the forest
> And the city is like a huge hunting horn.
>
> How sweet it is to jest before the end
> This is understood by the first and the last—
> Why, a man vanishes, leaving fewer traces
> Than a tragedian with a divine countenance.

There was an attitude in those poems, a vision, a sensibility quite new to me, but one that I instantly recognized and accepted:

> But now the main entrance thundered and the bell started barking—
> Springtime was ascending the stairs in silence.
> And suddenly each one remembered that he was all alone
> And screamed "I'm all alone!" choking with bile.
> And in the singing of night, in the roar of morning,
> In the indistinct seething of evening in the park
> Dead years would arise from their deathbeds
> And carry the beds like postage stamps.

I did not know enough about poetry at the time to recognize Poplavsky's sources, to discern his French influences: Baudelaire (who had a greater impact on him than anyone except Blok), Nerval, Rimbaud, Laforgue, Apollinaire, Breton. I did not know then, as I know now, that Boris Poplavsky was in a sense a very fine French poet who belongs to Russian literature mainly because he wrote in Russian. But much of his sensibility was also a verbal equivalent of the visual imagery I knew and loved in the work of the exiled Russian neo-Romantic painters Pavel Tchelitchew and Eugene Berman.[3]

An uncritical acceptance? I knew at once that much of what Poplavsky was doing was highly artificial. But I knew even then that artifice was a natural component of some of the finest art and had no objections. Despite its artificiality (and partly because of it), the book hit me with a wave of lyrical power I would not have believed possible, a wave that swept me off my feet and held me prisoner for many weeks. This was not like getting intoxicated on Blok's verbal magic, nor was it like the intense intellectual pleasure afforded by Pasternak's formal perfection and his freshness of perception. Poplavsky came to me more like a fever or a demonic possession. I went around reciting Poplavsky's lines by heart. I tried composing melodies to them. I discovered that stanzas 3 and 4 of his poem "To Arthur Rimbaud" could be conveniently sung to the tune of the clarinet solo from Tchaikovsky's "Francesca da Rimini," and I did sing them, obsessively. The next thing I knew, my mother, normally infuriatingly indifferent to poetry, was muttering Poplavsky to Tchaikovsky's music in an undertone while fixing dinner.

It was a heavy burden to keep to oneself at sixteen. I was fortunate indeed to have two older friends with whom I could share it. Alex and Eddie were almost as enthusiastic about Poplavsky as I. The three of us leafed through the fragments of his journals. We did not find his religious quest congenial, but the seriousness and depth of his spiritual experience got through to us and his ways of formulating it we also found impressive. Seeing that Russian poetry could be this closely allied with surrealism in painting, Alex was moved to write a few Russian poems, which were meant as literary parallels to his paintings. He submitted them to *Novoye Russkoye Slovo* and one of them was printed, not in that newspaper's Sunday poetry section as he had hoped, but as an illustration to an editorial which discussed the poor quality of Russian *émigré* poetry and asserted that surrealism as a whole was an unimportant trend, by now entirely passé and forgotten. Then Alex was drafted into the Army. He wrote me asking for the library copy of *Flags*. I sent it to him, he returned it, then he wanted it again, and it was lost in the mail. I ruefully paid the charges for the lost book ($2.50, I think). A few months later it turned up at Alex's training camp. When I tried to return it, I was told that there was no need, because the library had replaced it. I now had my own copy of a book by Poplavsky. . . .

But just who, exactly, *was* Boris Poplavsky?

Some biographical materials

Exhibit A: his father

[The vice-president of the Moscow Association of Manufacturers] was Yulian Ignatyevich Poplavsky, an extremely original and colorful personality even for the Moscow of those days.

Poplavsky was a musician. He graduated (with very high grades) from the Moscow Conservatory where he majored in piano and was one of the favorite pupils of Peter Tchaikovsky, with whom he was on intimate terms, as can be seen from his memoirs. I do not remember what it was that moved him to give up his musical career and take up industrial relations. [. . .] Poplavsky was a talented person; one seldom encounters such facility with word and pen. He could discuss any topic and could treat the most serious subject in a frivolous vein. His speech mannerisms, which corresponded to his manner of dress, irritated many and Poplavsky was widely disliked. It was said that he was "barred from the stock exchange." This seems to be factually correct: invitations were not extended to him and this would cause clashes between the Manufacturers' Association and the Stock Exchange Committee. He was also active in St. Petersburg where he was the representative of his organization, together with Jules Goujon [the president of the Manufacturers' Association] at the Convention Council. When a petition had to be drafted or a summary of a discussion prepared, he was irreplaceable and was able to draft them with the utmost ease and elegance. Gradually, people became accustomed to his manners, and he began receiving invitations to Stock Exchange Committee sessions, especially when labor problems were involved, inasmuch as the antiquated organization of the Stock Exchange Committee was falling behind the times in collecting current statistical data and the documentation pertaining to labor problems. Poplavsky's office on Myasnitskaya Street was excellently organized and the Association (it was in existence for only 12 years) was able to accumulate much valuable material.

> —A portrait of Boris Poplavsky's
> father, from Paul Bouryschkine,
> *The Merchants' Moscow*.[4]

Exhibit B: his sister

1. I can still see one [of these poetesses]—tall, feverish, everything about her dancing: the tip of her shoe, her fingers, her rings, the tails of her sables, her pearls, her teeth, the cocaine in the pupils of her eyes. She was hideous and enchanting with that tenth-rate enchantment which cannot but attract, to which people are ashamed to be attracted, to which I am openly and shamelessly attracted. . . .

2. I can say in general that I was met with kindness in this alien world of female practitioners of drug-addicted poetry. Women are in general kinder. Men do not forgive felt boots or having starving children. But this very same P——skaya, I am convinced, would have removed the sables from her shoulders had I told her that I had a starving child at home. . . .

3. I did not get to hear the feverish, fur-clad beauty recite her

poetry, but I doubt that cocaine could have disposed her to write of love. . . .

—Three glimpses of Boris
Poplavsky's sister Natasha, gleaned
from Marina Tsvetaeva's memoir
"A Hero of Labor" (1925).[5]
Tsvetaeva and Natasha Poplavsky
both appeared at a reading of
women poets in the cold and
starving Moscow of 1920.

Exhibit C: his biography

Boris Poplavsky was born in Moscow on May 24, 1903. His father was a free artist—musician, journalist, and a well-known social figure; his mother, née Kokhmanskaya, came from an old, cultivated, aristocratic family, had a Western European education, and was a violinist with conservatory experience. As a child, Boris Poplavsky was first looked after by his nanny, Iraida, and then by a German nurse and a French governess. Later, as an adolescent, he had Swiss and English tutors, and when he reached school age, he was taught by Russian university students, hired to give him lessons. He also studied music, but showed no enthusiasm; lessons in drawing, however, were always his favorites.

In 1906, his mother had to take the children abroad because of the severe illness of her daughter. They lived alternately in Switzerland and Italy, while his father remained in Moscow. While abroad, Boris forgot his native tongue to such an extent that, when he returned to Moscow, his family had to enroll him and his brother at the French *lycée* of Saint Philippe Néri, where he remained until the Revolution.

Boris took to reading early, . . . and it was hard to tear him away from a book. When his elder sister Natasha, a dazzlingly educated and talented girl, published a collection of verse in Moscow, where she was considered an avant-garde poetess, Boris, either through competitiveness or imitation, also began to practice writing verses in his school notebooks, accompanying them with fanciful illustrations.

When the revolution broke out in February 1917, Boris was fourteen years old. In 1918 his father was forced to travel to the south of Russia, and he took his son along. Thus, while still quite young, Boris had to part from his family and experience all the horrors of the civil war. In the winter of 1919, when he lived in Yalta, he gave his first reading as a poet at the Chekhov Literary Circle. And in March of the same year he and his father emigrated to Constantinople.

This period of his life can be summed up in two words: he meditated and prayed. All the money his father gave him, his own belongings, even his food, Boris gave to the poor; at times several homeless people would spend the night in his room: students, officers, monks, sailors,

320

and others, all of whom were literally refugees. In Constantinople, Boris attended a makeshift equivalent of high school, did a great deal of sketching, read a lot, occasionally took incidental jobs, and spent much time with the cub scouts at the Russian Hearth, which was organized by the YMCA.

At the same time, Boris saw life through a veil of profound mysticism, as if sensing the breath of Byzantium which gave birth to the Orthodox faith, to which he yielded himself unconditionally. In June 1921, his father was invited to Paris to attend a conference on Russian trade and industry. For ten years Boris lived in the Latin Quarter, during the last four on the Rue Barrault near the Place d'Italie. There he died in the little annex at N° 76-bis, located on the roof of the immense Citroen garage.

The exciting and intriguing city of Paris absorbed Boris so much that he left it only once, in 1922, to spend a few months in Berlin. There he moved in the avant-garde literary circles, often appeared at literary gatherings and artistic *soirées,* and made a number of literary acquaintances. The Poplavsky family gradually all assembled in Paris and Boris' life seemed to enter upon a normal course. He regularly attended the Art Academy at La Grande Chaumière and was later enrolled at the Sorbonne, majoring in history and philology. He immersed himself in philosophy and theology and spent long hours in the rare manuscript room of the Bibliothèque de Sainte Geneviève. He was a passionate book collector; he had two thousand volumes at his death. He regularly visited museums, where he would stay for days on end. He studied assiduously, practiced sports, and wrote. As in earlier days, he was interested in poetry, literature, economics, philosophy, sociology, history, aviation, music, and everything else. He was always in a hurry to live and work, and he sometimes dreamed of becoming a professor of philosophy in Russia . . . not merely when collective farmers got to wear top hats and drive around in Fords, as he put it, but when the persecution of faith would end and a free life of the spirit would begin.

His novel *Homeward from Heaven,* which is partly autobiographical, gives an idea of how Boris lived and worked in Paris. He frequently appeared at literary gatherings, debates, and conferences as the principal speaker or as a discussant; he was well known in literary and artistic circles. His close friends valued him as a religious mystic, a God seeker, and a perceptive philosopher and thinker. The last years of his life were profoundly enigmatic. Many found in him not only a friend but a source of support for attaining an ideological turning point in their lives. He was destitute at the time, but he would still share his last penny with the poor.

A tragically absurd incident brought his life to an end. On October 8, 1935, Boris met a half-mad drug addict, who under the pressure of his own adversity decided to commit suicide and wrote a suicide note, addressed to the woman he loved. He persuaded Boris, "on a dare," to try out a "powder of illusions," but instead, excited by the maniacal idea of taking a fellow-traveler along on his journey to the beyond, gave him a fatal dose of poison, taking one himself at the same time.

Boris left behind two parts of a trilogy in the form of two large novels, *Apollon Bezobrazov* and *Homeward from Heaven,* and sketches for the third part, *The Apocalypse of Therese.* Then there are three volumes of verse ready for publication, a philosophical treatise on logic and metaphysics, the essay "Solitude," a multi-volume diary, notations, drawings, letters, his favorite books which contain many jottings on the margins, and a great deal of other material, which so far has not been sorted out.

Paris, October 1935

—Yulian Poplavsky's biography of his son, slightly abridged.[6]

Exhibit D: a friend

I began writing verse quite early, and in 1920 Boris Poplavsky and I organized a Poets' Guild in Constantinople.

—Vladimir Dukelsky, alias Vernon Duke.[7]

Exhibit E: self-portraits

1. "Poverty is a sin, retribution, impotence, while luxury is like a kingdom in which everything reflects, extends, incarnates the slightest flutter of God's eyelashes. And nevertheless, stoically, heroically, Oleg managed to bring his life to a realization, extricated it out of its wraps, despite poverty, inertia, and the obscurity of his underground destiny. Having received no education, he wrenched one for himself from the stained, poorly illuminated library books, read while his behind grew numb on the uncomfortable benches. Anemic and emaciated, by abstinence and daily wrestling with heavy iron weights, he forced life to yield him cupola-like shoulder muscles and an iron handgrip. Not handsome, unsure of himself, he used his hellish solitude, know-it-all-ism, valor, asceticism to master that fierce eye mechanism which was able to subjugate, at times to his own amazement, female heads radiant with youth. For Oleg, like all ascetics, was extraordinarily attractive, and his ugliness, rudeness, and self-assurance only enhanced his charm. Life refused him everything and he created everything for himself, reigning and enjoying himself now amidst the invisible labors of his 15-year effort. Thus, in a conversation he would calmly and slyly radiate the universality of his knowledge, which astounded his listeners as much as did the ease with which he could, while sitting on a sofa, lift and toss

about a thirty-kilogram weight or a chair, held horizontally by its back in his hand, as he laughed at the gloomy, lifeless, unascetic, sentimental, disbelieving Christianity of the Paris *émigré* poets."

2. "You thought, Oleg, that you could at last do without God, rest from His insatiable demands; and see, now He is doing without you. . . . Look, nature is about to enter upon her sad, brief summer triumph and you were asleep, your heavy head full of the hot waters of sleep, and you dreamed of earthly, full-blooded, bearded life. Once again you were insolent to God, Oleg, and tried living without Him, and your face hit the ground, heavily, stupidly, clownishly. You finally awoke from the pain, took a look around, and see, the trees are already in bloom and have hung out their vivid, abundant new leaves. It is summer in the city and again you are face to face with God, whether you want to be or not, like a child that conceived the wish to hide from the Eiffel Tower behind a flowering shrub in the Trocadero garden and after walking around it was instantly overtaken by the iron dancer-monster that takes up the entire sky. You try not to notice it, but it hurts you to look at the white sky and a heavy, sweaty stuffiness is pressing on your heart. You are again in the open sea, in the open desert, under an open sky covered up by white clouds, in the intolerable, ceaseless, manifest presence of God and sin. And there is no strength not to believe, to doubt, to despair happily in a cloud of tobacco smoke, to calm yourself at a daytime movie. The entire horizon is blindingly occupied by God; in every sweaty creature He is right there again. Eyesight grows dim and there is no shade anywhere, for there is no home of my own, but only history, eternity, apocalypse. There is no soul, no personality, no I, nothing is mine; from heaven to earth there is only the fiery waterfall of universal existence, inception, disappearance."

—Two of Boris Poplavsky's self-
portraits as Oleg in his novel
Homeward from Heaven.[8]

Exhibit F: the critical response

1. . . . recently *The Will of Russia* (*Volya Rossii*) discovered the amazingly gifted B. Poplavsky. Of all his delightful poems it printed, not a single one could have possibly appeared in *Contemporary Annals* (*Sovremennye zapiski*)—they are far too good and uniquely original for it.

—Georgy Ivanov in *Latest News*
(*Poslednie novosti*), Paris, May 31,
1928.

2. Among the Parisians, Boris Poplavsky is particularly outstanding. Some of his poems (especially the one with the epigraph from Rimbaud that appeared in Volume 2 of *Poetry* and the "Manuscript Found in a Bottle" in *The Will of Russia*, No. 7) force one to stop and listen in

astonishment to the voice of a genuine and entirely new poet. What is interesting about Poplavsky is that he has severed all ties with Russian subject matter. He is the first *émigré* writer who lives not on memories of Russia, but in a foreign reality. This evolution is inevitable for the whole of the emigration.

—D. S. Mirsky (Prince Dmitry Sviatopolk-Mirsky), in *Eurasia,* Paris, January 5, 1929.

3. . . . Poplavsky's pseudo-naiveté and sleek imitation of the correctly grasped literary fashions. There is no point in mentioning Poplavsky's name next to the names of Blok and Rimbaud (and yet this has been done by Weidlé and Adamovich and Mochulsky).

The scribblings (*pisaniya*) of Mr. Poplavsky, whose critical articles are as deliberately insolent as his verse, would not even deserve mention were it not for the fact that these puerile and shrill scribblings found an echo in Georgy Adamovich.

—Gleb Struve in *Russia and Slavdom,* May 11, 1929; October 11, 1930.[9]

Exhibit G.

THE TRAGIC DEATH OF THE POET B. POPLAVSKY

The lower depths of Montparnasse have claimed the lives of two more young Russians. Under circumstances that are still being investigated, the poet Boris Poplavsky and nineteen-year old Sergei Yarko, well known in certain shady cafes of Boulevard Montparnasse, died of narcotics poisoning.

ACCIDENT OR SUICIDE? The police commissioner of the Maison Blanche quarter immediately initiated an investigation. At first, the possibility of a double suicide was not ruled out. But upon examination of the evidence, it became clear that the young men were the victims of a drug overdose. It is also possible that the drug, purchased on Montparnasse from nameless dealers, contained an admixture of some kind of poison.

Boris Poplavsky never thought of suicide. Sunday evening he visited D. S. Merezhkovsky and discussed literature and politics with him. On Monday he was seen on Montparnasse. His parents, with whom he had a conversation several hours before his death, categorically reject the possibility of suicide. Their son was a victim of "white powder" vendors.

Apparently Poplavsky and Yarko had been addicts for a long time. In the poet's wallet, his own photograph was found, bearing a revealing inscription: "If you are interested, I found a source of cocaine, etc. Reasonably priced: heroin 25 fr. a gram, cocaine—40 fr." This was written in Poplavsky's hand—apparently in some cafe, where he was not able to announce the news out loud to his friend.

NO FUNDS FOR BURIAL. At 4 P.M. yesterday, Poplavsky's and Yarko's bodies were taken to the Institute of Forensic Medicine for autopsy. The funeral is planned within the next few days. But there are absolutely no funds available for Boris Poplavsky's burial. His family is destitute. There is not a sou in the house. Boris Poplavsky's parents are appealing to all his friends and to all generous people to help them pay for a coffin and a burial plot for the poet whose life ended so tragically. Donations may be sent to *Latest News*.

—Selected passages from the
lengthy news story in *Latest News*
(*Poslednie novosti*), Paris, October
11, 1935.

Excerpts from "The Book of Blessings,"
Poplavsky's unpublished journal for 1929.

109. I need only those writers whom I can apply practically in my life, from whom I can learn a particular form of pride or pity and, of course, whom I can develop and alter in my own way. Chekhov teaches me to endure in a special way, not to surrender, to hope, for in Chekhov there is much that is Roman, there is much of "no matter what happens," of *quand même*. With Dostoevsky one can be ill and die, separate and perish, but it is impossible to live with him. As for Tolstoy, with his ancient Hebraic family idylls, I find him repulsive. But Chekhov I hope to put to use, after first rendering him harmless. How? By expanding and developing his admiration for the perishing, beautiful failures, by cleansing him of his disgusting squeamishness and his dignified contempt, contempt for what has failed, what has perished, i.e. extending him in a Christian or, more correctly, specifically Orthodox direction.

110. Chekhov is the most [Russian] Orthodox of Russian writers or, more correctly, the only Orthodox Russian writer. For what is Russian Orthodoxy if not absolute forgiveness, the absolute refusal to condemn which we hear in the voice of Sonya and of the Little Priest of the Swamps? [10]

111. Blok is also an Orthodox poet, the poet of absolute pity, angry at nothing, condemning nothing.

115. It seems to me that the closest work we have to the spirit of the Prometheus of Aeschylus is Chekhov's *Ivanov*. Let us note, *en passant,* that the Prometheus of Aeschylus is one of the most pretentious heroes in world literature. But then, is there anything more beautiful than heroic pretentiousness, for is not the perishing hero higher than the smugly successful hero? And is not the point of a perishing hero in his pretense at being a hero?

116. All my poetry is only the voice of Sonya, or at least I would like for all my poetry to be the voice of Sonya, consoling Uncle Vanya abandoned by everyone in the midst of the demolished estate.

325

123. Oh, how the lower strata of the *émigrés* are irritated and out-raged by the sight of an impoverished and merry friend of books and stars, with his tattered pants and a monocle in his eye! It is their enormous, base yearning for power that is outraged within them. What! He dares to be joyous, that owner of worn-out shoes? Isn't he in the same position as we? He has no money, no power, and he dares to be joyous. Where does he get his joy? Surely not from that bookish, intellectual stuff—the very thing that ruined Russia? From Culture and Social Conscience? Thus the poor people. And a huge disgust hangs suspended in perplexity from their curled lip, while the friend of the stars goes his own way in his worn-out shoes, waving his hand-some athletic arms in the air as he recites poetry to his neighbor.

124. The attitude of the wealthy *émigrés* toward the friend of the stars is even more base. What! We've done our best, we've achieved, we've recovered our own, and this one dares to be joyous while the seat of his pants is in patches? What was the point of our struggle?

125. But the attitude of foreigners is delightful. It can be seen from their glances in the street, for in them there still survive the ancient, beautiful ideals, merry and profound, of ancient stoical poverty. There was once this delightful philosopher—Anaximenes of Dorcrete seems to have been his name—a fine athletic old man. Diodorus tells us that he was once invited to some ritzy party, by some tyrant or other. Coming to the table, he bared himself and beshat the company and the table, and with this excellent deed he indubitably deserved his immortality. His other works were forgotten, but compared to this they could not have been important.

Poplavsky yesterday and today

When I first read *Flags,* I had no idea of Poplavsky's position in the Russian literary hierarchy. I had simply assumed that he was a poet as famous as Blok and Pasternak. I knew little about Russian poetry as a whole at the time, and there were many important modern poets I was yet to discover and read. It took me a few years to realize that apart from a small cult centered in Paris, almost no one had ever heard of his name. In the late 1940's my colleagues at the Control Council for Germany, Alain Bosquet and Edouard Roditi, were publishing a literary journal in Berlin. They asked me to write something about Russian poetry for it, "about somebody modern and famous, like Selvinsky or Bagrit-sky," as Roditi put it. I had no idea who Selvinsky and Bagritsky were, but I offered to write about the three poets who had been my favorites during my school years in Los Angeles. They let me, and I wrote three brief pieces on Khlebnikov, Pasternak, and Poplavsky; these were translated into German and published in *Das Lot,* Volume IV, in 1950, with a selection of translated poems by each of these poets. The overindulgent accompanying note identified me as the author of "numerous articles published in American newspapers and magazines," but apart from a few pieces in the college newspaper, this was actually my debut in print. I'm glad it had to do with Poplavsky and that I already then called him the most interesting poet produced by the Russian emigration between the two world wars.

By then I had already read his two posthumous collections of verse (they contain some astounding poems, but I found them on the whole a bit of a letdown after *Flags*); the published portions of his novels (*Homeward from Heaven* contains some of his finest lyrics, inserted between passages of prose and printed to look like prose); his paradoxical critical essays; the highly original short story "The Ball"; his pieces on painting and boxing. When in 1965 Nikolai Tatishchev privately published a new volume of Poplavsky's previously uncollected poems, *Dirigible of Unknown Destination,* my torch for the poet flared up again. The volume contained some of his most typical and most perfectly realized poems ("On the Frontier," for instance, with its striking central metaphor of a poet as a customs official trying to stop the two-way smugglers' traffic between the Land of Good and the Land of Evil; or "The Biography of a Clerk," with its transposition of the humiliated clerk of Gogol's "The Overcoat" and Dostoevsky's *Poor Folk* into a Kafkaesque and surrealistic tonality). I read a paper on Poplavsky's surrealistic techniques at a scholarly gathering in Washington, D.C., and published it as an article in *Slavic Review.* A few graduate students purchased copies of the *Dirigible* as a result, but I knew that, with one or two exceptions, I had failed to convince my fellow Slavicists of the value of Poplavsky's work. Just how badly I had failed was made clear to me by one of my most respected and discerning colleagues, who referred to him as a Parisian Vertinsky (a popular *émigré* nightclub singer) for the elect few.

Doing literary research in Europe in the fall of 1969, I made a point of seeking out and talking about Poplavsky with those who knew him or were his friends in an effort to reconstitute the reality of the man behind the poetry and the prose: the poets Alla Golovina and Sophia Pregel; the painters Ida Karskaya (a marvelously warm and compassionate woman and a far more important painter than I had previously realized) and Constantine Terechkovitch; the critic Georgy Adamovich; the literary scholar Sophie Laffitte (*née* Glickman, later Sophie Stalinsky and Sophie Bonneau); and of course Poplavsky's closest friend and the curator of his archive, Nikolai Tatishchev. All of them had observed Poplavsky at close range at one or another time in his life, all but the first two had poems dedicated to them in *Flags,* and all were willing to talk about him candidly and openly. Some day I hope to transcribe these interviews in full, but for the moment I can say that their sum total has helped me to formulate the two sets of polarities that I feel primarily motivated and shaped Poplavsky's literary art. The never-resolved dichotomy between poetry and painting is what accounts for the intensely visual nature of his imagery and much of his subject matter. According to Terechkovitch, Poplavsky thought of himself during his first few years of exile not as a poet but as a painter. In 1922, Terechkovitch and Poplavsky traveled together to Berlin to study art. In Berlin, Poplavsky met the leading Soviet abstractionists as well as Chagall, Tchelitchew, and Chaim Soutine. But everyone, and particularly his teachers and colleagues, kept assuring him that he had no talent for painting. At first he tried to ignore their verdict. When he realized that they were right, the result was a total nervous breakdown that kept him bedridden for several weeks. Not only his highly personal articles on art exhibitions and painters, which appeared later in the journal *Numbers* (*Chisla*), but much of his prose and poetry testify to his never-ending yearning for mastery of the visual arts. His literary development reflects not so much the development of Russian *émigré* poetry as the evolution of the Paris schools of painting in the late nineteen-twenties and early thirties—especially those of the surrealists and the neo-romantics.

The other central polarity has to do with his insatiable hunger for mystical experience (any kind of mysticism) and drug experience (any kind of drugs). It was his sister Natasha, that "dazzlingly educated and talented girl" his father wrote about, who introduced Boris to drugs by the time he was twelve. Her search for the ultimate high eventually took her to Madagascar, to Africa, to India, and finally to Shanghai, where she died in the late 1920's—of pneumonia, according to her father's biography of Boris, but of a hopeless opium addiction according to everyone else. Drugs remained a constant presence in Poplavsky's life, both in Berlin and Paris, and they (rather than imitation of his idol Rimbaud) account for the psychedelic swirling of images and the vivid, violent colors so typical of his verse. There are vast riches of authentic psychedelia to be mined in twentieth-century Russian poetry—Balmont and Khlebnikov are the names that come to mind most easily—but no one in the Russian tradition exploited the openings to other realities that drugs afford as systematically as did Poplavsky in the service of his poetry. There was, unfortunately, no LSD or mescaline to be had in those days and he had to do it the hard way. (A tremendous stimulus for writing much of *Flags* came when his friend, the minor poet Boris Zakovich, the "Pusya" of Poplavsky's journals, inherited a large supply of painkillers and mind-expanders from his dentist-father.) Those who are capable of appreciating the unique kind of beauty Poplavsky was thus able to glimpse and convey are the beneficiaries.

Poplavsky's religious quest was as intense as it was eclectic. A devout and loyal member of the Russian Orthodox Church (as his journals leave no doubt), he was powerfully drawn to Roman Catholic rite and lore, to Hindu mystics, to freemasonry, and to various forms of spiritualism. One of the most intense experiences of his life, according to Tatishchev, occurred in 1918, when he met Krishnamurti, who took his hand and addressed a few words in English to him. Poplavsky understood no English, but he was moved to tears. In Berlin he had several discussions about anthroposophy with Andrei Belyi. (His mother and aunt were close to Moscow anthroposophic circles.)

Boris Poplavsky was loved by a number of exceptional and

brilliant women in his day, but the central relationship of his life, its keynote, was what he himself called his love affair with God (*roman s Bogom*). This affair is the subject of many poems in *Snowy Hour;* it is basic to his novels, and it is vividly reflected in the portions of his diaries which his friends Dina Shraibman and Nikolai Tatishchev published after his death. It was also discussed in print by no less a thinker than Nikolai Berdyaev in his puzzled, perplexed, and not entirely sympathetic review of Poplavsky's journals.[11] I'll venture to say, with all due respect, that the celebrated philosopher simply failed to grasp the point of Poplavsky's mysticism. Like art, like drugs, mysticism was for Poplavsky both a way of expanding his personal vision and a means of transforming unbearable social reality. Poplavsky's lecture on Marcel Proust and James Joyce (he is the only Russian writer I can think of besides Vladimir Nabokov who responded creatively to *Ulysses*), of which I have the outline, concludes with a surprising prediction of impending social revolution in Western Europe, which would combine social, sexual, and personal-mystical elements. For Poplavsky, the reason the Soviet experiment turned Russia into a "vast, barbarous, snow-clad field" was that in its attempt to build a better society it suppressed the human spirit and its most precious manifestations. This was well understood by Poplavsky's friends Zinaida Gippius and Dmitry Merezhkovsky; yet one can easily imagine the shock that this conclusion of the Proust-Joyce lecture occasioned among the *émigré* audience when Poplavsky delivered it at the *Kochevie* Club on October 22, 1931.

Poplavsky's career in the world of *émigré* letters was brief and meteoric. Only six years separate his literary debut from his death. During that time he impressed some of the most important older writers-in-exile (Merezhkovsky, Khodasevich, Georgy Ivanov) and was acclaimed by the finest *émigré* critics (Mirsky, Mochulsky, Adamovich, Weidlé). He must have made an enormous impression on the *émigré* writers of his own age group, for he looms as a momentous presence in the subsequently written autobiographies and memoirs of Nina Berberova,[12] Yuri Terapiano,[13] Vladimir Varshavsky,[14] and V. S. Yanovsky.[15] Vladimir Nabokov has on two occasions singled out Poplavsky as the only poet of importance among the younger *émigrés*.[16] At Poplavsky's funeral, homage was paid to him by such diverse figures as Mark Aldanov, Alexei Remizov, and Vladislav Khodasevich, whose eloquent obituary of Poplavsky was later reprinted in a collection of his critical essays.[17] And yet, if we were to take a count, there would probably be fewer people in the world today who are aware of Poplavsky's existence than in 1935.

I am convinced that Boris Poplavsky has his readers somewhere. But where? Russians, either abroad or in the Soviet Union, don't seem to want to read him. When Olga Carlisle included Denise Levertov's fine translation of his poem, "Manuscript Found in a Bottle," in her book *Poets on Streetcorners,* the Moscow *Literary Gazette* took her to task for including this "tramp of whom no one has heard" among the other fine Russian poets in her anthology. Publication of a few excerpts from *The Apocalypse of Therese* in George Ivask's Russian literary journal *Experiments* (*Opyty*) in the late 1950's was met with similar scorn by Russian newspapers in Paris and New York. I tried submitting several of his unpublished poems and a highly interesting essay on Russian painting (which I obtained from Nikolai Tatishchev and which Jean Claude Marcadé carefully annotated) to the New York Russian literary journal *The New Review.* Two of the poems were published, with distorting "corrections" by the editor, while the remainder of them and the article were rejected after a two-year wait. In a personal letter to me, the editor of *The New Review,* Roman Goul, wrote that Poplavsky was "an utter madman" and proudly recalled how he and a group of friends once threw Poplavsky out of a Berlin beer hall.

And yet, as Vladimir Nabokov put it when I informed him of my interest in Poplavsky: "Yes, write something about him. He was, after all, the first hippy, the original flower child." This might simplify things a bit, but it is not wrong.[18] During the past few years young Slavic scholars in the West, those in their early twenties, have been repeatedly taking to Poplavsky like the proverbial duck to water. I've read with pleasure the intelligent papers Olga Bazanoff and Mike Hathaway wrote about him for

Vsevolod Setchkarev's seminar on *émigré* literature at Harvard, and Helene Paschutinsky's first-rate M.A. thesis on Poplavsky's imagery,[19] written under Sophie Laffitte's direction at the Sorbonne. I am excited about Anthony Olcott's Stanford thesis-in-progress.

Perhaps Poplavsky was an *émigré* in more senses than one. Caught between cultures, he was also trapped in the wrong historical period. Many young non-Russians today should have no trouble identifying with him and seeing him as one of themselves. As Emmett Jarrett and Dick Lourie wrote, when I sent them some trots of his poetry for translation: "He's dynamite . . ."

How to detonate him?

Notes

1. The passage corresponds to stanza VI of Edward Fitzgerald's version, where the nightingale speaks in Pahlavi and the rose is *sallow*. The notes to my (New York, 1888) edition explain that the rose was yellow in the first edition of Fitzgerald's translation and identify Pahlavi as the "old, heroic Sanscrit of Persia." This seems to suggest that Tkhorzhevsky was translating Fitzgerald into Russian, rather than the original Omar.

2. N. Tatishchev, "O Poplavskom" ("On Poplavsky"), *Krug* (*The Circle*), Vol. 3 (Paris, 1938).

3. "But Poplavsky's surrealistic world is created illegitimately, using means borrowed from another art, namely painting (some of the critics have pointed out that Poplavsky is actually a visual rather than a musical poet; his poetry has been compared to Chagall's paintings . . .)." Gleb Struve, *Russkaya literatura v izgnanii* (*Russian Literature in Exile*) (New York, 1956), p. 339. The observation is absolutely correct, but why is cross-fertilization between the arts illegitimate? Russian poetry of the twentieth century in particular has a deep-going and highly legitimate symbiotic involvement with both painting (Voloshin, Mayakovsky, Khlebnikov) and music (Belyi, Blok, Kuzmin, Pasternak).

4. P. A. Buryshkin, *Moskva kupecheskaya* (New York, 1954), pp. 256–57. This little-known volume is an astoundingly thorough and convincing record of the contribution made by the traditionally maligned and despised Russian merchant class to the development of Russian culture, literature, and the arts during the century preceding the Revolution.

5. Marina Tsvetaeva, *Proza* (New York, 1953), pp. 239, 240, 247.

6. *Nov'*, No. 8 (Paris, 1934), pp. 144–48.

7. Autobiographical note in the anthology *Sodruzhestvo* (Washington, 1966), p. 521. Although both wrote poetry at the time, it was the future composer of *Cabin in the Sky* and *Le Bal de Blanchisseuses* who considered himself a poet then, while Poplavsky saw himself as a future painter.

8. Fragments from *Homeward from Heaven,* in *Krug* (*The Circle*), Vol. 3.

9. Gleb Struve attacked Poplavsky's work vehemently when it first appeared in print, and he remains to this day Poplavsky's most consistent critical opponent. The only other adverse response to Poplavsky's literary beginnings in *émigré* criticism, Vladimir Nabokov's review of *Flags* in *Rul'* (*The Rudder*)—

which Nabokov subsequently repudiated (see note 16, below)—is far milder in both its tone and its conclusions. Although Nabokov took Poplavsky to task for his violations of meter, ungrammatical usages, and abuses of inappropriate colloquialisms, he ended the review with the admission that some of the poems in the collection "soared with genuine music."

In his later history of Russian *émigré* literature (see note 3), Professor Struve cites the highly favorable opinions of various important *émigré* writers and critics about Poplavsky's poetry with exemplary scholarly objectivity; he even seems to see some promise in Poplavsky's novels. But his ultimate judgment on Poplavsky can be summed up in this quote: "He was a gifted man and an interesting phenomenon, but he never became any kind of writer, no matter what his numerous admirers may say" (*Russian Literature in Exile*, p. 313).

10. I.e., Sonya from Chekhov's play *Uncle Vanya*, and the elfin creature from Blok's poem of that name, who prays with equal fervor "for the injured leg of a frog and for the Pope in Rome."

11. In *Sovremennye zapiski* (*Contemporary Annals*), Paris, 1939, LXVIII.

12. *The Italics Are Mine* (New York, 1969). Original Russian version, *Kursiv moy* (Munich, 1972).

13. *Vstrechi* (*Encounters*) (New York, 1953).

14. *Nezamechennoye pokolenie* (*The Unnoticed Generation*) (New York, 1956).

15. "Eliseyskie polya" ("Les Champs Elysées"), an excerpt from his memoirs, in *Vozdushnye puti* (*Aerial Ways*), Vol. V (New York, 1967).

16. "I did not meet Poplavsky who died young, a far violin among near balalaikas. His plangent tonalities I shall never forget, nor shall I ever forgive myself the ill-tempered review in which I attacked him for trivial flaws in his unfledged verse." *Speak, Memory* (New York, 1951), p. 216. This is repeated, with the addition of a quoted line from Poplavsky's poem "Morella," in *Speak, Memory* (an expanded version) (New York, 1966), p. 287.

17. "O smerti Poplavskogo" ("On Poplavsky's Death"), in *Literaturnye stat'i i vospominaniya* (*Literary Essays and Memoirs*) (New York, 1954).

18. His involvement with drugs and Hindu mystics are two of the more striking ways in which Poplavsky seems to foreshadow the hip culture, but that is by no means all. He dressed unconventionally, was never without a pair of dark glasses, thought bathing unnecessary, and would wear the same shirt for weeks on end. His favorite music was by Bach, Scriabin, and Stravinsky. A beard and long hair are the only ingredients that were missing, but that tonsorial style was inextricably connected with the priestly caste in Russian culture. There clearly would have been no point in Poplavsky's trying to pass for an Orthodox priest.

19. Particularly impressive is Mlle Paschutinsky's demonstration of the central function of the states of flying, floating, and levitation in Poplavsky's poetry, and of his systematic use of objects and beings capable of these states: fish, ships, dirigibles, balloons, submarines, interplanetary rockets, clouds, comets, and angels, as well as the role of Poplavsky's ubiquitous bridges, balconies, and towers, functioning as stepping-stones to flight and levitation. The resultant antithesis of lightness and heaviness is then used by Mlle Paschutinsky to construct a highly convincing and logical system that provides us with a key not only to Poplavsky's imagery, but also to the whole of his complex metaphysics. Should Poplavsky's poetry ever gain the wide readership it so very much deserves, Helene Paschutinsky's study will certainly become a fundamental source on this poet.

TWO POEMS BY NIKOLAI MORSHEN
translated by Richard Wilbur

1

A star in the sky. How many words and tears,
What promises, what wishes made upon it,
How many heart-cries! For what endless years!
What dashings-off of verse and rhyme and sonnet!

Yet to the clear mind, too, it signs from heaven:
The Magi followed it with reverence;
So did the navigators . . . Einstein, even,
Could not without some fixèd stars make sense.

Ah, to select a theme that once for all
Would captivate all men without exception—
Saint, atheist, hero, coward, freeman, thrall—
And then to realize one's high conception
On the night's canvas with a dot, just one.

What artist would not own himself outdone?

2

Nights rolled upon the river's face,
Volcanoes flared and overflowed,
And ferns which towered into space
With paleozoic flashes glowed

When, with his Slavic eye, there crept
A saurian from paludal slime—
My reptile ancestor—and stepped
On the dry land for the first time.

He did not then, of course, predict
The spate of future generation,
Of linked phenomena in strict
And inextinguishable relation
Or me, in that concatenation,
In whose world Planck and Blok connect!

But I . . . what breed am I, what kind?
What are my past, my destiny?
How should that far one be divined
Whose modest forebear I shall be,
Whose world's pure miracle to me,
Whose deeds, the manner of whose mind?

Hundreds of years will pass, perhaps
Millions, and then he will be there,
Remembering us across that lapse,
Our strange third partner, and our heir.

And then what magic time will do!
All distances will coalesce,
And all awareness flow into
The heaven of his consciousness.

From grey mist will materialize
His predecessors, one and all,
Whatever their degree or size,
No matter how obscure or small,

And to that joyous herd, that throng
Bound from creation and before,
You too shall certainly belong,
O my reptilian ancestor.

TEN POEMS BY ANATOLY STEIGER
translated by Paul Schmidt

1

Until the sun sinks into a green
Smoke and twilight starts to spread
We speak of nothing but summer.

Yet autumn will soon tell us
The truth, in a cold voice.

2

We believe in books, in music and poems,
We believe in the dreams we dream,
We believe in words (even words
Spoken to console us
From the window of a railway car) . . .

3

The dull rattle of shutters being lowered
So the cottage looks like someone blind,
And then, like a shot point-blank—
The roar of a motor in the garden out in front.

. . . And an endlessly accompanying glance:
Hopeless, melancholy, spaniel-eyed.

4

It must be an eternal arrangement:
Some people dissemble and lie,
While others help them do it
(Always seeing through it)—
And it's called love . . .

5

Friendship

i Where is he now, I wonder?
And what's his life like?
Don't let me sit by the door
Expecting a sudden knock:
He will never come back.

Was it to hurt me, or himself?
(Or maybe he was lucky.)

ii One dream remains—the thought of peace.
—Don't need friendship, all words are empty,
And that word's the emptiest of all.

(For friendship you need to have two.
I was one, the other was air: you.)

6

... Not an epilogue, but everything coming to an end.
We'll meet. I'll grow very pale.
Your arrogant face will flicker
With annoyance: "What a silly idea!"

At my arrival—a meaningless arrival,
Because I can't behave like all the rest—
What is this constant wanderlust?

Suppose, a variant: (The thought drives me wild)
A clumsy hug?

7

How do we break the habit of big words:
What does "pride" mean? What's "humiliation"?
(When you know perfectly well I'm ready
to respond to the first sign, the first call,
the first slight gesture.) ...

How can I shout, to be heard in that prison,
Beyond those ramparts, through those walls,
That not everyone has betrayed him,
That he is not abandoned, alone in the world?

I dreamed that I broke in to see you,
Sat on your bed and held you in my arms.
(Though he's long lost the habit, surely,
Of tenderness and soft, familiar words.)

Yet friendship exists, it really exists,
And tenderness of male for male as well . . .
It is not obligation, but particular nobility
To say so, with unwavering eyes.

9

Nobody waits at the foot of the stairs any more
Or takes our hand crossing a street, the way they did
When we were young. Nobody tells us about the mean
Ant and the Grasshopper. Or teaches us to believe in God.

Nowadays nobody thinks of us at all—
They all have enough just thinking of themselves,
So we have to live as they do—but alone . . .
(Impotent, dishonest, and inept.)

10

They will not ask us: have you sinned?
They'll ask us only: did you love?
With heads hanging,
Bitterly, we'll say: yes . . . Oh, yes,
We loved . . . Again and again . . .

THREE POEMS BY YURI ODARCHENKO
translated by Theodore Weiss

1

Claudia Petrovna,
Prepare the samovar.
Glistening like a copper star
That's spouting smoke,
It quakes with fiery love . . .

Tea at twelve sharp!

Shiny candies in crystal bowls,
Fresh napkins on the table,
Your napkins neatly monogrammed,
All your children at the table,

Claudia Petrovna!

Poppa, pacing his room,
Didn't sleep all night
And is late for tea.
But he himself ordered:

Tea at twelve sharp!

She went to the door. There
She turned. A mortal fear
In the clouded mirrors.
She fell to the parquet floor. Ah,

Claudia Petrovna . . .

2

Only for you my tea roses,
Only of you my random dreams,

You with your hovering smile,
You with arms rounding like swans.

Your hair is silk spinning,
Your voice a sleighbell all silver,

And the eyes in your taking face
Are two green tsetse flies.

3

The path I'm following
Is a surefire road to hell.

But from there, by a velvet ladder,
Warbling blithesome ditties,
I'll return to earth
Tucked out as a tomcat on the roof.

And I'll live with a little girl
In her little pink, prim bedroom,
And I'll be purring softly again
But about what nobody'll know.

THREE POEMS BY IGOR CHINNOV

1

July sparkled
quartz a whole crystal.
A patrol sped by
in a crimson blaze.

A soldier long dead
played a reed flute
and lilies twittered
for children.

And in napalm jetting
the village sparkled,
and an ebony palm
entangled the wing

of the very plane
which—yes, of course.
And the pilot sparkled
like a large star.

translated by Theodore Weiss

2

Pithecanthropi in the Pinakotek.
Orangutans in the Orangerie.
Pterodactyl's spirit revived in man.
Look: a gibbon in a helicopter.

And yonder in reactors, isotopes
Of uranium, of helium. A new experiment.
Look: Acropolis, pithecanthropus,
A flying saurian, a mindless robot.

Reactors, robots. Do not tease
Gorillas, mandrills, crocodiles.
Pluto, Urania. We are in the shadow
Of their terrifying realms, their hostile realms.

And soon, in an astronaut's rocket
The ravening troglodyte shall set forth.
And soon the pathfinders shall behold
The plesiosaur, the brontosaur.
Uranus, plutonium. And the troglodytes.
And the thermosaurian tomorrow.

translated by L. P. Izhorsky

3

All this bedraggled struggle . . .
Better to buy a cloud-pink
palazzo or a palazzo cloud itself.

Worries? What use are they
except to barter for a comet,
for Cassiopeia at the corner store.

Or, for less than the price
of a lottery ticket, to win
a good, golden hunk of immortality. O.K.?

translated by Theodore Weiss

Grasse diary
GALINA KUZNETSOVA

Galina Nikolaevna Kuznetsova joined the household of Ivan Bunin in Grasse in 1927 and remained there for several years. One of the young writers of the "Bunin school," she was a contributor to Paris émigré publications and published a volume of short stories in 1930. Her novel Prologue *appeared in 1933.* Grasse Diary * *contains her account of those years with Bunin in Grasse and Paris when Paris was the cultural capital of the Russian emigration and Bunin one of its central literary figures.*

May 19, 1927
Grasse

I have been living here nearly three weeks now and have not yet gotten down to work. In all, I've written two poems and no prose at all. I walk, gaze about, and promise myself first to enjoy the beauty of the surroundings as fully as possible and then, after that, to work, to write. But I am not succeeding even in getting my

ABOVE PHOTO: Nina Berberova, Galina Kuznetsova, and Ivan Bunin; Grasse, 1928. (Photo courtesy Nina Berberova.)
  * *Grasskii dnevink* (Washington, 1967).

fill of enjoyment. The deserted gardens, lying in terraces around our villa, lure me, for the most part platonically. I run there for a quarter of an hour, cast a glance around, and then hurry back to the house. However, I often walk in the open patio before the villa; I gaze and can't get enough of the valley, gently blue, which lies far below, by the sea. On the horizon are mountains, those wild Maures in which Maupassant roamed.

In the morning I cut roses—the fences are entwined with them —and expel the green beetles which are eating the heart of the flower. This last was taught me by Fondaminsky,[1] in whom there is a pleasant fondness for flowers, rare in a man. Usually I go on to fill all the pitchers in the house with flowers, which I. A. [Bunin] calls "occupying oneself with esthetics." He himself loves flowers, but from a distance. He says that on the table they bother him and that in general one should keep flowers only in those houses where there are many rooms and a whole staff of servants. This is a small example of his tendency always to exaggerate everything, a feature which is derived from his passionate, brusque nature. However, he does love fragrant flowers. Once he even asked me to cut a bouquet of heliotrope for him and place it in his study.

Bushes of this heliotrope grow under the windows of the villa Montfleury, which is located below our window and is at present empty. There on one of the terraces is an empty stone cistern. On the bottom of it, among branches and trash, lies a small skeleton of a cat, washed clean by rains. Obviously, it jumped in and couldn't climb back out. And although it must have died slowly and painfully, there is nevertheless in its little skeleton, in the tiny yellow bones of its hind paws, neatly folded under, a profound touching repose. It lies so quietly, and I involuntarily fall to thinking about death: what is this thing of which we are all so terrified? Perhaps the answer is in these clean little bones lying in the shade of a broad fig branch. It is as if they were a symbol of total peace, which was promised to every being on earth.

However, I. A. warned me not to speak of cats in the presence

344

of V. N. [Vera Nikolaevna Bunina, I. A.'s wife]. She has some sort of pathological fear of them. I. A. told how, the summer before last, he and Shmelyov [2] had killed a cat that took to visiting their villa and frightening V. N. I cannot say that this story made me very happy. I have a very friendly feeling for cats. I like their nimbleness and grace and the cautiousness concealed in the depths of the pupils of their eyes. Moreover, there is in them a certain aristocratic consciousness of their own worth.

I am writing, but meanwhile it has grown completely dark. The valley beyond the palm branches has become a dusky blue, and against its background stir the tiny leaves of the olive trees and the yellow bamboo which grows beneath the windows. A nightingale has awakened in the shrubbery. Nights here are splendid. I fall asleep to the exchange between the nightingales and the incessant passionate chorus of the unusual number of frogs that are here. But I have not seen a single one of them. We only hear them at night.

August 5, 1930

Yesterday we had dinner with Aldanov [3] and the Rachmaninovs under a boat on the sand. There was a real sandstorm, so there was nothing left for us to do but take ourselves to that comparatively quiet place and settle down. The "tramps' dinner," as I. A. called it, turned out to be rather unusual. The cutlets, tomatoes, cheese, and fruit were all served with sand, and there were only four glasses for all of us. The Rachmaninovs arrived when everything was laid out; they brought with them ham sandwiches and a bottle of Vichy water. I. A. introduced Aldanov to Rachmaninov. Aldanov was carelessly dressed: his trousers and shirt hung on him sloppily and his hair was hanging down. His wife had just left for Paris and he was a little sad.

Rachmaninov was especially gracious to him. By the end of the evening he had even invited him to stay with them in Rambouillet, assuring him that it would be very convenient for him to work quietly there, since he himself worked a great deal.

We were all invited to lunch the next day at Aldanov's in Juan-les-Pins. (When saying good-bye, he managed to whisper to me: "Be sure to bring the camera—you won't forget?")

Undated

First we had a swim at a small beach—the water was transparent, clean, delightful—then we went in the direction of Aldanov's villa. The Rachmaninovs overtook us in their car. V. N. and I. A. got in with them, and Tanya [4] got out and joined us. We went on, leisurely, on foot.

In Aldanov's living room, a round table already laden with hors d'oeuvres awaited us. We sat down: around one side, I. A., Aldanov, and Rachmaninov, closing the other, I, L.,[5] Tanya, and V. N. beside Rachmaninov, closing the circle. A pleasant breeze drifted through the half-open doors. Out of respect for the "celebrities" we were separated from the rest of the *pension* guests, who dined in the next room. Rachmaninov was very charming, gracious, and lively. He constantly turned to pass things to us, started conversations, and helped V. N. to serve the fish and chicken from a large platter.

After the roast, we were served dessert and coffee, the doors were closed, and we were left alone. Rachmaninov, who had drunk little and eaten very moderately, allowing himself only one extra cup of coffee, began to tell of his visit to Tolstoy. He spoke in a barely audible voice, almost a whisper, breathily, pronouncing "l" like "r."

"It is not a pleasant memory. . . . It happened in 1900. They had told Tolstoy that there is this certain young man who has stopped working, has been drinking for three years, and has despaired of himself; and yet he's talented and ought to be encouraged. I played Beethoven. There is a certain little piece with a leitmotif expressing the grief of young lovers who are being separated.[6] I finished and everyone was in raptures, but they were afraid to clap because they were waiting to see how Tolstoy would react. And he sat apart from everyone, his arms folded severely, and was silent. Everyone was quiet, seeing that he was not pleased.

Well, understandably, I tried to avoid him. But at the end of the evening I saw the old man heading straight for me. 'Pardon me,' he said, 'for what I have to say to you: that was a bad thing you played.' I said, 'But it was not something of mine, it was Beethoven.' 'So what if it was Beethoven? All the same it was bad. You aren't offended, are you?' At this point I came back at him impudently, 'Why should I take offense if even Beethoven can seem bad to you?'

"So I fled. They asked me to come again, and Sofya Andreyevna later invited me, but I didn't go. Up to that time, I had dreamed of Tolstoy as if he were happiness itself, and here it was all shattered. And it wasn't this that stunned me—that he didn't like Beethoven or that I played badly—but that he, the man that he was, could deal so harshly with a young beginner falling into despair, who had been brought to him for comfort. And I didn't go back. I was comforted later on by Chekhov, who spoke as a physician: 'Yes, but maybe it was that he failed to have a bowel movement that day and nothing more. And if you had come to him at another time, it might all have turned out differently.'

"Now I would go running to him, but there's nowhere to run. . . ."

"There, Sergei Vasilievich, with that last you have condemned yourself!" said I. A. "With a beginner, a young person, harshness is needed. If he survives, that means he has something to him, if not—good riddance."

"No, I. A., I completely disagree with you," said Rachmaninov. "If a young person should come to me and ask my advice, especially in a field other than my own, and if I should see that my opinion is important to him, I would rather lie. I would not let myself be inhuman."

An argument arose. I. A. defended Tolstoy, saying that he had been thinking of him "for a long time, for forty-five years" and that one cannot judge him by our usual standards; that he understood music if, in dying, he could say: "The one thing I will miss—is music." Rachmaninov, on the other hand, insisted that Tolstoy understood music poorly, that the *Kreutzer Sonata* does not contain what he found in it, and that Rachmaninov himself does not like it and never plays it.

At the close of the conversation, he asked me, "And are you working?" I answered, "Not right now, this is a vacation," and mentioned that I had published a book fairly recently. "What do you mean, fairly recently? That was a long time ago!" he exclaimed. "I do know when your book came out. You have to work every day."

Incidentally, he related how at Tolstoy's table he had said, "I don't believe in myself. I am afraid that I have little talent. . . ." To that Tolstoy had answered: "One should never think of that. That is nothing. Do you think that I never have doubts? Our work is not fun. Just keep working. . . ." [. . .]

We said good-bye in very friendly fashion, even though by then we were already a part of the large crowd that had gathered in the garden. Tanya invited us to visit her in Paris. Rachmaninov, holding my hand, said in farewell: "Well now, keep working. . . . Be sure you do. . . ."

November 14, 1930

We went to see the Merezhkovskys.[7] Dmitry Sergeich came out in some sort of white flannel jacket with black stripes, as always slightly stooping and clutching something to his breast. [. . .]

Zinaida Nikolaevna entered wearing brown, with her make-up in blotches. As always, she drawled something, chewing the end of her cigarette holder along with her words. She continually arranged her hair while supporting her head with a fragile, pale hand. For the first time since I have known the Merezhkovskys, their living room looked untidy: there was dust on the table; the water in the vase of chrysanthemums had not been changed, the chairs were out of place. The maid was ill.

We went out together. On the way, I talked mostly with Merezhkovsky. I asked him about something or other, and the conversation wandered from topic to topic.

"Things are going badly with us," he said, "and getting worse all the time. There is no one who amounts to anything. Oh, there are many with talent, but so what? One must bring something new into the world, even if only a grain of it, in any field whatsoever—poetry, criticism, journalism, memoirs, prose—but it must be new. Otherwise we have only imitators, repeaters. Who actually needs them? Take Flaubert—no matter how he wrote, how he sharpened a phrase, what use is there in his splendid phrase? In the end it even becomes irritating—and he gave us nothing new. Stendhal is another matter. How much that was new came in with him! Aldanov, if he'd devote himself only to journalism, could take his place in the first ranks. In England, for example, he would be a leading journalist. His best things are his political portraits and his notebooks. But his novels are ersatz. . . . Sirin,[8] now—here you have a real mimicry of talent. The creature looks just like a twig, is the twig itself, but in fact really isn't. His work may be a very delicate mimicry. And that in itself is a talent. Georgy Ivanov is a real poet. Of the two, Khodasevich and Ivanov, he is the more genuine. Now I am continually reading boring things. And it is a good thing that they are boring. For instance, there is Jouhandeau. Sometimes I am so bored with him that I put the book aside and pick up an adventure novel. Then, later on, I take it up again. There is *The Captain's Daughter*.[9] It is like a piece of candy. You swallow it and don't feel it. But what I need is an iron nail."

Another thing that was said was that in our age not everyone can be a writer, a poet, but everyone, if he wishes, may become a prophet. But the face of the emigration, the typical visage, is Mironov—of *Russia Illustrated* [*Illustrirovannaya Rossia*]. We walked along the embankment. He called my attention now to the "paradisiac green of the lawn," on which the delicate rays of the setting sun fell through the palms, now to the tall straight sail of a boat approaching the jetty. "Just like a butterfly wing!" On parting, he invited us to lunch.

I. A. went off somewhere for an hour while we stopped in at the furrier's and then drank coffee in a pastry shop. He does, after all, feel out of his element with the Merezhkovskys—they are his very opposite in everything. Later he said that, though Merezhkovsky played the charmer with me, much of what he said was said for the sake of paradox.

December 19, 1930

The other evening we were sitting in I. A.'s study and the conversation turned to Dostoevsky. I. A., who had undertaken to reread *The Possessed,* said: "So once again, for the umpteenth time, I decided to reread it, I approached it with an open mind. After all, the whole world is ecstatic about it, so I obviously had missed something. Well, I've gotten halfway through, and again it's the same thing. I feel that I'm being made a fool of, that I'm being taken for a dunce. And it doesn't move me at all. Endless talk and every minute 'everyone is expecting something' and everyone knows everyone else and they are all constantly gathering in one place and there is always one and the same heroine. And already two hundred pages, and still no one is possessed. No, it's bad! It's irritating!"

"What are you trying to say?" asked V. N.

"I am trying to say that clearly it is not I who am mistaken but the 'world'; that we are dealing here with a case of mass hypnosis. But not only do they not dare say that the king is naked, but they do not dare confess it even to themselves."

"Do you mean to say that Dostoevsky is a bad writer?" shouted Z.

"Yes, I do mean to say that. And you had better listen to me. I understand something in this matter."

"But how can you say such a thing? The fact that he doesn't like descriptions of nature—but that isn't his concern; that he hurries—that's because he had no time to polish, you know how he wrote."

"And I insist that he could write no other way and that he polished as much as he could and could go no further. Get what I'm saying: everything in him is so finished and polished that you cannot unravel one loop from that lacework. He could write no other way."

Z. jumped up and began to shout outraged refutations. V. N. said that Dostoevsky had explained to her much in I. A. himself and in the whole life of our household. I. A. stood his ground with unusual firmness and claimed as proof the fact that, no matter how many times he read Dostoevsky, a year later he remembered nothing.

A terrific uproar ensued. Roshchin [10] alone took no part in it. Resting his elbow on the table, he gazed at the illustration for some novel in the newspaper.

The argument of course led nowhere. Afterward, V. N. and Z. went upstairs, and the three of us remained below.

"And you, Captain, what do you think of Dostoevsky?" asked I. A. in the playful tone he and Roshchin always used with one another.

"It's of no concern to me . . . let him write as he pleases," replied the captain in a bass voice, matching I. A.'s. "What's it to me? Let him." We laughed.

November 3, 1932

An evening in Cannes. To the right against the sky stands out the huge flat stage set of the city and the mountains, cut out of dark, blue-grey paper. In this stage piece, now and then gleams an opening—a church tower, for example. Above all this is the golden sky. The sun has already set. The water is calm, smooth; freshness wafts from it. To the left, lights have come on around the bay, and the steel-blue water comes up to those sparkling palaces, the big hotels. We are talking about the Nobel prize.

I. A.: "No, precisely because we are so poor and because this money would save us, it won't happen. Things don't happen that way. It will go quite naturally to Valéry and it will change nothing much in his life. He already has a fine, cheap prewar apartment, cabinets of golden polished wood, in which there are heaps of splendid linen. In all respects it fits him (he's written some kind of cerebral, high-flown nonsense), but Mauriac, for example, it doesn't fit. But then, who would think of giving the prize to Mauriac?"

It was All Saints' Day. In the bus, people were standing in the aisles—I sat beside the driver. The grey ribbon of highway ran toward me, disappearing under the bus. Lit by brilliant sun, the road stretched under an awning of plane tree leaves, glowing through and through with all shades of yellow and brown. We stopped often. On the road before the Cannes cemetery, flowers were being sold everywhere. A crowd in black walked with arm-loads of tuberoses.

I. A. was depressed. Last night he had reread the first chapters which he had written of the continuation of *The Life of Arseniev.* At first he was rather satisfied with them, especially with the part about his growing intimacy with Lika. But then suddenly he lost his liking for it all.

Looking at him, I keep thinking how mysterious it is. Why couldn't he have written these chapters last year, for example? After all, the continuation was known to him all along. Why did he have to agonize for three years before sitting down to write what he had known beforehand—since, according to V. N., it all had really occurred in his own life? Indeed, it is a puzzle. Hadn't it ripened? Had he himself not been ready, not humbled sufficiently to describe what he calls that "insignificant life," that ordinary life? I look at him and keep thinking of this. Now that he has overcome the difficult barrier of introduction, he very quickly writes page after page, then polishes and adds after it has been typed up.

November 6

The business of awarding the prize is coming closer. The morning newspapers are becoming nerve-wracking. We await the French morning papers now in trembling. I. A. opens them first. I can imagine his agitation. If only that blow would fall as quickly as possible. Last year it was done earlier than expected.

This afternoon an imprudent (and perhaps thoughtless) tele-gram from Berlin, congratulations in advance, upset the whole house. We talked about it during our evening walk. In this situation I. A. behaves, as he himself said, naturally. There is no excessive nervousness—during the Gorgulov business [11] he was just as excited, and he bought even more newspapers. But of course he is restless nonetheless, especially after the unexpected and persistent appearance of Merezhkovsky's name in print.

But all the same, even today he wrote all day.

November 8

Awaiting the news of the prize has become painful. A clipping with a portrait of Merezhkovsky sent by some Argus of the press produced a depressing effect.

November 11

The prize went to an Englishman—Galsworthy. I felt a genuine relief, knowing that that secret torture of waiting, to which the whole house had been subjected during the last week, has ended. Now it is possible to occupy ourselves with the usual affairs, no longer to be anxious, to stop waiting for something, something which will not come to us Russians anyhow. Yes, in general, all that is from the Evil One, that anxiety about the prize, dragging on for two years now. Proof of that is the fact that literally the whole house, and I. A., it seems, more than anyone else, was relieved at the news of the awarding of the prize. With a sort of good-natured, relieved face, I. A. reviled the Swedes. We talked for five minutes in the dining room, and then he went to his study to write.

November 22

I. A. is writing three to four typewritten pages a day. He first writes by hand, and then before dinner gives them to V. N. to type. After that he makes his corrections and gives them to me to recopy on loose-leaf bond paper.

In the evening he goes walking with me and talks about what he has written. He writes literally all day, eats very little for breakfast, and drinks tea and coffee incessantly. This regime has been going on for a month, if not a month and a half. Needless to say, he is totally absorbed in his writing. Nothing around him exists. But our evening conversations are sometimes exceptionally interesting. And never before has his whole nature become as clear to me as in his present writing and talking.

Today during our usual evening conversation I touched a subject which has interested me for a long time: why did he develop so late, and why did Russian literature in general remain for so long primarily representational, a sort of virginal wilderness, while in the West they had been thinking abstractly for ages? I expressed the opinion that probably the country's nature and its particular features had an influence. As always when something fresh and interesting turns up, he became animated and began to develop my thought, saying that it probably came from the fact that the Russians were surrounded by the spectacle of things that were immense, sweeping, and eternal: the steppe, the sky. In the West, everything is crowded, enclosed, and from that fact was born a tendency to be inward, inside oneself.

"How strange that when traveling you always choose wild places, the ends of the earth," I said.

"Yes, wild indeed! And notice that I have been drawn to the necropolises, the graveyards of the world. That should be noted and deciphered."

November 15, 1933

I. A. has left and we came to our senses a little only as we were seeing him off. Even now I have not yet fully recovered, but I would like to make note of these five and a half days while the memory is still fresh. Thursday, the ninth, was a hard day: waiting. From morning on, everyone was depressed, secretly nervous, and tried all the more to keep busy, each with his own business. I went out in the morning to the garden to plant narcissus bulbs. I. A. sat at his desk, did not leave the room, and wrote, seemingly with concentration (the previous evening he told me that under the influence of what was happening he had begun to write with a kind of "boldness of despair"). The day was soft, with the sun seen through a white, almost wintry Russian sky. Between two and three I looked at the light falling widely and gently from the sky on the Esterel and thought about how, at that very moment, at the other end of the earth, Bunin's fate and the fate of all of us were being decided. And I thought also that I was no longer my normal self, and that sky and that day and the city below were no longer the same as usual. L. asked what to do in case the telegram came from Stockholm (we had decided to go to the cinema in the afternoon, so that the time would go faster and the decision come more quickly) and he himself answered that he would come after us.

At the cinema I. A. was nervous and in the beginning was unable to follow the film. It was cold in the theater and he was freezing. The first part ended. During the intermission we went out into the street and he went to the bar opposite to have a cognac, to warm up. When the second part began I looked around several times, but it was still too early to be anxious since it was only four o'clock. It was all the more strange (strange in that it had already been mentally lived through and now it was about to come true) when, glancing at a flashlight which suddenly appeared behind us in the darkness of the hall, I saw at the curtain the figure of L., pointing us out to the usher. "There, he's come," I said to I. A., suddenly forgetting L.'s name. Everything that followed happened somehow quietly, yet all the more stunningly. L. came up behind us in the darkness, bent down, and, kissing I. A., said: "Congratulations. A call from Stockholm." I. A. for a moment sat motionless and then began to ask him questions. We left immediately and hurried home. L. told how at four o'clock the phone rang, how he answered and made out, "Ivan Bunin . . . Prix Nobel . . ." V. N. was shaking so hard she couldn't understand a thing. Learning that Bunin himself was not at home, they promised to call back in half an hour, and L. ran to get us. At home we were met by V. N., flushed and excited in the extreme. She said that another call had come with congratulations from a Stockholm newspaper, which had tried to interview her. I. A. kept questioning her over and over, as if fearing a mistake. Then began almost incessant telephone calls from Stockholm and from various newspapers. Because of the great distance, no one understood anything, and it became my responsibility to speak, listen, and answer interviewers' questions, since I was the only one who could catch anything through the buzzing receiver. Around five o'clock came the first telegram from Chessin: [12] "Congratulations on the Nobel Prize. Out of my mind with joy. Chessin." Then came a wire from the Swedish Academy. Now we all believed it. But that was only the beginning. All evening the phone never stopped ringing with calls from Paris, Stockholm, Nice, and so forth. Already all the newspapers knew and hurried to get interviews. In the dining room sat Captain Brandt, a representative of the Swedish colony in Nice, who had come up from Nice to offer his congratulations. At dinner we drank champagne (including Joseph [13]). I. A. was terribly nervous, constantly getting angry with everyone, and in general everyone ran about and shouted.

After nine, I. A. and I went down to the city. In the park of Montfleury, in the dark, someone with an uncultured voice came up: "Do you know where around here is the villa Belvedere?" "Right here." "I'm looking for Bunin, who got the Nobel Prize today." "I am he." Magical transformation. A change of tone, bows, introductions. A correspondent from the Nice paper. But he was ignorant, spoke with a coarse accent, asked what they gave the prize for . . . he didn't even know that Bunin is a writer.

The interview was given right on the road while he walked down to Grasse with us. On the boulevard we were caught by two more journalists who had been looking for the Belvedere for two hours and had finally asked the chief of police, who was present (incidentally, a very nice, modest man of refined bearing). They took us into the offices of the *Petit Niçois,* brought something to drink from the cafe, and then began a hasty interview. Then the first photograph was taken, which appeared the next morning in *Éclaireur,* along with the interview, which mostly fell to me to give, since I. A. was so excited he couldn't answer everything immediately.

The next morning—beautiful, sunny—began with phone calls, telegrams, and more interviews. V. N. went to town to the hairdresser's, so we received everyone without her. The Prince and Asya,[14] in white, flew in with a huge bouquet of white chrysanthemums. We made them stay for lunch. "What fun, how interesting!" Asya kept exclaiming. "This is one of the happiest days of my life." The Prince, too, was unusually excited. They vied with each other in showering the French interviewer with information about all those present. Afterward we were all photographed at the table, which was arrayed with bottles. This time I. A. was amiable, touched, and very sweet to the journalists and photographers.

For some reason we went by car to Nice after lunch and of course got terribly tired. [. . .]

When I got home I found sitting there an important-looking elderly correspondent and R., the mayor of Grasse, who the evening before had sent a sheaf of luxuriant flowers, of which I. A. had said with horror, screwing up his face: "Why these flowers? There is something about them . . ." (he of course wanted to say "funereal"). The next day V. N. and I went to Cannes to buy a few necessities. Of late we have been dressed more than modestly. All this time there has been no money in the house. Only on Monday three thousand arrived from Paris by wire. I. A. has decided to go to Paris on Tuesday. We discussed this at length in his study yesterday, and he made pencil calculations. It turned out that fifty thousand would be required for the journey to Sweden. We all listened, and with one voice said that he must go to Stockholm alone.

On Tuesday we saw him off. It took him a whole day to prepare: as always he packed his things himself, allowing no one to help him, shouting, talking on the phone, reading the letters and wires that arrived. Dinner was festive, and at the table we talked about which writers should be given something from the prize money and how much, and we figured a little over a hundred thousand.[15] We were taken to the station by a taxi driver we knew. We arrived ten minutes before departure time. This time I. A. was traveling first class, in the sleeping car. The train left, we looked back at it . . . and came to ourselves only an hour later.

November 16

Yesterday passed comparatively quietly. [. . .] At four o'clock came I. A.'s first call from Paris. He arrived safely, was met at the station and taken directly to Kornilov's restaurant. There was a lunch which cost a thousand francs, and Kornilov refused to take any money, saying that it was an honor. He is staying at the Majestic. "I have a suite of several rooms, very quiet, and the charge will be only what they charge for the smallest room, since it is good publicity for the hotel that a Nobel laureate is staying there. Right now I'm going to the *Latest News* office, where the French press is waiting. I'll call again at six." But he hadn't called by six-thirty, when it was time for L. and me to go to the Kugushevs for dinner. [. . .]

November 17

All day yesterday and today there has been a terrible rainstorm with thunder and hail. We still haven't completely returned to our senses. I can't get used to my new situation at all, and I am literally terrified to allow myself even the most necessary purchase. (Yesterday, in spite of the rain, V. N. and I went to Cannes. Our return journey was fantastic, with the distant lights of Grasse ahead, in the darkness, behind the windows of the bus spattered with huge tears, and with the feeling that all is finished and that our life has turned a corner.)

Until late last night we rummaged in I. A.'s papers, his letters, pictures, folders, upon his request, looking for the old agreements with the publishers. And there was something terrifying in this for me, that now one might rummage in that which was usually guarded so jealously and locked away from everyone.

Again today there was a call from I. A. He said that he was taking Yakov Tsvibak [16] with him to Stockholm as his secretary, and that he planned to stay for the time being at the Majestic. He is continuously dined and wined, the papers are full of pictures of him at all ages, articles about him, and accounts of his stay in Paris.

I. A. called again. He said that he is receiving many honors, but that he is already very tired, isn't sleeping at night, and that he is very lonesome by himself. He still isn't outfitted for Stockholm, but the tailor who will make him tails, an overcoat, and so forth, has been in to see him. We must come to Paris in about a week for the big banquet in his honor.

He has already been filmed and has spoken over the radio.

November 28
Paris

The first evening is more or less quiet. I am alone. I went with I. A. to the "Moscow," where they treated us to caviar, sturgeon, shashlik, old Armagnac, and pineapples. They accepted no money, as is the custom now in Russian restaurants when Bunin is there. He gave the waiters a tip of one hundred and fifty francs.

Now it is almost midnight. V. N. is, as usual, not home yet. She will probably return sometime after midnight. She is running about to see her acquaintances.

It is late. The dusky old corridors of the Majestic are lit dimly. I never thought that I would stay here. But everything, as it comes true, is not the way you imagine it. On the ninth of November our life was fundamentally changed, not "magically," as some of our acquaintances are now saying but, all the same, changed. I don't know what will happen now. I. A. insists that I go with them to Stockholm, but I am hesitating. I'm at the end of my rope, worn to a frazzle, I sleep badly, and I keep thinking how good it would be to get a rest somewhere far from everyone and everything. . . . Besides that, I suffer from seeing all the blunders committed on all sides and blamed on Bunin, who is very little at fault for them, and up to now I do not rejoice at the change in our life.

December 1

Despite his fatigue, I. A. is nevertheless pleased and touched at the homage. He is trying not to drink, to save himself for Sweden. He himself took the trouble about my passport, but everything was arranged by Gustav Nobel. Yasha, "le magnifique," as Melita [17] calls him, takes on more and more the look of a commander. Sometimes his gestures are almost those of a general. He has a great influence on I. A., and for good reason. [. . .]

December 3

The send-off. *Train bleu.* Ten o'clock in the evening. A mob at the station.

In the evening after dinner in the dining car I stood in the corridor and gazed out the window. Night, an unknown country, already Belgium—a moonlit night, the gleam of a river beneath some pointed black cliffs. The train swayed. I stood, looked, thinking all the while. It seemed to be the first time this month that I have been alone for a few minutes. I've still not fully understood that the magic circle of our life has been broken, that we have left Grasse and are going to Sweden, where we never expected to be.

Night. I cannot sleep. I stood in the corridor with I. A., looking out the window. Our car is now the last one. The whiteness of snow, roads, tall gloomy trees, which are quite different from the ones in the south. Later: lights, factories, towers, and all this is alive with a strange, sinister life; something is flaming, something seems to be poured. Germany works even at night. At about one, we crossed the German border. Three Germans looked us over, looked to see what newspapers we had, but learning that I. A. is a *Nobelpreisträger,* they bowed and left. I. A. ordered a bottle of Riesling from the conductor and we drank it in his compartment. He was in high spirits and said that in the olden days he had always traveled this way.

December 6
Stockholm

The morning was grey and uninviting, with darkness and lights in the fir forests. At the last station before Stockholm, a nice young journalist hopped on and went with us to Stockholm. He asked questions and made notes with excessive, youthful earnestness, trying to maintain his dignity. At the station in Stockholm, we were met by a crowd of Russians and Swedes. Some Russian made a speech, proffered "bread and salt" on a silver platter with an embroidered towel, which someone deftly picked up right away. Several pictures were taken, bulbs flashed, while all around it seemed still dark. We left the station, and at the exit were met by a movie cameraman. Then we were driven along the snowy streets. My first impression of Stockholm was very pleasant: the embankment, the water, palaces, the ground barely whitened with snow. It isn't cold. In it all there is something half-forgotten, Russian, native to me. The Nobel house looks out on the canal and on the huge mass of the palace beyond. The apartment is splendid—pictures, armchairs, mahogany tables, and flowers everywhere. We have been assigned a separate apartment: three rooms and a bath. We are served by a Russian maid specially imported from Finland —young, bright, inquisitive.

Before sunset we were taken along the main street by Oleinikov, our host. The lights were already lit—here it gets dark by three o'clock—it was colder than in the morning. After Paris, which was bathed in light, Stockholm seems dark, in spite of the great number of street lights. However, in the light of the street lamp outside our room, the canal, iridescent with gleams of light, constantly reminds us of Petersburg. Our first big dinner, for forty, is planned for tomorrow, and the entire Nobel family will be present. This afternoon again there was an interview, this one by a serious young woman, modestly but well dressed. The young people here in general are pleasant, serious in appearance, but really young. In France the youth are not actually young. That race is too ancient for youthfulness.

The pictures taken this morning at the station have already appeared in the papers. One can see pale, blurred faces and the "bread and salt" with the long white towel, about which all the interviewers asked and then wrote, "ancient Russian custom." I am writing at the desk of Nobel himself. Before me is his portrait and his round crystal inkwell.

December 11

The most important ceremony, the awarding of the prizes, is over, thank God. At the moment he stepped out on the platform, I. A. was terribly pale and wore a sort of tragic, solemn look, as if he were going to the scaffold or to Holy Communion. His ashen face, next to those of the other three young laureates (thirty to thirty-five years old), attracted attention. Going up to the rostrum, from which members of the Academy had to deliver their lectures, he bowed low with marked dignity.

The ceremony of the entrance of the King and the royal family (before the entrance of the laureates) was very impressive and was accompanied by light music coming from somewhere in the ceiling. The hall was decorated only with Swedish flags, yellow and blue, in deference to Bunin, who has no flag. When the heralds signaled the entrance of the laureates with trumpet flourishes from the podium, the entire hall, including the King and royal family, rose to its feet. It seems this is the only occasion in the world when a king rises before anyone.

The first two, a physicist and a chemist, received the prize happily and simply. An ambassador accepted the prize for the third, absent, laureate. When Bunin's turn came, he rose and advanced from his place slowly, solemnly, as if on stage. Pictures were taken at the moment of handing him the medal and folder, and today all the papers have a splendid big photograph of that moment.

In the evening there was a banquet in the large hall of the Grand Hotel, where a fountain splashed in the middle. The hall is in ancient Swedish style, decorated with the same yellow-and-blue flags. In the center was the head table, at which the laureates were seated among the members of the royal family. (The head of V. N., with her heavy, glittering black necklace, was visible between the two heavy chandeliers at the center of the table.)

It was rather a torture to sit at table during the banquet. I was at the table closest to the head table. On both sides of me were important personages I did not know, and besides I was nervous for I. A.: in this huge, stiffly formal hall, before the court, he had to give a speech in a language that was not his own. I looked toward him several times. He was sitting with Princess Ingrid— large, beautiful, in a pale blue gown trimmed with sable.

The speeches began early. I. A. did not speak until very late, however, after the serving of the dessert (a very beautiful ceremony: a long line of waiters came bearing aloft silver platters on which, among chunks of ice, lay something delicate and heavy, surrounded by something pinkish, lacy, glistening, and translucent in the light of the chandeliers).

I was worried for him, but when he ascended to the rostrum and began to speak before the radio microphone, I calmed down immediately. He spoke superbly, firmly, with French stresses, with great awareness of his own dignity, and at times with a kind of persistent bitterness. It was said that, because of the poor acoustics, the microphone, and the Swedes' lack of familiarity with the French language, his speech was barely audible in the hall, but the external impression was splendid. The word *"exilé"* evoked a certain tremor, but everything went off well.

Today typewriters have been clattering in the reception room since morning. I. A. went to the bank to get the check. The weather continues to be sunny, dry, and generally wonderful. About noon every day soldiers march past the palace to the accompaniment of music.

A trip to Djursholm, outside the city, to the villa of one of the Nobels. It was a lovely automobile ride. There were Swedish-style houses in the woods, snow, frozen lakes on which young people and children were already skating. The house, which stood on a hill, consisted entirely of windows, beyond which were pines, a pale sky—an almost Ibsen-like landscape. We had lunch in a festive and neat dining room with (as everywhere else here) sliding doors, and then tea was served in a cozy corner of the living area under a lamp with a huge shade decorated with watercolors. Outside the windows it was already dusk—and new, thickly falling snow and a distant lake. We went out to have tea at another villa. The automobile was at the gate, and a chauffeur in a big woolly cap. Our hostess stepped carefully through the snow in white boots with white fur trim. It grew dark quickly; we passed through the carved wooden gate before an unfamiliar house, and in the house there was Swedish shipshape cleanliness, a fire in the fireplace, and a table laden with sandwiches and sweets. The sweet, flaxen-haired daughter of our hostess, fresh in a checked blouse with a large bow in front, poured tea for us.

At the marketplace this morning: fish, apples, flowers in glass boxes making one think of aquariums, wrapped from the cold in newspapers and warmed by kerosene lamps. There was a great number of wild ducks on the unfrozen spots in the canal by the bridges. We walked for a long time in the old city, which seemed to me like Gogol's Petersburg, with yellow buildings and street lamps on the walls. The cold of the snow underfoot made itself felt even through overshoes. How unaccustomed to it we have become!

December 18

I am in the salon of the ferry carrying us across to the German shore. Again it is quiet, grey, with the vibration of the engine underfoot and throughout one's body. I went walking on the spar deck: fresh air, gulls. The night was rather unpleasant, as nights on trains often are, and through my sleep came those strange, triple, glassy sounds which reached me through that snowy night on the last crossing before Stockholm. It seemed to me that they were some kind of warning signals. How excited I was then by that new country which I was to see. Alas! I saw it from the window of an automobile and did not really have time to enjoy it, for enjoying means to walk, look, listen, feel deeply and fully, and when was there time for all that? Dinners, dinners, formal teas, luncheons, stiffness, tension for days on end.

Yesterday Chessin showed us the city: in two automobiles we toured the best quarters of Stockholm and the local Bois de Boulogne. Real snow lay there. On the fiords people were skating, and the sky between the firs, oaks, and birches was amazingly soft, of a liquid, delicate blue. There were houses shingled in the local style, somber, dark red, some with pillars resembling the Russian style. How I would have liked to feel all that more completely, to live for a while in its midst!

We lunched in an old cellar-tavern in the old city, the "Golden World." There were candles in the windows, a Christmas tree at the end of the long, narrow hall, birch logs burning upright in the fireplace. Women in creamy rose-colored headpieces waited on table. The Swedish poet Bellman at one time frequented that tavern.

January 21, 1934
Paris

A strange feeling of emptiness, of the end. The noise of the last two months has completely died away. And much else, as if not yet realized, has also died away. Life was indeed profoundly changed, and it is necessary again to begin some kind of new existence.

In the wee hours I lay for a long time trying to fall asleep, but I wasn't able to. I got up late, with difficulty. I went to church, and here too was some kind of pain and emptiness, although the church was full, and dear, plump [Metropolitan] Evlogy lovingly blessed the crowd. I lit a candle and left, walking through fresh, chilled Paris to the Majestic.

What a feeling of mournful sadness and emptiness! So now everything is over: hopes, expectations, and the life that revolved around them.

The thought of Grasse doesn't frighten me but rather chills my soul . . .

February 13
Grasse

Fr. John (Shakhovskoy) [18] was here today. He left behind him a certain trace of goodness, which showed itself as a sort of temporary perforation in the crust already hopelessly hardened on my soul. I should like to know: is it true that something really emanates from people like Fr. John, or does it only seem so? Even assuming it is autosuggestion, people still try to restrain what is bad in them; they are ashamed of it, which means that something is already achieved. [. . .]

February 19

I personally have not yet had time to make sense of everything that has happened in these three months. Thus, from time to time some face or other that I had not thought of for all this while appears before me, or a place, or the atmosphere of some particular moment. To my surprise, I have spoken little of this even with I. A., although obviously for him it is as pleasant to remember all that happened as it was unpleasant for him to live through it. Going to Nice not long ago, he took a taxi and stopped at the Hotel Angleterre—to check in with his "old man," as he now calls the King of Sweden. Yet clearly he got little enjoyment from his brief fame in Sweden,[19] and indeed, it all passed with such stunning speed that it seems as if it were all a dream. And all the more so, since we live as we did before, and conversations go on as before about how money is scarce and we have to economize.

When I now look back on and remember these three months, I see that I. A. in reality received the prize all alone, that he somehow instantly withdrew into himself as soon as the telegram confirmed the message of the garbled voices on the telephone from Stockholm. Then, on some pretext, he left the house, went to the cathedral, walked for a long while in the garden of Montfleury, and, in his own words, adopted a "severe" attitude toward what was happening. Because of that he immediately became "severe" toward us, too, although inwardly he was, as he said, radiant and joyful.

But after having left for Paris, he did not retain that radiance. Those who met him there carried him off from the station to lunch in one of the most expensive Russian restaurants, and afterward, for about two weeks, bedlam continued. When we arrived, he was beside himself, perceiving nothing clearly and having wrong reactions to everything. On the journey he came to himself briefly. He reminded me of his former self when, standing on the rear platform of the Nord-Express, we looked at the snow of the receding track and talked of what had been and what would be. In Hamburg he lay the whole day in bed, sleeping off his Parisian fatigue. In Stockholm he behaved like an *enfant terrible* the entire time except in company, at banquets and in drawing rooms, where he was charming and irresistible, according to general opinion. But at home he was ailing, and we all fussed around him, and Oleinikov (who incidentally is not at all easy to get along with) more than once raised his eyes and hands to heaven.

He came to himself, actually, only here, and once more there appeared in him that which I love. These three months of his glory, swift as dreams, he has been absent. But all in all, much has happened during these three months. . . .

translated by Joan Delaney Grossman

Notes

1. Ilya Fondaminsky (his pen name was I. Bunakov) was one of the editors of *Contemporary Annals* (*Sovremennye zapiski*), the chief Russian *émigré* journal in Paris, established shortly after the Revolution. He died in a German concentration camp.

2. Ivan Shmelyov was an important traditionalist *émigré* novelist in the period between the wars. He wrote in the vein of both Dostoevsky and Leskov.

3. Mark Aldanov (pseudonym of Mark Landau) was a leading *émigré* literary figure for several decades. His novels have been translated into many languages, including English.

4. Sergei Rachmaninov's daughter.

5. The writer Leonid Zurov joined the Bunin establishment late in 1929 and served as Bunin's part-time secretary. He is referred to in this diary alternately as L. and Z.

6. Apparently the Sonata Opus 81-a (*Les Adieux*).

7. Dmitry Merezhkovsky, novelist and critic, and his wife, the poet Zinaida Gippius, were two of the most important figures of the Russian Symbolist movement at the turn of the century. Before the Revolution, Bunin belonged to Maxim Gorky's neo-realist *Znanie* group which opposed such modernist trends as Symbolism. In the emigration, he and the Merezhkovskys were brought together by their shared opposition to the Soviet regime; but the differences in their aesthetic and metaphysical outlook precluded any genuine intimacy or closeness.

8. Vladimir Nabokov's *émigré* pseudonym.

9. By Pushkin.

10. Nikolai Roshchin (pen name of Nikolai Fyodorov), who frequently stayed at Bunin's villa, was another younger writer of the "Bunin school," but considerably less talented than either Kuznetsova or Zurov.

11. The trial of the young Russian *émigré* who assassinated the president of France.

12. Serge de Chessin, journalist and author of a guidebook on Sweden.

13. The handyman.

14. The Prince and Princess Kugushev, friends of Bunin.

15. This indeed was done subsequently. AUTHOR.

16. Yakov ("Yasha") Tsvibak, better known under his pen name Andrei Sedykh, is a prolific *émigré* journalist, still active today.

17. Melita Levina, a friend of the author.

18. Now the archbishop of San Francisco.

19. Celebrations did continue, however; see *TriQuarterly* 17 (the Nabokov *Festschrift*), for a photograph of Bunin being feted by the Berlin *émigré* community in April 1934.

A note on Teffi
EDYTHE C. HABER

Nadezhda Aleksandrovna Teffi (1876–1952), best known as a writer of comic *feuilletons* and short stories, was, especially during the twenties and thirties, one of the best loved and most widely read of Russian *émigré* writers.

She was already popular in Russia, with a broad circle of readers, before emigrating in 1919. In addition to her stories, her many short, humorous plays enjoyed great success, while her poetry served to popularize (some say to vulgarize) the Symbolist movement. Before the October Revolution, Teffi's following was so wide that there were even Teffi candy and Teffi perfume.

After her emigration to Paris, Teffi occupied an important place in the *émigré* literary and journalistic community. Her *feuilletons,* which, during the twenties and thirties, appeared almost weekly in one or the other of the two Paris *émigré* newspapers, reached a very large and responsive audience. During the forties and early fifties (until her death in 1952), Teffi wrote less, because of old age and severe illness.

Her success as a writer of comic short stories is easily explained and well deserved, but her popularity as a humorist has tended to obscure the fact that she also wrote a large body of serious and seriocomic prose. As Teffi herself has written, "I was born in St. Petersburg in the springtime and, as everyone knows, our Petersburg spring is extremely changeable: now the sun is shining, now it is raining. Therefore, like the pediment of a Greek theater, I also have two faces, one laughing and one weeping."

Looking at the whole of Teffi's works, what strikes one most is the fact that, despite her "two faces," there is only one set of eyes looking out at the world from both the comic and serious works. Indeed, if constancy of vision is one of the traits which distinguish serious writers from mere entertainers, Teffi certainly falls into the former category. A surprisingly consistent world-view emerges in all her work, written over a very long time span.

In spite of her reputation as a humorist, Teffi's vision is anything but sanguine. Life is repeatedly portrayed as painful, dreary, empty. The highest of earthly values, love and beauty, prove to be fragile and fleeting. In her comic works, people fill the gap created by the loss of these through a variety of ruses, of which fantasizing and artificial posing are the most common. Thus, in "Time," one sees how the formerly beautiful and beloved Maria Nikolaevna has been transformed by time into a powdered and rouged "lump of pink fat" with blue porcelain teeth. The setting of this story is an expensive Russian restaurant in Paris serving traditional Russian foods and patronized by aging exiled Russian aristocrats who bear noble Baltic-German names and cling to the values and mannerisms of their pre-Revolutionary youth, complete with social snobberies and infantile nicknames.

As Teffi once wrote, "You know, living in a joke is not so much comic as tragic."

Time
NADEZHDA TEFFI

It was an excellent restaurant, with shashlik, pelmeni, suckling pig, sturgeon, and an artistic program of entertainment. The artistic program was not limited to Russian numbers alone—to "Bast Shoes" and "Bublichki" and "Black Eyes." Among the performers were Negresses and Mexicans and Spaniards and gentlemen of the indeterminate jazz tribe who sing incomprehensible nasal words in all languages while rolling their hips. Even avowedly Russian artists, after crossing themselves backstage, sang encores in French and English.

The dance numbers, which permitted the artists not to reveal their nationality, were performed by ladies with the most supernatural names: Takuza Iuka. Rutuf Yay-Yay. Hékama Yuya.

There were among them dusky, almost black, exotic women with elongated green eyes. There were rosy-golden blondes and fiery redheads with brown skin. Almost all of them, right down to the mulattoes, were Russian, of course. With our talents, even that isn't hard to achieve. "Our sister poverty" has taught us worse things.

The decor of the restaurant was chic. It is precisely this word that defined it best of all. Not luxurious, not magnificent, not elegant, but—chic.

Little colored lampshades, little fountains, green aquaria with goldfish, set into the walls, carpets, the ceiling painted with incomprehensible things, among which one discerned now a bulging eye, now a lifted leg, now a pineapple, now a piece of nose with a monocle glued to it, now a lobster tail. It seemed to those sitting at the tables that all these things were falling on their heads, but apparently this was just what the artist had intended.

The help was courteous. They never said to late-comers: "Hold on. What are you shoving for when there ain't no seats? This ain't no streetcar."

The restaurant was frequented as much by foreigners as by Russians. One could often see some Frenchman or Englishman, who apparently had already been at this establishment, bring in some friends with him and, with the expression of a magician swallowing a piece of burning cotton, empty a glass of straight vodka into his mouth and then, his eyes bulging, stop it in his throat with a *pirozhok*. His friends would regard him as a courageous crank and, smiling suspiciously, would sniff at their glasses.

The French love to order *pirozhki*. For some reason they are amused by this word, which they always pronounce with the stress on the *o*. This is very strange and inexplicable. With all Russian words the French use the stress characteristic of their own language, on the last syllable. With all words except *pirozhki,* which of course requires that last-syllable stress.

Vava von Mersen, Musya Riewen, and Gogosya Livensky were sitting at a table. Gogosya moved in the highest circles, although only in their outer periphery; therefore, in spite of his sixty-five years, he still answered to the infantile nickname Gogosya.

Vava von Mersen, who had also long ago grown up to an elderly Varvara, had a head of tightly wound dry curls the color of tobacco, so thoroughly cured that, were one to cut them off and chop them up fine, they could be used to fill the pipe of some undemanding skipper of the merchant fleet.

Musya Riewen was youngish, a mere child who had just been divorced for the first time, melancholy, sentimental, and delicate—which didn't prevent her from gulping down glass after glass of vodka, with no effect perceptible either to herself or to others.

Gogosya was an enchanting *raconteur*. He knew everyone and talked about everyone loudly and at length. Occasionally, at risqué moments, he switched, in the Russian manner, to French, partly so that "the servants wouldn't understand," partly because a French indecency is piquant while a Russian one offends the ear.

Gogosya knew just what to order in which restaurant, greeted all *maîtres d'hôtel* with a handshake, knew the names of the chefs, and remembered what he ate, when, and where.

He loudly applauded the successful numbers on the program, and shouted in a lordly bass:

"Atta boy! Good show!"

Or:

"Good for you, sweetheart!"

He knew many of the customers, gestured to them cordially, and sometimes hooted so the whole room could hear, *"Comment ça va? Is Anna Petrovna en bonne santé?"*

In a word, he was a marvelous customer, who filled three-quarters of the premises all by himself.

Opposite, by the other wall, a table was occupied by an interesting group. Three ladies. All three more than middle-aged. To put it bluntly—they were old.

The one in charge of the whole affair was small, compact, her head screwed directly into her bust, without the slightest hint of a neck. A large diamond brooch rested against her double chin. Her grey, excellently styled hair was covered with a flirtatious black hat, her cheeks were powdered with pinkish powder, her very modestly rouged mouth revealed bluish porcelain teeth. A splendid silver fox fluffed above her ears. The old lady was very elegant.

The other two were uninteresting and had evidently been invited by the smartly dressed old lady.

She chose both the wine and the courses very carefully, while her guests, obviously knowing a thing or two, also expressed their opinions sharply and defended their positions. They all attacked their food convivially, with the fire of genuine temperament. They drank sensibly and with concentration. They quickly became flushed. The main old lady filled out all over, even turned slightly bluish, and her eyes bulged and became glassy. But all three were in a happily aroused state, like Africans who have just skinned an elephant, when their joy demands that they continue dancing but their full stomachs fling them to the ground.

"What amusing old ladies," said Vava von Mersen, directing her lorgnette toward the merry company.

"Yes," Gogosya ecstatically joined in. "That's a happy age. They don't have to watch their figures, they don't have to conquer anyone or please anyone. If you have money and a good stomach, it's the happiest age. And the most carefree. You don't have to plan your life any more. Everything's been accomplished."

"Look at that one, the main one," said Musya Riewen, contemptuously lowering the corners of her mouth. "A bouncy cow, that's all she is. And I can just see that's the way she's been all her life."

"Life's probably been very good to her," Gogosya said approvingly. "Live and let live. She's merry, healthy, rich. Maybe she wasn't even bad looking once. Now, of course, it's hard to tell. A lump of pink fat."

"I think she must have been stingy, greedy, and stupid," Vava von Mersen put in. "See how she eats and drinks. A sensual animal."

"But still, someone probably loved her, and even married her," Musya Riewen drawled pensively.

"Someone simply married her for her money. You're always imagining something romantic which just doesn't occur in real life."

Tyulya Rovtsyn interrupted the conversation. He was from the periphery of the same circles as Gogosya, and therefore to the age of sixty-three preserved the pet name of Tyulya. Tyulya was also sweet and pleasant, but poorer than Gogosya, and everything about him was played in a more minor key. After chatting for a few minutes, he got up, looked around, and approached the merry old ladies. They greeted him happily, like an old acquaintance, and made him sit down at their table.

Meanwhile the entertainment program was following its normal course.

A young man came out on the stage, licked his lips like a cat who's eaten some chicken meat, and, to the howling and syncopated tinkling of the jazz band, performed an English song with a sort of pleadingly feminine cooing. The words of the song were sentimental and even melancholy, the tune monotonously doleful. But the jazz did its job without going into these details. And it sounded as if a sad gentleman were tearfully recounting his failures in love, while some madman was wildly jumping, roaring, and whistling and beating the tearful gentleman on the head with a brass tray.

Then two Spanish ladies danced to the same music. One of them uttered a shriek while running off, which considerably raised the spirits of the audience.

Then a Russian singer with a French name came out. At first he sang a French song and then, as an encore, an old Russian song:

> **Your humble slave, I'll go down on my knees,**
> **I do not struggle, ruinous fate, with thee.**
> **I'll bear disgrace, bitter indignities**
> **All for the joy of having you with me.**

"Listen! Listen," Gogosya suddenly pricked up his ears. "Oh, how many memories it brings back! There's such a terrible tragedy connected with that song. Poor Kolya Izubov . . . Maria Nikolaevna von Rutte . . . the count . . ."

> **Whene'er my gaze encounters your dear eyes**
> **I'm in the grip of tortured ecstasy . . .**

the singer uttered languidly.

"I knew all of them," Gogosya recalled. "The song was written by Kolya Izubov. Charming music. He was very talented. A sailor . . ."

> **And so are mirrored the e'er blessèd stars**
> **In the turbulent, unfathomable sea . . .**

the singer continued.

374

"How enchanting she was! Both Kolya and the count fell madly in love with her. And Kolya challenged the count to a duel. The count killed him. Maria Nikolaevna's husband was in the Caucasus at the time. He returned, and there was this scandal, and Maria Nikolaevna was nursing the dying Kolya. The count, seeing that Maria Nikolaevna was with Kolya all the time, put a bullet through his brain and left a death note for her, saying that he knew of her love for Kolya. The letter, of course, fell into her husband's hands, and he demanded a divorce. Maria Nikolaevna loved him passionately and was literally not to blame in any way. But von Rutte didn't believe her; he took an assignment in the Far East and left her. She was in despair, suffered madly, wanted to enter a convent. After six years her husband sent for her to come to him in Shanghai. She flew there, reborn. She found him near death. They lived together for only two months. He understood everything, he had loved only her all that time, and had been in torment. All in all, it's such a tragedy that it's simply amazing how that little woman could live through it all. At this point I lost sight of her. I heard only that she got married, and her husband was killed in the war. It seems that she perished also. Killed during the Revolution. Tyulya over there also knew her well, even languished over her in his time."

In the tu-u-urbulent, unfathomable sea.

"A remarkable woman. There are none like her nowadays."

Vava von Mersen and Musya Riewen maintained an injured silence.

"There are interesting women in any period," Vava von Mersen finally said through clenched teeth.

But Gogosya only patted her on the hand mockingly and good-naturedly.

"Look," said Musya, "your friend is talking about you with his old ladies."

Indeed, both Tyulya and his ladies were looking directly at Gogosya. Tyulya got up and approached his friend, and the main old lady nodded her head.

375

"Gogosya!" said Tyulya. "It turns out that Maria Nikolaevna remembers you very well. I told her your name, and she recalled you right away and is very glad to see you."

Gogosya was taken aback. "What Maria Nikolaevna?"

"Madame Nelogina. Well—the former von Rutte. Have you really forgotten?"

"Good Lord!" Gogosya grew agitated. "You know, we were just talking about her. Why, where is she?"

"Let's go over to her for a minute," Tyulya hurried him. "Your dear ladies will excuse you."

Gogosya jumped up, looking around in amazement.

"Why, where is she?"

"Why, over there. I was sitting with her just now. . . . We're coming, we're coming!" he shouted.

And the main old lady nodded her head and, merrily parting her strong fat cheeks with her painted mouth, gleamed affably with her even row of blue porcelain teeth.

translated by Edythe C. Haber

V. S. Yanovsky: some thoughts and reminiscences
HÉLENE ISWOLSKY

Though living in America, where most of his major works were published in Russian and English, V. S. Yanovsky is often mentioned, and likes to speak of himself, as belonging to the "Paris school" of Russian *émigré* writers. To be sure, he made his literary debut in the French capital, where I first met him, and though the style and content of his writings naturally developed and matured during the years, certain aspects of these works still reflect the moods of the 1930's, when the "Paris school" came to life. It was composed of young men and women who had been uprooted from their native land in their teens. Unlike the older members of the Russian emigration, they had but few memories of a secure life at home. They had left Russia when it was torn by war and revolution, and after that, life had meant long journeys, poverty, endless hardships and struggles. Then, just as they were gaining a foothold in the new land, their security and cultural growth were once more threatened. While their own country was barred to them by Stalinism, totalitarian doctrines acquired other monstrous forms (fascism and Hitlerism) raising the specter of war. All this accounts for the note of gloom, for the extreme sensitivity and skepticism of the young Russian writers in Paris, many of them talented but suffering from a deep awareness of tragedy and loss.

And yet the French capital, with its intense cultural life and atmosphere, was exciting and stimulating. Here was the center of great modern literature, art, philosophy, and religious quest. It was the time of Gide, Bernanos, Valéry, Joyce, and a galaxy of avant-garde painters and musicians. Paris had also become a refuge for many Russian intellectuals of the older generation, distinguished writers, poets, and literary critics, who contributed to the formation of the younger set. Russian *émigré* periodicals published, though sparingly, the works of this "junior class," which also brought out some books and collections of poems of its own.

Important, so far as spiritual values were concerned, were the circles connected with the religious thinker Nicholas Berdyaev and the great theologian, Father Sergei Bulgakov, who were both teaching in Paris. These circles followed the traditions of Russian Orthodoxy, at the same time renewing the approach to their faith. They were inspired by the religious thought expressed by Solovyov, Dostoevsky, Tolstoy, and Nicholas Fyodorov; the latter, as yet little known abroad, was the promoter of a "restoration of kinship among mankind" and of "the common task" of Christians. He was, as Yanovsky has often acknowledged, one of the catalysts of his own religious outlook on man, society, and the world.

The Russian Orthodox renewal of the Paris days was broadened and stimulated by Berdyaev's friend and follower, Ilya Bunakov-Fondaminsky, who sought to draw young writers out of their dark world of pessimism and agnosticism into the dimensions of a transcendent life. These young writers, as well as students, came to Fondaminsky's study circle, where they also met some of their seniors: the theologian and church historian, George Fedotov, and Mother Maria Skobtsov, a Russian nun who had started a home for the poorest Russian *émigrés*. She was at the same time a promoter of Russian literature and philosophy. I was a participant at many of these meetings.

It was at Fondaminsky's study circle that I often met V. S. Yanovsky, who was studying at the Paris School of Medicine and had already published several books. Even then he was concerned, as in later years, with the relationship of flesh and soul, of matter and spirit, and with the meaning of the medical profession. We were all interested in the ecumenical dialogue and invited Catholics and Protestants to our meetings. When Yanovsky and I came to New York in the nineteen-forties, our discussion group came to life again. With a few other friends who remembered the Paris days, we founded a publication entitled *The Third Hour,* to which Yanovsky contributed a series of essays. We also started ecumenical meetings, which still continue today. Both the publications and the meetings were inspired by our experience of the Paris days: the quest for humanism, social justice, and the transfiguration of a grossly material world through transcendent philosophy as well as action.

And such are the themes of Yanovsky's writings. In his books the reader finds, side by side, the stark reality of our times and the expectation of the *parousia*—the hope that one may defeat a mechanized and automatic civilization by a loving and gentle relationship in the name of "the common task." This lends Yanovsky's writings their seriousness of purpose and depth in his never-ending search for truth.

Struggle for perfection
V. S. YANOVSKY

He was almost thirty-five, the fateful age. At this period a man casually relinquishes the allegiances of his youth and begins to live "just so," from day to day, like everybody else. Before, he plays bridge or picks up a girl between two stages of growth, of important work; after, these pastimes become a goal around which life is more or less arranged. The creative impulse peters out; the world, it seems, cannot be—or is not worth being—changed. Henceforth he hangs on to life as a dead weight: a good citizen, a scrupulous taxpayer, hardened lava against which many reformers will bruise their heads. Christ died and was resurrected at the age of thirty-three. The saints at this stage of their life retreated into the desert, there to engage in deadly single combat with stubborn Satan. Dante found himself in a wood so impenetrable that even the memory of it would arouse terror (Virgil showed him the way out). It is a period at which people stray into wild, boggy, desolate places, and most are caught there forever; the best, for some reason, then pin all hope on their children.

This would probably have been Valerian L.'s lot, too, had not a minor circumstance come to his aid at the critical moment. For some time now he had been coughing in the mornings. A nasty cough. "I ought to see a doctor." And since the thought of death no longer revolted or depressed him, Valerian understood how far he had strayed from the living world into the world of matter. (It is the passionate fight with death that distinguishes the young, the alive, and the creative.)

But this ailment of his—the cough—worked in Valerian's favor. Realizing that it was caused by his intemperate use of tobacco, he somehow managed—without hysterics, without chewing-gum and other abominations—to give up smoking. As usually happens, friends and colleagues, inveterate smokers all, pestered him with questions: how had he done it, how should they go about it? Valerian tried his best to give detailed explanations, all the while aware that he was unable to convey the main thing—the element of miraculous accessibility.

"I analyzed my vice step by step and came to see how unfounded and accidental it was. I asked myself, Why do you smoke? For pleasure? But cigarettes had long ceased to give me pleasure. It was absurdly clear! And after clarity followed freedom." Others he also told that he had said a prayer, with rare success, after which liberation became immediately possible and welcome.

Be that as it may, for four months now Valerian had been abstaining and did not suffer in the least from this self-imposed limitation. Quite the opposite: his sacrifice had turned into a source of joy. It was not merely a matter of pride, male vanity, self-respect. There was still something else. His life had undergone a happy transformation. He showed more assurance, more kindness and reticence, as if constantly aware of the presence of a new, beneficial force. This is what some books call the liberation of inner energy: spiritual power which is gathered and immobilized around the passion-become-habit, is freed and spreads through the entire system. This was one explanation—a materialistic one. There were also other possible interpretations.

All this stimulated and encouraged Valerian. His former permanent exhaustion vanished as if by magic. After work, washed and refreshed, he would sit down at his desk, which was stacked with tidy piles of volumes in enticing covers: Jung and Thomas Aquinas, Nicholas Fedorov and Saint Teresa of Avila, Angelus Silesius and teachers of ancient esoteric schools. Of different periods and cultures, they dwelled amicably next to each other. Lovingly, in a fine, unhurried hand, Valerian strung together precious quotations, references, and commentaries in his notebook.

Before that, too, he had read books of this kind; but now, because of his newly acquired personal experience, they appeared in a different light, carried a special persuasiveness. Gradually he came to the decision to write a work of his own, a sort of synthesis of the digested material. "The basic shortcoming of contemporary man is his inability to face leisure. Herein lies one of the possible breaking points of our civilization," he asserted in his introduction.

The original plan was soon outgrown; he had to go into the question of education, which in turn led to the rearing of children, to family, church—an entire philosophical system would have to be constructed.

There was much that Valerian himself could not resolve; parts he left deliberately in an amorphous condition, entrusting his future reader with an active role: the book had to unfold in proportion to the personal effort and daily experience of each, and thus constitute an attempt at a collective creation, leaving room for later additions and corrections. Indeed, he was thinking of calling his work *The Struggle for Perfection*.

In this struggle of his, Valerian's past, his biography, came to play a definite, positive role and seeped into the very tissue of the book—his various occupations and travels, his failings, even his illnesses. Only now, it seemed to him, was he beginning to understand the hidden meaning in all those previous events. Light spread generously; minor incidents acquired color and value. Everything made sense. In short, Valerian had finally gained a measure of deserved happiness.

Secure in what was most important—no longer experiencing that fatal continuous wastage of life—he even found a certain satisfaction in his office, considering his hours there an exercise in developing inner strength, discipline, patience. Knowing that he himself was engaged in a difficult, important task, Valerian began to treat everyone around him as a potential ally. His faith in his own indisputable worth reassured him, and the strength he thus gained was of the kind that one is never tempted to abuse. (So will accomplished athletes move peaceably through crowds of pugnacious adolescents and aggressive, embittered breadwinners.) Ahead he discerned vast horizons: powerful mysteries would unveil themselves in proportion to his spiritual growth, and he would learn to use them for the good of all. He began to pray regularly, at the same time controlling his breathing according to a special method. His prayer—that of a happy creature—was exclusively one of thanks, since the joy of fruitful activity had been granted him.

Unfortunately, events in the outside world, as if conspiring against him, tried hard to break in upon Valerian's bliss and undermine his inner balance. Because of his work and personal connections, he was obliged to follow the political news closely; besides, he thought it immoral to escape from reality, to shut oneself up—in a box or in a monastery. And so those harsh, contradictory pieces of information, those editorials and headlines, increasingly disturbed Valerian and took up more and more of his time and emotions. Yet even at the height of one or another political crisis, he would be able to check himself and, feeling his own fullness again, draw on those new, genuine values within him. Ever stronger grew his conviction that he could see a beacon, that he possessed a compass, a criterion, and could distinguish good from evil, the open road from the dead-end, while those around him lacked that instrument and scurried about, blinded by passions and fear.

So it also seemed to him that evening at the meeting of the *émigrés*. Amid general confusion, irritating false predictions, and panicky rumors, he was the only one to preserve some serenity. Wishing to justify himself, he said he did not believe there would be a world war. It would all blow over again, as so many times before. Therefore one ought not to abandon one's accustomed work and thoughts. "It's so difficult to go back to it again!" For some reason his speech aroused the scorn of all those present. They accused him of delusions of grandeur, of cutting himself off from sacred, concrete reality, and, finally, of lacking the most elementary Christian compassion for other people. Somewhere, distinctly as always at night, a clock struck the hour. The room was stuffy and full of smoke; they kept drinking warmed-over tea. Anyway, all agreed on one point: this war would be a just one, heroic and meaningful. If the German barbarians threatened humanity, one had to finish them off, once and for all. To this each added personal misgivings, rumors about new weapons of mass destruction, secrets from general staffs.

The three left together: Valerian, Professor K., and a young physician. In a dark square, the huge, bright blotch of a freshly pasted poster stood out against a sad, autumnal fence. Several people were already trying to decipher the text, while excitedly yet softly exchanging views. Matches were struck; the wind immediately blew them out, but not before it had been possible to tear from the night, here the design of the state emblem, there disconnected, ambiguous, disturbing words. Someone produced a flashlight. Amid stunned silence, first one then another read aloud the puzzling phrases in officialdom's drab language. General mobilization.

"This is war," Valerian said, bewildered.

And those who for years had been predicting the catastrophe and who, just now, had debated for an entire evening the intricacies of battles, blockades, and sagacious strategies all at once went limp as if turned into mollusks. The miracle had not occurred. Suddenly everyone became aware of the hostile silence of the night and, beyond it, of yet another silence that carried with it the icy breath of interplanetary voids.

Professor K. had recently published a book on the conquest of Turkestan which had been well received. Therefore he considered himself a military expert. Although of marked civilian appearance, he had taken to using expressions such as "lines of communication," *"têtes de pont,"* "breakthrough." Now, however, not quite appropriately, he developed a severe case of diarrhea. Yielding to a sacrificial impulse, the young doctor carried him off, almost in his arms; they vanished into the night, hoping to find a cab somewhere.

As a matter of fact, there seemed to be exceptionally few cabs about, and those few sped along the boulevards, obviously not looking for customers. The passersby, while perhaps not so few in number, were almost imperceptible—shadows clinging to fences and walls and noiselessly crossing the streets. The hushed city resembled a sick or wounded animal which has dug itself in and, doomed, is listening to the hunter's horn and the barking of the dogs, real or imagined. A gust of wind swept across the avenues, plazas, and bridges. One felt: the gates are wide open, the soul is unprotected, nothing is secure.

Stopping in front of a still-lighted shop window, Valerian tried long and painfully to remember something. "Oh yes!" it finally came to him. He entered, bought a pack of cigarettes, and lit one—without pleasure or particular desire; inhaling deeply, he smiled an awkward smile, as if witnessing his own execution.

Now this central part of town appeared completely dead. He stopped at a monumental church, turned his back to the popular saint. And from there he saw God. Before him stretched a tree-lined avenue, ending in a graceful plaza that resembled a precious vase. Beyond, the wings of a bridge (above the narrow, dark Seine) came to rest against a palace. All this lay on the palm of the night in limitless, frozen, mummified rest and sleep. And there, in the distance, he saw God. Not the God of Abraham, Isaac, and Jacob. And not the God of the poor and meek. But the God of the Romans and Greeks, the God of cities, temples, palaces, and viaducts; the God of measures and weights, of symmetry and forms; the God of carvers and things carved; the God of soldiers and providers.

"Yes, yes, after all we have been living in a pagan world. This new collapse will perhaps lead toward salvation. What is my life in this whirlwind! The storm has not reached us yet and already everything is falling apart. I wanted to; as Christ is my witness, I

385

tried," he declared solemnly. "But now everything is shaking and there is no stable point left. Why," Valerian decided all of a sudden, "it would even be a sin to look for one."

Greedily, hastily he smoked one cigarette after another, while a stream of joy spread through his body. "Against the Germans it will be tough, of course. If I'm lucky they'll send me to Austria or some such nation. It would be good to get to Hungary: the Tokay and the girls there are first class."

His very walk changed: liberated from an age-old burden, erect, putting all his muscles into play, he advanced with athletically soft steps, casting keen, brutal glances to all sides, as if already considering as his home any place where he would make a fire. He eyed the people who passed him under the lights. Women—legs, hips; men—potential resistance. The elderly (and some occasional children) he contemptuously dismissed.

A feeling of lightness and tangible happiness invaded Valerian: how many complex adventures the future held in store for him! (A bear or an elephant probably experiences the same joy when his trainer takes the roller skates off him.) "I wanted to; as Christ is my witness, I tried," he still repeated mechanically from time to time.

The sky slowly brightened. Above, in the transparent, icy dome, innocent white clouds rushed about. There were no bombs yet, no searchlights or shell bursts, but the clouds were already scurrying in fright, circling aimlessly, pitifully around and around—perhaps for the reason that the wind, shifting at dawn, was striking at once from opposite directions.

translated by Isabella Levitin

from the novel
American experience
V. S. YANOVSKY

The operation

The operation had been set for March third: at the doctor's apartment, under local anesthesia. . . . Sabina was to leave directly for home and stay in bed. Should she start hemorrhaging or should her temperature rise, they were to call some other doctor, preferably a competent one, or go straight to a hospital, but give away nothing.

"You see," Sabina explained on the eve of the operation, "before the law I am as responsible as he is. Therefore we must keep quiet, whatever complications there are."

Bob thought, it would be enough to make the surgeons alone responsible, to put an end to the whole racket.

And the day came. At three o'clock in the afternoon Bob was impatiently pacing up and down a side street off Second Avenue. Wind, bitter cold. The sun shone more lazily than in February, dimly illuminating a fantastic landscape: a frost-burned city—dull houses, flat roofs, factory smokestacks, and a man waiting for his beloved at the doorway of a dubious specialist.

Frozen and in despair, Bob prayed: "Make it fast. Let her come now and let it be finished!"

There she was, Sabina! In her short fur coat and the fur hood, looking like a child, like a schoolgirl: waiting for her at home would be her parents, cocoa, and *David Copperfield*.

Bob disappeared into the entrance hall, let her go past him, and then caught up with her and firmly grasped her arm; without stopping she walked on, swiftly and impassively.

They climbed the dark, neutral, untended staircase to the top floor of the squalid, seemingly deserted house. In New York there are many such houses: without a past, without a future, houses which do not arouse curiosity about their tenants.

Doctor Spart opened the door himself, cast a hostile look at Bob, murmured something in answer to their greeting, and led them through a long corridor, several large, bare rooms, and a few that were furnished but obviously not in use. . . . They ended up in a large, freshly whitewashed office with a gynecological table in the center and glass cabinets along the walls.

"Did you take a bath?" Spart asked. Bob answered, pulling himself up as before a commanding officer:

"Yes, Sir, she did."

"Get undressed!" And then: "It is understood, in case of complications you won't look for me; you won't find me anyhow. . . . Without wasting time you take her to a hospital. Right?"

"Yes," Bob agreed. "But I wanted to ask, couldn't she rest here for a couple of hours instead of going right away? . . ."

"No," Spart said, "she has to go home while the anesthetic is still working. Get undressed!"

He was heavyset, shaggy, grey, with an unshaven face that looked swollen from sleep. He went about distributing instruments, cotton, syringes—some to the right, some to the left, in accordance with what was obviously a definite, established routine.

"They were sterilized at the hospital," he explained. "It will be all right. Still, I don't understand why people refuse to have children."

Odd sounds—as of a grown person jumping on one bare foot?

—could be heard from behind the door. The doctor hurriedly ran out. "Lie down there. I won't be a minute," he said.

Sabina obediently lay down: in her sweater, half naked. And now she looked at Bob, for the first time all day, perhaps for the first time in many weeks—as if the scales had fallen from her eyes! He stood at the head of the table, a concentrated smile on his face; listening, it seemed, to an ever-growing, dull, accustomed pain. Close above her Sabina saw his eyes—the same as they used to be in moments of intense happiness. He had grey-blue eyes which, under the influence of a strong emotion, would change their shade brusquely, turn a deep blue. She recognized them and the feeling which they always aroused in her; there, before her, was what she needed most in life—generously gathered and offered! "Bob." He noticed the change in her expression, bent even closer, and began to whisper, rapidly, insistently:

"Remember, there is no inertia, no predestination, no fate. A Christian can begin all over at any moment, turn back, rectify, salvage. You can still jump off this wretched table—a free act of your great soul—the bridge is not yet burned!"

She did not listen and frowned in annoyance: why these speeches? His eyes were more convincing; they explained it better. How clumsy and childish he still was. But most of all he was hers —her own, her love.

"Let's go," exclaimed Sabina, suddenly coming to her senses. Holding his breath, his face distorted, he lifted her off the table, and, confusing the different garments, helped her dress.

"We are leaving," Bob said roughly as the doctor came back into the room. "I can take care of your expenses. Do you understand? We are leaving, there will be no operation!" he shouted angrily, for Spart did not answer.

"I understand," the doctor finally said and broke into an unexpected smile. But there was no one to appreciate this miracle: scrambling into their coats as they ran, pushing open the wrong doors, Bob and Sabina rushed out.

"This way, this way," Spart howled, protecting the inhabited rooms of his apartment from intrusion, "to the right. . . ."

A misunderstanding

The slamming of the door told Spart how relieved they were to escape from his house.

Whistling something familiar and old-fashioned, he painstakingly cleared up the office, putting things back in their place and locking some of the instruments into a secret safe. For a man with such an oddly blown-up body, he moved quickly and lightly. He washed his hands for a long time under the faucet, only to wipe them dry with a torn, greasy towel. Then he went out, locking the office door. As he passed one of the rooms, he stopped and carefully looked in. There, curled up on her bed, the crumpled end of a blanket pressed to her bosom, lay his wife. As usual, she was gently rocking an imaginary creature to sleep. In her derangement, this piece of blanket represented her husband, although at the same time he was also high in a corner near the ceiling, to which spot she sent smiles and glances—a grey-haired, disheveled, unwashed, wrinkled woman with the happy eyes of a bride. Making kissing sounds, giggling bashfully, smiling coquettishly, wiggling her withered little body—this was how she flirted with her chosen one.

In silence Doctor Spart observed her from the threshold. It came to him for the first time in all the years of her derangement: there was a logic to his wife's illness! He, her husband, had not justified her love, hopes, expectations. . . . She had gone into another world, carrying along the ideal mate in her arms. He smiled. Such theories reassured him—regardless of the implications.

He remembered another abortion—hers—in Europe. They were very young then, students. Although aware of all the difficulties, he wanted the child but she decided it was too soon. How far away it all was—and how near: alive still, painful. It happened in Vienna, before the war. But it could have been yesterday and in Shanghai. "If only we had had the wisdom and faith to run, to behave like this silly couple," he thought. (So will a dilettante chess player blame one move for the loss of a game—but give the move back to him and he will make a similar mistake right away!) "Yes, but events would have developed differently," Spart told himself, "perhaps still not successfully, but at least unsuccessful in another way. For there could be nothing worse than my life. There simply has been no life."

The doctor moved on to his large, unaired, gloomy study filled to overflowing with a collection of seemingly superfluous objects. He felt a familiar pain in his heart and sat down on the sofa, pressing his hand to his chest. "This is how I am going to die some day," flashed through his mind. "Here. Alone. I shall be lying on this sofa or I shall slide down onto the rug. A day or two, perhaps more, will go by before anyone notices, knocks, breaks in the door. Police, witnesses. . . . One sees such pictures in the paper: overcome by fumes . . . suicide . . . coronary. Yes, that's how it will be. Not today, of course," he decided from habit, "but soon, very soon." He was massaging his chest with a sticky, bloated hand. The thought of death no longer frightened or outraged him. But he did like his quiet comfort, his peace. The room —unmade bed, dust, smells—only seemed to be in disorder; in fact he could immediately find anything he needed. And then, abruptly, he would be expected to move on from here, board a train in the middle of the night, jostle, with many changes, going somewhere—in the cold, with all the discomforts of travel: muddy coffee, hot dogs, rude conductors, arguments with customs officials. . . . This was how death now appeared to him: a questionable, difficult journey, fourth class, with an expired passport.

"They are fools, these children," he again remembered his runaway patients. "They will be sorry. But still and all—there ought to be more such fools."

Doctor Spart had studied in Vienna. He had wanted to practice surgery but slid gradually into doing abortions. Why? Any "honest" practice would have brought him no less! At the hearing his honorable colleagues denounced him, put him to shame. Honorable. . . . They did the same things but kept up appearances. Idealists! He, Spart, at least treated patients for free sometimes, at his own risk. But they would sell themselves for five dollars; they injected vitamins and hormones, cut out appendixes and tonsils. Racketeers! One sort of racket is legal and the other not. That's all. But Brutus is an honorable man.

At the time, the board formally acquitted Spart. Laws. Bastards. There was not much reason for living. And it was not even worthwhile dying. "But this woman! One could love her! And the Negro. He had something in him. As if, bleeding from a cut artery, plugging it with a finger, he was continuing some deadly struggle. Stupid, but there is something attractive in stupidity. My handicap is rather the lack of stupidity. I believe it's the first time something like this has happened to me," Spart thought, and smiled again. "As long as they don't regret it and come back tomorrow."

For Spart, nighttime was painful. He went to bed early, at seven or so. He would awake around eleven, lie in the dark, listen to his heart and to himself, thinking his mirthless thoughts; would switch on the light, leaf through a book, play chess with an imaginary friend, walk about the apartment, bring his wife water or an apple, again stretch out on the sofa to remember and curse invisible foes and detractors. Toward morning he would sink into a fitful, unhealthy sleep.

His yellow, puffed face resting high on a pillow, Spart was just about to reach for a second phenobarbital when there was a shrill ring, followed by loud thumping. Spart clutched the ends of his bathrobe together with shaking hands and rushed toward the door, turning on every light along the way. Uncertain of his voice, he opened the door without a word and saw Robert Caster standing on the threshold.

"Doctor," Bob said, out of breath, "please, doctor—a hemorrhage."

Spart led his visitor to a chair, sat him down, and asked him to explain coherently what had happened. . . .

Suddenly, for no apparent reason, Sabina had felt ill; Bob had been trying some home remedies when he saw that she was lying in a pool of blood. "Save her," Bob implored. "Use all that life and science have taught you. After all, it cannot have been an accident that we came to you!"

"You want me to treat your wife?"

"She is not yet my wife."

"That makes no difference. But do I understand you correctly: you did not come back for an abortion?"

"Of course not! We must save them."

"Wait for me," the doctor said softly. "Give me five minutes," and, throwing off his robe, he began to dress. Grey, large, barrel-chested, he looked impressive, and even his beard—those straggly, disheveled strands—was no longer repulsive or frightening. His entire air—strict, prophetic—inspired confidence. "I am coming," he muttered. "What is five minutes? I have been waiting for you all my life—and you cannot wait five minutes! I will deliver this baby! I will pull him out with pincers! I'll be his godfather, do you understand? You can't stop me, young man!" He took a threatening step toward Bob. "If you only knew what sometimes happens in life, young man . . ." and he burst into tears: awkwardly, grimacing helplessly.

translated by Isabella Levitin in collaboration with the author

Alla Ktorova: a new face
OLGA HUGHES

Alla Ktorova belongs to the generation of writers now associated with the early post-Stalinist years, but her literary biography is considerably different from that of her more illustrious contemporaries. With the remarkable exception of Alexander Solzhenitsyn, success generally came to the younger prose writers of that generation more slowly than it did to the poets. Unlike the poets, they could not recite their works before the thousands in Mayakovsky Square; new prose works, disseminated through underground channels in the Soviet Union, are also at a disadvantage in comparison to verse. In addition, Alla Ktorova started publishing only in the sixties, and, what is more important, not in Russia, but in the West. The situation of Russian letters being what it is, contemporary Russian literature is rarely judged on its purely literary merits, and even the best known and most established writers lose the greater part of their appeal for a Western reader as soon as they find themselves in the West. In Alla Ktorova's case there are two more reasons for her work being very little known in the West: she is not overtly concerned with politics (as

many of her compatriots who find their way to the West are)—
she is primarily a short story writer; and her highly original and
rich prose is almost untranslatable.

Alla Ktorova's literary output comprises ten stories and a short
novel. She writes about life in contemporary Moscow, mostly
during the fifties, both before and after Stalin's death. The period
from the end of World War II to 1953 serves as a prelude and a
contrast to the years following; there are occasional references to
a more remote past, the thirties and the nearly prehistoric twenties.
Alla Ktorova's stories are about the everyday life of ordinary
Soviet citizens, who are used to living under the totalitarian
regime; they are very much aware of the punitive system functioning in their state, and they are not immune to the fears and dan-
gers common to their compatriots. This is only one of the
components of their lives, however, and does not constitute Alla
Ktorova's primary interest. The only period of mass arrests to
which many references are found in her work is the campaign
against the "rootless cosmopolitans" that was stopped short by
Stalin's death.[1] The relative prominence of this particular campaign in her stories points to one of the fundamental traits of her
writing: her subjects and localities are largely circumscribed by
her own experience. However, the temporally and spatially limited
world of the stories gains a great deal precisely from this limitation
—the author has an intimate knowledge of whatever she touches.
There are no generalizations and they are not needed. The wealth
of characters and detail—which at times almost overwhelm the
reader—invariably fall into their proper places and cause the
reader to draw his own conclusions and to form his own generalizations.

The author's conscious approach to writing is not concealed
from the reader. He is taken into the author's confidence: she
comments on her writing, admits her concern about choosing the
appropriate approach, and states pointblank that she does not
intend to write according to the "accepted literary rules." In one
of her earlier stories, the narrator (a high school teacher of
literature) comments on her attempt to write the story according

to the rules which she was taught and which she herself used to teach to her students:

Dénouement, exposition ... Exposition, dénouement ... there are also the development of action and a climax: this is the way every story, tale or novel is constructed. ("Georgie's Lane," *Grani*, 53, 1963, page 3.)

This approach is unsuccessful, for the story emerges "protozoan-unicellular," as we are told. Implicitly, the desire to avoid the expected, not to follow the accepted literary norms, is present in all Alla Ktorova's work, but it is made more explicit at the beginning of her longest, most ambitious, and most successful work, a short novel *The Face of Firebird* (Washington, 1969).[2] In this work not only is her manner fully developed, which makes it easier to formulate those "rules" that the author is trying not to follow, but the whole first chapter is devoted to descriptions of the author's attempts to write this work. She is reminded by her friend that her subject is losing its actuality with the passing of time; she searches for inspiration; reads about birds—although the Firebird of the title has nothing to do with real birds; comments on the difficulty of choosing the epigraph, and in the process provides us with a list of those she rejects; and discusses the genre of the work. The make-believe seriousness of this self-consciousness can be taken as a tongue-in-cheek attitude. But in reality it provides some important insights into Alla Ktorova's art.

The work is subtitled "Scraps of an Unfinished Anti-Novel"—the author's intent is not to write a "perfect novel." This reference to the genre par excellence of Socialist realism is not accidental.[3] Despite the subtitle, the work, although fragmentary in nature, is a finished whole and Alla Ktorova does tell a story. But there are conscious deviations from the "accepted" literary norms, deviations which would make the publication of *The Face of Firebird* in the Soviet Union inconceivable on purely literary grounds.

The most obvious of those deviations is the deliberate disruption of the time sequence. In the course of the narration there are multiple jumps—both backward and forward. References to subsequent developments, known only to the author, are deliberately confusing. Many things can be understood only on a second reading. Flashbacks depict not only the childhood of the narrator and her friend Firebird, but the history of their families from the time of Napoleon's invasion and the Moscow fire of 1812. The whole story is told retrospectively, *after* the narrator's friend leaves Moscow and settles with her French husband in Paris, and even the details of their early friendship are seen in the light of Firebird's departure. The narrator's marriage in the last chapter turns out to be a prosaic conclusion to the story of her friendship with Firebird, but the husband, who is shown as the epitome of dullness, philistinism, and careerism, is referred to by name in the opening pages.

By those multiple shifts, Alla Ktorova succeeds in creating an impression of a simultaneity of events: the reader does not simply follow the story, but is forced to see the events with both the narrator's past and future experiences in mind. This is accomplished in part by careful selection of material: only those events, whether past or future, which have a bearing on Firebird's story and the narrator's part in it are shown. Another contributing factor to the reader's acceptance of the disrupted time sequence is the frequency and unpredictability with which the narrative is interrupted.

Other traits that place Alla Ktorova's work outside the Socialist realist tradition are the absence of a "positive hero," a quite "improper" message, and her very original but at times unkempt language. Each of these elements requires a more careful examination.

Compared to the protagonists of the Socialist realist as well as Russian nineteenth-century novel, all Alla Ktorova's characters are peripheral. They are women (single, married, divorced, abandoned, widowed), children, adolescents, retired elderly men and women, Jews, and members of other national minorities.[4]

Males appear as adolescents ("Georgie's Lane") or as retired people ("The Little Clowns," *Grani,* 59, 1965). Adult males are usually episodic; quite often they provide the local color (Ivan Mordvinov in *The Face of Firebird*), or fill the traditionally female role as an incarnation of philistinism (Gennady, the husband of the narrator in *The Face of Firebird,* Tyomka in "The Little Clowns"). If the plot requires the existence of husbands or not very old fathers, their roles remain secondary at best. Firebird's father, whom the narrator admires greatly, is spoken of as being highly superior to his naive and simple-minded wife, but he is removed from the central action of the novel. When his daughter decides to marry a foreigner, he is sent on an extended business trip. Similarly attractive, but distant, is Klara's husband in "Klara the Terrorist." Another category of adult males is made up of government officials. They are usually dumb and pedantic, or double-faced and threatening if they happen to work in the State Secret Police.

This conscious deviation from the main line of development is somewhat reminiscent of Leskov. Alla Ktorova's characters are drawn from those groups of the population (sex, age, social status, nationality) which would have only secondary roles in the works belonging to the main line of development. The parallel goes beyond this reversal of the preference for protagonists, and Alla Ktorova is aware of it. In one of her later stories ("Tais," *Mosty,* 15, 1969), a reference to Leskov's "righteous men"—which here turns out to refer to a woman—is unmistakable. But Alla Ktorova does not let herself or her readers carry this parallel too far. The "righteous" Tais, who saves and adopts a Jewish orphan,[5] refuses to see her old friend, the narrator, who presumably comes on a visit from abroad, for fear of her neighbors.

The narrator plays an important role in all of Alla Ktorova's works. It is always a young woman easily identifiable with the author: she is usually a native Muscovite, very often a student ("Klara the Terrorist," "The Little Clowns"), or a young schoolteacher ("Georgie's Lane").

In *The Face of Firebird,* the narrator and the protagonist appear as doubles. They are not only friends who spend their school years together and whose friendship continues after their graduation, but they even look alike. Vladya, the narrator, wears Firebird's clothes, and they are often taken for twins. This becomes especially apparent after Firebird's departure, when various people mistake Vladya, the narrator, for Nika, the Firebird. It can be conjectured that some autobiographical material was used for both Firebird and Vladya (Alla Ktorova worked as an interpreter and married an American tourist; moreover, her first name is Victoria, which brings her even closer to Firebird, whose Christian name— Nika—is the Greek version of victory), which would justify this partial identification. The same device is used in one of the stories ("The Little Clowns"), where the narrator at one point merges with the central character. This merging, or rather splitting the autobiographical character in two, gives the author a possibility of utilizing both the first- and the third-person narration.

A multitude of episodic characters in Alla Ktorova's stories helps create an "atmosphere" of the surrounding life. Some friends and neighbors in the communal apartments materialize only in order to listen to the main characters talk, or to provide the support for the "accepted" view with a few words, or to enable the author to contrast the "uneducated" vs. "educated" manner of speech. Those characters are usually given names, and some colorful details about them are included. One character is brought in only to tell the narrator of the increasing danger of Firebird's situation: he identifies himself by name and whispers his warning, after which he disappears never to appear again.

It is not unexpected that as a consequence of the near-banishment of males from Alla Ktorova's world, love interest is also either absent from her stories or comes in only peripherally. This should be added to the "deviations" from the traditional novel. Firebird and Vladya are "in love with love," and that does not require the presence of significant male characters. We are not led to believe, however, that love does not exist in the lives of the characters—only that, in the period of their lives on which the author chooses to concentrate, it does not occupy an important place. In most of Alla Ktorova's stories the place of prominence is given to friendship between young females, one of whom is invariably the narrator. In some of the stories, the narrator's friend and protagonist is an older woman ("Tais," "The Abominable Snowman").

The central episode in *The Face of Firebird* (if there is such a thing as a central episode here) is Firebird's departure from Moscow. She marries a Frenchman with whom she is supposedly madly in love. It is her love that helps her to overcome all the difficulties placed in her way by Soviet bureaucracy. But her French husband is no more than a *deus ex machina.* He appears in the flesh only at the airport just before Nika boards a plane for Paris.

Some time after the dramatic events of Firebird's marriage and departure from Russia, the narrator marries also. If Firebird's marriage was right out of a fairy tale (marrying a foreigner, a Frenchman, and leaving with him for Paris!), Vladya's is robbed of all excitement and romance. She decides to marry because her aunt and her friends think that she should (a highly improbable development, given Vladya's character, ability, and achievement). The man she marries is looking for a wife because he has reached that age and position in life when he can not only afford to marry, but when married status as such can bring certain advantages, particularly the possibility of being allowed to travel abroad. The husband is shown as a careerist and an opportunist. This marriage is provided with all the stock disadvantages, the foremost of them being the mother-in-law who comes from the provinces for extended visits.

Not long after her wedding, Vladya collects her belongings and goes back to her aunt; but at the very end of the novel there is a tentative, projected reconciliation with her husband. The author's view penetrates the future: she will not only return to her husband, but is seen in her later role of a well-to-do, overdressed, and over-fed woman (it is clear that the dull husband proved to be a success in this respect), who is overprotective of her small child. This is only a projected conclusion, for actually we don't know what happens to the narrator and the protagonist in the end, but Alla Ktorova likes to point out different possibilities.

Alla Ktorova is a past master at depicting the nuances of the change from adolescence to young adulthood, the process which is often accompanied by an increased attachment to material goods. She does not stop, however, at this commonplace truth, and the conditions of life in the Soviet Union which help brutalize people are also brought in. In "The Little Clowns" the narrator marries and quickly turns into the philistine that her husband is; in their desire for material comfort they do not stop at anything. In the end they move into the apartment of an old friend, whom they have succeeded in driving out of it. But, this, apparently, was the only way the couple could get an apartment. The narrator, who is not quite at ease with her conscience after the transaction, remarks: "All people are alike, when they are incited to a taste for blood" (*Grani,* 59, 125).[6]

The variety and the diversity of characters in Alla Ktorova's stories justify the variety of her language. The language of her stories is very unlike the smooth "literary" language of Soviet writers that admits a limited number of colloquialisms and vulgarisms. Alla Ktorova is highly aware of what she is doing in this respect. At the beginning of *The Face of Firebird,* the narrator receives a letter from a school friend of hers and Firebird's who describes her impressions of a Mexican art exhibit in unmistakable "officialese." The infuriated Vladya composes her reply in the same language. The source of this style is indicated: she leafs through several widely read magazines. The language of both letters differs markedly from the language of Alla Ktorova's characters. The language of Alla Ktorova's stories is based on contemporary colloquial speech; it presents a mixture of styles and levels, and reflects various social, cultural, and ethnic backgrounds. The author depends heavily on dialogue and utilizes a variety of features characteristic of spoken language: diminutives, exclamations, ellipses, and so forth.

Characterization is achieved mostly through language: different characters each have a highly·individualized manner of speech. An attempt is made to convey various degrees of colloquial admixtures: a number of gradations of uneducated speech is represented with typical mispronunciations (reflected orthographically), mangling of unfamiliar words (here Leskov comes to mind again), and predictable hypercorrections; in a class by itself is the language

401

of uneducated Jews. In all these categories, a very clear distinction between the generations is made: the incorrect usage is typical of the old and the uneducated, and it either upsets or amuses their children (the mother in "Klara the Terrorist" mixes up the grammatical cases, and one of her daughters patiently corrects her through the years without any visible results). Another widely represented subdivision is the contemporary slang, which is used mostly by the young. Needless to say, most of these distinctions are lost in translation. Another feature of contemporary spoken Russian—the use of generally accepted and understood abbreviations (usually for various government offices and institutions) is also well represented. The degree of its acceptance in the language is demonstrated by the fact that many of the abbreviations are inflected.

One of the sources of the exceptional variety of Alla Ktorova's language is her use of names. The form of address in Russian (the use of patronymics and the variety of diminutives) can convey the minute nuances of the relationship between the speakers. Here Alla Ktorova displays an astounding virtuosity: in her stories, names are made to reflect upon the social origin and education of the speaker (Evdeniya Yuryevna), and even on the political climate of the times.[7] In translation, this variety of names, although serving a definite purpose in the original, can only confuse the reader. The narrator's name is "Vladilena" (a contraction of Vladimir Lenin), but she is more often addressed as "Vladya," "Vladenka," and at times "Vladka" or "Vlad." At one point her name and patronymic—"Vladilena Mikhailovna"—are used. In the case of the protagonist of *The Face of Firebird,* the use of various forms of her name goes beyond the mere display of the author's virtuosity.

In general, Alla Ktorova's stories abound in literary references and quotations ("The Little Clowns" especially). This is also true of *The Face of Firebird.* Some of the quotations are identified; others are easily identifiable. There are many which provide only a glimpse, or a hint, of a certain literary association. There are many quotations from popular songs, both Soviet and pre-Revolutionary, and some come from the colloquial sentimental songs that are a part of the urban folklore. All quotations, semi-quotations, and mere hints are well integrated into the fabric of the text.

In *The Face of Firebird,* a large part of Chapter One is devoted to a selection of a proper epigraph. Various poems by Blok and Balmont are suggested and eventually rejected; assorted "bird" information is brought in. Searching for inspiration, the narrator comes to Moscow's bird market on the day of Annunciation, when traditionally birds were bought in order to be set free. She rereads those works of Russian literature that have even the remotest connections with birds, and reminds herself of various birds in art and music—all this in search of inspiration for her novel about Firebird. The bird in the quotation which actually is used as the epigraph to the novel is not a real bird, but "the White Bird of Youth that flew into the grey mist . . ." (from a song by Alexander Vertinsky)—a symbol of youth, youthful imagination, intoxication of youth.

The novel, essentially, is about youth. It is a nostalgic view of youth from the vantage point of a young adult who is faced with the complexity of life and looks back at her rather protracted adolescent years as a golden dream. In this connection another quotation among those sampled sheds light on the story—a line from Blok: "Can't there be truth in a fairy tale?" Her youth appears to the narrator more like a dream and a fairy tale because it ends when she parts with the friend and double of her youth. Nor can Firebird come back to visit her home town and her friends— she lives now in a different world. In Russian, the word "firebird" has very strong fairy-tale associations, and in the story there are other elements pointing to fairy-tale connections. The work opens with a list of *three* reasons for the gloomy mood of the narrator. The first two are quite realistic, but the third—being upset because her shadow overtakes her—transports us into the world of fairy tales where a reason like this would have significance. Also, *three* times in Firebird's life all Moscow talks about her: when she falls off a balcony, when she escapes from the collapse of the China Wall, and when she escapes from the penalties she might have incurred for marrying a foreigner. She escapes danger three times and proves to be victorious, as could have been predicted·by her name.

Alla Ktorova's characters are neither "building socialism" nor are they moving toward a "bright future." If anything is idealized in *The Face of Firebird,* it is the protagonist's and the narrator's youth—viewed retrospectively. Both the present and the future do not seem to have much excitement in store: the life of an adult is filled with responsibilities; whether happy or unhappy, successful or not, it is different from the exhilarating and intoxicating adolescent years of Firebird and Vladya. The narrator's gloomy mood at the beginning of the novel is largely due to her longing for her past. Her love for Moscow—its history, architecture, people—and her thoughts about her Moscow forebears serve as a strong connecting link between the past and the present in the novel. As a child she was discovering Moscow, unconsciously assembling piece by piece her Moscow which now, as an adult, she loves, and she is conscious of this love.

The reader learns many diverse facts and details of the everyday existence of Alla Ktorova's characters, among them a search for "living space" in overcrowded Moscow; a detailed description of new transistor radios made in the U.S.S.R. and said to be better than the foreign ones; doubts of the girl at the loan desk of the Lenin Library whether the books by Bruno Jasieński can be given out to someone without a special authorization; and the relations between neighbors in a communal apartment. Such seemingly unpretentious descriptions tell the reader a lot about the reality of life in present-day Russia. The class distinctions in a "classless society" are conveyed by humorous genre scenes: the Zharovs' maid is very much opposed to Firebird's new friendship with Vladya, a child of lower social standing; Aunt Dashonka and her friends pronounce judgment on the intelligentsia's strange habit of not going to the public baths. The author does not write all this off as the "survivals of the past," for in the closing chapter, the projected view of the narrator shows her preventing her own child from playing with the children of a lower social rank.

Almost casually, the narrator's past and the misfortunes of her family are recounted: the father, a class-conscious worker and a

Proletarian poet, "disappeared" in the thirties; the mother died soon after; the younger boy was sent to a state children's home; the daughter—the narrator—was taken in by her father's cousin, the young childless widow Dashonka. As usual, Alla Ktorova does not elaborate; the information is conveyed without emphasis or overstatement.

Sometime in the late fifties, the narrator and her aunt move to a new apartment. The description of the housewarming party includes the chatter of Vladya's friends from which the reader learns that the apartment was a part of reparations paid during Khrushchev's de-Stalinization program to the families of the "illegally repressed." Typically understated, it is a savage passage: most of Vladya's friends are in the same situation—they are comparing notes and rejoicing because justice has been done to them and because their living conditions have improved considerably. But there is something spine-chilling about this scene of the happy chatter of a group of young people on the graves of their fathers: the natural egotism of youth appears here as truly cynical and brutal. Vladya's father actually returns from the labor camp. The daughter does not recognize the father; he tries to take the situation lightly, attempts to joke, but breaks down. This highly emotional scene is saved from becoming sentimental by a comic touch —the inclusion of sincere, but almost ridiculously "colloquial," remarks of the aunt and her friend.

A description of the simple comforts of Vladya's new apartment (it is always warm, and they share it only with one other person) merges imperceptibly into a comment on her pleasure in her new furniture: "I love to sit at home alone and listen to occasional creaks of my new furniture: Czechoslovak couch-bed, Finnish desk . . ." (*The Face of Firebird*, p. 18). Do the "occasional creaks" reflect upon the quality of the furniture? Does the fact that it is not made in the U.S.S.R. convey something about the domestic production of furniture or Soviet trade relations? Or is the country of its origin mentioned simply in order to add to the precision of the description? One thing is clear: by not sparing Vladya, Alla Ktorova confirms the nearly universal rule that the desire for a reasonably comfortable existence easily turns into a materialistic attachment to creature comforts and an appetite for acquisition. A description of Vladya's new living quarters becomes a comment on the human condition in general.

The story of Firebird's marriage and departure—besides reminding the reader of the well-known facts that, under Stalin, marriage to a foreigner was considered treason and that, in post-Stalinist times, exit visas are not granted automatically—brings in some highly instructive information. Of her friends, it is only Vladya and her mother's friend Syusya who bravely continue to see Firebird after her plan to marry a Frenchman is revealed. Her other intellectual friends have reasons to fear for their own safety. Vladya remains steadfast in her devotion to Firebird, although she is called in to the State Secret Police and not too subtly reminded that her father was only recently rehabilitated. The interior decorator Syusya by chance happens to be working in the apartment of a relative of some highly placed official and uses this opportunity to plead her friend's cause. But it is the help of Vladya's picturesque nonintellectual friends that proves to be decisive. The jobs of Frau Olga, Tolka the Hero, and Ivan Mordvinov place them close to those in power: Frau Olga works in an Intourist hotel, Tolka the Hero is a chauffeur for some official in the State Secret Police, Ivan works on a special farm that supplies fresh produce to the summerhouses of the top state officials. The implication is that all three are trusted by the state. They not only have access to those who can help Firebird, but are very conscious of their power and speak of it in terms of "human rights."

Despite the general fragmentation, there are never any loose ends in Alla Ktorova's stories: the long and numerous digressions do not prevent the author from returning to the temporarily abandoned line. The result of interrelating various episodes, characters, and above all the narrator's past and present can be compared to an intricately woven braid, where the bright golden thread of past youth and friendship is just as noticeable as the dark grey of the present of adult chores, responsibilities, and relationships. There is also a multi-colored thread of the author's sparkling humor and sharp observation of detail, and an ironic one—whatever color the reader chooses to assign to it. The ostensibly isolated segments of various threads fall into a pattern—it is not accidental that the pointillist technique in painting is mentioned early in the novel.

Alla Ktorova's work deserves more attention from the Western reader (Russian *émigré* critics have praised it unanimously); it is tempting to conjecture what direction her writing will take in the future. The possibilities are many, but fortune-telling is a precarious occupation. It is better to end with a wish of success to a very promising writer. As for prediction, we should not worry; we have a pledge in Alla Ktorova's "literary face," which like the face of Firebird has many expressions—some foreseeable, others quite unexpected.

Notes

1. The story "Klara the Terrorist" (published in the Russian-language magazine *The New Review* [New York], 63, 1961) has the protagonist appear in two chronologically and psychologically well-defined periods—before and after her arrest and labor-camp term in the early fifties.

All the stories of Alla Ktorova were published in Russian. As far as I know, only one, "My Sister's Applegarth," appeared in English translation, in the collection *Russia's Other Writers* (New York, 1971).

2. This article is primarily devoted to that work; whenever other stories are referred to, the source is given in the text.

3. This subtitle is hardly acceptable to any orthodox and cliché-ridden mind: in a recent catalogue of the very publishing house where Alla Ktorova's novel appeared, it was listed as "*Sketches* of an Unfinished *Novel.*" If accidental, the change demonstrated an automatic translation into more acceptable terms. *Ocherki* ("sketches") for *obryvki* ("scraps") perhaps was looked upon as a "correction" of a "misprint."

4. Here Alla Ktorova also surprises her readers, because it is not the Jewish intellectuals that attract her attention (although, to be sure, one can find some in her stories), but the older and the uneducated ones, the more picturesque types. The most striking among them is the protagonist of "The Abominable Snowman" (*Grani*, 67, 1968)—a Jewess who is a kindhearted thief and black-marketeer.

5. This is reciprocated by the Jewish protagonist of "The Abominable Snowman," who adopts a not very attractive Russian boy and showers him, and eventually his family, with her love.

6. "My Sister's Applegarth" (originally in *Grani*, 55, 1964) explores various "legal"—and rather unexpected—ways of procuring an apartment, or, more properly, "living space."

7. The protagonist of "The Abominable Snowman" changes her name during Stalin's anti-Semitic campaign of the early fifties from *Fruma Moiseevna* to *Grunya Alekseevna*. The two components of the new name by themselves are very Russian, the first name having a definite "folksy" ring. But the combination (a diminutive followed by a patronymic) betrays both her Jewish origin and her lack of education.

The face of Firebird: scraps of an unfinished anti-novel
ALLA KTOROVA

For Zoya, Vera, and Lida

From abroad I received a new, small white volume of Vertinsky's lyrics published in Germany. Incredible as it might seem, this book was passed by the censors. It is a very handsome edition, and I am extremely happy with it, despite the fact that I am in complete agreement with Gogol that the moon and everything else that is made in Hamburg is made very poorly indeed. . . .

Over the first poem on the opening page there is a handwritten inscription: "Enter this in my album of maxims. . . ." *

In my beautiful hand I wrote:

> **It's delirium. It's a dream.**
> **Sweet deception of old days.**
> **The white bird of our youth**
> **Has vanished into the haze.**

The lower the sun sets, the longer the human shadow becomes. And mine at the moment is long, very long, misshapen, dark and skinny, like Don Basilio. I measure it with my steps: one, two,

---

* Firebird adored maxims. After she departed on her own for the Crimea, she bombarded me with letters, asking, "Any new maxims?" AUTHOR.

three. And I come up against the wall—the China Wall,* the area where Firebird and I spent our childhood and youth.

Between the second and third brick, on a microscopic, slanted piece of dirt, a weed gently sways. Should I call over Klavka Beryozkina, the botany teacher from Public School 617, and ask her if it's a plantain?

Why are you so disturbed by a plantain? By a miserable hick of a weed, of interest to no one but rabbits?

The English say that if plantains grow in front of the house of a person who has gone away, it means he will never return to his native land . . .

> *I refuse to exist*
> *In a bedlam of non-humans*
> *—Marina Tsvetaeva*

Chapter VI: Lilac dream

Lilac? Or perhaps simply a rabbit's deceptive doze? With just one eye closed and his ears twitching?

It happened exactly at the time in our lives when Firebird and I were suddenly tormented by an indefinable longing. For hours on end, with mud-splattered stockings, we roved over our beloved Ordynka Street and wondered what we could do that would absolutely astound everyone. Go to the barber shop and have ourselves shaved bald? Buy a hovel and grow pumpkins? Or cover up our pale legs? †

Just after the distribution of work assignments in May, when Firebird was told that since she was not married she would be left without an assignment, or, if it was really impossible for her to get along without work, she could go to Chapaevsk as a foreign-language teacher or work as a stewardess for Aeroflot (Martha Shishkina and Rosa Yevstigneeva work for them, why on earth can't you?)—just then, after she had run in tears from the office of the director, where the assignments had been made, a heavy man with a huge bald pate followed her out into the corridor, went up to her, and said in a dignified manner:

---

* The remnants of an ancient wall in the center of Moscow near the Kremlin, now a tourist attraction. TRANSLATOR.

† Paraphrase of a one-line poem by Valery Bryusov. TRANSLATOR.

"Strogov is my name, Vasily Alexandrovich Strogov. I represent the National Committee on Foreign Cultural Relations. Don't be upset, comrade. Don't sign up for Chapaevsk or anywhere else. You'll be all right. They only threaten to take you to court. There is no such law. Come to work in our organization. I like your face."

Firebird gleefully beat her wings.

"But why didn't you say it in front of the commission—that you would be glad to take me?"

"Oh, you child. As if such a thing were possible. It would only make a mess of everything. They would say she did not distinguish herself in the Communist Youth League, that she did not carry out any social work. They would say, we have married women, women who are more deserving and are left without an assignment, and you are asking us for her. It would do no good. Do not tell anyone, and toward the end of August come to see me and we'll formalize it."

Thus Nika Zharova,* who was nicknamed Firebird, started to work as an interpreter of English, French, and German in one of the most interesting institutions in Moscow.

This was the happiest period in her life. Whether for better or for worse I do not know, but it was this period that brought so much commotion into our lives that for a while we lost anything resembling peace of mind.

First of all there occurred certain most interesting events, followed by new thoughts and, most important of all, by concerns of an extremely serious nature.

Firebird was furiously busy at work, starting early in the morning.

"Zagorsk, Zagorsk, I have been on the phone half an hour."

"Father Alexei?" she shouted joyously into the receiver, when she was finally connected with Zagorsk, "This is Nika Zharova. From . . . Yes, yes."

I was sitting in the corner, as a person who had come to see

* "Zhar" means "fire" in Russian; "Zhar-ptitsa" is the firebird of Russian folklore. TRANSLATOR.

employee Zharova "on personal matters." But I cannot describe how amazed I was listening to all of this; despite my fondness for comparisons, I cannot conceive of a single one that would be appropriate.

"So, Father Alexei," Firebird was saying, her feathers aflutter, "well, I have a group of fifteen today, all Americans. We'll see you at three o'clock sharp, okay?"

A fifteen-year-old nephew of some friends of mine, Slava, said bashfully to me, "Vladya, can't you ask your friend to borrow a stick of chewing gum from one of those Americans?"

Rudik, a friend of Slava's, was prodding his companion in the side.

"No, Slava, instead of chewing gum it'd be better if she let us see those Americans put their feet up on the table."

In the evening the events were relayed to me, Syusya, Emka, and Aunt Tamarochka.

"This Frenchman, traveling deluxe. He says: 'My God, why do they keep carting us around girls' cemeteries" (this was followed by hysterical laughter on our part, since he had in mind the necropolis of the New-Virgin Cemetery), " 'and to these ancient fortresses and monasteries? I want to see and talk with living people, not corpses. Why don't you rather invite me to your place for cocktails?' "

Syusya and Tamarochka shuddered as one person.

" 'No, I can't,' " I told him. " 'My father is at home sick. But why don't you like the monasteries? We want to show foreign visitors that we have freedom of religion, and that all people who want to can . . .' "

" 'Freedom. Such weird creatures in the monastery, so gloomy, and what a stench. You know, it's really like the fourteenth century. Why do they say "Mother Russia"? It would be far better to say "Grandma Russia." ' "

That slayed us. I believe it was just then that a gut in my stomach burst from laughter. I'll surely have to have an operation.

Firebird had her own private thoughts during all the turmoil. Once she said to me:

"This cute little Indian, a writer from India, said to me: 'You see, none of you believe in God, but then explain to me why you are always screaming: "Oh, my God! Oh, good Lord!" Why don't you say instead: "Oh, my Lenin! Oh, my Stalin!" And finally, "Oh-h-h, my Kh-ru-shh-chev." ' "

The N. Sisters came from Paris. Important old ladies. The daughters of a famous Russian theoretician of Marxism. They were supposed to be received by Khrushchev himself, and yet they were given so little black caviar that they put it out on the windowsill to make it last longer.

The sisters looked into the face of Firebird for a long time, and then they suddenly decided they did not want their former interpreter, Dina Slobozhan, but wanted a new one, Firebird. Only Firebird. That is, of course . . .

If you would be so kind . . .

Please forgive us . . .

Beg your pardon—if it is at all possible . . .

"Mademoiselle is bright, mademoiselle is charming, mademoiselle is be-au-ti-ful!" they sang out modestly.

George Pukhov, the interpreter for a small Japanese atomic scientist, brought a large package to the Bureau addressed "To Nika Zharova."

"Before he left, my Nip asked me to give it to you. I don't know what's in it, I didn't open it."

George humphed.

"By the way, it seems strange—how did he ever get to see you? I don't remember him sitting at your table even once. They say that you're real popular with the Yankees, too."

In the package Firebird found a small flight bag packed with oranges and a beautiful man's sweater. The enclosed letter said:

Dear Nika:

I never thought Russia would be the place where I would see the most beautiful Japanese flower—Lilac Dream. This flower is you. I am leaving you the sweater only because it is a little over the baggage allowance on the plane. I would be very happy to see you again, and hope I shall.

Your I. Takahashi

Firebird looked out the window. She was delighted: the sweater would be perfect for Tamarochka for the winter. How soft it was! It did not weigh more than two hundred grams.

"Can you imagine what he thinks about our standard of living when he leaves a 'girl-flower' a man's sweater!" said Leonid Zolotarev, one of the interpreters.

"N-n-no, I can't take it," wailed George Pukhov. "A flower? Nika, a beautiful Japanese flower? Did he know about the coat?"

The coat had been quite a story.

That year, after some eight years, Firebird had finally had a new coat made for herself. Fitted at the waist, made out of fine dark blue worsted. And she had ordered a matching cap in the shop on Stoleshnikov Lane. Her joy over the coat was so boundless that when I implored her not to go alone at night to a remote suburb to visit her ailing nanny, Katya, for fear she might be raped in that neighborhood, she said:

"So what if they rape me! Just so they don't get the coat!"

And though that sounded like a well-known joke, Firebird was not joking.

The beginning for her was exactly the same as it had been for old Akaky Akakievich Bashmachkin in Gogol's *Overcoat*. The thief, a powerful, light-haired fellow of about twenty, grabbed Firebird by the collar and said: "Take it off, or else. One sound and . . ."

But the end was one Akaky Akakievich could never have imagined.

Firebird swung her arm, clothed in the new worsted, and gave the thief such a blow across the snout that he fell to the ground and howled in a frightful voice.

The victim (Firebird) ran as fast as she could to the train, afraid they would arrest her for murder.

In this respect, I declare quite frankly and want it to be understood—Firebird and I have absolutely nothing in common. If I had been in her shoes, I would have begged, "Oh, please—oh, dear—oh, have mercy—please, please take everything, just don't kill me. . . ."

When she heard this story, Anna Davydovna, the mother of our Emka, shook her head bitterly for a long while: first forward and backward, then backward and forward, then left to right and right to left.

"Well, Nika, I see you'll never get married."

"Why is that?"

"It just is," was Anna Davydovna's retort. "That's what it comes to. If a young girl can knock a sturdy man off his feet, it means she has a heavy hand. And only old maids have heavy hands. Just mark my words, none of you—not you, with all your looks, not Vladya, still less my Emka—none of you will ever get married."

"Why do you bring up Vladya?"

"Why? We invited her over a few days ago. There were a lot of young men here. We asked her over on purpose, of course, so that she could meet some people. She had hardly opened the door when she started yelling so that the entire hallway heard her: 'Where are my prospective husbands? Where are they?'"

Nonetheless, despite her heavy hand, the opposite sex besieged Firebird from all sides.

A beanpole of a Czech waited for her after work and chased after her to the trolley

"Comrade, dear comrade . . ."

Undoubtedly he wanted to accompany her home and along the way declare his love to "Comrade Firebird."

Vasily Alexandrovich Strogov, her boss, addressed himself to a group of Hungarians that had crowded around Firebird's table:

"Friends, you can go to the other interpreters. It makes absolutely no difference who serves you."

"No, no, it absolutely does make a difference," said the tallest, most handsome of the group, who also spoke the best Russian, as he stepped forward.

"Neki jó arca—NEKI JÓ ARCA—this is why it makes a difference."

In Hungarian this means "What an attractive face!"

In order to round out this theme, it must be added that after every "gift" left for Firebird (*Jolie Madame* perfume, lipstick with pop-out mirrors, one-size-fits-all stockings, and so forth), after every letter with a foreign postmark, addressed to the charming interpreter, Miss Jarson, and after every occasion when more than "ordinary interest" was shown, she was immediately called in to see the Boss-Puppet.*

"Well, then. And what are his political views?"

"He had a very, very high opinion of the new houses on Kaluzhskaya Street."

"He did?"

"He had high praise for the milk-vending machine on Chekhov Street and the packaged crisp-fried potatoes."

"Hmmm. So? What's your personal opinion?"

"A highly refined person in every respect."

The last comment of Firebird was jotted down by the Boss-Puppet in some kind of notebook. She put her signature under it. And the book was passed higher up—from one Boss-Puppet to another, according to the chain of command.

All these talks with Puppets naturally were to be kept in strict confidence, but both she and the other interpreters discussed them in great detail, not only with each other but even with outsiders—such as myself, for example.

They made fun of the Puppets, for whom, lethargically doing their duty, they described, both aloud and in writing, their conversations with foreigners, each fibbing as best he could.

Moreover, it was obligatory for them to give an account of themselves and answer the following questions in writing:

1. Who are your friends? Their names?
2. What do you like, what are your interests?
3. What is your purpose in life?
4. How do you reply to foreigners when they inquire how you feel about your country?

Firebird and I worked together on answers to these intellectual questions. Here are our answers:

* Ironical nickname for bureaucrats, from Mayakovsky's play *The Bathhouse*. TRANSLATOR.

1. My friends are people who are not so much activist as they are truthful, and they are not opportunists, but people with heart. Their names: Susanna Semyonovna Syurmul and Marianna Kadyrova (Mogilevkina before she got hitched). I have no other friends.

2. Best of all I like fruit-flavored candies (like Chekhov used to), and I get carried away by Gumilyov's poem "The Giraffe." I also take an interest in nature, music, and placitude.

3. My aim in life is to find the Thatch Hut.

4. When foreigners ask me how I feel about my country, I answer them: "My motherland is where the most beautiful clouds pass by."

A bit apprehensive, I said to Firebird: "Won't he guess that we're making fun of him? Especially the Thatch Hut, and the clouds?"

"Not a chance," Firebird answered coolly, "because, first of all, the serious and the idiotic are mixed together here, and, second, these Puppets—every last one of them—are all genuine morons."

I sniffed doubtfully.

"Yes, of course. 'What are his political views?' That is all he knows."

Firebird then said something that I had thought about a great deal myself.

"I'll tell you, Vladya. My colleagues and I have talked it over a million times. We would have nothing, nothing at all against that institution. As Kozma Prutkov wrote, 'The police right there in the life of every state are.' It's the same abroad. It's that way everywhere, so it's necessary. We would have nothing against them if they only had human faces. As it is, all those phizzes have something criminal in them. You should see them. Their little caps. Their tattoos. No, I'm going to write it all down. They won't guess. . . ."

For a very long time not only the Puppets, but even I, could not guess. Why that was, I do not know. And to this day no one believes that for nearly a year I had no suspicions—not Aunt Tamarochka, nor Dashonka, nor the writer Osetintsev, nor an American correspondent.

Only Syusya Syurmul believes me. Because she remembers how the two of us once came together to the locked room of the Zharovs and suddenly saw a letter that had been tucked behind the doorknob by the mailman—a light-blue and white letter with blue and red margins. Air mail! "From over there! From A-B-ROAD!"

The words "from over there, from ABROAD" were chattered by Syusya. Then she grabbed the letter and tried to slip it under the door, so the neighbors would not notice it (especially that witch Rafalovskaya).

The Bird is merry and gay
Strutting down calamity road,
With no notion along the way
Of what the dark shadows forebode. . . .

"Vladya," Syusya said hoarsely, finishing the lyrics, with which I unfortunately was not familiar, "Keep in mind that if they find out she is getting mail at home instead of at work, we will be the first to get it for not reporting it to the proper authorities."

Syusya nearly collapsed onto the neighbors' trunk.

"Oh, I don't feel well, I don't feel well at all," she lamented, "the way a person destroys herself, just flies off into the flame. I am not even talking about Tamarochka. I can imagine the kind of St. Bartholomew nights, the kind of Walpurgis nights she lives through, the poor mother, every time she sees those envelopes."

After that incident I only dimly began to comprehend the situation.

"Tupupernats, tupupernats, tupupernats, tuts-nats, tuts-nats," sang sly Firebird merrily as she hurried somewhere, thrusting out her legs. But she did not say a word about her own strange affairs and secret doings. I saw that she was deliberately wallowing in individualism and not telling anyone about anything.

No matter how much I hinted that, as a close friend, I expected the disclosure of a secret, Firebird pretended not to understand a thing.

"Syusya, do you know anything?"

"And you, Vladya, do you know anything?" Syusya replied, slightly offended." When you have to ask a dressmaker what a dress costs, Syusya does it for you, because it's 'embarrassing' for you. When you have to ask that highway robber Soloukhin to come and repair the meter, your fool Syusya does that too, because she's bolder. But when it comes to something important, when the advice of an experienced person who's been through hell and high water is really needed . . ."

"But at least you tried asking her about it?"

"Well, yes. Yes, I tried."

"And what happened?"

"Nothing. A Mona Lisa smile, and she's quiet as a chicken with its head cut off."

In those terrible, muddled days, a new entry appeared in the Firebird's album of maxims:

> **I refuse to exist**
> **In a bedlam**
> **Of non-humans.**
> **(From the poetry of Marina Tsvetaeva)**

All her friends, to say nothing of mere acquaintances, abandoned Firebird. They were frightened.

Emka Kukui moaned over the telephone:

"Vladya, really, now! I would do anything on earth for her, anything at all. But I'm afraid. Really, with that fifth question * of mine, can I afford to get mixed up in something like this? Mother's going out of her mind from fright. Merely because we're friends. You know, Uncle Senya was just rehabilitated."

I bumped into Klavka Beryozkina in the self-service cafeteria at the Hotel Moscow. Wiggling her tray and her behind, she tried to slip into the dining room, feigning not to notice me.

"Klavka! Aren't you ashamed?"

The tea on her tray started to splash violently onto the neighboring table.

"Now listen, Vladya. Dad isn't retired yet, he still works at the police department." Klavka started nervously rubbing the amber necklace which she wore around her neck to prevent goiter and

---

* "Fifth question" on official forms refers to nationality. Emka Kukui is Jewish. TRANSLATOR

cravenly blinked her short eyelashes. "Tell Firebird that I asked Grandma to pray for her at church. I gave her three rubles of my hard-earned money for candles. Just in case. Might help. Who can tell the devil's ways? . . ."

Klavka looked at me warmly with her grey, slightly protruding eyes.

How Firebird's happiness staggered at first! How her fate could not find its way!

"Fate's a robin, bobbity bobbin," mumbled the dismayed Dashonka. "If it was somebody else, I wouldn't say a thing. That'd be that, but I feel sorry for her."

"Shut up, will you."

"I'll give you shut up! Who do you think you're talking to? You carrion."

That was her latest fashionable invective, which she hurled at anyone who came along, and most often at me.

"She sits, like a . . . And instead of all the nonsense, you should invite her over for tea. Have them both come over. I'm not afraid of anyone. Tell them both to come over for tea."

She noticed that my frown grew even deeper, and added rather pathetically:

"Tell her Dashonka will get her favorite fruit-flavored candies, come payday. Not the cheap loose stuff but the best three-layered kind, that comes in a box."

After that good-natured squabble, we both cried terribly for half an hour. Our nerves were worn down to a nylon frazzle.

They sent Firebird from Pontius to Pilate, from Pilate to Pontius.

Some said:

"Really, now, how does that depend on me? If it did, all right! You may leave right away!"

Others growled:

"Citizen Zharova" (they at once started calling her "citizen" instead of "comrade"), "you apparently do not fully realize what you have done. It is a good thing that Stalin's times have passed.

Otherwise . . . If his law were still in force, it would be so much the worse for you. It is tantamount to betraying your country."

Only a few had enough courage to regard Firebird with sympathy, and, certain that no one else could hear, they would pass along words of comfort:

"Keep your ear to the ground!"

"Don't give in! Stay bright-eyed and bushy-tailed!"

Many persons, including a sizable number of former friends, were burning with impatience:

"Any news? Will they arrest her? Or simply a public Court of Honor with public condemnation and dismissal from work?"

Firebird, who in any other situation could have fought off seven mad dogs, shed plaintive child's tears.

"Come on now, Firebird," I pleaded with her, "don't show them any tears, cry yourself out at home. They are not all swine, there are some decent ones. Look at Frau Olga and her important position—still she called me specially when she found out."

Firebird hopefully opened her swollen eyes.

"She said you should not argue with anyone, you should implore them modestly. She advised to write to HIMSELF."

I did all I could to put Nika on the right track.

"Ask, but don't demand, don't fight. You bow down to anyone, if you have to. Come on, Nika, you angel, you darling, just play the part of an orphan of the storm."

"The Duke knew how to faint and liked to? Is that what you mean?" Firebird said indignantly.

To my horror, she did not want to purchase her happiness at the cost of groveling, flattery and loathsome promises, and she desperately insisted:

"No, don't tell me some of them are good. I hate them all, every one of them now, every single one! From first to last."

Sitting in a worn armchair in the Zharovs' room, in the bass voice of a Moscow match-maker from some Ostrovsky play, I shook the walls with curses never heard there before, the chief of which sounded like "Chuck it."

Aunt Tamarochka would unhappily rejoin every time: "Again!"

And Syusya Syurmul gently calmed her:

"Tamarochka, dear! What can you expect from the grand-daughter of a coachman?"

I have to express my admiration for Aunt Tamarochka and Syusya Syurmul. For Aunt Tamarochka because, despite the very definite expectations of Firebird and myself, she behaved like a human being instead of like a philistine. She astounded us all, and most of all her own daughter, Firebird.

We expected tears, wailing, hysteria, something on the order of, "I said so, oh, if I hadn't said so! But it was I . . ." and so forth, but all she did was learn and repeatedly sing the last lines from an old Vertinsky record ("In a Small, Dusty Town"):

> **Tatata-tatatata-tatata-tatatata**
> **Driven through the city first,**
> **Lying stiffly in the hearse . . .**

Syusya told me in secret that Aunt Tamarochka had said to her:

"Tell my family that under no circumstances do I want to be cremated. I'm afraid. I want to be next to my mother in Pyatnitsky Cemetery."

The sacrifice that Syusya made during those three horrible months was evident by the fact that she stopped using mascara; she was afraid that it would run because of the tears which never ceased flowing, and so would burn her eyes.

"Oh, I don't feel well, I don't feel well at all," she lamented melancholically when I remained alone with her. "Vladya, what should we do? Who do we run to? How do we save them?"

Firebird's father at that time was on an extended business trip.

Although to this day not a single one of us really knows where salvation came from, I am sure half the credit must go to the interior decorator, Syusya.

"Oh, Tamarochka," she said, as she carefully pressed her outspread hands to her chest, "you know I am only an interior decorator and deal mostly with women. Oh, Tamarochka! But I'll talk to everyone, Tamarochka, everyone, I'll hint, I'll *mention it to them all!*"

She would drop by in the morning and then disappear, telephoning to Naryshkinsky Square every half hour.

"My God, I can barely breathe. Any good news? Or nothing at all yet?"

Finally she came, her cheeks rosy and glowing, and whispered two words:

"It's crystallizing!"

This meant she had been asked to do a job "up there." She was to design the interior of a new apartment for the cousin of—was it Khrushchev's wife, or Kozlov's wife, or of Furtseva herself?

"Tamarochka, relax. That's it. That's about it. The main thing in an affair like this is to make a personal request. Don't worry, I'll ram it down their throats. Everyone likes romantic stories, especially women, and I don't see anything criminal here. Much less political."

Kary Kadyrich Kadyrov, a deputy of the Council of Nationalities, Fanka's son-in-law and Marianna's husband, energetically shook his black watermelon of a head.

"I will tell everyone that I know her, that she is in every way a Soviet person, that I know no one more attractive."

Marianna, agreeing with every one of her husband's words, shook her curly locks.

Fifty times a day, Ivan Mordvinov would form his eyebrows into triangles:

"How are we to understand this? Give hope first, then scoff? So he should go, she should stay? Not on your life! Bring it to a clash and signal to the higher-ups. It's pretty clear: someone below is in charge of it. If important people found out about it—they sure wouldn't pat them on the head."

"Important people," fumed Dashonka, "important people . . . By the time you get to them, to your important people, you've run yourself ragged. A lamb should leave the wolves alone. . . ."

But then . . .

I received a telephone call at work.

422

"It's me," announced the baritone voice of Frau Olga. "When you come to see me I'll give you such good news you'll die, you'll pass out, and you'll wake up in tears. I said I'd do it for her if it kills me. Because she's such an awfully sweet child . . ."

"Oh, Frau Olga, darling, please, right now . . ."

"Not on the telephone. Come over."

"Well, at least give me a hint, at least. . . ."

"Come over!" she bellowed mercilessly over the phone.

And when I saw her personally she reported exactly the same news that Tolka the Hero had brought to the Zharovs' apartment:

"Don't cry, you little fools. Everything'll be okay." He took off his boots, went to the door, closed the safety lock with both paws as quietly as possible and whispered:

"They had me and Olga Ivanovna in. They asked for an objective evaluation of Nika's character."

"Well?"

"I said okay, and I mean okay. We gave such a favorable evaluation—she'd never guess . . ."

"Do you think something will come of it?"

"How else? Yesterday I saw Nikolai Konstantinov, an operative. He said this case is already causing some commotion. I had said that the main thing was to make more noise. So it was. Yesterday there was a reception at the Indian Embassy. People sitting around, eating, drinking. The daughter of the ambassador, a cute young Indian girl, got up, went to Khrushchev himself, and bluntly asked him right in front of everyone about this case. Why, she asked, don't you let them? You'll see. Any day now."

That winter was not at all what we had expected. They say that when there is a hot summer there will be a cold winter, and when there is a cold winter, expect a hot summer. Everything was just the opposite. I cannot recall such a hot summer, or such a mild winter.

Who is there, in the crimson beret? * Who is it, wearing the pea-colored overcoat? It is I.

* A fragment of a line from Pushkin's *Eugene Onegin*. TRANSLATOR.

On a warm completely springlike day in January, from six o'clock in the evening on that certain day, I am on guard, like a sore thumb, in front of a grey building with a bas-relief, bearing the inscription: ALL OF OUR HOPE IS BASED ON PEOPLE WHO FEED THEMSELVES.

I spend my time both "here" and "there." What I do "here," I am writing now; everything I say "there" I will also write.

This is what I say "there":

"Of course, of course, if I notice anything suspicious, I will report it. Before, I did not even know anything."

"Wasn't your father just recently rehabilitated?"

"Yes, but I barely know my father."

"No, no, I was just talking. It doesn't pertain to the present case. Here we hold you in very good regard."

Yes, they hold me in very good regard, but every time they politely invite me by telephone to some address for "a talk" with some callous character (I do not know his name, because his signature is nearly unintelligible) I feel like gagging and get dizzy all over.

On nights like that I barely drag myself home.

Once, at precisely such a time, I heard a voice behind my back:

"Don't turn around, Vladya. It's me, Kostya." But this part has already been described in the chapter "My Friend Firebird."

A French soldier who survived the battle at Waterloo went insane. He said that he had been killed in that battle and that only his shadow remained on earth. I am the French soldier who was killed at Waterloo. It seems to me that my own shadow runs in front of me, looks into my face, looks for me, looks and does not find me. . . .

I put my heart in a heavy wheelbarrow—I cannot budge it.

Ever since the TU-104 carried Firebird away I have not been able to sleep without sleeping pills.

And when I do sleep, I dream of myself.

Or suddenly I hear:

"Is anybody here, or not?"

424

Into the window crawls the peasant who haunted Anna Karenina in her dreams.

I scream loudly.

"I won't touch you, I won't. Call your hubby, mum, call Yakov Mikhailovich, my axle's broken. . . ."

I see myself married to my grandfather, the Moscow cabby, Yakov Mikhailovich Kolotushkin.

But why do I converse with my nocturnal visitor in English?

Then suddenly I hear someone saying:

"In the Colorado River Valley, in the distant, strange, weird valley of the Colorado River. . . . How the hell did you get there? You are afraid of me, you are bored. . . . The deep red canyon, on its bottom the slow-flowing gray Colorado River. . . ."

"Remember, Vladya, that pretty friend you had? You always were together, like Orestes and Pylades, like Siamese twins. With that strange male * name."

"Nika Zharova?"

"Yes, yes. Where is she now?"

How can I tell my old friend, the film director, Efrim Borisovich Geller, all that happened to Firebird without his running to the other side of the street in fright and without his looking as though he were about to faint from astonishment—because he had heard about the whole saga but had no idea that it had happened to her?

So I start to spin a comical story for him, knowing that he likes and collects them.

"First of all, the girl with the man's name—that's nobody but me," I jabber in a lively way. "Marianna came to see me yesterday, do you remember, from our old apartment? Her husband, Kary Kadyrich, was with her. For a long while he looked over Nika's photos, which she sent to me, and then he said—no, first he clacked with his tongue, Uzbeks always clack with their tongues, and he said right in front of his wife: 'No, I guess I've really be-

* Nika and Vladya are most common as boys' names in Russian. TRANSLATOR.

425

come Russified. If I still were a true Easterner, I'd never have given away such a beauty to another country.' "

When I drop by at Firebird's old place of work, from a distance I notice that old goose, the cleaning woman, Auntie Masha—certainly a person who's gotten out of touch.

"Oh-h-h-h, damnation," cackles old Masha, "I thought you were somebody else. I almost had a fit. Oh-h-h."

"Why, what happened?"

"I thought you was her. I thought she came back."

"Who?"

"Nika. Nika Zharova. The Firebird. Who else?"

We take a seat on the wooden bench in the hallway.

"Aunt Masha, I've brought you some pastry. Want an eclair?"

"I can't, it's Lent."

"Well, anyway, take it. God will forgive."

"Well, all right. When I'm in Zagorsk, I'll atone for it."

I always come to see Auntie Masha to squeeze the latest news and gossip out of her. Every time, I bring her either a jar of pickled chanterelles, or some gherkins, the pimply kind, or a small package of cocoa, which she adores.

These gifts, these edible bribes, always make her talkative.

"How about Strogov? Did he blame her? Abuse her? Threaten her? I suppose he fears for his own position now?"

"No, Vladya, here's how it was," Auntie Masha mumbles with evident relish, "I dunno about when he was alone, but in front of others he didn't abuse her. They told him not to."

"Who told him?"

"Come on," says old Masha, "as though you don't know who gives orders here to do things and not to do things."

"That's right."

"It's right, but it isn't right. So he didn't abuse her, but he said: 'What did I see in her that time at the distribution of assignments? I don't know myself. There'd been girls a thousand times purtier, says he. As for love . . . What is this love business? She

426

simply decided that she'd be better off there than here, she simply decided to get herself a good setup. That's all.' "

"Really?"

"Yes, so he doesn't abuse her, but here's what I'll tell you. When all of us first heard about it we was scared out of our wits. We had a general closed meeting concerning this business: all of us, Strogov and two other men in plainclothes. The younger of the two of them said: 'It's not her who is at fault, comrades, but all of us. How did we let it get by?' "

"Really?"

"The absolute truth—I'm not lying. After the meeting, Strogov says to me: 'Auntie Masha, you must be watchful too! When there's nothing to do, you should watch your co-workers, watch who has long talks with which foreigners, who has long chats with who else and who does what else with whom.' But I don't give a hoot for what he says. . . ."

Auntie Masha tells me all I need to know.

"Yes, Strogov was worried at first. The first days. But later . . . He got the word. Took it easier. And how did she manage to get together with him? he wondered. Not even very good at French, English is her main language. And in any case, no good could come of it. As though there aren't enough examples . . ."

"That's true," I drawled, "but they certainly won't pat him on the head for it; it did, after all, happen in his office, so he must worry about his job."

"No. Why should he worry? He covered himself—he wrote an explanatory letter, and we all signed it. . . ."

Since childhood I have hated my birthday, the anniversary of my birth. I am glad when my old friends forget it, and I don't tell it to my new friends. I never thought about my years before, and I did not fear them.

Now I go up to the chest of drawers, look into Dashonka's old, "most exact" mirror, peer into a face that is far from what it used to be, and I shudder at the thought that a "round number" is approaching and that I will soon be thirty.

I look at the former Communist Youth League activist, Auntie Masha, and think, what will I be like in half a century?

I close my eyes and see a dark grey, distressing day. A church. A humpbacked old woman emerges from it dressed in rags. With shaggy eyes. With a bunch of radishes in her hand.

It is I.

Auntie Masha roused herself.

"And that Japanese? The Lilac Dream? Remember? He used to come here every day with his interpreter? I remembered one thing concerning."

She snickered.

"Big deal, in Japan! Why right in those places near the Volga we have a flower like that too. But it's not called 'lilac dream,' it's called 'violet dream.' When you smell it, you could doze right off to sleep. Grows by creeks. But the flower itself is so tiny, so modest looking! Nothing to admire . . . Nothing but a smell . . . Nothing but a dream . . ."

translated by Daniel Bures in collaboration with Olga Hughes and Simon Karlinsky

A note on Konstantin Korovin (1860-1939)
TATIANA KUSUBOVA

When Korovin's name is brought up in the context of literature, the usual reaction is: "You mean Konstantin Korovin? But wasn't he a painter and not a writer?" This response reveals and summarizes the posthumous fate of an unusually gifted man whose earlier fame as a painter and stage-set designer overshadowed his later efforts as a writer.

Korovin came from an impoverished Moscow merchant family. He studied art in the Moscow School of Painting, Sculpture, and Architecture, and upon graduation became a very successful painter. Historians of Russian art place him among the best Russian Impressionists. As a member of the Mamontov circle and later as chief designer for the Imperial Theaters, he revolutionized techniques of stage and costume design. When the Revolution broke out in Russia, he fled to Paris. But life as an *émigré* proved to be difficult, and Korovin found it impossible to adjust to the demands of a foreign country. It was even harder for him to adjust to the new trends in art, and he remained faithful to Impressionism. However, contrary to the claims of Soviet art historians, he produced very interesting works during this period, both as a painter and as set designer. An evaluation of him as a painter during his emigration will be possible only after a thorough examination of the works he produced in exile.

In the early 1930's Korovin embarked on a totally new career, and it is this new career that interests us here. Driven by the hardships of *émigré* life and spurred on by friends who knew him as an extraordinarily gifted *raconteur,* Korovin started to write his fragmentary memoirs. At this time he was already seventy years old. From 1930 to his death in 1939 he was a regular contributor to most of the major Russian *émigré* newspapers.

The central theme of Korovin's semifictionalized memoirs, so typical of *émigré* writers, is his memory of Russia and the people he knew when he was young. He reminisces about his early encounters with Anton Chekhov (Chekhov's brother Nikolai was Korovin's fellow student at the art school) and the painters Savrasov, Serov, and Levitan. He writes about his role in the Mamontov opera productions and how he was a witness to the birth of the career of the famous Russian basso, Chaliapin. Other articles tell of meeting Ostrovsky, Tchaikovsky, and Gorky. Like Turgenev, Korovin was an avid fisherman and hunter; he wandered around the Russian countryside in the Vladimir region, observing the life of Russian peasants at the turn of the century and on the eve of the Revolution. Many years later, in Paris, these impressions would become the central theme of many of Korovin's stories.

As a painter, and as an Impressionist, Korovin sought to evoke a certain atmosphere through his use of color. He abhorred tendentiousness in art, and, like Levitan, Serov, and Savrasov, revolted against the compulsory bias in Russian painting which found its expression in the art of the *Peredvizhniki.** When Korovin started to write his memoirs he applied his techniques of painting to literature. His main purpose was to convey an atmosphere of the past through colors, characteristic detail, and vivid settings.

* The Wanderers, a group of academic realist painters admired more for their social commentary than for their art. EDITOR.

During his nine years of literary activity, Konstantin Korovin received some favorable reviews, particularly for his book of memoirs about Feodor Chaliapin (*Chaliapin. Vstrechi i sovmestnaya zhizn'*, Paris, 1939). His stories and memoirs, which were never collected in book form, received no attention after his death, and his reputation continued to rest primarily on his achievements as a painter and stage designer. Interest in Korovin's memoirs has been revived since the 1960's, however, and various stories have been printed in *émigré* newspapers abroad and in special magazines in the Soviet Union. The first collection of Korovin's memoirs (*Konstantin Korovin vspominaet*, Moscow, 1971) has recently been published in the Soviet Union. "My Encounters with Chekhov" is the first translation of Korovin into English.

My encounters with Chekhov
KONSTANTIN KOROVIN

1

It all took place, if I'm not mistaken, in 1883.

On the corner of Dyakovskaya and Sadovaya Streets in Moscow there was a hotel called Oriental Rooms, though no one knew what was Oriental about it. It had very shabby furnished rooms. Three bricks hanging on a rope were attached to the front door to help it close more securely.

Anton Pavlovich Chekhov lived on the first floor, Isaak Levitan —who was at the time still a student at the School of Painting, Sculpture, and Architecture—lived on the second.

It was spring. Levitan and I were on the way home from our school on Myasnitskaya Street after our final painting exam. We had both received silver medals—I for drawing, he for painting.

As we went into the hotel, Levitan said to me, "Let's stop in at Antosha's [i.e. Chekhov's]."

Anton Pavlovich's room was filled with smoke. There was a samovar on the table, surrounded by bread, sausages, and beer. The couch was strewn with papers and lecture notebooks: Anton

Pavlovich was preparing for the final examinations at the university, after which he would become a doctor.

He was sitting on the edge of the couch wearing a gray jacket of the type many students wore at the time. Some young men whom we didn't know were in the room with him. They were university students.

The students were talking heatedly—there was an argument going on—drinking tea and beer, and eating sausage. Anton Pavlovich sat quietly, only occasionally answering the questions put to him.

He was extremely handsome. He had a large, open face with kind, laughing eyes. When talking with someone, he would sometimes fix his eyes on him for a moment, only to lower them immediately and smile his own special shy smile. His whole appearance—his open face, his broad chest—inspired in people a special sort of confidence. It was as if he emanated waves of warmth and protection. Despite his youth, despite his adolescent appearance, he even then made you think of a kind old man whom you could approach and ask about the meaning of life, tell of your sorrows, and confess something very important, the kind of secret everyone has somewhere down deep. Anton Pavlovich was simple and natural; he was unpretentious and lacked the least bit of affectation or self-admiration. Innate modesty, his own special sense of measure, even timidity were always a part of his character.

It was a sunny spring day. Levitan and I asked Anton Pavlovich to come to Sokolniki Park with us.

We told him about the medals we had received. One of the students present asked, "Well, are you going to wear them around your neck the way doormen do?"

It was Levitan who answered. "No, they're not meant to be worn. They aren't used for anything. They're awarded at graduation as a sign of distinction."

"Like the ribbons dogs get at dog shows," added another student.

The students were different from Anton Pavlovich. They loved to argue, and they were in some peculiar way opposed to just about everything.

"If you have no convictions," said one student turning to Chekhov, "you can't be a writer."

"No one can say, 'I have no convictions,' " said another. "I can't understand how anyone could not have convictions."

"I have no convictions," replied Chekhov.

"You claim to be a man without convictions, but how can you write a work of literature without any ideology? Don't you have an ideology?"

"I have no ideology and no convictions," answered Chekhov.

These students had an odd way of arguing. They were apparently displeased with Anton Pavlovich. It was clear that they could not fit him into the didactic turn of their outlook or into their moralizing ideology. They wanted to guide, to instruct, to lead, and to influence. They knew everything. They understood everything. And Anton Pavlovich was plainly bored by it all.

"Who needs your stories? Where do they lead? They don't oppose anything. They contain no ideas. The *Russian Bulletin,* say, would have no use for you. Your stories are entertaining and nothing else."

"Nothing else," answered Anton Pavlovich.

"And why, may I ask, do you sign your stories Chekhonte? What's the point of such an outlandish pen name?"

Chekhov laughed.

"And when you get to be a doctor," the student added, "you'll be ashamed of having written without ideology or protest."

"You're right," answered Chekhov, still laughing. Then he added, "Let's go to Sokolniki. It's a beautiful day. The violets will be in bloom by now. We can breathe fresh air and enjoy spring."

So off we went to Sokolniki.

At Red Gate we took a horse-drawn omnibus and rode past the train stations, past Red Pond and all the wooden houses with green and red iron roofs, out along the outskirts of Moscow.

On the way, Levitan continued the interrupted conversation. "What do you think?" he asked. "Take me, now. You see, I too have no ideology whatsoever. May I or may I not be an artist?"

"Impossible," the student replied. "A man cannot exist without ideology."

"What a crocodile you are," Levitan said to the student. "What am I supposed to do now? Give up painting?"

"Yes, give it up."

Anton Pavlovich entered the conversation with a laugh. "How can he give up painting? No! Isaak's a sly one. He won't give it up. After all, he's got a medal around his neck. Now he's on his way to a Stanislaus, and a Stanislaus isn't that easy to come by. That's what they say: I've got a Stanislaus, so don't punch me in the nose."

We laughed. The students were angry.

"What sort of ideology is it if I feel like painting pine trees in the sun or a spring landscape?"

"Allow me, but your pine tree is a product, see? A building product, you see? Timber belongs to the people. It's something nature creates for the people—you see?" The student was wrought up. "For the people!"

"But it makes me sick to see a tree being chopped down. Trees are every bit as alive as we are, and birds sing in them. They— those birds—are better than we are. When I paint, I don't think of trees as timber. I can't think that. You really are a crocodile!" said Levitan.

"And why are singing birds better than us, pray tell?" asked the student indignantly.

"Yes, this offends me too," said Anton Pavlovich. "Isaak, you must prove why."

"Be so kind as to prove why," insisted the student seriously, looking at Levitan with his piercing eyes and with an air of extreme importance.

Anton Pavlovich laughed.

"This is all so stupid," snapped Levitan.

"We'll be at Sokolniki soon. We're getting close."

A lower class woman who was sitting next to Levitan held out a red Easter egg to him, saying, "You're a handsome boy. [Levitan was very handsome.] Eat this egg. My father died forty days ago. Pray for him."

Levitan and Chekhov burst out laughing. Levitan took the egg and asked what her father's name was so he would know for whom to pray.

"Are you a priest, son? Is that what you are?"

The woman had had a few too many. "They are students, that's what they are. What a bunch. A book under their arm and that's all they own. I declare . . ."

We arrived at Sokolniki Circle.

Getting out of the omnibus, the woman who was sitting next to us turned to Levitan and said in farewell: "Pray for my father. His name was Nikita Nikitich. And when you graduate from the seminary, you will have beautiful hair. Come to Pechatniki. Everybody knows Anfisa Nikitishna. I'll give you a good meal. Even though you're scholars, you don't seem to get much to eat."

Anton Pavlovich laughed. The students were serious; they seemed depressed. It was as if Old Woman Woe were trailing at their heels. They were full of obsessive ideas. Something heavy and contrived was weighing down on them like some compulsory duty that had fettered their youth. They lacked simplicity and the ability to yield simply to life's moments. And that spring was so beautiful! Yet when Levitan referred to the beauty of the forest —"Look, how beautiful"—one of the students responded, "Nothing special. Nothing exciting. A forest, so what? What's so beautiful about it?"

"What would you know about it, you dodo!" Levitan replied.

We walked along a path.

The forest was mysteriously beautiful. Highlighted by the rays of the vernal sun, the tops of the pine trees glittered with reddish sparks against the deep, dark blue sky. There was a constant whistling of thrushes and in the distance the cuckoos were mysteriously reckoning how many years each of us has left on this enigmatic earth of ours.

The students, with lap rugs around their shoulders, also became more lively and began singing:

> **Raise your glasses to the one**
> **Who wrote "What Is to Be Done." [1]**
> **Drink a toast to him and to his great ideal...**

Anton Pavlovich and Levitan walked side by side; the students were up ahead. At a distance their long hair—long hair was stylish at the time—was plainly visible against the background of the lap rugs.

"What's that flying over there?" one of them cried out, turning to Levitan.

"It's probably a falcon," answered Anton Pavlovich jokingly.

Actually it was a crow.

"I doubt that Sokolniki has any more falcons," added Chekhov. "I've never seen a falcon. [2] Oh, my fair falcon! What are you thinking of, my falcons? Falcons and falcon hunts must have been popular throughout medieval Russia."

By this time we had come to the edge of the forest. There was a path for the railroad tracks in front of us, and some tables covered with tablecloths soon came into view. A large number of people were drinking tea, their samovars steaming. We too sat down at one of the tables. Drinking tea was the thing to do at Sokolniki. The hawkers came up to us immediately.

Their trays were covered with rolls, biscuits, sturgeon fillets, and smoked sausage.

"Take your pick, good people."

A group of extremely drunk merchants—they looked as if they came from the Okhotnyi Ryad Market—had taken seats around a nearby table and were looking us over in a most unfriendly manner.

"You're students," said one of them who was very drunk, turning in our direction. "You're the ones who ... and if you dare ..." And he showed us his fist.

Another tried to convince him not to bother us.

"Don't pick on them. What do you want? Maybe they're not even students. What do you want?"

"The servant serves; the loafer loafs," said the glassy-eyed drunk in our direction.

It was clear they had no love for us. Their puzzling enmity toward us "students" was breaking through to the surface.

Anton Pavlovich took out a small notebook and quickly noted something in it.

I remember his telling me on the way back: "Spring has a kind of yearning to it. Deep yearning and anxiety. Everything is alive, but there is an incomprehensible sadness in all nature, despite her new life."

And after we had said good-bye to the students, he said to Levitan and me, smiling, "Those students will make excellent doctors. They are lovely people, and I envy them having their heads full of ideas."

2

Much time had passed since our Sokolniki walk. It was the spring of 1904, and shortly after I arrived in the Crimea, in Yalta, I went to see Anton Pavlovich Chekhov at his home in Upper Autka. When I went through the gate, what did I see in front of me, in the front yard, sticking out his neck, standing on one foot, but a live crane! When he saw me, he spread his wings and began hopping around, dancing an animated dance as if to show off all the fancy steps he could do.

I found Anton Pavlovich in his room. He was sitting by the window reading a newspaper, *New Times.*

"What a nice crane you have," I said to Anton Pavlovich. "He does such an amusing dance."

"Yes, he's a most remarkable and most kindly creature. He loves us all," said Anton Pavlovich. "You know, he flew back to us this spring. He flew off for the winter to find other, well, different climes, off to the hippopotami, but he's come back for a visit. We love him so, Masha and I. Isn't it strange and mysterious—flying away and flying back again? I don't think it's only for the frogs he's always killing here in the garden. No, he's proud, and besides he's happy to be asked to dance. He's an artist, and he loves to hear us laugh at his amusing dances. Artists like to play in different places and then they fly off. My wife, for instance, has flown away to Moscow, to the Art Theater."

Anton Pavlovich picked up from the table a piece of paper rolled into a short tube, had a fit of coughing, spit into it, and threw it into a jar filled with solution.

Everything was neat, clean, bright, and simple in Anton Pavlovich's room; it looked somewhat like a sickroom and smelled of creosote. On the table were a calendar and many photographs inserted fanlike into a special stand—portraits of actors and acquaintances. The walls were also adorned with photographs— once again portraits, but this time people like Tolstoy, Mikhailovsky,[3] Suvorin, Potapenko, Levitan, and others.

Maria Pavlovna came into the room to say that the cook had fallen ill and was in bed with a bad headache. At first Anton Pavlovich paid no attention, but then all of a sudden he stood up and said, "Oh, I'd forgotten. I'm a doctor, aren't I? Of course I am. Let me go see what is the matter with her."

And he went into the kitchen to have a look at the patient. As I followed him, I remember noticing how stooped his frame had become under the impact of the illness; he was thin and his sharply protruding shoulders bore witness to the grave ailment undermining his strength.

The kitchen was off to one side of the house. I stayed outside with the crane. He had begun to dance again and enjoyed hopping up and down so much that he spread his wings, flew up and around the garden, and landed again in front of me. "Craney, craney," I called, and he came right up to me and looked at me from the side with his penetrating eye, probably expecting a reward for his art. I offered him my empty hand. He looked at it and screamed something. What? "Cheat!" probably, or something worse. After all, I hadn't paid him for his performance.

Later I showed Anton Pavlovich some new work I had recently done in the Crimea, hoping to entertain him a bit—pictures of large ships asleep in the night. He asked me to leave them with him. "Leave them. I want to look at them again alone," he said.

Anton Pavlovich was planning to go to Moscow. I advised him

against it; he looked very ill and had a husky cough. At dinner he asked me, "Why don't you drink wine? I would if I were healthy. I do so love wine."

Everything about him bore the stamp of illness and distress.

I told him I wanted to buy a small plot of land in the Crimea and build myself a studio on it. Not in Yalta, though somewhere in the vicinity.

"Masha," he said to his sister, "how about giving him our plot? Would you like a plot in Gurzuf right by the cliffs? I lived there for two years, right by the sea. Listen, Masha, why don't I give the land to Konstantin Alexeyevich? Would you like it? The only problem is that the sea is eternally roaring there. Would you like it? There's a cottage there. I'd be happy to have you take it."

I thanked Anton Pavlovich, but I too would have been unable to live right by the sea. I can't sleep so near the sea; it gives me palpitations.

That was the last time I saw Anton Pavlovich Chekhov.

Later I did live in Gurzuf; I built myself a studio there. And from my window I could see the cottage by the cliff where Anton Pavlovich had once lived. I often painted that scene: roses . . . and Anton Pavlovich's cottage standing out cozily against the seascape. It conveyed the mood of a far-off land, and the sea roared near the poor little cottage where the soul of a great writer had dwelt, a man who had been poorly understood in his time.

More than once Anton Pavlovich had said to me, "Women don't like me, you know. Everyone thinks I'm a scoffer, a comic writer, but they're wrong. . . ."

translated by Tatiana Kusubova

Notes

1. I.e. Nikolai Chernyshevsky, the radical critic and novelist of the 1860's, framed and sent to Siberia by the tsarist government.

2. The name of Sokolniki Park is derived from the Russian word for "falcon." Chekhov quotes several traditional formulas associated with falcons in Russian folktales and folksongs.

3. Probably the minor novelist Nikolai Garin-Mikhailovsky, with whom Chekhov was friendly at the end of his life, rather than the famous and powerful Populist critic of that name who repeatedly tried to discredit Chekhov with liberal readers and to wreck his literary career.

Mozart:
theme and variations
VLADIMIR MARKOV

If only there could be found a spot here, where men had ears, a heart to feel, and at least a little understanding of music.

—*from* Mozart's letters

Two hundred years ago. The twenty-seventh of January, eight o'clock in the evening. Probably never among the "earth-born" (Tyutchev) has there been someone so uncommon.

Sequences of thirds were picked out on the harpsichord at the age of three; he composed his first minuet at five; as an eight-year-old—his first symphony; his first opera was written in his twelfth year. Europe was charmed by the child virtuoso, empresses kissed him on his chubby cheeks, learned Englishmen conducted scientific research on him. Then things got difficult, and they grew ever more difficult. Just when he ceased being a child prodigy and began to create true miracles. There were, of course, grand (if short-lived) successes: *The Marriage of Figaro,*[1] the concertos for Vienna. A handful of connoisseurs always knew his worth. But, as his merry hero sings: *"Molto onor, poco contante."* And not

441

always was there even much honor. It seemed that fate and men conspired to strike him down again and again. Metaphorical blows there were a-plenty; one was literal, when Count Arco kicked his behind down some stairs. Nor was this proud man and lover of the good life made for humiliation and poverty. Over a year before the end, he had come to wait for death. He died a beggar, in debt, a spiritual wreck, all his strength expended—feverishly, hurriedly finishing the composing of what he still could. He was buried in a common grave for paupers. No one has yet been able to find this grave.

Soon after his death, he became really famous. True, for his first love, Aloysia, Mozart remained merely "a nice little fellow." But his wife, Aloysia's sister, soon realized that Mozart was a great man (incidentally, she was a sweet but limited creature, who in her own way loved Mozart very much). She squandered his manuscripts, destroyed a great many letters, and crossed out lines in others: the nineteenth century was just beginning and had its own conception of morality and its own opinion about the relationship of that morality to greatness.

The nineteenth century revered Mozart. Whether it understood him is another question. He and Raphael were always referred to as the summit of perfection (only in our time has a different painter been found whose name goes incomparably better with Mozart's—Watteau). Schumann called Mendelssohn the Mozart of the nineteenth century (the way Ostrovsky is dubbed the Russian Molière). Not that the century really knew Mozart well: only an insignificant portion of his works were performed, the "unquestionably great" works—that is, three of the forty symphonies, one or two of the more than twenty remarkable concertos for pianoforte. His operas were staged at times in an altogether outrageous manner: at the beginning of the century *The Magic Flute* was performed in Paris with music from various works, not only by Mozart, but by Haydn too. Tamino sang the Queen of the Night's first aria, and the Queen herself, on the other hand, sang Donna Anna's vengeance aria from *Don Giovanni.* Finally a shepherd (where did he come from?) and a totally unidentifiable

Mona sang a duet (!) to the music of Don Giovanni's "champagne" aria. In time this sort of thing came to an end, as a growing academic conscientiousness took over. They even began to attach the real finale to *Don Giovanni*—with no letup, it's true, in the complaining and lamenting that it "lowered the dramatic quality." The "amoral" and "preposterous" *Così fan tutte* was barred from the stage. In short: there was no love for Mozart. And all through the nineteenth century there could be heard the strumming of thousands of poor little girls, whose feet did not reach the pedals, and who with no enthusiasm banged out the Sonata K. 545, secretly hating this Mozart, since at the mention of his name their music teachers invariably produced some sound resembling an exclamation point and an expression of sedate, stupid rapture.

There's no point in painting the picture too black. Many great composers were drawn to Mozart, among them such opposites as Chopin and Brahms, Wagner and Tchaikovsky, Rossini and Richard Strauss. And not only composers: Stendhal, Balzac, Ingres, Delacroix. Goethe understood Mozart, the way he understood everything; it was he who said that only Mozart could compose the music for his *Faust*. Let us not forget that Pushkin's tragedy and the story by Eduard Mörike were written in the nineteenth century.

An unexpected discovery of Mozart is occurring in our time. A shift is taking place within the Bach-Mozart-Beethoven triad. The nineteenth century put Beethoven in first place; at the beginning of the twentieth century there was a tendency to reserve this place for Bach; and now Mozart is mentioned more and more as number one. But the triad itself is "eternal"; one can hardly speak seriously about a fourth candidate for this company. Perhaps it is still too early to analyze the meaning of the shift. Although it *is* possible to assert that if you are searching for man in music, then your composer is Beethoven; if music for you is a means of communion with God, you will hardly bypass Bach; but if you want music from music, then the name Mozart acquires for you a special significance.

This authentic musicality was our first and most important discovery in Mozart. We are speaking here, of course, not about "art for art's sake," not about mathematics, not about abstraction, but about limits correctly divined. Musical meaning does not coincide with a "résumé of content," whether of plots (in opera), or of "ideology" (in symphonies). From the point of view of "content," *Così fan tutte* is an absurd anecdote, *The Magic Flute* a hodgepodge. But as soon as their music reaches you . . . The musical meaning of Mozart is harbored not only in the change of keys and their selection, the type of modulations and so on, but in peculiar "nooks," which more often than not do not coincide with the main incidents of the plot. An example might be the Count asking the Countess' forgiveness in *The Marriage of Figaro,* or Fiordiligi's part in the farewell quartet. These "nooks" are especially numerous in Donna Anna's role.

The second thing that we discovered in Mozart is his true humanity. This does not contradict the fact that we linked the human with Beethoven. In Beethoven, man is a rebel and is alone, the favored hero of the Faustian age, Man with a capital M, the master of nature, which has a "proud sound," and so forth. In Mozart there is everything valuable that has been accumulated by the human community, man in his modest and disciplined communication with his own kind—of which life has actually consisted (not "ought to consist") from time immemorial. From this point of view there is no music more humane and more human. A French traveler through the jungles of the Amazon played for the most savage people on earth records of boogie-woogie and military marches, and did not make the slightest impression on them. A Mozart symphony "did not cover their faces with a mask of fear . . . it revealed the inmost recesses of their hearts." We needed two hundred years to figure out Mozart. In spite of the established conception of the unclouded Olympian quality of Mozart, in our time drama was discovered in him (how could it have been missed earlier?). In this, our opinion coincided with that of his contemporaries, who considered his music passionate and melancholy. When the shadows were found, the light also began to sparkle in a new way. Here is one of the explanations of our gravitation toward Mozart, a gravitation toward the opposite: our horror has patches of light, his light has dark "nooks." Verbal labels reveal little, and in the majority of cases one cannot even say whether he is joyful or sad: at times the one and the other are in inseparable conjunction. At any rate, the common misunderstanding—that Mozart is typical rococo—has come to an end. Goethe's words about Mozart's "demonic spirit" no longer sound like a paradox.

Even in high school one learns that it is more difficult to depict the "positive characters" than the "negative characters" (of course it is the "positive" Chatsky that is mentioned). God knows how much Soviet critics have written about the "problem of the positive hero," but the problem is still there—and not only because they were talking through their hats. Mozart solves the problem with the greatest of ease, both on the everyday level (the finale of *The Marriage of Figaro,* with its triumph of decency), and on the more elevated (*The Magic Flute*). In the latter, with a stunning escape from stereotype, good is entrusted to the villain's voice, the bass; and evil, to the coloratura soprano—which makes everything sparkle with new colors. It is interesting that up close even Mozart's religious beliefs turn out to be deeper than those of the romantics: they pondered faith, he had faith. These religious beliefs are unconscious, but profound and firm (just like Pushkin's), and all his work is an unending paean to the Creator. It is enough to listen carefully to the orchestral introductions to almost all his concertos: there is pure joy in them. Joy, precisely, and not gaiety; the joy of the acceptance of life. Now Beethoven's *Freude,* as we all know, is not joy at all, but the pseudonym of *Freiheit,* which has brought precious little joy to the world.

Attentive listening also reveals in Mozart a great novelty of musical language, surprises at every turn. Not for nothing did his contemporaries consider him a "modernist." Critics of those days called Mozart a "musical Daedalus," constructing "labyrinths without entrances," saw in him "an inclination toward the unusual," found that he "goes too far" and that he "leads the listener between overhanging cliffs into a prickly forest where flowers are found only rarely." They often lamented that Mozart's music was oversaturated (as if he were Richard Strauss), and Emperor Joseph II complained that in *The Marriage of Figaro* Mozart drowns out the singers with his orchestra (as if he were Wagner). A feeling of modernity is not lost even to our ears. It's not even a question of dissonances and chromaticism. Try listening to the finale of the "Jupiter" without thinking about fugue, or about development—listening to pure sound: in places it is pure Hindemith. And the minuet from the G-minor Symphony that everyone knows: as on the canvases of Picasso, behind the first minuet there appears a second, one of a "different color" (hysterical, piercing), one that does not coincide with the outlines of the first.

The growth of interest in Mozart, and especially the flooding of the market with diverse records, has also revealed a generic variety that is comparable with no one else's. In this respect, how monotonous in comparison with him are the public's favorites— Verdi, Chopin, Tchaikovsky. Even a great lover of Mozart, who knows his *Don Giovanni* down to its last Italian comma, can for years on end discover in Mozart's boundless *oeuvre* masterpieces that were previously unknown to him: now a pianoforte quartet, now a concert aria, now a motet, now a German dance.

Finally, one more interesting fact is being discovered: rarely is there anything in the music that has come after Mozart which is not already there *in* Mozart. In the overture to *The Magic Flute,* specialists find the whole history of music from Bach to Debussy. But one need not be a specialist to discern Chopin, Schumann, and others in individual passages. All of Beethoven may be found, even the Beethoven of the last quartets. Mozart's admirers may rightfully insist that other music (both before and after) need not even have existed.

Many fine books about Mozart have appeared in our time. Their value lies not only in biographical research or analysis of his works. Their authors more (Blom, Einstein) or less (Sitwell, Ghéon) professionally attempt to transmit a general impression of Mozart's music, but mainly they attempt to pay mankind's overdue debt and to make him a declaration of love. But not one book succeeds in re-creating a living image of Mozart the man. This image must be sought on the pages of the few memoirs and, still better, in his remarkable letters. These letters deserve a place among the major works of literature. In them there are keen portraits, word-play that approaches metalogical language (*zaum'*), a plentiful supply of that laughter we know from *Così fan tutte* and the horn concertos. Like Pushkin in his poetic epistles, Mozart transforms himself depending on who his addressee is: deferential with his father (*"Mon très cher Père"*); indecent and "futuristic" in letters to his Augsburg lady cousin; playing the blissful, silly fool in letters to his wife, letters full of that charming banality without which there is no mutual connubial happiness. As a true artist he views the world straight on, distinctly, and he expresses it without moralizing, with a Hemingway-like laconicism: "I saw them hanging four lads in the cathedral square. They do it here the way they do it in Lyon." As a true artist, he is not inclined to exaggerate the significance of this world: "I didn't go to look at the hot-air balloon. First of all, I can picture very well to myself what it is." And besides, as a true artist, he takes note of the eternal and so very contemporary situation: "No one any longer knows or values moderation and truth. In order to achieve success, you either have to write so simply that any cabby can whistle the melody, or else so incomprehensibly that it is liked precisely because any other rational being cannot possibly understand it."

It is interesting that Mozart was not an intellectual, in contrast to many of his colleagues (both then and later). One could count on the fingers of one's hands the number of books he read. On the other hand, he liked to dance, to dress up, to possess fine things. He loved to play billiards, to drink grog. Despite a life that turned out unhappily and absurdly, any chip on the shoulder (so familiar to us) is absent. He is simply and healthily sure of his genius, without Beethoven's aggressiveness ("Prince Kaunitz told the Archbishop that people like me are born only once every hundred years").

Faith in himself, faith in God, a wonderful family. He could have repeated after Goethe: "Vom Vater hab' ich die Statur. . . . Vom Mütterchen die froh' Natur." * Everything started out so well: they loved and respected each other, a great success, firm founda-

* "From my father I have my stature . . . from my mother my cheerful nature." EDITOR.

tions. But the whole family was fated to take the same inscrutable path to misfortune, just as was Wolfgang. And so his sister Nannerl dies a lonely, paralyzed old woman; Leopold ends his life in disillusionment, conscious that not one of his hopes had been realized; his mother dies in muddy Paris, like a displaced person in an alien, incomprehensible environment, not wishing to call in a French doctor.

It is difficult not to mention the works themselves. But how is one to write about music? "After the cadenza the second theme returns," or "This awakens such and such images in the soul"? The first is not enough, the second doesn't apply. For this reason you cannot meaningfully speak in words about his most perfect works, the pianoforte concertos (from the ninth to the twenty-seventh, one better than the other). It is easier to say something about his operas, with their Shakespearean mixture of tragedy and buffoonery (but more successful than in the Bard of Avon). It is precisely in his operas that we find his most elevated pages (thus *The Magic Flute* stands on a par with *Fidelio*) and those most full of frivolity (thus *The Marriage of Figaro* anticipates *Der Rosenkavalier*). And those separate "nooks"! How many there are in *Don Giovanni,* the most enigmatic opera in the world, which has been called "the eighth wonder of the world," "the Hamlet of opera," and "the perfect opera." One of the first to discover these "nooks" was E. T. A. Hoffmann, and the end of these discoveries is not in sight. And in that same *Magic Flute* who can forget the meeting of the heroes after the trials, the jagged rhythm of the mad Pamina's phrases, the musical train of the gown of the Queen of the Night, and the transition from Darkness to Light just before the finale? This opera is an encyclopedia of music, from Papageno's little ditty to the mystical duet of the Men in Armor and the echo of Bach (*O ew'ge Nacht*).

One cannot formulate a general impression of Mozart. He escapes definitions, and probably always will. His very simplicity is deceptive. His contemporaries considered him complex. The musicologist Eric Blom says that anyone can compose several measures

448

of a Mozart-like melody, but let him try to develop it. And indeed, compare the "Lacrimosas" in the *Requiems* of Verdi and Mozart. The first begins more beautifully, melodically more substantially, and more opulently, but after several measures, Verdi no longer knows what to do with the melody; it is precisely in the development that Mozart shows what he is capable of. In general, his simplicity often only accompanies the complexity (again, as in Pushkin). He writes about his concertos: "Here and there are spots which afford pleasure only to the connoisseurs, but even a nonconnoisseur will be pleased without knowing why."

Mozart wrote subtle quartets and pretty little waltzes for dancing parties in an equally beautiful way; for a church organ, and for a mechanical clock or something called a glass harmonica. He once wrote for an orchestra consisting of two flutes, five trumpets, and four drums. The most interesting thing is that what we call "hack work" never resulted; it is all first-rate music. He would write to order, would follow the fashion, would not express his heart (his most radiant works were written in the most difficult times), would borrow from himself and from others, would entertain—the one thing he did not do, it appears, was to write "for eternity."

One can say that Beethoven's music is music of birth and of conception (this is especially clear at the beginning of the Seventh and Ninth symphonies), and that Schubert's music is music of pure motion (most evident in his C-Major Symphony). What about Mozart's music? "Flawless" is a word that conveys nothing. It would be incorrect to speak of "perfection." One can speak of an "aristocratic quality," "purity," and so on, and be immediately refuted. The critic Turner calls him an "enigma," and the pianist Schnabel, "the most inaccessible of the great masters." He's considered a classicist, but he's also called a romantic (Graf). For many, Mozart is full of light; others insist that at the core of his music there is death (Ghéon).

His death mask was not preserved (Constanze said: "Thank God, that hideous thing got broken," and she swept up the pieces).

His portraits, like his works, do not resemble each other. No one knows where he is buried, and no one knows how he played the cadenzas in his concertos. Nor does anyone really know in general how to play him. In the well-known G-Minor Symphony, if tragedy is emphasized, things go wrong; if it is not emphasized, things are wrong again. The *Requiem* is to be explained neither by tradition, nor by Catholicism, nor by theatricality, nor by Romanesque architecture. Nor by the fact that the degree of Mozart's authorship is undetermined. Nor can it be explained by freemasonry: when the mezzo-soprano begins *Judex ergo cum sedebit*—what does it have to do with freemasonry? It's simply chills up and down the spine.

One thing is clear: despite all obstacles, mankind has stumbled upon Mozart and now will not let go, no matter how fashions may change. All we can do is to delve deeper into what has been found, to unearth the riches. In the same way they will some day stumble upon Pushkin. The Russians have him; beyond the borders of Russia almost no one knows him. With Mozart it is the reverse: Europe and America have found him, Russia still has not.

> *He and Mozart adore Moscow.*
> *—Mandelstam*

First variation

Any informed person could easily write an extensive dissertation and prove with unassailable facts that in Russia Mozart was loved, valued, understood, and often performed. Didn't Glinka say about *The Magic Flute:* "I never have enough of it"? Peter Tchaikovsky wanted a monument to Mozart placed on every street corner. His brother Modest was the originator of the phrase "words sweeter than the sounds of Mozart," which found its way into a line of Blok's. It's worth listening to Nezhdanova singing the second aria of the Queen of the Night: she not only brilliantly manages the vocal acrobatics, but she may be the only one to convey what is snaky-scaly-evil in this role. Finally, as a curio, it can be noted that in 1842, in *The Muscovite,* Mozart was called a "Bohemian Slav," and his operas "Germano-Slavic."

There are facts still more significant. A member of the "Green Lamp" and a Nizhny-Novgorod landowner, Alexander Oulibicheff, published in 1843 his three-volume *La nouvelle biographie de Mozart suivie d'un aperçu sur l'histoire générale de la musique et de l'analyse des principales oeuvres de Mozart* * (it came out in Russian only at the very end of the century). The book is verbose, but in places amazingly to the point. In the most difficult part, the evaluation and the analysis of the works, it has not by any means lost its importance even in the present day.[2]

Should one mention Pushkin's tragedy, with its virtuoso use of iambic pentameter without caesura? But one should also speak of Rimsky-Korsakov's opera to its text, a unique occurrence (an opera about Mozart!) in the annals of music.

No less interesting are Mozart's biographical connections with Russia. It was precisely in Prince Golitsyn's salon (*"sans doute grand mélomane et peut-être musicien"*) † that Mozart played his pianoforte concertos when he was at the height of his fame. "Big-nosed Paul" (as Mozart calls him in his letters), the future auto-crat of All Russia, was traveling at that time in Europe under the name of the Comte du Nord, and Mozart placed great hopes on his stay in Vienna: in honor of the heir to the Russian throne *The Abduction from the Seraglio* was to be given, but for some reason it was canceled and replaced by Gluck's *Alceste*. True, they say that, in the presence of this same Paul, Mozart did participate in a contest between pianists. When Mozart traveled to Berlin, he played in the Russian embassy. In Dresden he spoke with the am-bassador, Prince Beloselsky, about the possibility of a trip to Russia; and according to other sources, Andrey Razumovsky, who wished to get him for the all-powerful Prince Potyomkin, a great lover of music, carried on negotiations with him in Vienna; Mozart died, and Sarti went in his place. Apparently it was in connection with these negotiations that Mozart bought, in 1790, a *Geo-*

---

* *The New Biography of Mozart Followed by a Review of the General History of Music and an Analysis of Mozart's Principal Works.* EDITOR.
† "Undoubtedly a great music lover and perhaps a musician." EDITOR.

451

*graphisches und topographisches Reisebuch durch alle Staaten der österreichischen Monarchie nebst der Reiseroute nach Petersburg durch Polen.** Another curious fact: Nannerl's notebook, with Wolfgang's first minuets, somehow found its way into the possession of a Russian lady of the high nobility, who returned the notebook to Salzburg one hundred years after brother and sister played from it. All these are interesting and at times convincing facts. Undoubtedly one could add much more to them. And still . . .

And still one is rather uncomfortable saying, "Mozart is loved and understood in Russia." Deep down, one feels that this is not so. And almost any one of the foregoing statements needs correction.

Glinka, for instance, stubbornly disputed that Mozart's *Don Giovanni* was a great work. Tchaikovsky was in raptures over Mozart, but wasn't it only because he saw in him the ideal counterbalance to the "Moussorgskianism" he hated? In his inner musical nature there is no composer who is more a diametrical opposite of Mozart than Tchaikovsky. Tchaikovsky is convincing only psychologically, and at times he is not responsive to the logic of musical development. In his two deliberate imitations of Mozart— the "Pastorale" in *The Queen of Spades,* and the "Variations on a Rococo Theme"—if Mozart is present, then it is only the one invented by the nineteenth century, whom those piano-playing little girls so rightly hated. If Tchaikovsky understood his beloved Mozart in just the way he expressed it in these two works, we are justified in concluding that he loved not Mozart but someone else invented during "sleepless nights" (Apukhtin). Both of these compositions are imitations of little interest, imitations of some abstract *Zopfmusik.* At any rate, Tchaikovsky did not succeed in perceiving Mozart creatively (that is, in grasping for himself the underlying principle, and not simply copying the style). On the other hand, a composer who was infinitely distant from Mozart

* *Geographical and Topographical Travel Book Through All the States of the Austrian Monarchy and Also the Route to Petersburg Through Poland.*

452

in his personal make-up, Richard Wagner, took the principle of his music drama from *The Marriage of Figaro,* as he states in one of his letters.

Not a single Russian singer built a reputation on Mozart, even though Russia had its own small Wagnerian *pléiade.* Listen to how crudely and stylistically wrong Chaliapin is in his interpretation of Leporello's catalogue aria (although he has no difficulty at all with Rossini's Don Basilio). And in general Mozart was performed in Russia rather little, rather seldom, rather pedantically and as if the musicians were duty-bound.

Oulibicheff is one of those exceptions which confirm the rule. Much more influential and much more truly expressing the general Russian point of view of music, Stasov, for instance, called the overture to *The Magic Flute* "an exceedingly dry and boring balancing act, with a theme that goes over and over the same ground in a very ridiculous fashion." (Oulibicheff devotes a separate chapter to it and calls it "the crown of all instrumental music, *nunc et in saecula."*)

Recalling the fruitful activity of the Mozart Society in Paris, Pablo Casals' festival in Perpignan, the famous productions of the operas of Mozart in the little English town of Glyndebourne, the innumerable "opera workshops" of American young people, which put on even *La Finta Semplice*—one must admit that the Russians have never done, and are not doing, anything like it.

Nor has the situation changed in recent years. Mozart is almost never presented on stage. Only occasionally are his operas heard in concert performance. For *The Marriage of Figaro,* Leningrad music lovers were indebted to the visiting conductor Fritz Stiedry, without whom no one would even have thought of producing this opera. Only a small selection of the symphonies and concertos of Mozart are performed, and, more often than not, uninterestingly. It is hardly by chance that the most widely known piece of Mozart's in Russia now is the little lullaby "Schlafe, mein Prinzchen, schlaf' ein," which wasn't even composed by Mozart but by the little-known and forgotten composer Bernhard Flies. Is it worth adding that in the *Great Soviet Encyclopedia* Mozart is allotted a pitiful four columns between "Mokhoobraznye" (Bryopsida) and "Mocha" (urine)? The article is not crude, but faceless. Along the way, of course, we learn that the Archbishop of Salzburg "slighted his musicians in a rude way, and treated them like serfs," and that in opera bouffe Mozart "was attracted by the . . . folk-like and song-like quality of the musical language." Finally, the prominent Russian musicologist of recent times Asafiev (Igor Glebov) admits that Mozart has not been fortunate in Russia. Of course one can always refer to the teachers of music, the conservatory professors, and even the nonmusicians who sincerely love and even understand Mozart, but all this is too sparse to make much of a difference. The ordinary musical Russian John Doe does not love Mozart, and what is worse has a false impression of him. Alas, too often for him Mozart is material for piano exercises, whose tra-la-la does not touch his heart. At best, he is unsure of Mozart, the way he is unsure of where to put the stress in his name. But you cannot ignore John Doe. After all, it is precisely he who is beginning to make Mozart popular in Europe and America. But not in Russia. Of course the approaching two-hundredth anniversary of his birth will stir up a certain commotion in Soviet musical circles. An issue of the journal *Soviet Music* will be devoted to Mozart, an article will appear in *Pravda,* about how only in the U.S.S.R., etc., etc. But then everyone is familiar with the true character of such campaigns.

What is the source of our Russian lack of attention and lack of understanding? That same Asafiev begins his well-known work about Tchaikovsky with the words: "The world perceived by the great Mozart is radiant, radiant and joyful is his music, fleeting is the grief that it evokes"—as if he had never listened to, say, *Don Giovanni* (to say nothing about many other things). In Russian music, grief was always painted with such heavy strokes that Mozart's restrained grief appears "fleeting." But it is not only because Russians are accustomed to excessive emotional coloring that they are hindered in their approach to Mozart. The flowering of Russian music in the nineteenth century coincided with the idealization of the "folk." [3] "Folk" music was used not as one of the components, but was used rather as the foundation. Opera and the symphony are the result of a complex evolution on a higher level, and are in no way linked with folklore, or they include it only occasionally. Russian composers filled both these genres with folklore material, which by its very nature is not susceptible to musical development and is able to exist only in a static form. The symphony, for example, is the purest product of musical thought; it is unthinkable without a musical idea. The very best Russian symphonist was Tchaikovsky. He left behind deeply sincere compositions, often well constructed, full of beauty (and in the Sixth Symphony, emotional depth). But spiritually they are all naive.

Pure "feeling" and an eclectic "folk spirit" ruined the higher musical genres, deprived them of musical substance. Unfortunately for Russian music, at the time when it was flourishing, Russian philosophical thought was only awakening or, in any case, had little influence on the society. Russian composers followed the then fashionable spiritually negligible "social" ideals. The musical leaders (Stasov) were aesthetically helpless, and were crude realists. Under the circumstances, only one path remained—history, the epic; [4] by itself it led nowhere, it failed to compensate for the lack of spirituality, and let loose an uncontrollable flood of pseudo-folksy clowns and buffoons.* The spiritual renaissance unfolded later, and for music it was already too late. True, Moussorgsky in *Khovanshchina* divined Russian spirituality. Rimsky-Korsakov also came close to it in his *Legend of the City of Kitezh*, even though the task was beyond him.

Was not this whole complex an obstacle on the path to Mozart?

But perhaps one has to insist, the way Russian thinkers like to do, that Mozart is yet to be in Russia. Just as everything that has never been in Russia before is yet to be. There are reasons for such optimism, and the first of them is that the Russians have Pushkin. Pushkin's lifelong interest in Mozart is not accidental. Mozart's name makes its first appearance in his lyceum verse:

* E.g., Skula and Eroshka in *Prince Igor,* Duda and Sopel in *Sadko,* Varlaam and Misail in *Boris Godunov.*

> ... Or on the resonant piano
> At your dextrous hands
> Mozart is brought to life.
> ("To My Sister," 1814)

And later, in his tragedy, Pushkin, through Salieri, provides a most precise evaluation of the music of Mozart:

> What depth.
> What audacity and what just proportion!

(Let us note the sequence in which these qualities are placed.) Nor let us forget the epigraph to "The Stone Guest."

Much more important is the general similarity between Mozart's character and Pushkin's. One can enumerate endlessly the qualities of Pushkin's muse that are kindred to Mozart's: universality, sense of measure, and so forth. Pushkin lived in the eighteenth century for only half a year, but this half year turns out to have been decisive. "Byronism" and "nationality" do not change the picture: they are a tribute to the times. This is why Pushkin, despite forced proofs to the contrary, establishes neither a tradition nor a school; rather, he contains within himself everything that came before and will come after. Exactly like Mozart. The fact that Pushkin wrote "Czar Saltan" does not make him "national," but *also* makes him national. Likewise Mozart just incidentally created German opera. Generally, the universality of Pushkin is not a Russian characteristic; it is the basic quality of men of eighteenth-century culture, and Dostoevsky, in his Pushkin speech, was mistaken.

In Pushkin's verse there are the same "nooks," the specks that are decisive, just as in Mozart. Such are "indifferent nature" and "empty heavens." With the same aristocratic elegance, Pushkin expressed truths that seemed to be known to all, self-evident, but in essentials he is just as enigmatic as Mozart. The writer Ghéon finds in Mozart "joyful sorrow" (*cf.* Pushkin's "my sorrow is radiant"). As noted above, Pushkin and Mozart resemble each other in the character of their religious beliefs. And is not Pushkin's "rabble" the *gemeine Pöbel* of *The Magic Flute?* By the way, speaking of the rabble, both of them suffered from the condescending patronage of their crowned masters, who considered themselves connoisseurs. Both of them were better subjects than those others were masters. The biographical parallels can be extended. The most interesting of them: both were drawn to death in the last year of their lives. Even in their habits and characters, they had something in common: both liked to gesticulate and to play the fool.

But Pushkin is not the only token of the future acceptance of Mozart by the Russians. In his inner musical nature, Glinka is closer than any other Russian composer to the author of the *Don Giovanni* whose worth he did not appreciate. The "national" tendency here too mixed up all the cards, pushing Glinka externally, "ideologically" along the path common to his epoch. . . . Similarly Pushkin did not appreciate Racine, who was in his blood, but was fascinated with the infinitely distant Byron (and Glinka, with Berlioz). The Stasov school contributed to the perversion of Glinka's image, and in the general chorus that is still heard today there was drowned the just observation by the critic Laroche that Glinka had an "impeccably graceful, crystal-clear style that made him the Russian Mozart." One can find that same humanity in Glinka, the same universality, and even the same "nooks" as in Mozart. But in comparing them it is better to begin with the art songs or the instrumental chamber music, and not with the *Kamarinskaya*. In the art songs, by the way, the polarity between Glinka and Tchaikovsky is immediately revealed. Although both have an inclination to a personal "vulnerability," Glinka always knows when to stop; he instinctively subjects his emotions (qualitatively similar to Tchaikovsky's) to music.

If one attempts to express in one word what unites Pushkin and Glinka with Mozart, there comes to mind the hackneyed word "classicism"—the classicism of artistic nature, and not of school or movement; inner rather than formal.

Second variation

The word "classicism" has been brought up. The volumes analyzing this term cannot be counted. If we choose the path of meticulous scholarly selection, we shall end up with dozens of varied and contradictory classicisms and neoclassicisms. T. E. Hulme speaks of this, asserting that it is dangerous to oppose classicism and romanticism to each other: there are five or six kinds of antitheses involved. Keeping this danger in mind, one can still attempt to isolate several traits which usually differentiate the classics from the romantics.

For the romantic, creative "vulcanism" is characteristic—the lava of his "soul" processed only minimally; selectivity is found only rarely. With the classicist, on the other hand, the architectural element is dominant, the work is constructed, and is not an outpouring. Racine wrote his tragedies in prose, and only later did he rework this prose into verse [5] (for which Khodasevich would have immediately disqualified him).

Another typical trait of a romantic is that he is at odds with tradition, often rejects it, or openly rebels. This quality has especially degenerated in our time, when revolutionism has become a mass-production item. In the past, romantic rebellion still contained some elements of Fronde, but nowadays its extreme plebeian nature is evident to everyone. Such a plebeian quality, by the way, often accompanies negation. A classicist, on the contrary, furnishes an example of freedom of movement within limits set by tradition. In Anatole France's fine phrase, he "carries his chains as if they were garlands of flowers." Aristocratic qualities are inherent in a classicist.

The romantic strives to step beyond the limits of his art and this world. His aim is *Aufschwung,* and if possible a breakthrough into the beyond. Ideally, he is always transcendental. The classicist knows exactly where to stop.

Romanticism is very often combined with an escape from its

surroundings, and with an extreme individualism. This escapism can be expressed in different ways. At times its tendency is toward populism—a pastoral, Karataev-like tendency toward a fusion with the folk and, through them, with nature. (It is indicative that Mozart was not interested in folk music at all.) At times the romantic flees into the past, historical or mythical. And lastly, after Ludwig Tieck, it became fashionable to escape into art. In this instance, a romantic often appears in the toga of neoclassicism (such was Stefan George). A classicist is part of human society. He is social, and as a rule has good manners. Let us recall the famous incident when Goethe moved aside with a bow and gave way to the emperor's retinue, while Beethoven, without being deflected, barged right through a crowd of dukes. Beethoven was a true romantic, and the paradox of his last years, when he embraced mankind in his Ninth Symphony and reached the limits of loneliness in his quartets, is not accidental. A similar picture is presented by the contrast between the sociable Pushkin and the socially unbearable Lermontov.

Of course all these traits determine nothing, and they cannot be used as a yardstick or as litmus paper. This is only an attempt to establish the most general tendencies, which are far from being binding. Classicists can have a romantic profile (Brahms), and, vice versa (Alfred de Vigny). Besides, many traits that are usually associated, say, with romanticism are not its monopoly. One should not, for instance, classify as romanticism everything that is dramatic and emotional by nature (and this is usually done). Such an individual-quality as melancholy, or reverie, is for some reason always perceived as romantic. An inclination toward the unusual is also not always a sign of romanticism, and nowadays more than one critic classifies Shakespeare with the classicists (had Voltaire but known!), which is quite convincing. On the other hand, such a "classical" trait as economy of artistic means can be found in romantics (Schumann, the late Lermontov), although it "becomes" a classicist incomparably better. Of course it is typical of Mozart that he considered the monologue of the Ghost of Hamlet's Father much too long, and in response to the emperor he proudly retorted that in *The Abduction from the Seraglio* there are exactly as many notes as are necessary. At times everything exchanges places: Pushkin the classicist is interested in the "folksy," and Khodasevich, a romantic in classicist's clothing, was ready to bite heads off in the defense of tradition (although he failed to see the pure Racinian beauty of Griboyedov). So, however one may try, loose ends will remain, and it is impossible to find a pattern that fits everyone.

Of greater importance are the echoings between the great geniuses of classicism. At one time classicist aesthetics asserted that in imitating the ancients one imitates nature. Nature here, of course, is not romantic. But even if this assertion were sophistry or pure absurdity, the method established by it is the only correct one. Only thus is art preserved through the centuries—from Sophocles through Racine to our time, like an unbroken chain stretching through the ages, but not always visible. This is why some of the apparently casual facts are so important: that one of Mozart's early operas, *Mitridate,* is based on a Racine text; that the critic Romain Rolland finds the qualities of Racine's heroines in one of Mozart's best known pianoforte sonatas. That Pushkin, in the manner of Racine, kills Boris' son offstage. All these are signs of the link passed from generation to generation or, more correctly, an eternal fellowship. Chronology, therefore, plays no role. Stendhal, like Pushkin, lived in the nineteenth century, but is rather more typical of the eighteenth. Batyushkov, a forerunner and a teacher of Pushkin, goes beyond the latter in combining classical traits with romantic ones. This is why Pushkin could not understand him at times and criticized his romantic "lily-of-the-valley" from classicist positions. And afterward came Lermontov's lineage. There was no Pushkinian tradition, although anyone could claim him.

If one forgets schools and programs entirely and, rather than analyzing, looks closely at these few classical geniuses who echo each other, then among other observations, two stand out especially.

For the romantics, usually, there exists this world and the other, an absolute one. For them art is only a means to attain the absolute. If this means for some that reason does not perform its function, it is simply discarded, and a direct contact with the other world is established: philosophical, religious, mystical—through thought, prayer, revelation. But romantics who lack the strength and daring construct a peculiar, artificial world of "art for art's sake," where the shortcomings of this world are minimized and the disturbing truths of the other world are removed. A classicist also has a third world, and it is also to some extent the world of art, but never is it art for art's sake. The tendency here is in general not a problem: this art may be for God, for men, for oneself. It is important that it stays within its limits, which are precisely known. The third world is where true artists abide—some always, others whenever they can manage to. It is not a matter of what an artist expresses or depicts (God, our world, his "soul"), but where he abides while doing this. If he does not rise above the facts and emotions of our world, the result is what we call, or must call, "realism" (Gorky, Tchaikovsky); if he crosses into the beyond, we have pure romanticism (early Blok). Classicists live in the third world, where the images of our world acquire an ideal state, and the images of the other world acquire substantiality, and both of these attain form or (what is the same thing) are filled with beauty. The limits of this third world are beautifully sensed not only by Mozart, Racine, and Pushkin, but also by Dante (recall Pushkin's praise of the plan of the *Inferno*), Milton, and Shakespeare (with a few exceptions). Byron does not have this sense, neither does Khlebnikov; Blok senses these limits poorly. Beethoven often manages to remain in this world, but at times slips into "realism" (the Sixth Symphony) or crosses the limits of this world (the Ninth Symphony). Breaking through the limits in either direction is a transgression. Mozart knew this very well and often ridiculed "depiction" in music [6] (Fiordiligi's aria "Come scoglio"), and this is the reason he didn't go to see the balloon. Nor did he make an attempt to reach into the beyond, and there is great wisdom in this, which is the reason his *divertimentos* (to the accompaniment of which the guests of the Archbishop of Salzburg rattled their knives and forks) contain more genuine music than certain acknowledged masterpieces which never disappear from concert programs.

The other observation establishes the characteristic trait of genuine classicism which is even more indisputable. In Rainer Maria Rilke's well-known poem "Archaïscher Torso Apollos" there is an enigmatic hemistich, which after a detailed description of the sculpture brings the poem to an unexpected conclusion: *"Du musst dein Leben ändern"* ("You must change your life"). Its meaning is the indispensable condition for the perception of classical art.

There are works of art that strike some chord in us. They remind us either of something we've seen before or something that happened to us in the past, or else they touch some inner nerve, or they invite us to assume vicariously the position of the hero, to experience everything that he experiences. Unfortunately this is the most widely spread but, at the same time, the falsest perception of art. This is the quality exploited by Hollywood films; in the final analysis, surrealism, the contemporary variety of romanticism, is based on it. Here belongs the music that penetrates you, that flatters you, that intoxicates you. On a lower level are gypsy songs; on a middle, Tchaikovsky and Rachmaninov; on a higher, Wagner. For the perception of such art, no special premises are needed, nor is taste needed. It either fits you or it does not; you either accept it, or you do not; you "understand" or you do not. *De gustibus non est disputandum.*

In a classicist work, there are no microbes that enter you and infect you with it. You have to approach it on your own; you must, in Rilke's words, "change your life." Phèdre and the Tonya Smirnova with whom you were in love at the age of fourteen are not one and the same. A Mozart quintet doesn't make one recall a song that one heard "at the dawn of misty youth" (Koltsov). A Poussin landscape is not affecting (perhaps only in the Pushkinian meaning of this word). With classicism one must not transplant oneself into the work, but rather forget oneself for the duration, to become different. Merezhkovsky, who wrote little about music, once let fall in this respect a just observation: "Music makes man neither good nor bad, it makes him different." If with Beethoven you suffer and rejoice, then with

Mozart you feel a communion with another, better world—this is the source of that extraordinary joy his music brings. Classicism cannot be for the masses, its demands are too great. If it is difficult to partake of it, then it is more difficult to create it. Rather, one cannot create it if one is not born a classicist. And we are all born romantics. However, we have a duty at least to school ourselves to appreciate classicism, for in its highest manifestations it is more valuable than romanticism.

But we love our romanticism, our innate laziness pushes us toward it, we are more comfortable with it. Classicism repulses us with its dryness, its "intellectuality," [7] while romanticism attracts, infatuates, and entices (you can't help recalling that "attraction" is "a kind of malady" [Griboyedov]) with "comprehensible" joy and "familiar" sadness, [8] in other words that which we classify as "emotion," as "feeling."

We have hardly touched on what is called realism. It is a contradictory term which often expresses nothing. Poetry, for instance, is more realistic than prose in the sense that in every epoch it searches for a more truthful correspondence between art and its time (to write nowadays "like Pushkin" would not be an anachronism, it would be a lie). In prose (in speaking of realism, one usually speaks of prose), the depiction of external reality is considered realism. (Although what do we know about so-called "external reality," and why is the truthful portrait of the "soul" not realism? However, it is usually called romanticism.) Close up, realism in its best examples turns out to be nothing but romanticism which some simple-minded "leading" critic of the past just couldn't figure out. Thus Gogol (long listed among the realists, contrary to common sense), the Rousseauist Tolstoy, Dostoevsky, Flaubert with his roots in "The Temptation of St. Anthony," Balzac, and Dickens turn out to be romantics. Realism generally, of whatever variety it is, cannot be opposed to romanticism (in that case it would become classicism); realism is the direct development of romanticism, along the line "depiction—reflection—expression." Only it is not the inner or the beyond, as in the pure romantics, that is depicted (photographed), but the external and the this-worldly. The frequent coincidence of romantic and realistic traits is therefore not something extraordinary, but an entirely legitimate phenomenon (Gorky). And a romantic is often a simple photographer of the "soul," that is "phenomenal" and not noumenal—which according to his title he is supposed to be. If we turn to realism in its worst examples, we shall find simply a depiction of the familiar in substitution for genuine, unique truth; it is outside art, for it is outside the idea. Such, for instance, is the painting of the *Peredvizhniki* ("Wanderers").

Contemporary mass culture, which holds us all captive, is the consequence of the romanticism that so luxuriantly blossomed forth more than a century ago and that has become so commonplace in our time. Only the genuine classicism of the masterpieces of human art can withstand it. But we have lost the ability to arrive at a true overall evaluation. In the realm of aesthetics one ought to restore order, not so much in matters of philosophy as in matters of taste. It is on the best examples that taste must be trained for a long time if this ability is to be regained. So-called good taste does exist, and about it *est disputandum*. It must be developed by listening, reading, looking, "changing one's life." And then there will appear not only the general ability to evaluate genuine masterpieces, but there will also be the possibility of creating new classicist works (and not only "neoclassicist" ones). Mozart is the best means to the achievement of this ideal.

> *Death, the true goal of our existence, the best friend of mankind. The image of it does not frighten me, but soothes and calms me.*
>
> *For me everything is cold; as cold as ice.*
>
> —*from* Mozart's letters

Third variation

The most persistent of man's dreams is the fulfillment of his wishes. The Good Fairy, Mephistopheles, even Czar Dodon: "Your first whim I shall fulfill, as if it were my own."

Should the fairy ask me into what moment of the past I should like to be invisibly transported . . . Go ahead and ask: I have a wish all prepared—to a private concert at Count Esterhazy's. Well, let's see—where is Turner's book? . . . Here it is! Let's say Friday, March 5. How can one imagine a Viennese salon of 1784 and not appear like Gogol's blacksmith Vakula? Chandeliers, lace handkerchiefs, parquet floors, wigs—all this of course. It never occurred to me that candles could be so bright. The orchestra is already finishing the introduction to the E-flat Concerto. Mozart at the keyboard, with that mixture of excitement and assurance that is familiar to performing artists, that special feeling of inner freedom. He is waiting for the beginning of his part.

But for some reason, one would like to escape this glitter, although it is precisely here-and-now that is his happiest moment, his genuine success, what men call fame. Everybody is talking about him, he is invited everywhere. But he also had a more modest, more durable happiness. Perhaps it's better to be transported to Salzburg to the little room on Hannibalplatz? To hear him and Nannerl play piano four hands. Leopold listens sternly, the Abbé Bullinger in the corner with his kind smile.

No, that's not it. Now I know for sure, Fairy, the moment I want. This is final. December 6, 1791, Tuesday. Hurry, it's quarter past four already. Not to St. Stephan's; the funeral service is over. We'll catch up with the procession on one of the streets. Heavens, what rain! There it is, a three-*gulden* hearse. The mud barely has time to run off the wheel before that spot is in the slush again. The pine coffin is jostled about, is getting soaked. Several umbrellas, turned-up collars, mufflers; perhaps not even a dozen people. Everyone is bundled up to his nose; what weather! Who's that waving his arms and telling a story? It must be the good Deiner from the Silberner Schlange on Kärtnerstrasse:

—This started a long time ago. I remember as if it were today: in November he came to the Schlange. The main room was full of Italians, raising a din. . . . These Italians (Deiner looked cautiously at the gentleman in the green camisole and lowered his

465

voice), he was fed up with these Italians. He asked that he be taken to a room to be alone. . . . They wanted to give him beer right away. He said he didn't want any. Give me wine. They bring him wine. He doesn't drink the wine. Then our waiter comes running to me, says: Mozart's in a private room, asks for wine, doesn't drink it. I went in, and I see: he's sitting, his wig disheveled, pale. In that room there are trees all over the wall. And he's looking at those trees, and doesn't seem to see them. *Grüssgott,* I say. He answers: *Grüssgott.* I'm not feeling well, he says, And then: have my wine, Joseph, he says. He always called me "Don Primus" for a joke, but now—Joseph. I say to him: You drank too much in Bohemia, Maestro, and now you've gone and ruined your stomach. And he says: My stomach is better than you think. I, says he, have learned to swallow much worse. There's something cold coming over me, he says. The music will soon be over. He makes me drink his wine. Then, he says: Come to our place in the morning, we have no firewood. I come the next morning, and he's already taken to his bed. Nothing today, Joseph, he says. Today, he says, we have to do with doctors and apothecaries.

Who else is out in all this dampness? His brother-in-law Lange —open face, kind eyes. It was he who painted Mozart's portrait. Another brother-in-law, Hofer. Kapellmeister Roser, musicians, the singers from *The Magic Flute* that is filling the theater to capacity every night. And there goes Süssmayr, Mozart's devoted student. Mozart taught him, one pauper the other, without pay. Until the last moment, Süssmayr was sitting on his parti-colored quilt, and he listened to how the *Requiem* was to be finished. I hear his thoughts: I'll have to finish the "Hosanna" all by myself . . . and I remember the accompanying figures in the "Agnus Dei" well, but the chorus melody he never sang very clearly. . . . In general, in certain places, I'll have to use the earlier material: toward the end, for instance. On the other hand, what he said about the "Lacrimosa" I remember to the last detail.

And again the voice of the chatterbox Deiner:

—Sophie Haibel, his sister-in-law, said: before he died, he was annoyed by the canary, but he didn't let them take it away. Then suddenly he says: I have the taste of death on my tongue. That's what he said: on his tongue. And just before he died, he puffed out his cheeks as if for a trumpet: he kept thinking about his *Requiem.* Constanze couldn't stand this *Requiem,* once she even hid it. Yes. . . . When he was dying, outside there was a horrible storm, worse than now. He died sometime after midnight. I was the one who wrapped him in his death shroud. It's supposed to be a black one for them, the Masons. . . .

Why didn't it occur to me earlier that the man in the green camisole was Salieri? There's no doubt—Antonio Salieri. Let me take a look at his face: big watery eyes, large hooked nose, a contemptuous mouth. After Pushkin I imagined him different. Why did you come to his funeral, Salieri? You never stopped plotting against him, not only in Vienna but even in Prague. Oh, yes, you did stop intriguing after your so-called voluntary retirement. Proud man! You did not want to be dismissed by the new emperor and hastened to forestall him. You have changed completely since then: Remember, at the premiere of the *Flute,* to which Mozart invited you, you kept whispering "Bravo" to him after every number. Only there's this stupid rumor about poisoning which this idiot Constanze Mozart started. When Schwanenberg brought this gossip to you, you flared up and said: "Fools! How did he earn the honor?" Still this rumor keeps bothering you. That's why you came to the funeral—in this weather. So you'd be seen.

I'm putting you in my private hell, Salieri, together with the Duchesse de Chabot who made Mozart wait for two hours in a cold room, together with the Count Arco, who threw him out. The Emperor Joseph II is also there (what salary did you pay him, Your Majesty? Your favorite composer was Salieri, by the way). And of course Hieronymus Colloredo, the Archbishop of Salzburg, is also there. Oh, not only the acquaintances of Mozart are in this hell. There, for instance, is Benckendorff, with his august sovereign, Nicholas I.

Salieri went up to the tall gentleman who was walking along

under an umbrella all by himself: "It is a great loss for music, for all of us, Herr Baron, isn't it? However, had he lived any longer, all we composers would soon be without a roof over our heads."

Baron van Swieten, the imperial librarian and a music lover ... He was the only one to subsidize Mozart's concert when no one else wanted to listen to him any more. This man is a riddle to me. After all, he loved Mozart's music. Mozart directed his house concerts right up to the end. It was for him that he completed the unnecessary reorchestration of Handel's oratorios, for which posterity so reproached Mozart. And for all this, Mozart got not a *kreutzer*. But wasn't the baron aware of his circumstances? What is he thinking about now? About how this morning he sternly counseled Constanze, stupefied with grief, to have her husband buried at the lowest possible cost, in view of the difficult financial situation of the family? He will take care of everything personally. It will cost 11 *gulden,* 36 *kreutzer,* including the hearse. . . . Despite her state (entirely understandable, of course), her eyes swollen from weeping, Madame Mozart is an attractive woman. She's not beautiful, but very feminine. . . .

Deiner continues his story to the chilled musicians (the singers have already left the procession: they can't afford a cold, they have to sing tonight): —Yes, Frau Constanze stayed at home. She's completely undone. Sees nothing, hears nothing. At first, she seemed to have lost her mind: threw herself onto her husband's bed—wanted to "catch the infection" and die herself. Herr Baron van Swieten advised her not to attend the funeral. She couldn't have anyway, unless we all took turns carrying her. She and her husband were like children. Once I dropped in late at night; there they were dancing around the stove in the dark. It's cold, they said. I brought them some firewood. . . . What a storm, gentlemen. Rain and snow together. My feet are wet through already. If it's this muddy here, outside the Stubentor it will be up to our knees. We'll not be able to pass unless we take a boat. It would be better if we all stopped by the Silberner Schlange, it's not far. We'll warm up there. The hearse will get there without us. As for Herr Mozart, the storm will not get him now. But we are still alive— Lord, have mercy on us sinners.

And now there's no one walking behind the coffin. The hearse is covered with wet snow. Some post or other splattered with mud. . . . Some shutter is squeaking and slamming in the wind against a window: bang, bang, and bang again. . . . No one around. No one . . . How could I have missed you, Goukerl? You were here all the time, trotting along while I was studying those mortals who have scattered now. Your coat is wet and matted from the rain, your paws all muddy. Preoccupied and business-like, there you are running alongside.

You probably don't know that your master had another dog, Bimperl, when he was a boy in Salzburg. When Wolfgang went to Paris with his mother, it kept thinking that Leopold and his daughter would some day not return to the house. And then when they did come back from their walks, after all, Bimperl would jump for joy right up to the ceiling.

Here's St. Mark's Cemetery, Goukerl. The driver has gone into the gravediggers' hut. No one's coming. It's doubtful that they'll bury him today. It's already dark, past five. The weather's getting worse. When the storm quiets down a bit, they will drag the coffin to the common grave, and fill it in tomorrow. In the meantime, your master is being treated like a dog. . . . Forgive me, Goukerl, this nasty human expression.

You will stay here, of course. You can't even think otherwise. Tomorrow you, half-alive, dirty and wet, will be kicked into the same grave; the gravediggers like their jokes.

And I have to leave now. The fairy has granted me only so much time. Don't think, Goukerl, that I'm making up an excuse: honest to goodness, I've got to go back. However, the reproach in your eyes is deserved, by me and by everyone. People were never noted for fidelity or gratitude. And in my time, they will even stop writing about these qualities in novels.

Farewell! The wooden box and the ball of wet fur grow blurry and disappear. . . . I'm back in my own home. I turn the soft lights on, put on a record, start it going, press the button. Sit down in a comfortable chair, stretch out my legs. The sweet sounds of Mozart fill the room.

1956

translated by Olga and Robert Hughes

Notes

1. Incidentally, even in them the "rabble" did not participate: "May 1, 7 o'clock in the evening—at the opera: *The Marriage of Figaro.* Libretto by Daponte, music by Mozhardt. Luise with us in our box. A most boring opera." (From the diary of Count Zinzendorff.)

2. Interesting is one of the author's notes: "More than one melodic phrase and more than one modulation in *The Abduction from the Seraglio* make me think that Mozart knew our folksongs."

3. Here and following, the quotation marks imply no irony, but simply attempt to present this word in its usual narrow, folklore, peasant, beard-and-balalaika meaning.

4. Borodin was the one who felt this path out instinctively and with particular success: his Second Symphony is the only original, and is the most Russian, one in our music. Had there not been his chemistry and his stupid "social" involvement, it is Borodin who could have created authentic Russian music. Of the other giants, Glinka in his musical nature was a European, a man who took the wrong path, and Moussorgsky was a genius, but not a musician.

5. This is what Nekrasov did with "Princess Volkonsky," but—"the devil of a difference!" True, he reworked someone else's prose into verse.

6. It is known that Schumann, after listening to Mendelssohn's Scotch Symphony and thinking that he had heard the Italian, said: "It depicts Italy so well that one doesn't even have to go there."

7. It is interesting that the Austrian critic Ambrose, in *The Limits of Poetry and Music,* considers that the music of the romantics is intellectual (because they force music to become the voice of emotion), and the music of the classicists is the music of the soul (because it is pure musical beauty in which the soul seems to be bathed).

8. There is another special kind of sadness that seems to cover old works with a patina, irrespective of their contents. Especially in music, especially when there is a flute. The tears of time?

Contributors

Alfred Appel, Jr.'s books include *The Annotated Lolita* (a McGraw-Hill paperback) and *Nabokov's Dark Cinema* (Oxford). He is currently on a Rockefeller Humanities Fellowship and is writing a book on American film and culture, 1941 to the present.

Brant and **Charty Bassett** are employed by Voice of America in Washington, D.C.

Daniel Bures is the author of *The Negative Potential,* a volume of poems, and *The Mind Machine,* a collection of short fiction.

Mirra Ginsburg is an editor and translator living in New York. Among her publications are Bulgakov's *Master and Margarita, Heart of a Dog* and *Flight* (all Grove), Zamiatin's *Dragon* (Chicago), *We* (Bantam) and a collection of his essays, *A Soviet Heretic* (Chicago), Andrei Platonov's *Foundation Pit* (Dutton), and Dostoevsky's *Notes from the Underground* (Bantam).

Joan Delaney Grossman is Chairman of the Department of Slavic Languages and Literatures at Berkeley. She is the author of *Edgar Allen Poe: Study in Legend and Literary Influence* (JAL Verlag, West Germany). Her most recent article is "The Portrait of Anna: Keystone in the Arch" (*Criticism,* Winter 1976).

Edythe C. Haber has taught Russian literature at Brandeis and Tufts Universities. Her most recent articles are "Nadezhda Teffi" in *Russian Literature Triquarterly,* no. 9 (Spring 1974) and "The Mythic Structure in Bulgakov's *The Master and Margarita*" in *Russian Review,* XXXIV, no. 4 (October 1975).

Olga Hughes is an Associate Professor of Slavic Languages and Literatures at the University of California, Berkeley. She is author of *The Poetic World of Boris Pasternak* (Princeton) and of articles on Marina Tsvetaeva and Nikolai Gogol.

Robert P. Hughes has published articles on Osip Mandelstam (*The Nation*), Vladimir Nabokov (*TriQuarterly*) and Alexander Blok (*California Slavic Studies*) and is co-editor of the Collected Works of Vladislav Khodasevich (Ardis Publishers). He is Associate Professor of Slavic Languages and Literatures and of Comparative Literature at the University of California, Berkeley.

471

Helene Iswolsky has published a translation of Mikhail Bakhin's study of Rabelais, and is the author of two memoirs on Marina Tsvetaeva.

L. P. Izhorsky has spent some time in the Near East. His main occupation is travel. When last heard from, he was in Greece and, with the help of friends, hopes to move soon to an even more intriguing region.

Simon Karlinsky is the author of a critical biography of Marina Tsvetaeva and editor and annotator of *Anton Chekhov's Life and Thought* (both University of California Press). His most recent book is *The Sexual Labyrinth of Nikolai Gogol* (Harvard University Press).

Tatiana Kusubova is an Assistant Professor of Russian Literature at Princeton University. She is the author of a dissertation on Konstantin Korovin as a writer.

Isabella Levitin is married to V. S. Yanovsky and is a translator of his work into English.

Ron Loewinsohn teaches American Literature at the University of California, Berkeley. His most recent collections of poems include *Meat Air: Poems 1957-1969* (Harcourt Brace) and *Goat Dances: Poems and Prose* (Black Sparrow Press).

Vladimir Markov teaches Russian literature at U.C.L.A. His most recent book is *Russian Futurism: A History* (University of California Press). He received the 1968 P.E.N. Club award for the best translation of the year for his *Modern Russian Poetry* (with Merrill Sparks), published by Macgibbon and Kee, London, and Bobbs-Merrill. For Fink Verlag in West Germany he has edited re-issues of Khlebnikov, Balmont and Kuzmin.

Vladimir Nabokov's most recent books are *Transparent Things, Look at the Harlequins!* and *Details of a Sunset* (all McGraw-Hill).

Anthony Olcott is the author of a doctoral dissertation on Andrei Platonov, and has taught Russian literature at Stanford University and the University of Virginia.

Paul Schmidt is Associate Professor of Slavic Languages and Literatures at the University of Texas, Austin. His most recent book is *The Complete Works of Arthur Rimbaud in Translation* (Harper & Row).

Alex M. Shane has published articles and reviews in the *Slavic and East European Journal, Slavic Review, Russian Literature Triquarterly* and the *Modern Language Journal.* His *The Life and Works of Evgenij Zamjatin* was published by the University of California Press in 1968. He is Professor and Chairman of the Department of Slavic Languages and Literatures at the State University of New York at Albany.

Elizabeth Shepard is a Research Associate at the Center for Slavic and East European Studies at Berkeley and the author of "Pavlov's 'Demon' and Gogol's 'Overcoat'" (*Slavic Review,* 33, June 1974).

Theodore Weiss has published seven collections of poetry, most recently *Fireweeds* (Macmillan). His *The Breath of Clowns and Kings: Shakespeare's Early Comedies and Histories* was published by Chatto & Windus, London, and by Atheneum.

Richard Wilbur was recently elected to the American Academy of Arts and Letters. His latest books are *The Mind Reader: New Poems* and *Responses: Prose Pieces 1953-1976* (both Harcourt Brace Jovanovich).

V. S. Yanovsky is the author of *Of Light and Sounding Brass* (Vanguard Press) and *The Dark Fields of Venus* (Harcourt Brace Jovanovich) and of seven novels published in Russian.